Kris Jamsa s
STARTING
with

Macromedia®

Dreamweaver®

UltraDev™

Check the Web for Updates:

To check for updates or corrections relevant to this book and/or CD-ROM visit our updates page on the Web at **http://www.prima-tech.com/support**.

Send Us Your Comments:

To comment on this book or any other PRIMA TECH title, visit our reader response page on the Web at **http://www.prima-tech.com/comments**.

How to Order:

For information on quantity discounts, contact the publisher: Prima Publishing, P.O. Box 1260BK, Rocklin, CA 95677-1260; (916) 787-7000. On your letterhead, include information concerning the intended use of the books and the number of books you want to purchase.

Kris Jamsa's
STARTING
with

Macromedia®
Dreamweaver®
UltraDev™

PRIMA TECH

JMG™
Jamsa Media Group

JIM HOBUSS

A Division of Prima Publishing

Prima Publishing and colophon are registered trademarks of Prima Communications, Inc. PRIMA TECH is a trademark of Prima Communications, Inc., Roseville, California 95661.

Publisher: Stacy L. Hiquet

Associate Marketing Manager: Jennifer Breece

Managing Editor: Sandy Doell

Technical Reviewer: Dan Ransom

Editorial and Book Production: Argosy

Cover Design: Prima Design Team

Macromedia, Dreamweaver, and UltraDev and trademarks or registered trademarks of Macromedia, Inc. in the United States and/or other countries. All other trademarks are the property of their repective owners.

Important: Prima Publishing cannot provide software support. Please contact the appropriate software manufacturer's technical support line or Web site for assistance.

Prima Publishing and the author have attempted throughout this book to distinguish proprietary trademarks from descriptive terms by following the capitalization style used by the manufacturer.

Information contained in this book has been obtained by Prima Publishing from sources believed to be reliable. However, because of the possibility of human or mechanical error by our sources, Prima Publishing, or others, the Publisher does not guarantee the accuracy, adequacy, or completeness of any information and is not responsible for any errors or omissions or the results obtained from use of such information. Readers should be particularly aware of the fact that the Internet is an ever-changing entity. Some facts may have changed since this book went to press.

ISBN: 0-7615-3268-4

Library of Congress Catalog Card Number: 2001088960

Printed in the United States of America

01 02 03 04 05 BB 10 9 8 7 6 5 4 3 2 1

To Diane

The little boat of you and me went sailing on the deep blue sea. We weathered winds and crashing waves, and we were strong and true and brave. And we were still in love, so we kept sailing on the deep blue sea, the little boat of you and me. I am so in love with you.

Acknowledgments

I set out to write this book because of Mark Ace, President of Ace Communications, and I wish to thank him for the opportunity to manage a project whose purpose it was to create a Web-delivered training course on UltraDev that is now available at eHandson.com. Although the Web-based training course we developed is a very high-level presentation of the use of the UltraDev product, it nonetheless inspired me write a book that was more comprehensive, with better lessons and examples.

From that idea I approached my agent, Carole McClendon of Waterside Productions, to find a publishing company that was interested in a book on Dreamweaver UltraDev targeted for the beginning to intermediate user. As an agent, Carole has been and continues to be a very dominant presence in the technical publishing industry, and I am fortunate to have her represent me. Carole put me in contact with Dr. Kris Jamsa. From the first contact with Kris, he has been a strong advocate for this book, and I want to thank him for his dedication and perseverance to see it through.

Caroline Roop was the editor on this book, and she did a very splendid job in that role. This is the seventh book I've written, and the sixth to be published. Of all the editors I have worked with, Caroline has been the most professional, diligent, and accommodating. I would like to thank her for making the final stages of this book proceed as smooth as they did. And finally, I'd like to thank Stacy Hiquet, who is the publisher at Prima Publishing. Stacy has affirmed that it is more important to do the right thing at all times, even if doing the right thing doesn't necessarily save the most money or make the most financial sense. The practical application of morality and decency don't have dollar signs attached to them, and honor and decency are priceless commodities. These are lessons that I knew.

Contents
at a
Glance

Part III — Using Database Access Components of Dreamweaver Ultradev

Part IV — Extending Dreamweaver UltraDev

Part V — Finatus

Contents

Part I — Fundamental Concepts

Part II — Getting Started Using Dreamweaver UltraDev

Part III — Using Database Access Components of Dreamweaver Ultradev

Part IV — Extending Dreamweaver UltraDev

Part V — Finatus

Part I

Fundamental Concepts

Lesson 1

Introducing Macromedia Products and the Role of Dreamweaver UltraDev

The World Wide Web (or simply the Web) has become the place where people and businesses interact, in a variety of ways:

◆ **Person-to-person (P2P).** A Web site that lets a person or small group of people further their individual pursuits. A family, for example, might build a site that lets others view family pictures, read about the family's current events, and so on. I have a personalized Web site for my family and friends that you can view at www.teleport.com/~jhobuss/Personal.htm.

◆ **Person-to-business (P2B).** A Web site for an individual or small group of people for the purpose of self promotion and/or personal gain. Examples of P2B Web sites include a Web site that describes individual professional accomplishments developed by someone seeking a job, and a Web site offering homemade wares for small-scale distribution. I have a professional Web site to promote myself to potential employers at www.teleport.com/~jhobuss/Professional.htm.

◆ **Business-to-consumer (B2C).** A Web site for potential consumers of a company's products. Some of the first nongovernmental sites put on the Web were "brochure" sites that companies used to promote their products and services to potential customers. Examples of B2C sites include The Macromedia Web site at www.macromedia.com and the Oracle Web site at www.oracle.com.

◆ **Business-to-business (B2B).** A business Web site designed to help other businesses. Most B2B sites on the Web have pages that are only accessible and useable by other businesses.

Pages on a B2B Web site may provide a company's vendors with access to the company's current inventory levels so that the vendors can determine when to deliver new products to the company. Normally, the site password protects such pages, which restricts user access. The Web sites at www.macromedia.com and www.oracle.com each contains pages that are only accessible by businesses.

Across the Web, designers and programmers employ Macromedia products to create Web sites in all four of these categories. Today, Web site developers create and deploy Web sites at the rate of one site every 12 minutes, a phenomenal pace that is expected to continue for years. In the four months prior to beginning the writing of this book, I worked on Web sites in each of the preceding four categories.

This lesson will introduce you to Macromedia, the company that sells and supports Dreamweaver UltraDev. As you will learn, Macromedia did not actually develop the software, but rather it purchased a product named *Drumbeat*, which became Dreamweaver UltraDev. You also will learn about the products that are sold and supported by Macromedia that work very well with UltraDev, and you will learn how to download free of charge fully functional evaluation copies of all of Macromedia's products. By the time you finish this lesson, you will understand the following key concepts:

◆ Macromedia is a company whose products and solutions enable the development and maintenance of rich, engaging, and personalized Web experiences for visitors of Web sites.

◆ There are specific products available from Macromedia that embellish the Web experience for site visitors. Dreamweaver UltraDev is the development environment that pulls all of these related products together.

◆ UltraDev is an evolutionary product, spawning from an earlier product called Drumbeat.

◆ Macromedia added many useful functions to Drumbeat when it incorporated it into the Dreamweaver user interface.

◆ Using UltraDev, you can build dynamic and interactive Web sites that include access to data stored in most types of databases, including, among others, Oracle, Sybase, MS Access, and MySQL.

◆ You can easily incorporate Java, JavaScript, Java Beans, Active Server Pages (ASP), and VBScript code in your Web sites by utilizing the UltraDev interface.

Macromedia: The Company and Its Products

Macromedia is a company that delivers award-winning products and solutions that give developers the power to develop and implement engaging and effective next-generation Web sites. These products include Web authoring and graphics creation tools that provide integrated solutions for mission-critical Web operations.

Headquartered in San Francisco, CA., Macromedia is a $250+ million software company that employs over 1,200 people. *Fortune* magazine has recognized Macromedia as a *Fortune* e-50 company. You can reach Macromedia at:

Macromedia
600 Townsend Street
San Francisco, CA 94103
Phone: (415) 252-2000
Fax: (415) 626-0554
Web: www.macromedia.com
Customer Service: customerservice@macromedia.com

Macromedia has formed strategic partnerships with a variety of companies, enabling it to deliver tools that let developers build compelling and effective Web-based experiences while managing the challenges of authoring, producing, delivering, and personalizing those Web sites. In the process of doing this, Macromedia has created impressive statistics demonstrating its success:

- Macromedia Dreamweaver is the standard platform for professional Web site production, with 70 percent market share (source: *PC Data*, March 2000).

- The Macromedia Flash Player has 250+ million users, and across the Web, users download Flash at the rate of 1.4 million times per day. According to a study done by NPD Research, titled "Flash Penetration," 90 percent of all Web users have the Flash viewer installed

- Seventy-five percent of all professional Web developers use one or more Macromedia products (source: Macromedia/IDC. IDC is an industry research division within Macromedia).

- Macromedia provides solutions for e-branding, e-commerce, e-learning, e-marketing, e-merchandising, news and information publishing, entertainment, and online advertising.

From standalone products for Web authoring and graphics creation to integrated solutions for mission-critical Web operations, Macromedia offers the technology and services that enable developers and enterprises to create successful Web sites. Table 1.1 briefly describes various Macromedia products. For specifics on each product, visit the corresponding Macromedia Web site.

Table 1.1   Products offered by Macromedia

Product Name	Description	URL
Aria	Provides tools for intelligent e-business decisions with real-time Web analysis.	www.macromedia.com/software/aria/
Authorware	Used to produce rich-media training materials.	www.macromedia.com/software/authorware/
CourseBuilder for Dreamweaver	Used to create Web-based interactive training materials.	www.macromedia.com/software/coursebuilder/
Director Shockwave Studio	Used to develop Internet destinations that draw site hits using powerful multimedia elements.	www.macromedia.com/software/director/
Dreamweaver	High-productivity tool for the development of Web sites.	www.macromedia.com/software/dreamweaver/
Dreamweaver UltraDev	Used to create dynamic, database-driven Web applications using technologies like ASP, JavaServer Pages (JSP), and ColdFusion Markup Language (CFML).	www.macromedia.com/software/ultradev/
Fireworks	Used to design, develop, and optimize Web graphics for easy and efficient integration into HTML pages.	www.macromedia.com/software/fireworks/
Flash	Used to create vector-based animations that add "punch" and "action" to your Web sites.	www.macromedia.com/software/flash/
Flash Player	Used by visitors to Web sites that have Flash components on them. This is a free product.	www.macromedia.com/software/flashplayer/
Fontographer	Used to create and modify fonts that are viewable across multiple platforms in a consistent manner	www.macromedia.com/software/fontographer/
FreeHand	Used to create eye-catching illustrations, logos, graphics for Macromedia Flash, site storyboards, and design-intensive documents.	www.macromedia.com/software/freehand/

(continued)

Table 1.1 *(continued)*

Product Name	Description	URL
Generator	Used to deliver dynamic content graphically.	www.macromedia.com/software/generator/
LikeMinds	Used to deliver highly accurate product recommendations, personally relevant content, and targeted promotions for each individual Web visitor.	www.macromedia.com/software/likeminds/
Shockwave Player	Used by visitors to Web sites that have Shockwave components on them. This is a free product.	www.macromedia.com/software/shockwave/
SoundEdit 16	Used to create audio for dissemination on Web pages.	www.macromedia.com/software/sound/

NOTE: *You can also download a fully functional 30-day unlimited use version of any of the products listed in Table 1.1 by visiting the links specified.*

Evolution of Dreamweaver UltraDev

In 1998, Macromedia had developed and was selling a product called Dreamweaver, version 1.0. In a January 20, 1998, review of Dreamweaver, John Garris of *PC Magazine* wrote:

It (Dreamweaver) builds visually appealing, cutting-edge Web pages using style sheets and DHTML without forcing you to sacrifice control over the source code. Dreamweaver will certainly appeal to graphically oriented designers with these tools, but it may also represent a new direction in hybrid-WYSIWYG editors once it ships. The shipping version is to integrate our Editors' Choice code-based editor, HomeSite, to make Dreamweaver a potentially unbeatable combination of power and ease.

One of the best features of Dreamweaver is its "Roundtrip HTML" editing, which lets you create Web pages using either graphical tools or a raw HTML editor without any difference in the output. Dreamweaver is the only WYSIWYG editor in this review whose graphical tools don't produce modified HTML code, so editing the underlying source is easy. You can switch back and forth between environments, and Dreamweaver will update the other environment automatically.

In the same issue of *PC Magazine,* John Garris wrote the following about a product called Drumbeat that was sold by a company called Elemental Software, Inc.:

> An impressive new release that offers strong drag-and-drop capabilities, Elemental Software's Drumbeat 1.01 ($699 list) most resembles NetObjects Fusion in this roundup, which is good if you want to create a Web site and not worry about fine-tuning, but bad if you need to have more control over your code. Drumbeat is great if you want to add JavaScript to your Web pages, but it is not as complete as NetObjects Fusion, lacking some important basic features such as page import and HTML table editing.
>
> With Drumbeat, you simply drag and drop HTML elements directly onto your Web page. Drumbeat lets you specify precisely where you want all your HTML objects to appear. You can also have Drumbeat automatically position your objects along gridlines to ensure proper alignment of page elements. Furthermore, Drumbeat's extensive tool palette contains a number of customized objects, such as timers and navigation buttons, as well as standard HTML objects.
>
> Drumbeat's similarity to NetObjects Fusion stems from your not generating HTML when you build pages. Instead, you modify a Drumbeat project file that has all the information needed to build your Web site. With your site finished, you "publish" it and Drumbeat generates the HTML pages. It can publish to a local directory or to a remote FTP server.

The similarities between Macromedia's Dreamweaver and Elemental Software's Drumbeat were extensive in early 1998. In fact, they were reviewed by *PC Magazine* (www.zdnet.com/pcmag/features/htmlauthor/rev3.htm) as competing products.

In June 1998, Elemental Software released version 2.0 of Drumbeat. On May 17, 1999, authors Rob Brooks-Bilson and Gordon Benett wrote the following comments about this release:

> Elemental (Software) hits the ball out of the park with its visual RAD tool for Web design, which does for ASP and DHTML what tools like Symantec Visual Café did for Java. Drumbeat delivers a tsunami of next-generation features that raise the bar for data-driven page design.
>
> Through SmartElements (a component in Drumbeat 2.0), Drumbeat makes it possible to create sites of three distinct types:
>
> ◆ Static—With manually entered content—your basic collection of HTML pages. Static sites offer low interactivity but can be deployed on any platform.
>
> ◆ Database-derived—HTML pages populated from data tables at publication time but static thereafter.
>
> ◆ Database-driven—ASP pages populated from data tables on the fly. Data-driven sites built with Drumbeat must run on an ASP server such as IIS."

As seen in the previous reviews, Elemental Software built in features and capabilities in the transition from version 1.0 to version 2.0 of Drumbeat that allowed for database access. This was the critical feature added to the product that made for an easy decision by Macromedia to buy it, and Elemental Software, Inc. In a July 12, 1999, press release, Macromedia stated:

> *Elemental's strength in dynamic Web application development with products like Drumbeat and eStore Builder, combined with Macromedia's leadership in professional Web publishing with products like Dreamweaver and Generator, will enable Web developers to more efficiently create dynamic Web sites for e-commerce, corporate intranets and personalized content. The addition of the Elemental products to Macromedia's Web publishing product family provides the first and only standards-based end-to-end solution of award-winning Internet software for efficiently creating, producing and maintaining dynamic Web sites that automate the process of linking database information to Web applications with reusable code.*

In late 1999, Macromedia released Drumbeat 2000, which was an incorporation of the product purchased from Elemental Software into the Macromedia family of products. In this release, user interface changes were made, and some integration was accomplished to allow Drumbeat to integrate more closely with other Macromedia products, most notably Dreamweaver.

Then, on June 7, 2000, at the JavaOne 2000 Conference in San Francisco, California, Macromedia announced the release of Dreamweaver UltraDev with the following press release:

> Macromedia, Inc. (NASDAQ: MACR), a leading provider of solutions for compelling and effective Web sites, today shipped Macromedia Dreamweaver UltraDev, the visual solution for rapid Web application development. Dreamweaver UltraDev is the first application to allow visual creation of data-driven Web applications across industry leading server technologies, such as Sun Microsystems' JSP, Microsoft's ASP, and Allaire's CFML.

> The following industry vendors announced support for Dreamweaver UltraDev: IBM, Sun, ATG, Allaire, BroadVision, BlueMartini, Cache/Intersystems, Documentum, and WebGain.

> Dreamweaver UltraDev will empower developers to work more efficiently when creating Web applications across their choice of databases, application servers, and operating systems," said Beth Davis, vice president of product marketing at Macromedia. "The depth and breadth of support for Dreamweaver UltraDev by industry leading corporations is a true testament to the fundamental need for a flexible, rapid Web application solution that supports the Web's heterogeneous environments."

> The product shares the core architecture of Macromedia Dreamweaver, the market-leading visual Web authoring environment for professional Web developers. Due to that shared architecture, Dreamweaver UltraDev can be easily extended and customized to work within any development environment using Java technology, JavaScript programming language, HTML, XML, and C.

Role of Dreamweaver UltraDev

Dreamweaver UltraDev allows you to build Web sites that incorporate database access. As shown in Figure 1.1, it extends the capabilities of other HTML development tools to allow you to design powerful Web site solutions that incorporate Component Object Model (COM) objects (such as JavaBeans) while accessing SQL databases via an Open Database Connectivity (ODBC) connection.

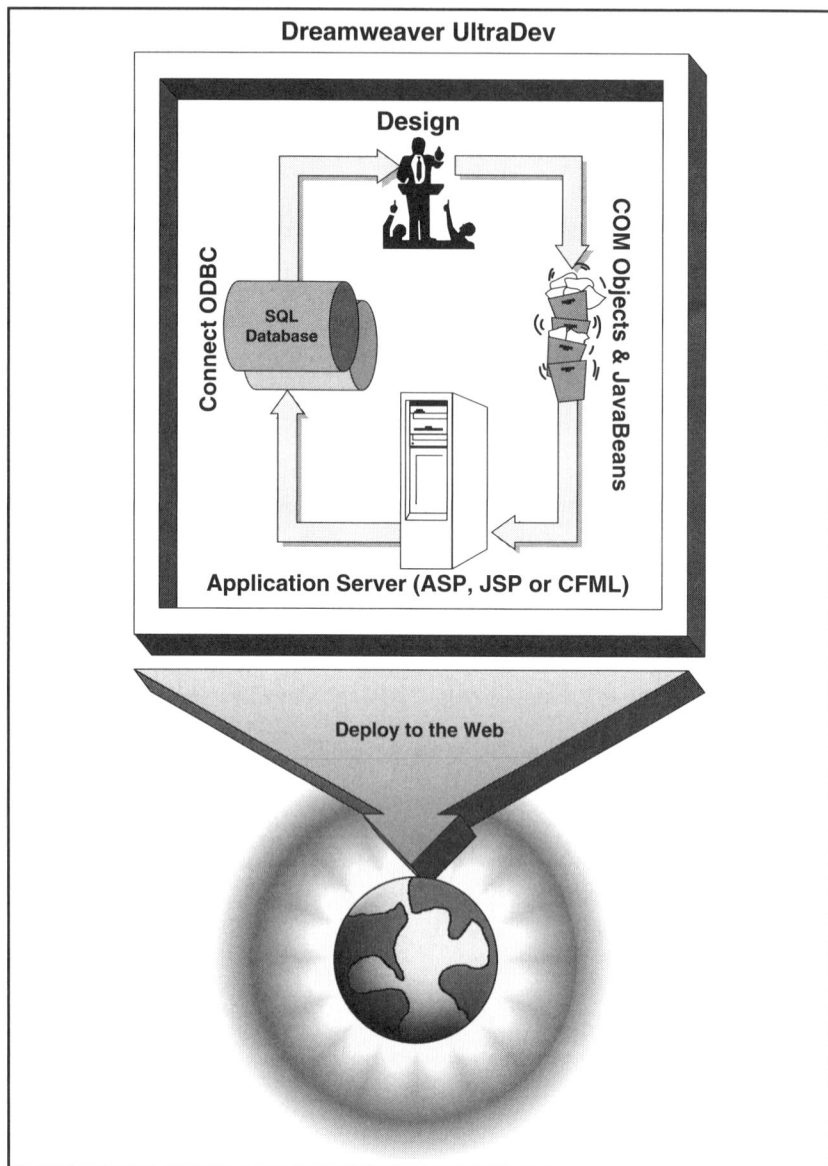

Figure 1.1

The Dreamweaver UltraDev model

With Dreamweaver UltraDev, you can build Web sites that offer personalization, such as www.expertcity.com; news and information, such as www.invehicleproducts.com; a high degree of customer interactivity, which you will find at www.netaid.org; and e-commerce, such as www.winecask.com.

Dreamweaver UltraDev, hereafter referred to simply as UltraDev, extends the features of Dreamweaver by providing the following capabilities:

♦ Generates ASP code

♦ Generates CFML code

♦ Generates JSP pages

♦ Quickly generates database-driven forms and reports

♦ Supports roundtrip server markup

♦ A built-in set of objects for connecting to databases

♦ Live data preview

♦ Connection to databases using JDBC, OLE, and ODBC

♦ Query Builder, to simplify database search operations

♦ Binds attributes and text to databases and server scripts

♦ Dynamic data formatting

What You Must Know

This lesson introduced you to Macromedia, Inc., the company that sells and supports Dreamweaver UltraDev. You also examined the products that are sold and supported by Macromedia that work very well with UltraDev, as well as how to download free and fully functional evaluation copies of all of Macromedia's products. In Lesson 2, "The Basics of Dreamweaver UltraDev," you will get to know UltraDev and learn the key operations you will perform when you work with UltraDev on a regular basis. Before you continue to Lesson 2, however, make sure that you understand the following key concepts:

◆ Macromedia's products and solutions enable the development and maintenance of rich, engaging, and personalized Web experiences for visitors of Web sites.

◆ Macromedia provides a variety of products Web designers can use to embellish the Web experience for site visitors. Dreamweaver UltraDev is the development environment that pulls all of these related products together.

◆ Macromedia evolved Dreamweaver from a product it purchased named Drumbeat and eventually named its enhanced software UltraDev.

◆ UltraDev gives you the ability to build dynamic and interactive Web sites that include access to data stored in most types of databases, including, among others, Oracle, Sybase, MS Access, and MySQL.

◆ You can easily incorporate Java, JavaScript, Java Beans, ASP, and VBScript code in your Web sites by utilizing the UltraDev interface.

Lesson 2

The Basics of
Dreamweaver UltraDev

In Lesson 1, "Introducing Macromedia Products and the Role of Dreamweaver UltraDev," you learned about Macromedia's various product offerings, and the role and evolution of the UltraDev product. In this lesson, you will learn about the architecture of the Web at a very high level. It is necessary that you have this knowledge to have an understanding of the role that UltraDev has in this environment. Then, you will examine the UltraDev product at a high level. You will also take a tour of the user interface and examine some of the main features. By the time you finish this lesson, you will understand the following key concepts:

◆ The current architecture of the World Wide Web (WWW, or simply the "Web") involves a number of different technologies and architectural components.

◆ To simplify its user interface, UltraDev provides a number of key visual elements.

◆ The UltraDev interface is easy to use and heavily takes advantage of the What You See Is What You Get (WYSIWYG, pronounced "wizzy-wig") paradigm.

◆ Most of the elements in the UltraDev interface employ a point-and-click approach for rapid use of the tool.

Understanding the Architecture of the World Wide Web

When Web servers came to prominence in 1990, there were relatively few sites in the world. There has been a phenomenal explosion in the number of Web sites and pages of information located on those Web sites since then. Estimates by NEC Research place the current number of Web pages on the Internet at over 500 million.

Nowadays, if you are a multinational company, then you must have a Web presence: businesses are investing hugely in Web technology, paying large sums of money to graphic artists and Web developers to see that their sites are noticed. As well as information provision, companies are quickly coming round to the idea of using the Internet as a retail medium. For example, Dell Computer Corporation has spent millions on its very successful Web site. Also, more and more smaller companies competing in the global community are looking to the Internet as a means of getting some competitive advantage by exposing their products and services to an international market at a previously unthinkably low cost. HTML's interactive nature lets businesses provide information in creative ways that hold their customers' attention.

Over 350 million people worldwide are currently wired to the Internet—a significant increase from the 1,000 or so people who were hooked up in 1983. According to Pegasus Research International, business-to-consumer commerce over the Internet is an $8 billion industry today, and is likely to grow to $65 billion by the end of 2002.

The basic architecture of the Web is two-tiered, with one tier being the Web client that displays information content, and the other tier being a Web server that transfers information to the client. From here, other architectures are possible:

◆ **Three-tiered.** A Web client, Web server, and application or database server

◆ **Four-tiered.** A Web client, Web server, application server, and database server

◆ *n*-**tiered.** Any combination of architectural components that delivers content over the Web

Macromedia's Dreamweaver product allows for the creation of Web sites that primarily support a two-tiered architecture (although different architectures are possible, the two-tier model is most common). The Dreamweaver UltraDev product, because of its ability to create Web sites that incorporate databases, most commonly fits into a three-tier (or possibly a four-tier) model. These architectures depend on the following key standards and architectural components:

◆ HTML (*Hypertext Markup Language*). Encodes document content. HTML was first released as a standard in 1990, with specification level 0.0. The current HTML specification, proposed by the W3C (*World Wide Web Consortium*) organization on Dec. 24, 1999, is level 4.01. You can view a full copy of this specification at web3.w3.org/TR/html401/. Across the Web, users view HTML files using Web client browser software, such Internet Explorer and Netscape Navigator. Current HTML standards let Web designers embed images, sounds, video streams, form fields, and complex text formatting. Designers can also embed references to other objects (documents, images, sounds, video, and so on), called *hyperlinks*, to other objects within HTML by using URLs (see the following bullet). When a user clicks his or her mouse on a hyperlink on a Web page, the browser takes a specific action as described in the hyperlink by the type of URL.

◆ **URIs (*Universal Resource Identifiers*).** Name remote information objects in a global namespace. There are two types of URIs: URNs (*Universal Resource Names*) and URLs (*Universal Resource Locators*). There are several different types of URLs: file URLs, FTP URLs, Gopher URLs, news URLs, and HTTP URLs. If you're interested in reading the specification on URLs, you can find it at www.w3.org/Addressing/URL/url-spec.html. URLs may also be relative to a directory or offsets into a document. CGI programs (described later in the list) may be embedded in URLs and are typically identified by the passed parameter that appears in the URL that follows the question mark (?). An example of a passed parameter to a CGI program listed on a URL is www.amazon.com/exec/cgi-bin/search-handle-form? NewBooks.

◆ **HTTP (*Hypertext Transfer Protocol*).** Defines the rules that programs must follow to transfer images across the Web. HTTP is an application-level protocol with the lightness and speed necessary for distributed, collaborative, hypermedia information systems. It is a generic, stateless, object-oriented protocol that can be used for many tasks, such as name servers and distributed object management systems, through extension of its request methods (commands). A feature of HTTP is the (MIME) typing of data represented and displayed on Web pages, allowing systems to be built independently of the data being transferred.

◆ **CGI (*Common Gateway Interface*).** Provides a standard for interfacing external programs with Web servers. The Web server interprets the request to execute a CGI program, as identified in the URL passed from the client's Web browser, and in turn initiates the execution of that CGI program, passing any parameters to it that need to be passed as coming into the Web server from the URL.

◆ **Helpers/plug-ins.** Helpers are applications that run external to a client machine's browser, while a plug-in runs within the client machine's browser. These plug-in components extend the capabilities of HTML while also allowing designers to build Web sites that are very individualistic.

◆ **Java/JavaScript.** Provides a cross-platform (runs on Windows, the Mac, as well as Unix) programming language modeled after C++ from Sun Microsystems. Java programs embedded in HTML documents are called *applets* and are uniquely specified in the HTML code. Programmers create and compile Java applets into a platform-independent bytecode that a user's

Web browser later downloads and executes. Browsers that support Java are termed *Java-enabled*. JavaScript is a scripting language designed for creating dynamic, interactive Web applications that link together objects on both the client and server machines. A client-based JavaScript can recognize and respond to user events such as a mouse click, form input, and page navigation. A server-based JavaScript program can exhibit behaviors similar to CGI programs.

Taking a Closer Look at UltraDev

As you have learned earlier, UltraDev is a tool that encompasses many useful features. First, UltraDev provides you with an HTML editor. As you will see later in this section, UltraDev gives you a number of different ways (you will look at two of them in this section) to do any specific task. UltraDev is also a Web authoring tool, a Web site management tool, and a Web application development and maintenance tool.

In HTML parlance, you format a document using a starting and ending tag pair. For example, using the start bold `<B>` and end bold `</B>` tags, the text `<B>`This is bold `</B>` appears within a browser window as `This is bold`, with the tag pair being `<B>` and `</B>`.

HTML requires a tag pair for each and every attribute or action on a Web page. The first-generation Web authoring tool created by software companies to help with the building of Web sites was an HTML editor, because there were significant encumbrances in remembering and placing tag pairs appropriately. HTML editors freed people from having to remember the maze of HTML tag pairs required to format a Web page. The second generation of these Web authoring tools brought a WYSIWYG visual interface to the design. With these second-generation tools, Web developers not only did not need to remember HTML tag pairs, but also could see exactly what the results were of certain HTML tag pairs.

Even with the second generation of HTML editors, production Web developers still needed to hand-code (known as *hard-coding*) some HTML to enable certain attributes on their Web pages. The current generation of HTML editing tools provides a rich WYSIWYG interface to HTML, but also provides an easily accessible interface to hand-code HTML. UltraDev is in this class of tools.

Figure 2.1 shows UltraDev's WYSIWYG interface to HTML, with the HTML text editor appearing in the foreground window. For now, don't be concerned with how you get here. The point is the ease with which you can easily move from the graphical editor to the text editor. Moving from the WYSIWYG editor to the text editor is a process of clicking on the icon that appears in the lower-right corner of the graphical interface (the icon that the mouse pointer is on).

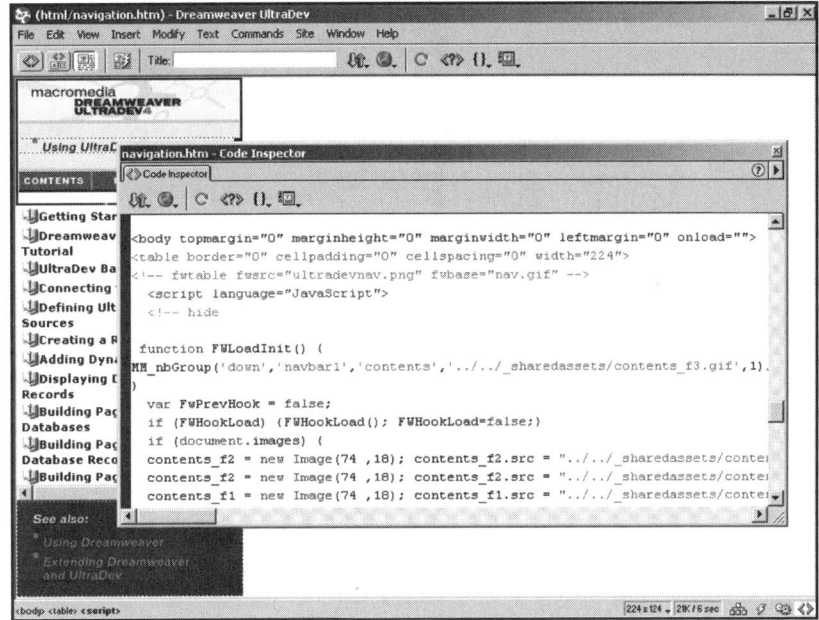

Figure 2.1

UltraDev's HTML text editor over the WYSIWYG editor

As you read earlier in this section, UltraDev is also a Web authoring tool. A Web authoring tool enables you to create complex Web applications having dynamic HTML that includes interactivity and animation. As you can see in Figure 2.2, inserting an image on an existing Web page is a matter of clicking on the Insert menu item, and then on the Image submenu item, and then selecting the name of the image to insert onto the Web page (this step is not shown in the figure). Again, do not worry that this lesson is not yet giving you step-by-step instructions at this point. Rather, the important thing is to understand what features and functions are available for your use.

UltraDev gives you a number of tools to manage your site. Lesson 8, "Setting Up an UltraDev Site," presents this information in detail. As is the case with all of the features and components in UltraDev, establishing a site is a very simple process. As you can see in Figure 2.3, which is a configuration screen that is accessed by just two mouse clicks, creating a site is a process of defining configuration parameters for six categories. After you have done this, click your mouse on the OK button. UltraDev, in turn, will create your site.

NOTE: *Changing a site configuration parameter is much simpler using Ultra-Dev than using other tools of this type. Other tools require you to go through a lengthy process of exporting your site to a metafile, defining a new site, and then importing the metafile into the new site. As you will see in Lesson 8, "Setting Up an UltraDev Site," these steps are not required in UltraDev.*

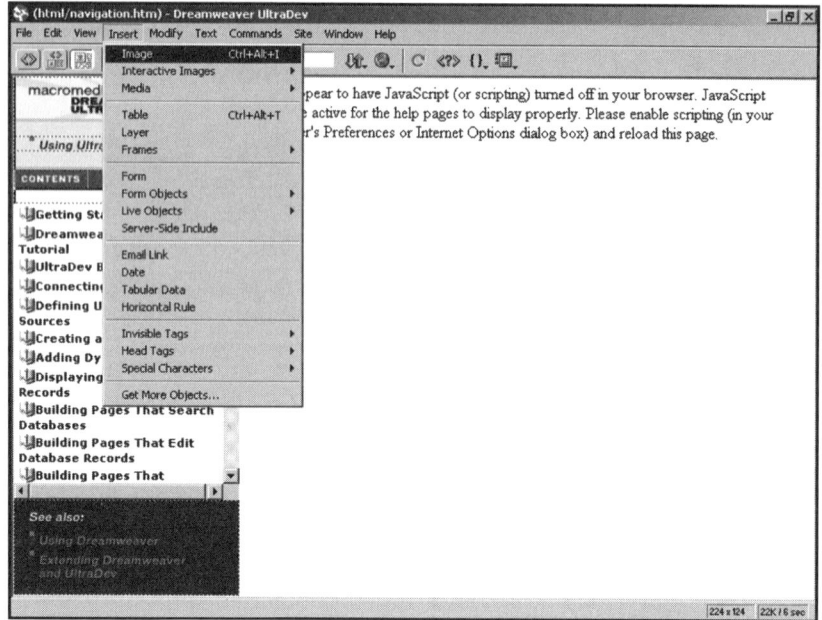

Figure 2.2

UltraDev is a powerful Web authoring tool.

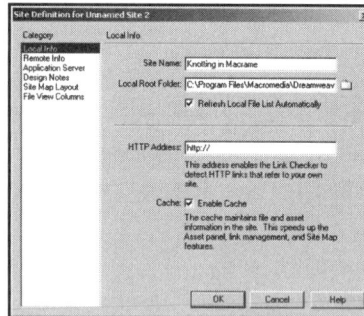

Figure 2.3

Creating a new site in UltraDev is very easy.

The most significant component that extends the Dreamweaver product to make it the UltraDev product is UltraDev's ability to read data from and write data to external databases. This component makes UltraDev truly a fully featured Web application development tool. Beginning with Lesson 16, "Setting Up for Database Interaction," you will learn how to configure the settings to attach a Web site to an external database, and then to access and manipulate that data within UltraDev. But for now, simply examine Figure 2.4 and you will find that the creation of a connection to an external database is an easy process of completing a form.

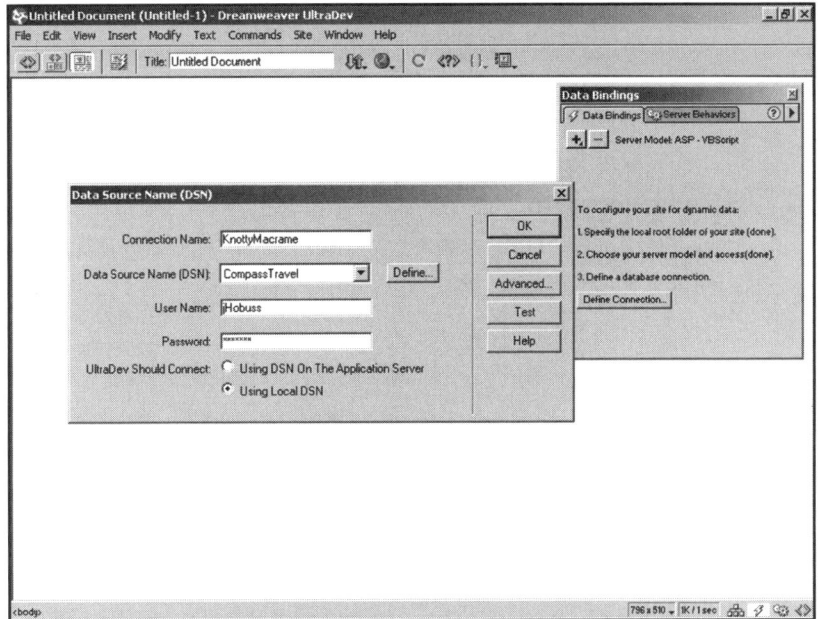

Figure 2.4

Establishing a database connection to a Web site is easy in UltraDev.

Examining the UltraDev User Interface

NOTE: *The information in this lesson provides an overview of the UltraDev interface, rather than a tutorial on how to use the interface. To start, it is important that you understand what the features and components in the product are before you learn how to use each of them.*

One task that Web designers repeatedly perform is the process of inserting objects (such as text, graphics, objects, and behaviors) onto a Web page. After the designers place these objects on the page, the designers often frequently manipulate the objects in one way or another. As you will learn, UltraDev excels at both of these activities. The UltraDev graphical user interface (GUI) has a number of windows, panes, editors, and palettes available to make these two processes simple.

Entering Text

The glitz and punch on Web sites usually comes from the graphics, audio, and visual components that appear on the page. These components are added to a Web site primarily to make the site entertaining. People do not usually visit Web sites to be entertained, though; rather, users normally visit sites for information, and the means by which that information is communicated on a Web site is primarily by the words (text) that appear on the pages.

Although you will learn how to add text to a Web page in Lesson 9, "Laying the Groundwork for an Application," for now recognize that to add text you simply click on the Web page where you want to insert text and type the text. As you can see in Figure 2.5, UltraDev gives you the ability to modify any of the attributes for that text in a single screen interface, called a Text Property Inspector.

NOTE: *In UltraDev terminology, you set properties of certain components using inspectors, and all the elements that appear on a page are manipulated using an inspector.*

Figure 2.5

Inserting and manipulating text is easy in UltraDev.

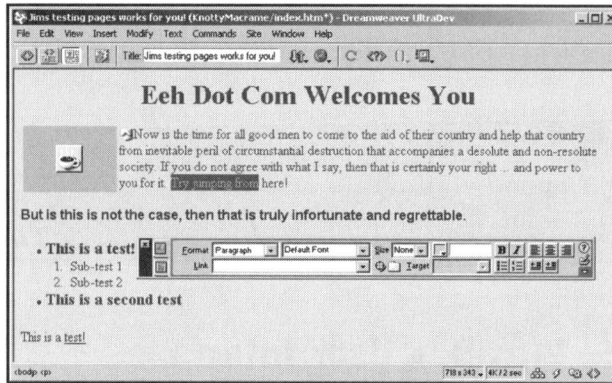

Modifying Any Object with a Click of Your Mouse

In UltraDev, you can easily manipulate any object (such as text, JavaScript, and audio/video components) that appears on a page by double-clicking your mouse on the object and then modifying the attributes that you desire by using the Inspector that UltraDev pops up onto your screen display. As you can see in Figure 2.6, double-

Figure 2.6

Manipulating the attributes for any object on a Web page is a double-click away.

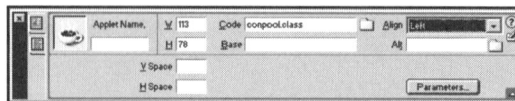

clicking your mouse on the JavaApplet icon (the one that looks like a cup of coffee) launches the Java Applet Property Inspector.

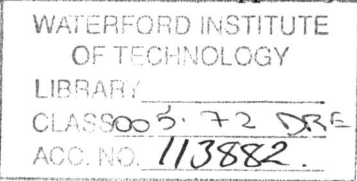

Customizing Your Interface

UltraDev gives you the ability to customize the user interface to better suit your needs in a number of ways:

◆ **Launcher.** Using the Launcher, shown in Figure 2.7, you can open and close various windows, property inspectors, and palettes. After you open an object, you can move the object to any place on your desktop (including outside of the UltraDev workspace). You can later dock the object at a specific location, so that each time you open the object, it appears in the same location.

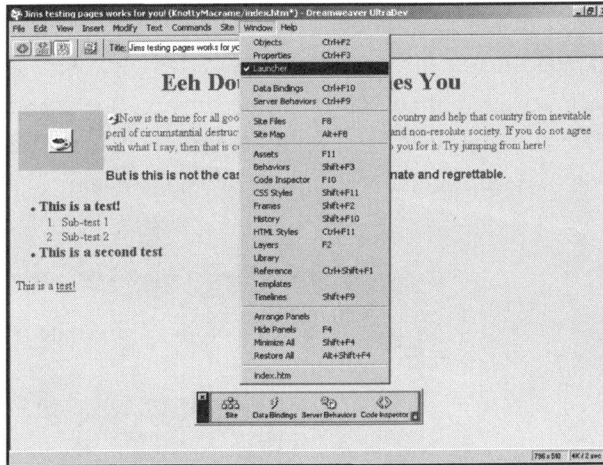

Figure 2.7

The Launcher lets you open and close windows, property inspectors, and palettes.

◆ **Customizable Objects Palette.** The Objects palette, shown in Figure 2.8, lets you easily pick and place an object on a Web page. The Objects palette shows you UltraDev's default Objects palette, which UltraDev creates during the installation. As you will learn, UltraDev provides iconic representations of many of the types of objects that you will want to place on a page. There are some objects that you could place on a page that are not on the Objects palette. If you are placing a large number of a certain object on your pages, you can add that object to the Objects palette.

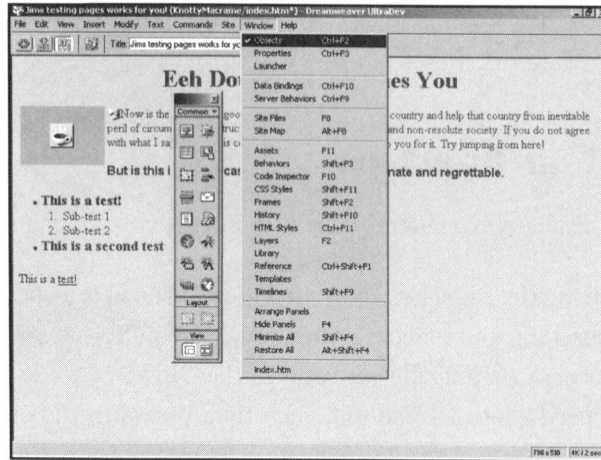

Figure 2.8

The Objects palette displays the most commonly used objects, and is customizable.

◆ **Defaults.** There are a number of objects that you will place on your site that you will want to have look and/or function in a consistent way. Examples of these are page properties, cascading style sheets (covered in Lesson 13, "Controlling Page Layout"), and others. As shown in Figure 2.9, UltraDev gives you the ability to set certain site preferences. UltraDev gives you other ways, discussed throughout the book, to modify defaults for various objects and entities.

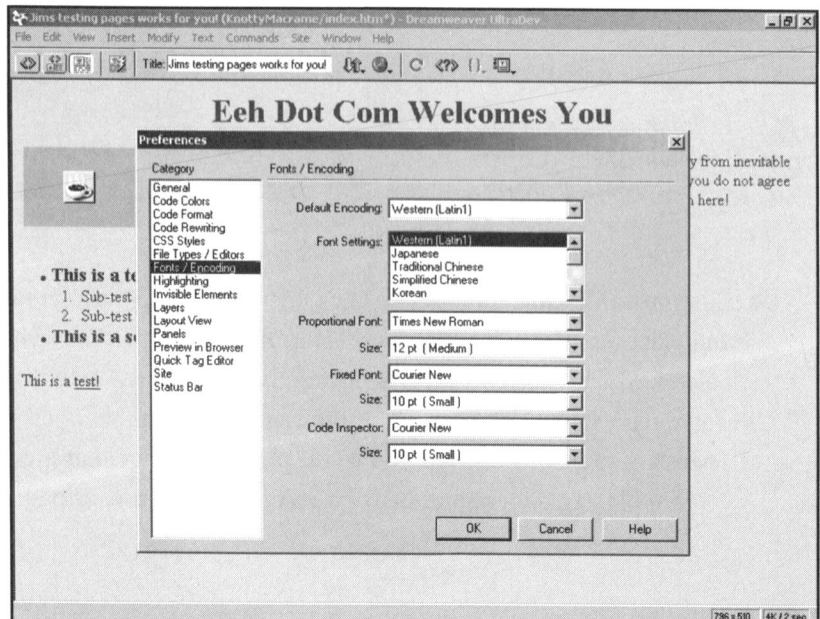

Figure 2.9

You can adjust site preferences for many elements in the Preferences window.

Selecting Tags Is Easy

UltraDev gives you powerful abilities to create HTML without actually coding HTML. There are times, however, when you'll find it necessary to either select a specific HTML tag or modify the tag by writing a bit of HTML code. To accommodate this, UltraDev also gives you the ability to modify HTML code, or to see the HTML code that is created for any element on the Web page. You do this by using the Tag Selector, shown in Figure 2.10.

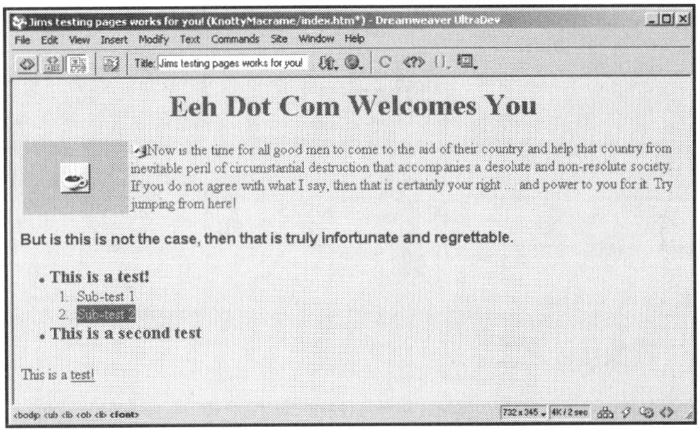

Figure 2.10

Use the tag selector to see what HTML code is created for an object.

Within the figure you will see the highlighted text on the Web page, and the HTML code UltraDev created to produce that element.

Exploiting Superior Layout Control

UltraDev gives you four mechanisms that you can use to control the layout of your Web pages with the precision of a desktop publishing program:

◆ **Tables.** You can create tables with rows and columns, placing text and graphics in the cells of the table. You also have the ability to merge cells.

◆ **Layers.** Using native HTML commands, you have limited control over the placement of objects and text on a Web page. Starting with HTML specification 3.0, you can place layers anywhere on a Web page, down to specifying the exact pixel where the top-left corner of the layer is located. UltraDev allows you to specify layers and to position those layers wherever you want on the page, including overlapping other layers.

◆ **Rulers.** As shown in Figure 2.11, rulers appear on the top and left margins of a Web page being manipulated in UltraDev. You have the ability to specify the increments on the ruler in pixels (shown in the figure), inches, or centimeters.

◆ **Grids.** Also shown in Figure 2.11 are grids that appear as horizontal and vertical lines on the Web page. These only appear while the page is being viewed in the UltraDev interface. You can specify the grid distance in pixels, inches, or centimeters. You can also specify if you want objects appearing on the page to snap to the nearest grid.

Figure 2.11

Rulers and grids are two of the mechanisms in UltraDev to control placement of objects.

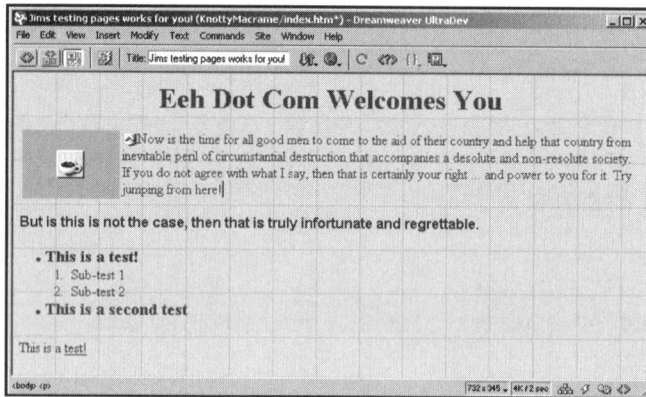

NOTE: *Lesson 13, "Controlling Page Layout," examines all the UltraDev facilities you can use to control page layout.*

Playing Back Active Content

Most Web site development tools give you the ability to preview the page and/or site you're working on before publishing it to a Web server. UltraDev gives you this ability by pressing the F12 function key from the application workspace. Most other Web site development tools lose their ability to show active content, though, when they preview pages, which means that Flash, Fireworks, or any other object that requires a plug-in will not show its active content. UltraDev remedies this and allows you to preview a Web page exactly as it will be seen in a user's Web browser.

Taking Advantage of Multiple Browser Support

When you create a Web site, you rarely know with certainty what browsers users will be viewing your site with. A possible exception to this is an intranet site built for a company that maintains strict controls on the software and browsers installed on employee machines.

NOTE: *An intranet site is a Web site that is viewed by a targeted group of people. Most intranet sites are secured behind a company's firewall, and the firewall restricts access to the site. In early 2000, I worked on an intranet Web site for Hewlett-Packard Company that was only accessible by people in its manufacturing group.*

You need to be concerned not only with the different types of browsers that people will be using to access your Web site, but also with the version of each type of browser. Each version of Netscape Communicator, or Internet Explorer, supports different HTML and Web standards from previous standards.

As you will learn in Lesson 29, "Browser Targeting," there are a number of features in UltraDev that assist you in making sure that your Web site is viewable by different browser types and versions. One of those features is shown in Figure 2.12, which shows you a screen that is used in the process of determining browser compatibility with your site.

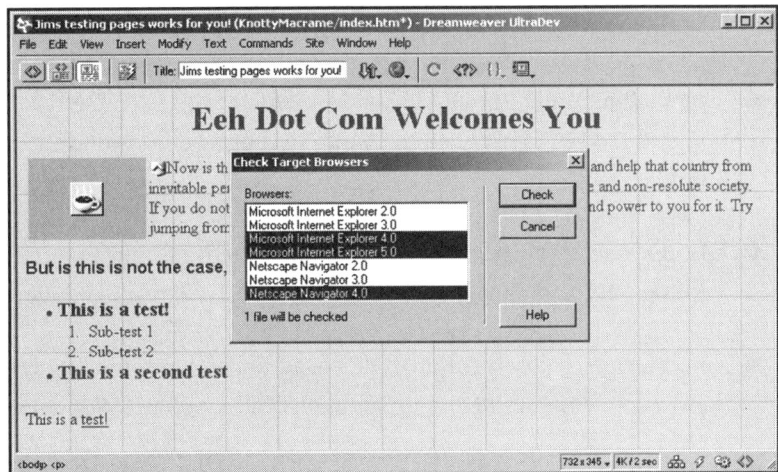

Figure 2.12

Selecting the types and versions of browsers your site is compatible with is easy in UltraDev.

What You Must Know

This lesson introduced you to the architecture of the Web, including a description of two-tier, three-tier, and *n*-tier architectures. You learned about the components of an UltraDev application that work in each of these tiers. Then you learned about some of the more beneficial components of UltraDev, like the text editor, palettes, and HTML editor. You learned that UltraDev gives you tremendous control over the look and feel of the user interface, as well very precise control over the placement of the objects that appear on your Web pages. You then learned that UltraDev is unique in that it gives you the ability to view the animated components of your Web site in a preview mode, without having to publish the page to a Web server beforehand. Finally, you learned that UltraDev has facilities to target your site for certain browsers, and to check the content of your Web site against one or more browser types. In Lesson 3, "Installing Dreamweaver UltraDev," you will learn the steps you must perform to get Dreamweaver UltraDev up and running on your system. Before you continue to Lesson 3, however, make sure that you understand the following key concepts:

♦ A two-tier Web architecture is one in which there is a Web browser component accessing a Web server component.

♦ A three-tier Web architecture is one in which there is either an application server or a database server component, in addition to the two components comprising the two-tier Web architecture.

♦ The most prominent standard and architectural components that control and manage the Web environment are HTML, URLs, HTTP, CGI, Helper plug-ins, and Java/JavaScript.

♦ There are a number of key visual elements of the UltraDev user interface, including HTML text and the WYSIWYG editor, point-and-click object modification, and a customizable user interface.

♦ UltraDev gives you control over the placement of objects on a Web page much the same as desktop publishing tools give you control over the printed page.

♦ You can view/hear execution of video, audio, and graphical elements on your Web page in Preview mode, without having to "publish" the page on a Web server.

♦ You can target a specific group of browsers that your Web site will support. You can also check your Web site for compatibility with one or more different browser types and versions.

Lesson 3

Installing Dreamweaver UltraDev

In Lesson 2, "The Basics of Dreamweaver UltraDev," you learned about the architecture of the Web. You also learned about the UltraDev product at a high level, including some of its more beneficial features and capabilities. In this lesson, you will learn the minimum hardware and software requirements needed to install UltraDev on a PC or Macintosh workstation. You will learn where to get a fully functional 30-day evaluation copy of the product as well. You will also be guided through the process of installing UltraDev. By the time you finish this lesson, you will understand the following key concepts:

♦ Depending on whether you install a server or workstation implementation of UltraDev, your system requirements will vary.

♦ To help you get started quickly, you can install a 30-day free trial copy of UltraDev from the CD-ROM that accompanies this book, or you can download the software from the Macromedia Web site.

♦ Installing UltraDev on your system is a very straightforward process.

Understanding Your System Requirements to Run UltraDev

The minimum system requirements you must have to install and run UltraDev are based on the operating system that is running on the server and the operating system that is running on the workstation. The following sections present the configuration specifications that Macromedia recommends as minimum requirements. To improve your system's performance, note the author's recommendations, which this book presents within parentheses.

System Requirements for a Server to Run UltraDev

If you are running Windows NT Server, your system must be running the following software:

◆ Sun's Java Development Kit version 1.1.8.

◆ Microsoft's Access ODBC driver. The driver is normally installed with NT Server by default. You can also get the driver by installing Microsoft Data Access Components (MDAC) version 2.1 or higher or by downloading the driver from Microsoft's Web site, at www.microsoft.com/data/download.htm.

System Requirements for a Macintosh Workstation to Run UltraDev

Macromedia recommends that, as a minimum, you have the following installed on a Mac that is running Ultra-Dev:

◆ Power Macintosh PowerPC at G3 level or higher.

◆ MacOS 8.1 or later.

◆ 48MB of RAM. (Author recommends 128MB of RAM.)

◆ 30MB of free hard-disk space.

◆ Color monitor capable of 800 × 600 resolution. (Author recommends at least a 17-inch viewable area.)

◆ CD-ROM drive.

◆ Mac OS Runtime for Java (JRL) version 2.2, which you can download at Apple's Web site: www.apple.com/java.

System Requirements for a Windows-based System to Run UltraDev

Macromedia recommends that, as a minimum, you have the following installed on a Windows-based system that is running UltraDev:

♦ Intel Pentium −90. (Author recommends at least 300MHz—any Intel-compatible chipset.)

♦ Windows 95/98, or Windows NT 4.0 with service pack 3.0 or later. (Author recommends *not* installing UltraDev on a Windows 95 machine.)

♦ 48MB of RAM. (Author recommends 128MB of RAM.)

♦ 30MB of available disk space.

♦ 256-color monitor capable of 800 × 600 resolution. (Author recommends at least a 17-inch viewable area.)

♦ CD-ROM drive.

♦ Sun's Java Development Kit, version 1.1.8, which you can download from Sun's Web site at java.sun.com/products/jdk/1.1/jre/download-jre-windows.html.

Additional Software Requirements

Macromedia also recommends the following software, according to your requirements:

♦ **Shockwave 8.** If your Web site is going to run Show Me movies, you will need to install Shockwave 8. You can download and install this from Macromedia's Web site at www.macromedia.com/shockwave/download.

♦ **Web server or application server.** To run dynamic pages, you need a Web server or an application server that supports Microsoft's Active Server Pages (ASP), Sun's JavaServer Pages (JSP) version 1.0, or Allaire's ColdFusion.

♦ **Database.** Web applications that require database access need a way to receive and store data on a database server. If you are building an application that needs this ability, you will need some sort of database system on which to store the data. UltraDev can connect to any database that provides ODBC or JDBC connectivity. This includes file-based databases such as Microsoft Access and Lotus Approach as well as enterprise databases such as Oracle 8i, IBM's DB2, Sybase's SQL Server, and Microsoft's SQL Server.

Installing UltraDev

As shown in Figure 3.1, you can download a 30-day fully functional copy of any of Macromedia's products from its Web site. In addition, the CD-ROM that accompanies this book provides a 30-day time-locked fully functional version of UltraDev. To install UltraDev from the CD-ROM, perform the following steps (these instructions assume you are using a Windows-based PC):

NOTE: *Macromedia strongly recommends that you exit all Windows programs before beginning the installation process. As a rule, you should heed such recommendations. So, close all Windows programs (such as MS Outlook, MS Word, Internet Explorer or Netscape Communicator, and so on) before you proceed with the installation.*

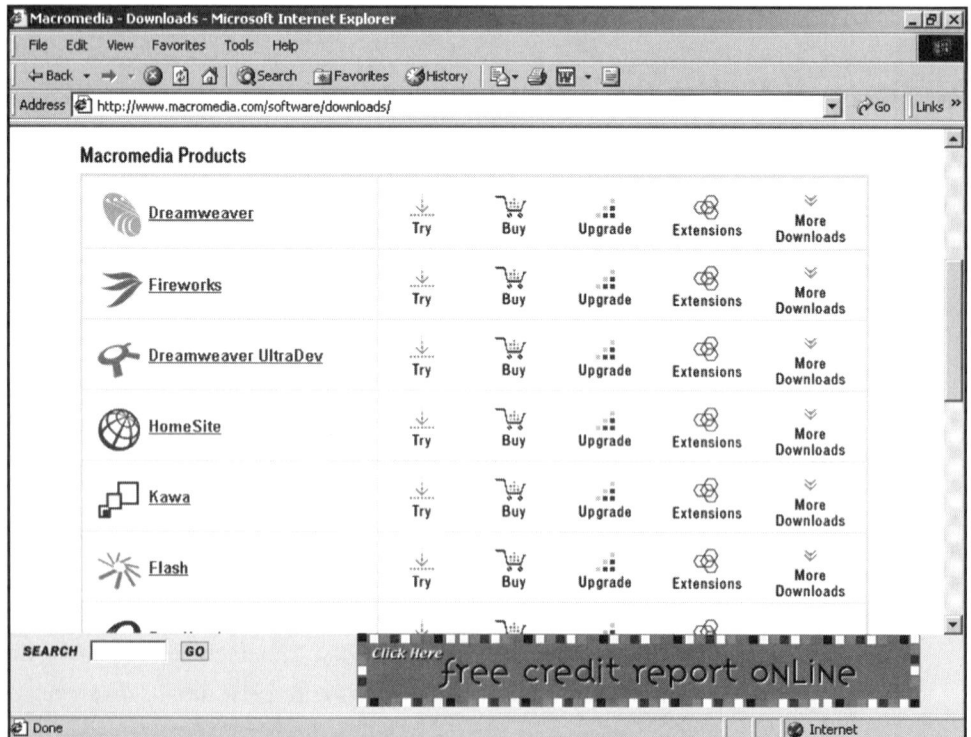

Figure 3.1

The Macromedia page where you can download a trial copy of any of its products

1. Place the CD-ROM that accompanies this book in your CD-ROM drive, and close the door.

2. From your Windows desktop, double-click your mouse on the My Computer icon. Windows, in turn, displays the Exploring – My Computer window, which is divided into two panes. The left pane shows you folders, and the right pane shows you the contents of (files contained within) the selected folder. In the left pane, locate the icon that represents your CD-ROM drive. On many systems, this is either the D or E drive.

3. Within the Exploring – My Computer window, double-click your mouse on the icon representing your CD-ROM drive. In the right pane of the Exploring – My Computer window, Explorer displays a number of folders, including one called Macromedia Demos, that reside on the CD-ROM you just inserted in your CD-ROM drive.

4. Within Explorer, double-click your mouse on the Macromedia Demos icon to display the folder's contents within the right pane. The folder should list three files.

5. Within the right pane, you will see a file named Ultradev-trial. Double-click your mouse on this icon. Windows displays the first installation screen, as shown in Figure 3.2.

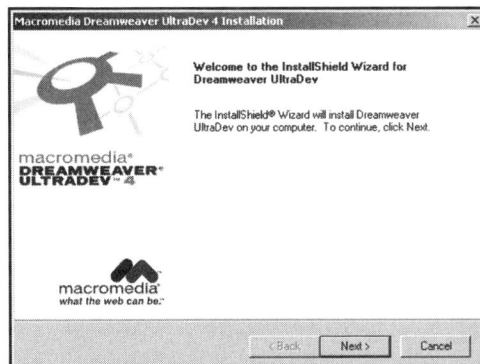

Figure 3.2

The UltraDev installation program Welcome screen

6. Within the Dreamweaver UltraDev Welcome window, click your mouse on the Next button. The installation program displays the Software License Agreement window, as shown in Figure 3.3. Read this agreement before proceeding.

Figure 3.3

Read the Software License Agreement before proceeding.

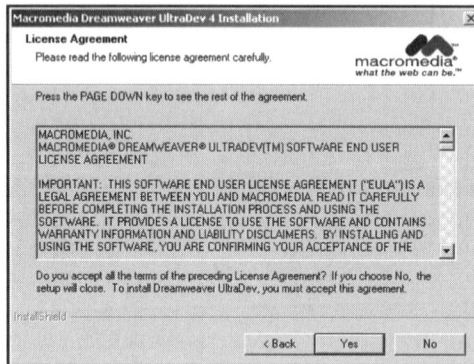

7. Within the Software License Agreement window, after you have read the information the window contains, click your mouse on the Yes button, provided you agree with the terms of the license agreement. The installation program then displays the Location window, as shown in Figure 3.4.

Figure 3.4

The Location window lets you specify where the Setup program installs UltraDev on your disk.

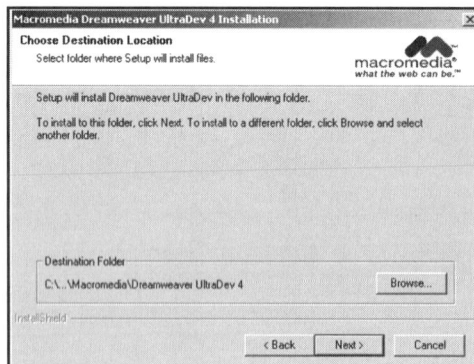

8. Within the Location window, you have the opportunity to change the location where the installation program will place the software. If you want to change this location from the default, click your mouse on the Browse button and then select a different directory location. Assuming the default location of C:\...\Dreamweaver UltraDev is appropriate (as shown in Figure 3.4), click your mouse on the Next button. The installation program displays the Default Editor window, as shown in Figure 3.5.

Figure 3.5

Associate file types to open in UltraDev on the Default Editor window

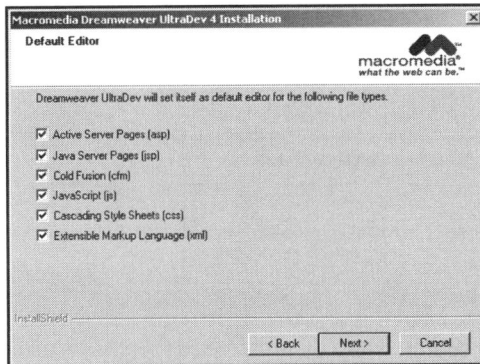

NOTE: *The selections you make in the Default Editor window determine what program is launched when you click on any file in Windows Explorer that has one of the listed file extensions. For example, one of the file type selections is .jsp, which stands for Java Server Pages. If you want Dreamweaver UltraDev to launch and load a file that you click on in Windows Explorer that has a file extension of .jsp, you would select this file type.*

9. Within the Default Editor window, select as a minimum Web Pages and Cascading Style Sheets. After you select the items you desire, click your mouse on the Next button. The installation program displays the Start Menu – Program Folder window, as shown in Figure 3.6.

Figure 3.6

The Start Menu – Program Folder window is where you specify where you will launch UltraDev, beginning with your Start button.

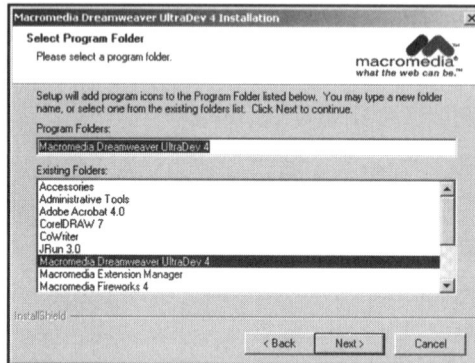

10. By default, the installation program tries to install an entry within a program folder named Macromedia Dreamweaver UltraDev. You can accept this default program folder, type in a name of a new program folder in the textbox below where it says Program Folders, or you can select one of the existing folders on your computer that list in the box that is titled Existing Folders. After you make your selection, click your mouse on the Next button to see the Start Copying Files window, as shown in Figure 3.7.

Figure 3.7

The final point of debarkation— clicking Next begins the copying of files to your computer.

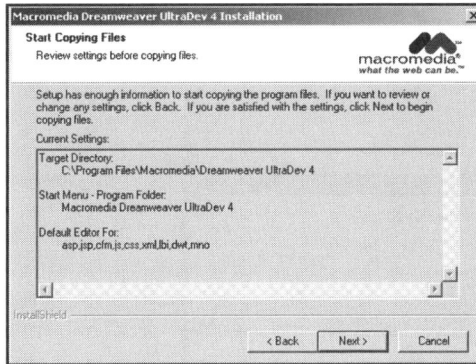

11. Within the Start Copying Files window, you will see the settings you established on previous windows, specifically the location of the Target Directory and the name of the Start Menu – Program Folder. If you want to change either of these settings, click your mouse on the Back button to the appropriate window and make the change. Otherwise, click your mouse on the Next button to begin the actual installation process. The installation program displays a window that looks similar to Figure 3.8, which shows the names of the files as they are being installed on your machine.

Figure 3.8

If you are a very fast reader, you will be able to see the names of the files as they are copied to your computer.

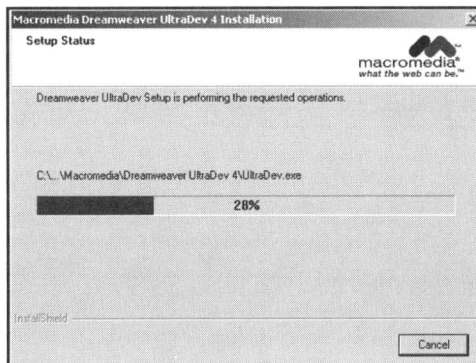

12. When the installation process is complete, your screen displays a Setup Complete window, as shown in Figure 3.9. Click your mouse on the Finish button to complete the installation and setup process.

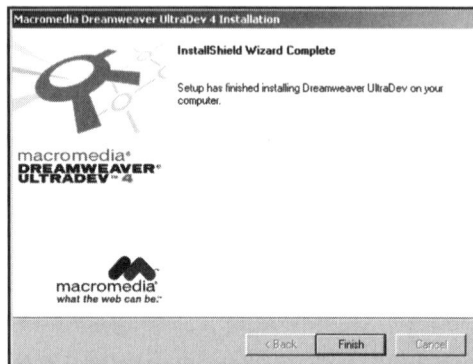

Figure 3.9

You are done! The installation is complete and you can begin using UltraDev.

What You Must Know

This lesson described the minimum hardware and software requirements needed to install and run Dreamweaver UltraDev on either a Macintosh or Windows computer. It also described the components that need to be installed on the server, if you are going to be using the product to access databases located on the server. Also, you were guided through the process of installing Dreamweaver UltraDev on your computer. In Lesson 4, "A Hands-on Tour of Dreamweaver UltraDev," you will roll up your sleeves and start putting UltraDev to work. Before you continue to Lesson 4, make sure that you understand the following key concepts:

◆ Depending on your system type, the requirements your system must meet to run UltraDev will differ.

◆ Before you can use UltraDev to access files that reside on a server, you may need to install additional software components.

◆ You can get a free 30-day fully functional copy of Dreamweaver UltraDev from Macromedia's Web site and the CD-ROM that accompanies this book.

◆ The installation process of Dreamweaver UltraDev is straightforward. You have the option in the installation process to pick a folder where the system components are placed and to direct where in Start Programs you will launch the product.

Lesson 4

A Hands-on Tour of Dreamweaver UltraDev

In Lesson 3, "Installing Dreamweaver UltraDev," you learned about the minimum hardware and software requirements needed to install UltraDev on a PC or Mac workstation. You also learned how to install Dreamweaver UltraDev. In this lesson, you will learn about the UltraDev interface, and the various components of that interface that assist you in building high-quality, fully functional Web sites. By the time you finish this lesson, you will understand the following key concepts:

◆ The UltraDev work area is comprised of various components.

◆ Within UltraDev, the Document window is where you perform most of the work on individual Web pages.

◆ The status bar, which appears at the bottom of the Document window, provides valuable tools and information that help you manage your Web site and work with each page.

◆ Palettes and inspectors are facilities in UltraDev that extend the functionality of the product well beyond most other Web site development toolsets.

◆ The Objects Palette is a tool that lets you click and reclick to place various objects (such as images, rollover images, tables, navigation bars, and so on) on a Web page.

◆ The Property Inspector is a useful tool for displaying the properties of any object you select on the Web page.

◆ The Launcher is a specialized palette containing buttons that open and close the remainder of the UltraDev palettes.

◆ UltraDev employs two forms of menuing. The first is an easily recognizable system that not only is very much Windows/Apple-like, but is also consistent with other products sold by Macromedia. The second type consists of the various context menus that pop up whenever you right-click on any object on a Web page.

NOTE: Copying This Book's Companion CD-ROM to Your Machine

Beginning with this lesson, you need to open and work with various components that reside on the CD-ROM that accompanies this book. Each lesson in the book has examples that are included on the CD-ROM. Within the CD-ROM, you will find a folder named Lesson Examples.

Beneath this folder you will find subfolders for each lesson in the book, named Lesson 04, Lesson 05, and so on. Take time now to copy the entire contents of the Lesson Examples folder on the CD-ROM onto a folder on your machine named Lesson Examples. Moving the files to your disk is important, especially in the earlier lessons of this book, so that examples work on your machine as described in the lessons.

In Lesson 8, "Setting Up an UltraDev Site," you will learn how to adjust site-specific information so you can place a site in any folder you want. But for now, if you make sure that you create a folder called Lesson Examples and place the contents of the folder called Lesson Examples on your CD-ROM in it, examples will work just fine.

Understanding the UltraDev Interface

To get started, you will start UltraDev, and then load a Web page into UltraDev, by performing these steps:

1. Start Dreamweaver UltraDev. The steps you must perform depend upon whether you are using Windows or the Mac and the location on your disk within which you installed the UltraDev files.

2. Within UltraDev, click your mouse on the File menu and select Open. UltraDev displays the Open dialog box.

3. Within the Open dialog box, click your mouse on the drop-down list box next to the Look In field to select the folder that contains the source file (the Web document) you want to open. The dialog box, in turn, displays a pop-up Explorer-like window of the folders and directories on your system.

4. From within the Explorer-like window, select the disk and folder where you placed the contents of this book's companion CD-ROM.

5. Within the Lesson Examples folder, click your mouse on the folder titled Lesson 4 and you will see a folder named Images and a file named Index.html.

6. Click your mouse on the file named Index.html, and then click on the Open button to load the file into UltraDev.

The UltraDev interface is comprised of a number of objects that you can select and position wherever you like. When you open UltraDev and load a Web page, you start your work within the Document window, as shown in Figure 4.1.

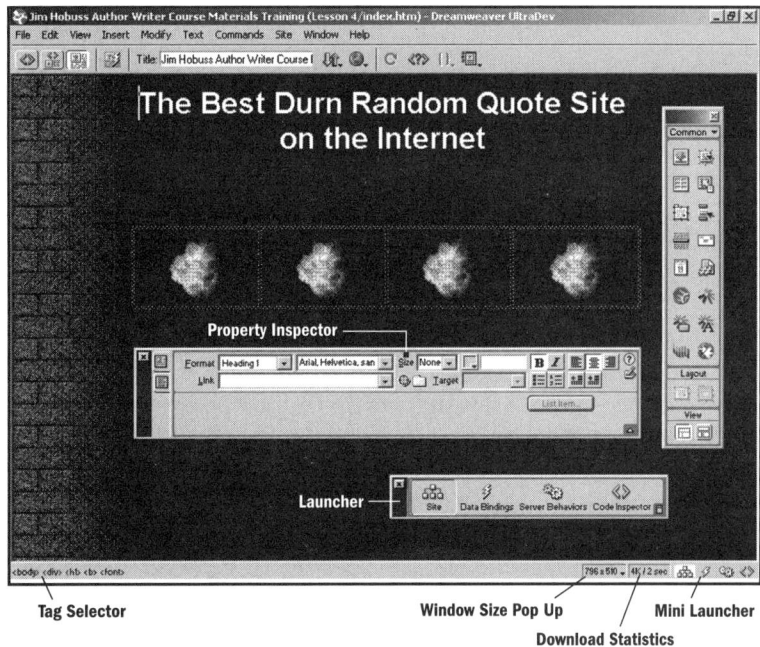

Figure 4.1

The Document window and some of the UltraDev objects and palettes

NOTE: *When you open UltraDev for the first time without loading a page and assuming you have no sites defined, you see an empty Document window. However, if you have Web sites set up in UltraDev, when you first launch the product, you see the Site window, which is a navigation tool that lets you easily work with one of multiple Web sites on your machine.*

If you do not see objects within the Document window, as shown in Figure 4.1, perform the following steps to view them:

7. Within the Document window, click your mouse on the Window menu. UltraDev displays the Window submenu pop-up.

NOTE: *Three submenu items are listed at the top of the Window submenu: Objects, Properties, and Launcher. If all three of these are checked, you are ready to continue. To display an item, click your mouse on one of these three submenu items that does not appear with a check mark.*

8. Within the pop-up menu, notice that when you click your mouse on a Window-menu item, the submenu then disappears. This is alright.

9. Repeat Steps 1 and 2 until UltraDev displays the three objects within the Document window similar to that previously shown in Figure 4.1

The following sections examine some of the objects that appear within this window in more detail.

The Title Bar

Within UltraDev, the title bar contains the name of the site you are working on, plus the name, in parentheses, of the page that is loaded in UltraDev. Within Figure 4.1, the name of the page loaded in UltraDev is *index*, which you loaded from the Lesson04 folder. When you open UltraDev for the first time without a page loaded, you will see a document title of *"Untitled"* in the title bar. As you load new pages into the Document window, you will see the name of the page appear in the title bar.

The Menu Bar

The Menu bar in the UltraDev product looks very much like the Menu bar in other Macromedia products. You will get very accustomed to the features and capabilities available through the Menu bar options. As this section describes the functions available on each of the menu items located on the Menu bar, click your mouse on the appropriate menu item. The UltraDev Menu bar is comprised of the following menu items:

◆ **File menu.** Enables you to perform actions on files and general site management and handling.

◆ **Edit menu.** Provides commands that let you quickly modify a Web page and undo modifications made that you want to easily remove.

◆ **View menu.** Enables you to turn certain features (such as rulers, grids, layers, and so on) on and off.

◆ **Insert menu.** Contains the same objects that are selectable on the Objects palette. Used to select a specific object type (such as a table, image, layer, and so on) for placement on your page. As you may have observed already, the UltraDev interface frequently gives you more than one way to perform a specific action.

◆ **Modify menu.** Two acts are repeatedly done by Web designers: placing objects on a Web page, and modifying those objects once placed. The Insert menu (or the Objects palette) is used to place an object on a Web page. The items listed on the Modify menu let you modify existing objects on a Web page.

◆ **Text menu.** Because Web sites originated as primarily text-heavy pages, and the reliance on the written word on Web pages has remained a significant element of Web pages, since Ultra-Dev provides the Text menu with options to manipulate, place, and format text.

◆ **Commands menu.** Provides commands to create and execute user-definable code that is capable of manipulating almost any element (text, graphic, or otherwise) on a Web page. UltraDev gives you the ability to execute commands that ship with the product, create and execute your own commands, or even to manipulate the commands that ship with the product to create a unique and desirable behavior.

◆ **Site menu.** The majority of the work to build a Web site is the creation of the actual Web pages. After these pages are built, they frequently are modified numerous times throughout their life. As the number of pages on your site grows, and as the length of time that a page stays on your site increases, and as the number of links to existing pages on your site increases, the ability to manage these myriad relationships can become complex. The Site menu gives you tools that assist in the management of your overall Web site.

◆ **Window menu.** Gives you the ability to manage the UltraDev objects that you have access to (such as palettes, Properties, Behaviors, and so on).

> **NOTE:** *All the UltraDev windows and objects are opened by pressing a specific key combination, in addition to clicking on the appropriate object type in the Window menu. To close an object that is open (such as the Properties window), simply press the same key combination that opened the object in the first place. In the case of the Properties window, for example, you would press the Ctrl+F3 keyboard combination.*

◆ **Help menu**. UltraDev ships with one of the best Help facilities that I have seen in a commercial product. In addition to standard Help capabilities, you have access to connect to the Macromedia site to update components of the UltraDev product installed on your machine.

The Status Bar

The status bar, which appears at the bottom of the Document window, is comprised of four different elements:

◆ Tag Selector

◆ Window Size pop-up menu

◆ Download Statistics

◆ Mini Launcher

The Tag Selector, which resides at the far-left side of the status bar, provides easy access to the HTML code that is involved with any object on the page. If you want to see the HTML code generated for any particular object on your page, click your mouse on that object and the Tag Selector will show it to you. There are two HTML elements to the Tag Selector. The first is HTML generated to support the Web page up to the object selected, and this is displayed in a normal font. The second is the HTML generated for the selected object, and this displays in a bold font. In Figure 4.1, you see two HTML tags, a <body> tag and a <p> tag.

Try clicking on various objects and in various sections of the page loaded in UltraDev. You should see how the Tag Selector changes to represent the HTML for the object selected.

NOTE: *In Lesson 14, "Scripting and UltraDev Actions," when you examine scripting and behaviors, you will see that the Tag Selector has more value than what is presented here. The Tag Selector is a useful navigation tool to move from object to object in your Web page.*

The Window Size pop-up menu shows the current screen resolution in UltraDev. As shown in Figure 4.1, the screen resolution is 794 × 540. Also notice the down arrow in this object in the Status bar. Click on the down arrow. A pop-up menu displays, as shown in Figure 4.2, that lets you select a different resolution for your Web page. This is a very convenient way to test the layout of your page at different monitor resolutions.

Notice in the pop-up menu that there are two sets of numbers in each row. The leftmost pair of numbers is the *estimated* browser window dimension, and the rightmost pair of numbers, the ones in parentheses, is the screen resolution. The reason why the browser window dimensions are less than the associated screen resolution is that the browser interface takes up some of the available screen space.

The last submenu item in the pop-up menu is Edit Sizes. Clicking your mouse on this item takes you to the status bar category in UltraDev preferences where you can create your own (or edit an existing) window size. As is the case with most of the features in UltraDev, there is another way to access this facility; in this case, by clicking your mouse on the Status Bar item in the Preferences submenu that is located on the Edit menu.

Figure 4.2

The Window Size pop-up menu allows you to resize the screen and approximate the viewable area of a browser.

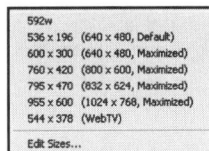

```
592w
536 x 196   (640 x 480, Default)
600 x 300   (640 x 480, Maximized)
760 x 420   (800 x 600, Maximized)
795 x 470   (832 x 624, Maximized)
955 x 600   (1024 x 768, Maximized)
544 x 378   (WebTV)

Edit Sizes...
```

The third item in the Status Bar, Download Statistics, shows two pieces of information that are very valuable when determining how fast your page will display in a browser. The first piece of information is an estimate of how large the page is, in bytes of data. In Figure 4.1, you see that the page, as drawn, is approximately 21,000 bytes. The second piece of information is the amount of time it will take to download the page given a particular modem's speed. The default modem speed is 56Kbps (kilobits per second). From the Download Statistics in Figure 4.1, you see that a user viewing this Web page using a 56Kbps modem speed to connect to the Internet will take 6 seconds to download and view this page in their browser.

As shown in Figure 4.3, you can adjust the target modem connection speed to get an idea of how responsive your Web page will be. To access this Window, perform these steps:

1. From the Menu bar, click your mouse on the Edit menu item. UltraDev displays the Edit submenu items.

2. Within the Edit submenu items, click your mouse on the Preference submenu item. Ultra-Dev displays the Preferences window.

3. Within the Preferences window, click your mouse on the Status bar item. UltraDev displays a window that looks very much like that shown in Figure 4.3.

4. Within the window, click your mouse on the Connection Speed drop-down list box to select a different connection speed. After you select a different connection speed, UltraDev closes the Preferences window.

Figure 4.3

The Status Bar item on the Preferences window is where you change the target modem connection speed.

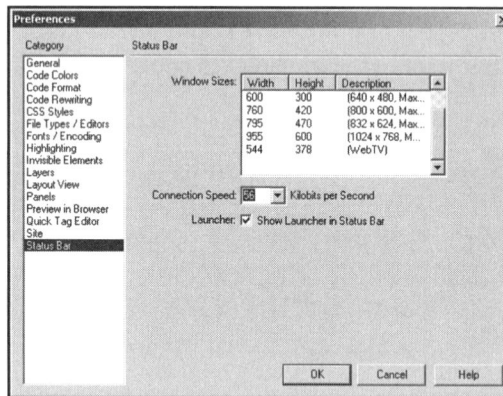

Using the directions listed here, try adjusting the connection speed from what is shown. As you change the connection speed, you will see the effects of your change within the Download Statistics section of the status bar.

The last item on the status bar, the one furthest to the right, is the mini-launcher, which is where you go to begin the execution of any of the palettes on the Launcher. You will examine the facilities available on the Launcher in this lesson's section "Understanding the Launcher."

The Property Inspector

Within UltraDev, the Property Inspector displays all the properties for a given selected object. For example, the Property inspector previously shown in Figure 4.1 is displaying a paragraph's properties.

Within the Property Inspector, you can easily change an object's attributes. As you might guess, there are attributes specific to a block of text (such as Font, Size, and so on) that are different from an image that is selected (image name, background color, and so on).

For now, try clicking your mouse on one of the graphics that appears within the Web page, and watch what happens to the Property Inspector. You may see one of the object's attributes change. At this stage, do not be concerned about how you change any of the specific attributes for a selected object, as we will cover that in detail later. Click your mouse on any of the words in the title of the page. You will find that the Property Inspector changes the object's appearance.

If you look at the lower-right corner of the Property Inspector, you will see an arrow pointing up. You will see this as the circled arrow in Figure 4.4. Click your mouse on that arrow and the Property Inspector collapses. At the same time it collapses, the arrow changes appearance to a down arrow. Next, click your mouse on the down arrow. UltraDev gives you the ability to remove clutter from your screen by limiting what items appear within the Property Inspector to (what the folks at Macromedia believe are) the most commonly modified attributes for every object.

Figure 4.4

The Property Inspector showing the maximize/minimize button

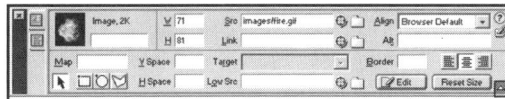

The Objects Palette

NOTE: *In Lesson 26, "Customizing Dreamweaver UltraDev," you will see how to create your own objects and include those objects on the Objects palette. Placing customized objects on the Objects palette lets you improve your efficiency using UltraDev by reducing the number of keystrokes you need to execute to insert a customized or unique object on a Web page.*

The Objects palette lets you place one of 56 types of objects on a Web page. And, even though there are 56 default objects on the Objects palette, as discussed in the previous note, you can manipulate these to a greater or lesser number. UltraDev groups these 56 objects within the following six categories, as shown in Figure 4.5:

♦ Characters

♦ Common

♦ Forms

♦ Frames

♦ Head

♦ Invisibles

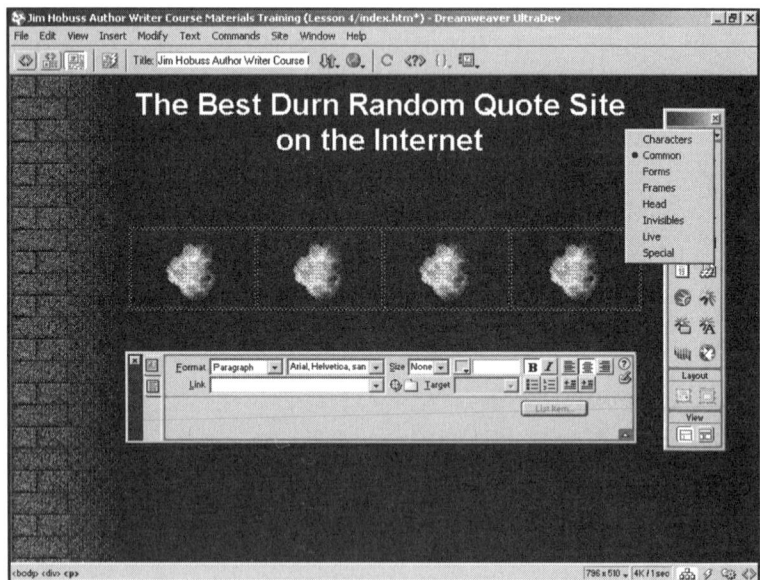

Figure 4.5

The six panels comprising the Objects palette

Assume, for example, you must place a trademark symbol (™) following the words "The Best Durn Random Quote Site" that appears as a heading of this Web page. To do so, you would use the Objects palette as follows:

1. Within the Objects palette, click your mouse on the small down arrow that appears next to the Common panel name. UltraDev displays a pop-up menu that contains the six panels that comprise the Objects palette.

2. On the panel list of the Objects palette, click the panel named Characters. You will see the complete Characters panel display in the Objects palette.

3. Place the insertion point on the page where you want the character you are about to select placed. Position the icon for your mouse pointer after the *e* in the word "Site" that appears in the line "The Best Durn Random Quote Site," and then click the mouse button once. You will see the pointer start blinking at this spot.

4. The leftmost icon in the second row of the Characters panel should be a button with a trademark symbol (™). Click your mouse on that icon one time. UltraDev inserts the trademark symbol on the page at the insertion point, and your Document window should look very similar to Figure 4.6.

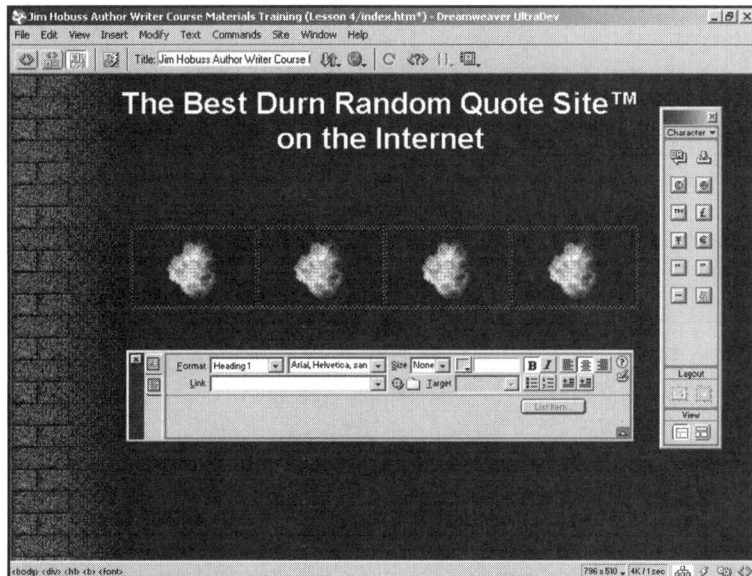

Figure 4.6

The Document window after inserting a trademark symbol

NOTE: *An alternate way to place an object from the Objects palette on your Web page is to grab and hold the object (click your mouse on the object and do not release the mouse button), and then slide it over to the location on the Web page where you would like to place it. As you work with UltraDev, you will develop your own preferences on how you like to accomplish certain tasks.*

The Launcher

The Launcher is a special palette containing buttons that open and close other UltraDev palettes. If an Ultra-Dev palette is closed when you click on the button representing that palette, the palette will open. If you click on the button representing a palette that is currently open, the palette will close.

NOTE: *There is a small orientation button that appears in the lower-right corner of the Launcher. Clicking this button alternates its display between a horizontal and vertical orientation.*

Do not be concerned with the functions and use of the various palettes that appear on the Launcher, because these will be discussed later. The important concept to understand here is that the Launcher is a special facility that allows you to launch and close other palettes from it with a single click of the mouse.

By default, UltraDev displays four palettes in the Launcher: Site, Data Bindings, Server Behaviors, and HTML Source. You can customize (add or remove) the palettes that appear in the Launcher. Assume that you want to include the Objects palette in the Launcher. To include the Objects palette within the Launcher, perform these steps:

1. Within the Menu bar, click your mouse on the Edit menu item. UltraDev displays the Edit menu.

2. Within the Edit menu, click your mouse on the Preferences submenu item. UltraDev, in turn, displays the Preferences window.

3. Within the Preferences window, click your mouse on the Floating palettes category. Ultra-Dev displays the floating palettes in the right side of the Preferences window.

4. Within the Preferences window, click your mouse on the plus button (+) that appears next to the Show In Launcher section. UltraDev, in turn, displays a pop-up menu showing all the available palettes in normal text. The pop-up menu will disable the currently selected

palettes. Click your mouse on the Objects item. UltraDev closes the Preferences window and you see the Objects Palette showing as a button in the Launcher, as shown in Figure 4.7.

Figure 4.7

The Launcher, with the Objects palette included

An Alternative Way to Access Menus

The menu items that appear on the Menu bar are a convenient and typical way to access certain features and facilities in the UltraDev product. The items that appear in the Menu bar are static, meaning they do not change at all (although they may become enabled and disabled, they never change).

Using the context menu shown in Figure 4.8, UltraDev gives you the ability to access a custom set of menu items for any type of object that you might select on a Web page.

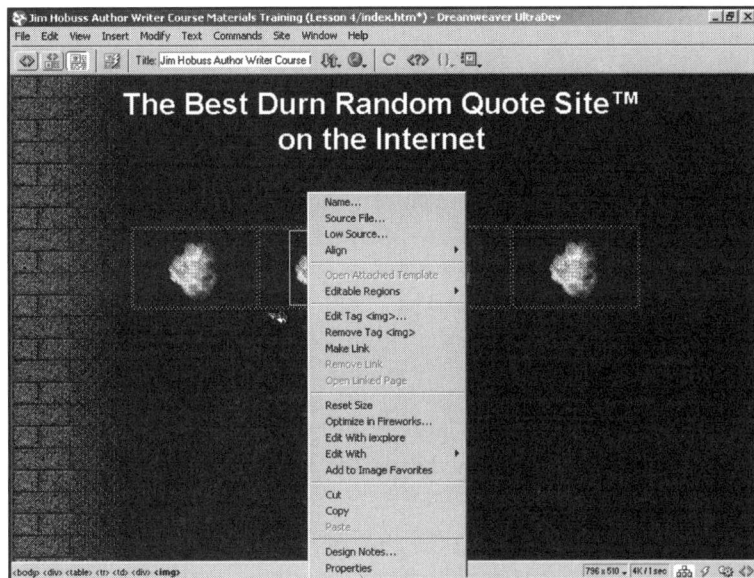

Figure 4.8

To access the context menu, right-click your mouse on any object that appears in the Document window.

The product architects at Macromedia decided what functions a developer would most likely need to access when working on each object type that could appear on a Web page, and developed these context menus to list those functions.

What You Must Know

This lesson described the UltraDev interface, and the various components of that interface that assist you in building high-quality, fully functional Web sites. In Lesson 5, "Additions to Dreamweaver That Make It Ultra-Dev," you will learn about the features Macromedia, Inc., added to the Dreamweaver product to create UltraDev.

Before you continue to Lesson 5, make sure that you understand the following key concepts:

♦ There are a number of facilities in the UltraDev work area that assist you in the creation and maintenance of your Web page and objects that appear on those pages.

♦ The Document window is the pane where you see your Web page pretty much as it would appear in a browser, and where you launch many of the other components in the UltraDev interface that help you.

♦ There are many uses for the status bar, which appears at the bottom of the Document window, including a Tag Selector, a Mini Launcher, information about the size of your viewable window, and document statistics.

♦ Palettes and inspectors are facilities in UltraDev that allow you to set properties for objects, open other palettes, and add audio/video content to your Web pages.

♦ With the Objects palette, you can click and re-click to place various objects (images, rollover images, tables, navigation bars, and so on) on a Web page.

♦ The Property Inspector allows you to display the properties of any selected object on the Web page.

♦ The Launcher is a "specialized" palette that contains a set of buttons that let you open and close the remainder of the UltraDev palettes.

♦ Two forms of menus are used in UltraDev. The first is very much Windows/Apple-like, and is accessible on the Menu bar. The second type is the various context menus that pop up whenever you right-click on any object on a Web page.

Lesson 5

Additions to Dreamweaver That Make It UltraDev

In Lesson 4, "A Hands-on Tour of Dreamweaver UltraDev," you learned about the interface to UltraDev, including palettes, inspectors, and menus. As you will recall, Macromedia, Inc., did not create the UltraDev product from scratch, but rather purchased a software program named Drumbeat and then added new features that it integrated into its Dreamweaver software to create UltraDev. In this lesson, you will examine the features in the UltraDev product that extend it from the Dreamweaver product.

By the time you finish this lesson, you will understand the following key concepts:

♦ UltraDev is an extension to Dreamweaver, and the two products are sold separately by Macromedia.

♦ Some of the extensions to UltraDev are for the purpose of enabling it to interface with databases.

♦ Some of the menu items in the Dreamweaver interface have submenu items added to them to provide necessary UltraDev functions.

UltraDev's Roots Are in Dreamweaver

In July 1999, Macromedia, Inc., purchased a company named Elemental Software, and in turn acquired Elemental Software's product called Drumbeat. The Drumbeat tool lets Web developers access corporate data stores. In late 1999, Macromedia released its first version of Drumbeat, which it called Drumbeat 2000. In this release, Macromedia made some changes to the user interface and integrated Drumbeat more closely with other Macromedia products, most notably Dreamweaver.

Then, on June 7, 2000, at the JavaOne 2000 Conference in San Francisco, California, Macromedia announced the release of Dreamweaver UltraDev. Sold as an add-on product to Dreamweaver, UltraDev is billed as a tool that makes it possible to create sites of three distinct types:

♦ **Static.** This is a basic collection of HTML pages. Static sites offer low interactivity but can be deployed on any platform.

♦ **Database-derived.** HTML pages populated from data tables at publication time, but static thereafter.

♦ **Database-driven.** ASP pages populated from data tables on the fly. Data-driven sites built with Drumbeat must run on an ASP server, such as Microsoft Internet Information Server (IIS).

UltraDev extends the capabilities provided in Dreamweaver by providing the following additional capabilities:

♦ Generates ASP (*Active Server Pages*) code

♦ Generates CFML (*ColdFusion Markup Language*) code

♦ Generates JSP (*JavaServer Pages*) code

♦ Generates database-driven forms and reports quickly

♦ Roundtrip server markup

♦ Provides a built-in set of objects for connecting to databases

♦ Live data preview

♦ Connection to databases using JDBC, OLE, and ODBC

♦ Query Builder

♦ Bind attributes and text to databases and server scripts

♦ Dynamic data formatting

With UltraDev, Macromedia made a strategic decision to discontinue selling Drumbeat in any form, and is expected to drop support for Drumbeat soon. Therefore, at the present time, purchasers have the following options when deciding which Web site development tool to purchase:

◆ **Dreamweaver.** Used if the Web site does not support database access.

◆ **Dreamweaver UltraDev.** Used if the Web site needs to support database access.

◆ **UltraDev Upgrade.** Used if the user currently has a registered copy of Dreamweaver and needs access to the capabilities in UltraDev.

Interface Differences Between Dreamweaver and UltraDev

The following are the four areas in the user interface design of UltraDev where the developers at Macromedia placed access to various facilities that extend the Dreamweaver product to the UltraDev product:

◆ Data Bindings palette

◆ Launcher

◆ mini-Launcher

◆ Menu items

Using the Data Bindings Palette

The Data Bindings palette, shown in Figure 5.1, is a pop-up window that lets you add dynamic content to your page. The Data Bindings palette consists of two tabs: the Data Bindings Inspector and the Server Behaviors Inspector.

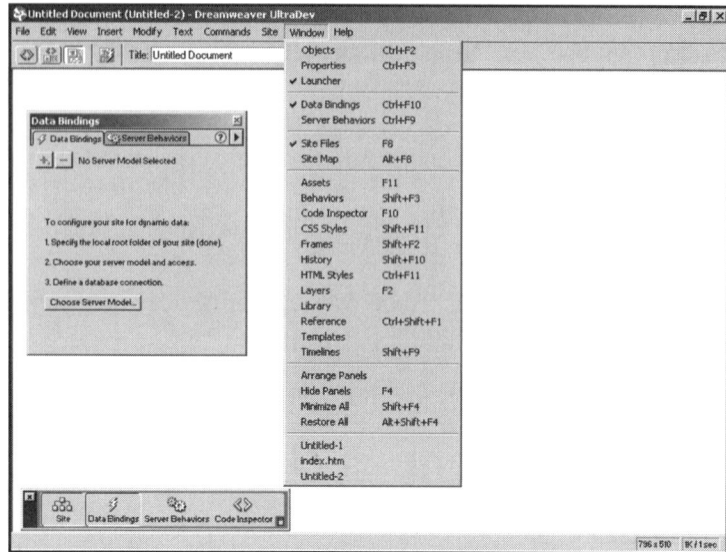

Figure 5.1

The Data Bindings palette is one of the UltraDev-specific interface objects.

Accessing the Data Bindings Palette

For ways exist to access the Data Bindings palette:

◆ Click on the Window menu Data Bindings submenu item (as previously shown in Figure 5.1).

◆ Press the Shift+F10 key combination at any time you are working in the UltraDev interface.

◆ Clicking on the Data Bindings icon (the one that looks like a lightning bolt) that appears on the Launcher, which is also shown in Figure 5.1.

◆ Click on the Data Bindings icon (again, the one that looks like a lightning bolt) that appears on the mini-Launcher at the bottom of the document window.

Understanding the Data Bindings Palette

Whenever you create a Web page that accesses data stored in a database, regardless of whether the Web page updates the data or only reads the data, that Web page is termed *dynamic*. The aspect that makes it dynamic is that, theoretically, the data retrieved from the database can change from one moment to the next. There needs to be some way to connect the Web page you create with the data stored in the database. This mechanism is contained within the two tabs of the Data Bindings palette: the Data Bindings tab and the Server Behaviors tab.

Using the Data Bindings Tab

Within UltraDev, you use the Data Bindings tab to establish various types of connections to your database.

The Data Bindings tab shown in Figure 5.2 looks slightly different from the Data Bindings tab previously shown in Figure 5.1, because I created a database connection to a Microsoft Access database before taking the screen shot seen in Figure 5.2.

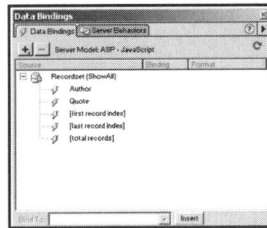

Figure 5.2

The Data Bindings tab on the Data Bindings palette

Within Figure 5.2, you will notice the plus (+) and minus (−) buttons at the top of the Data Bindings tab. These buttons provide you with access to screens that let you add and delete data sources. A *data source* is another term for a database.

Using the Server Behaviors Tab

Within an UltraDev database, a server script is a set of instructions that tells your database server what to do with the data retrieved from the database, for placement on a Web page. It also tells the database server when you must write information to the database from the Web page. For example, the sample database you will use throughout this book contains various quotes attributed to different people. If you want to retrieve all of the quotes in the database attributed to Mark Twain, you could create a server script to only extract the records from the database that pertain to quotes made by Mark Twain. In this way, you transfer from the database server to the user's Web page only the data the page will display.

The Server Behaviors tab, as shown in Figure 5.3, is the mechanism in UltraDev that lets you establish and maintain server scripts.

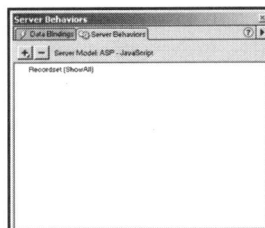

Figure 5.3

The Server Behaviors tab on the Data Bindings palette

As you will learn, UltraDev ships with a library of prewritten server scripts, and there are facilities that let you write your own scripts. Within Figure 5.3, you will notice plus (+) and minus (–) buttons at the top of the Server Behaviors tab. These buttons provide you with access to UltraDev's library of server scripts.

Understanding UltraDev Differences in the Launcher

Within UltraDev, you use a facility called the Launcher to access some of the more commonly used UltraDev components. Referring to Figure 5.1, you access the Launcher in one of two ways: by clicking on the Window menu Launcher submenu, or by pressing the Shift+F11 key combination at any time you are working in the UltraDev interface.

The two icons on the Launcher that are new to the UltraDev interface are the Data Bindings icon (the icon that looks like a lightning bolt) and the Server Behaviors icon (the icon that looks like two gears). Clicking on either of these icons launches the Data Bindings palette, with either the Data Bindings or Server Behaviors tab enabled.

Understanding UltraDev Differences in the mini-Launcher

The mini-Launcher is a component in the Dreamweaver UltraDev product that gives you quick access to some of the more commonly used facilities.

Figure 5.4 shows the mini-Launcher that is pre-configured for the Dreamweaver product. Although this lesson will not delve into the specifics of what each icon does, notice how much different the mini-Launcher for Dreamweaver looks from the mini-Launcher for UltraDev, which is shown in Figure 5.5.

Figure 5.4
The Dreamweaver
mini-Launcher

Figure 5.5
The UltraDev mini-Launcher

Within Figure 5.5, notice the two icons that provide you with access to the Data Bindings tab and the Server Behaviors tab on the Data Bindings palette. You can use these icons to quickly specify which relational database management system (RDBMS) you are using, as well as how you want the RDBMS system to return data to the Web pages you create within UltraDev.

Understanding UltraDev Differences in the Menus

There are changes to four menus that transition Dreamweaver to UltraDev:

- ◆ **View.** Lets you view portions of your site or Web page, or attributes of a component or control on a page.

- ◆ **Modify.** Lets you modify an attribute specific to your site, a page on your site, or a component or control on a page.

- ◆ **Window.** Gives you access to different palettes and UltraDev components.

- ◆ **Help.** Starts the UltraDev online help utility.

The following sections discuss changes to each of these Menu items that exist between Dreamweaver and Ultra-Dev.

Using the View Submenu

Within UltraDev, the View submenu provides you with access to view different palettes and controls within UltraDev that describe and format the way you view your site pages.

As shown in Figure 5.6, there are three new submenu items to the View menu in the UltraDev interface:

- ◆ **Live Data**. Allows you to view a sampling of data directly retrieved from the database.

- ◆ **Refresh Live Data**. Allows you to refresh the view of sample data retrieved from the database.

- ◆ **Live Data Settings**. Allows you to view and modify the way your site connects to the database.

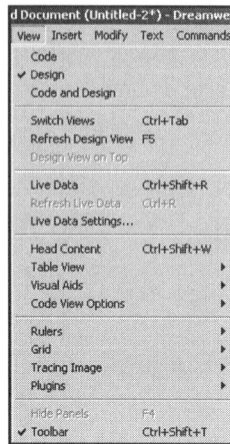

Figure 5.6

New View submenu items to support UltraDev functions

The Live Data submenu lets you establish the ability to view the dynamic content on your page while you work on the page. The Live Data window works with the Web server that hosts your remote site. UltraDev borrows the server to run the page and display the results in the Live Data window. The ability to view dynamic content while you work is a powerful capability when you design and develop your pages.

Within the UltraDev interface, the Refresh Live Data submenu option lets you refresh the display of data that shows in your document window. By clicking on the Refresh Live Data submenu item, you direct UltraDev to extract the data from the database to display it within the document window.

The Live Data Settings submenu item lets you modify any of the settings previously established for the connection to your database.

Using the Modify Submenu

Within UltraDev, the Modify submenu lets you access and modify different palettes and controls that describe and format the way you work with your site pages. As shown in Figure 5.7, there is one new submenu item to the Modify menu in the UltraDev interface: Connections.

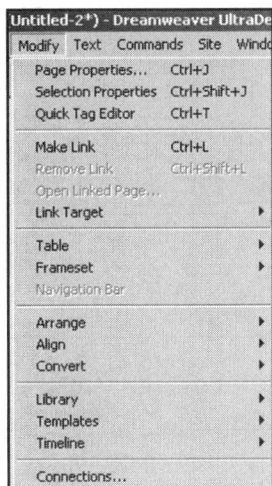

Figure 5.7

New Modify submenu item to support UltraDev functions

As previously discussed, you must establish a connection to a database before your Web page can access data on that database. In actuality, you must create at least one, and possibly two, connections to each database that is accessed from a Web site. These connections are as follows:

◆ **Run-time database connection.** Points your Web pages to the location and name of the database to access when the pages are accessed from a user's browser.

◆ **Design-time database connection.** Points your Web pages to the location and name of the database to access when the pages are being developed and before they are placed into "production" status.

UltraDev lets you create a run-time database connection and an optional design-time connection. Both of these database connections are established by clicking on the Connections submenu item on the Modify menu, which opens the Define Connection window, shown in Figure 5.8. Because your run-time connection is your deployment connection, you must always create one. You should create a design-time connection if it's impractical or impossible to access the deployment database at design time.

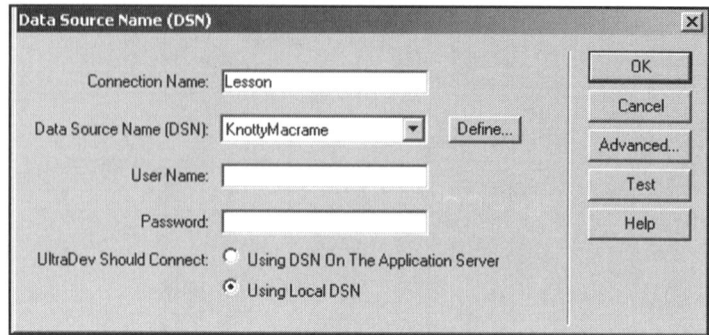

Figure 5.8

The Define Connection window

If you use a file-based database program, such as Microsoft Access or Lotus Approach, you can place a copy of the database file on a system that's easily accessible, and then create a design-time connection to it. While you work, UltraDev will display information from the database copy—information such as table and field names, stored procedures, and so on.

NOTE: *The database examples in this book use the MS Access database, which UltraDev views as a file-based database.*

You must also create a design-time connection if you cannot connect to the database using the run-time technology. For example, Macintosh users developing ASP sites (thus using ADO technology to connect at run time) cannot use ADO to connect at design time, because the Macintosh does not support ADO. Macintosh users must use JDBC technology to connect at design time (often connecting to the same database as the run-time connection).

Using the Window Submenu

Within UltraDev, the Window submenu lets you access different UltraDev facilities that give you access to components specific to your site.

As shown in Figure 5.9, there are two new submenu items to the Window menu in the UltraDev interface:

◆ **Data Bindings.** A descriptions of how the site connects and attaches to data stored in the database.

◆ **Server Behaviors.** These are behaviors that execute on a Web server and are triggered by specific events initiated by a site visitor.

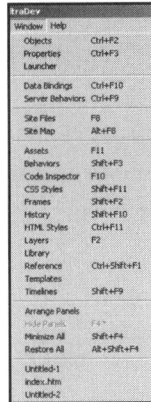

Figure 5.9

New Window submenu items to support UltraDev functions

These two submenu options launch the Data Bindings tab and the Server Behaviors tab on the Data Bindings palette, respectively.

Using the Help Submenu

UltraDev provides you with an extensive online help facility, which you access using the Help submenu. As shown in Figure 5.10, there are five new submenu items to the Window menu in the UltraDev interface:

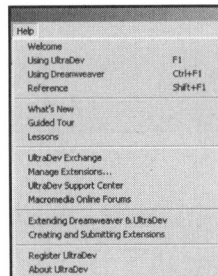

Figure 5.10

New Help submenu items to support UltraDev functions

◆ **Using UltraDev.** Provides access to HTML-based help that is fairly high level, but is useful to be familiar with.

◆ **Guided Tour of UltraDev.** Provides access to HTML-based help that is more extensive than Using UltraDev. There is a Search component in this facility that is nicely developed.

◆ **UltraDev Tutorial.** Provides access to HTML-based help that is written in a tutorial style. This is probably not going to be as useful to you as the Guided Tour of UltraDev option.

◆ **UltraDev Support Center.** Provides access to Web pages maintained at the Macromedia site that are written to disseminate information specific to features in UltraDev. A screen capture of this site is shown in Figure 5.11. The Search facility on these pages is very well implemented.

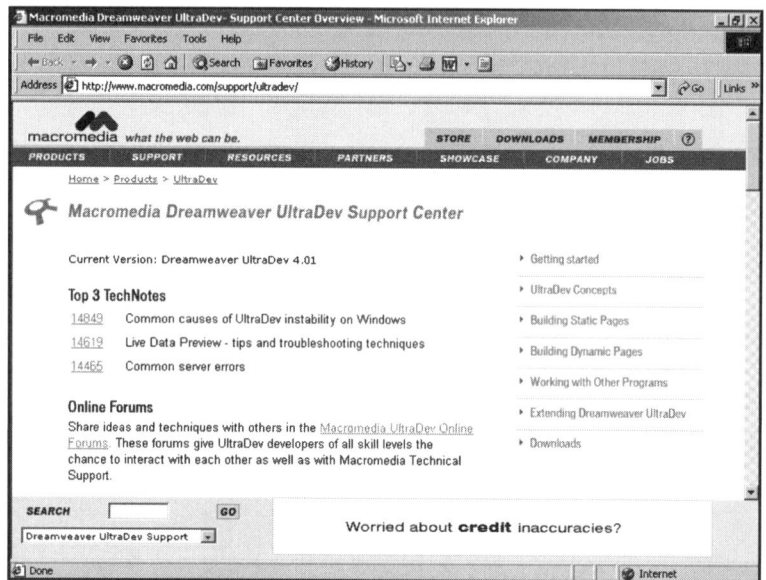

Figure 5.11

The UltraDev Support Center

◆ **UltraDev Exchange.** Provides access to Web pages maintained at Macromedia that are maintained to be a place where you can get easy-to-install extensions, learn how to get the most out of them, and even create your own. Extensions let you easily add new features to Dreamweaver UltraDev. Each extension has its own page that includes the extension, a short description, user reviews, and a discussion group where you can post questions and get support for an extension.

What You Must Know

This lesson described the features in the UltraDev product that extend it from the Dreamweaver product. You learned about these first at a high level, and then how these extensions are distributed through the various menus, palettes, and objects. In Lesson 6, "Understanding Database Basics," you will learn about the major types of databases, and how to write the code necessary to work with the data stored in a SQL database. Before you continue to Lesson 6, make sure you understand the following key concepts:

◆ UltraDev is an extension to Dreamweaver, and the two products are sold separately by Macromedia.

◆ The single most significant component in UltraDev that extends it from Dreamweaver is its ability to interface with databases.

◆ Some of the menu items in the Dreamweaver interface have submenu items added to it to comprise the UltraDev interface.

Lesson 6

Understanding
Database Basics

In Lesson 5, "Additions to Dreamweaver That Make It UltraDev," you learned about the features and components in UltraDev that extend the functions and facilities found in Dreamweaver. In this lesson, you will learn about databases, the component that extends Dreamweaver to UltraDev.

By the time you finish this lesson, you will understand the following key concepts:

◆ The relational database is one of three types of databases, and is currently the most popular database architecture.

◆ Many different types of components comprise a relational database.

◆ A database is comprised of tables, rows, columns, and attributes.

◆ A database schema describes the layout of the data contained within the database, and the relationship between data components.

◆ Structured Query Language (SQL) is the language used to interact with relational databases.

◆ The three parts to any SQL statement and the types of actions you can perform on data in a database using SQL.

Introduction to Database Management Systems

A database management system (DBMS) is a suite of programs and utilities that typically manages large, structured sets of persistent data, offering ad hoc query facilities to many users. The DBMS may be an extremely complex set of software programs that controls the organization, storage, and retrieval of data (fields, records, and files) in a database. It also controls the security and integrity of the database. Likewise, the DBMS may be a very simple entity consisting of nothing more than a single file containing information.

The DBMS accepts requests for data from the application program or Web server and instructs the operating system to transfer the appropriate data.

When a DBMS is used, information systems can be changed much more easily as the organization's information requirements change. New categories of data can be added to the database without disruption to the existing system.

Data security prevents unauthorized users from viewing or updating the database. Using passwords, users are allowed access to the entire database or subsets of the database, called *subschemas* (pronounced "sub-skeema"). For example, an employee database can contain all the data about an organization's employees, but one group of users may be authorized to view only payroll data, while others are allowed access to only work history and medical data.

The DBMS can maintain the integrity of the database by not allowing more than one user to update the same record at the same time. The DBMS can keep duplicate records out of the database; for example, no two customers with the same customer numbers (key fields) can be entered into the database.

Database design is the process of deciding how to organize this data into record types and how the record types will relate to each other. The DBMS should mirror the organization's data structure and process transactions efficiently.

Organizations may use one kind of DBMS for daily transaction processing and then move the detail onto another computer that uses another DBMS better suited for random inquiries and analyses. System design decisions are made by database administrators and systems analysts. Detailed database design is performed by database architects.

Understanding Database Types

There are three main types of databases in use today:

♦ Hierarchical

♦ Flat-file

♦ Relational

The following sections discuss each of these.

Understanding Hierarchical Databases

Hierarchical databases were quite popular in the 1970s, 1980s, and into the 1990s, long before the Internet became popular. The most notable hierarchical database is one sold by International Business Machines (IBM) named Information Management System (IMS). A hierarchical database is easiest to conceptualize if you think of a family tree, with the trunk of the tree having one or more main support branches, and each of these main support branches having one or more secondary branches, and each of these secondary branches having one or more twigs. Figure 6.1 illustrates how a developer might construct a hierarchical database to contain data specific to movies.

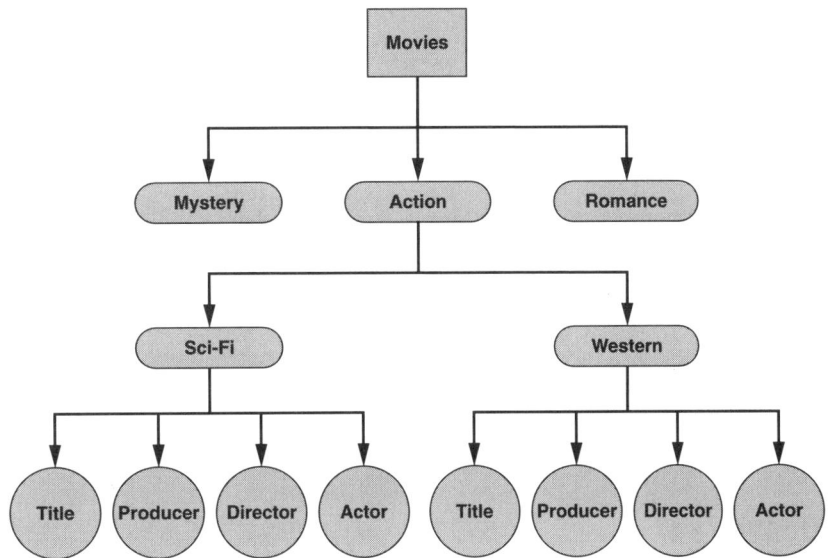

Figure 6.1

A hierarchical database storing information about movies

Understanding Flat-File Databases

A flat-file database is one in which all the information you need or want to keep is stored in a single file. This is a useful form of database for most kinds of general, day-to-day information, such as a telephone book or a recipe book. Flat-file databases typically do not allow for combining information from several database files. Figure 6.2 is an example of a flat-file database.

Figure 6.2

A flat-file database storing movie information

Rec #	Title	Type	Sub-Type	Producer	Director	Actor
1	Jaws Goes To The Races	Action	Adventure	Benchley	Romanoff	Dreyfuss
2	SpaceTrek Odyssey	Action	Sci-Fi	Reagan	Nixon	Clinton
3	Wizard of ID	Action	Sci-Fi	Roosevelt	Jackson	Dreyfuss
4	Gunfight At The Not OK Corral	Action	Western	Cagney	Whatzit	Clingon
5	Clash of the Twin Peaks	Romance	True Story	Diane	Catherine	Matheny

Understanding Relational Databases

Sometimes all the information of interest to a business operation can be stored in one table. For example, suppose the only data you must maintain about your office supplies is a description of each item, its supplier, and the quantity on hand. It would be enough to have one office supply table with those data items (description of each item, supplier, and quantity on hand) as the fields.

More often, though, business applications involve many tables. In a typical personnel application, there might be one table for employees, another for information about work hours, and another for the departments in the company.

This is what makes a relational database management system, or RDBMS, so powerful. It stores data in one or more tables and enables you to define relationships between the tables. The link is based on one or more fields common to both tables.

For example, Figure 6.3 reorganizes the data contained in the hierarchical Movie example previously shown in Figure 6.1 into a relational structure consisting of multiple tables.

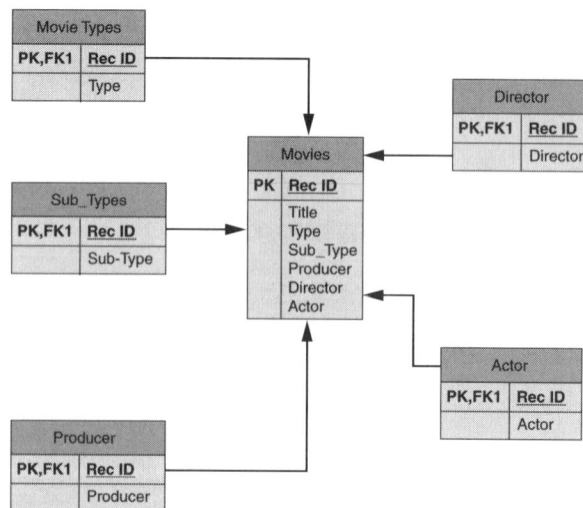

Figure 6.3

A relational database structure to the Movie example

There is a Movies table that contains links to other tables, such as the Studio, Director, Actor, and Producer tables. In the Studio table, each studio has a unique number associated with it, and this number is what is stored in the Movies table. Likewise, each person identified as a director in the Director table has a unique number, and this number is what is stored in the Movies table. This same structure follows through to the Actor and Producer tables. The relational database is the one most commonly supplying data to Web sites.

NOTE: *It is not necessary that the linking fields have the same field names. What's important is their value and what they represent. The "linking" of fields that have different names is the responsibility of the DBA or data architect.*

Understanding Database Elements

Relational databases are comprised of one or more components called *tables*. A table is a physical collection of data where each data element is identical to other data elements. In Figure 6.4, the Quote table does not contain the names of Shakespearean actors, or models of automobiles. The table contains information specific to the quotations stored in the database.

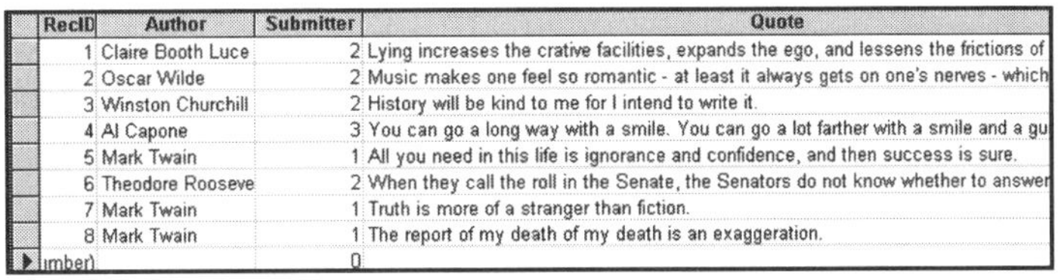

Figure 6.4

Relationship between table, row, and column

RecID	Author	Submitter	Quote
1	Claire Booth Luce	2	Lying increases the crative facilities, expands the ego, and lessens the frictions of
2	Oscar Wilde	2	Music makes one feel so romantic - at least it always gets on one's nerves - which
3	Winston Churchill	2	History will be kind to me for I intend to write it.
4	Al Capone	3	You can go a long way with a smile. You can go a lot farther with a smile and a gu
5	Mark Twain	1	All you need in this life is ignorance and confidence, and then success is sure.
6	Theodore Rooseve	2	When they call the roll in the Senate, the Senators do not know whether to answer
7	Mark Twain	1	Truth is more of a stranger than fiction.
8	Mark Twain	1	The report of my death of my death is an exaggeration.
umber)		0	

Understanding Data Elements

Tables consist of one or more rows of data, where a row is synonymous with a record. Each row of data represents one instance or occurrence of a unique congregation of data. In Figure 6.4, there are eight rows of data, with each row representing one quotation stored in the Quote table.

Rows in a table are comprised of one or more columns. A column contains a finite and discrete piece of data. In Figure 6.4, you see there are four columns in each row of data in the Quote table. These four columns are named RecID, Author, Submitter, and Quote. Each column in the row is unique from other columns in the same row.

Whereas Figure 6.4 shows the names of the columns in the table along with a brief description of the type of data stored in each column, Figure 6.5 shows the actual data stored in each row in the table. Note that there are eight rows in the table, and each row contains the same set of four columns as every other row. The data in each row/column combination may be different, but there certainly is order and consistency in the layout of this table.

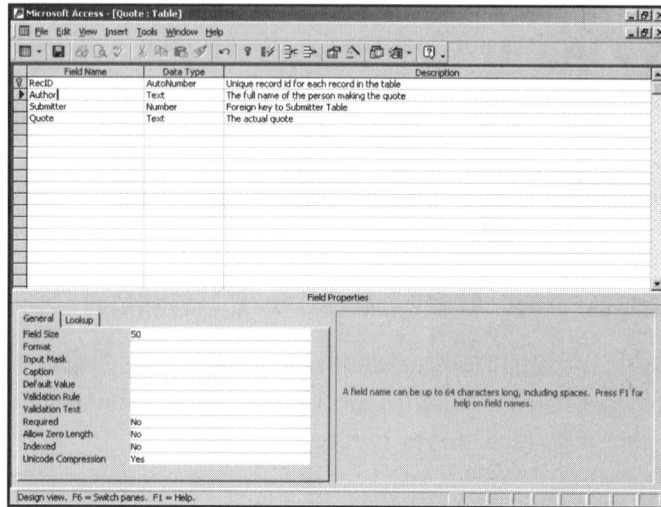

Figure 6.5

Data contained in the Quote table

Each and every column is comprised of one or more attributes. These attributes control how the data is stored and manipulated within the database, as well as how it is edited and displayed on a form (or Web page). As you can see in Figure 6.6, there are a number of attributes defined for the Author column in the Quote table.

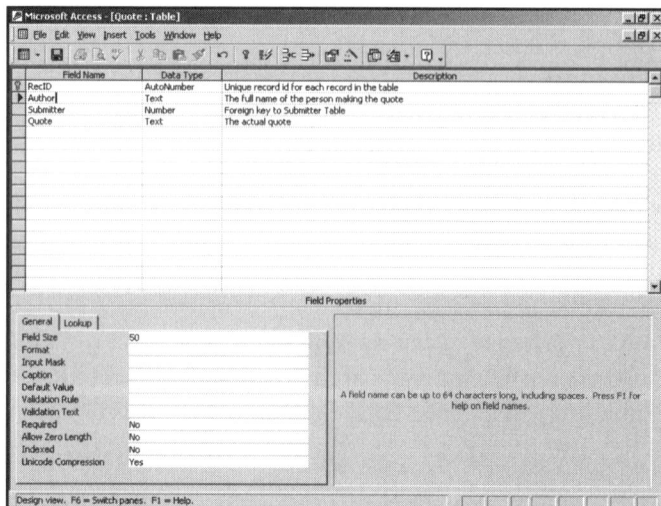

Figure 6.6

Columns are comprised of one or more attributes.

Understanding Sorting and Index Elements

Most RDBMS products include the capability of automatically storing and retrieving data in a predefined sort order, which is convenient because you do not have to bother with making sure that the data is entered into the database in any particular order to retrieve it in a specific order. In other words, if you want the names of employees retrieved in a report in alphabetical order, you can tell the database to do this, without regard to entering the names in the first place in alphabetical order. This is called *sorting*. When you identify a specific column in a table to sort on, that column is designated as an index.

In our example in Figure 6.4, you can see there are three rows in the table in which the Author is Mark Twain. If an index was defined on the Author column in the Quote table and you wanted to see the quotes stored in the table for which the author is Mark Twain, then you could very quickly and accurately search for and find these three rows of data in the table.

To be sure, if you didn't have an index identified on the Author row, you could certainly query the database and extract exactly the same information as if you did have an index on this column. The difference is that with the index, the RDBMS would only scan through and read the three rows of data that satisfied the request. Without the index on Author, the RDBMS would read through all the rows of data in the table and filter out the rows where the Author is not Mark Twain. Certainly, in a database where there are only eight rows, the time difference is negligible. But as the size of the database grows, the efficiency in using an index increases.

Relating Two or More Tables

Columns that establish a link between the tables in a database are essential in a relational database. Using numbers or text numbers in tables makes it possible to relate tables, to join them to create reports that contain information from two or more tables. As you can see in Figure 6.7, the Quote table is joined with the Submitter table. The column named Submitter in the Quote table is joined to the column named RecID in the Submitter table.

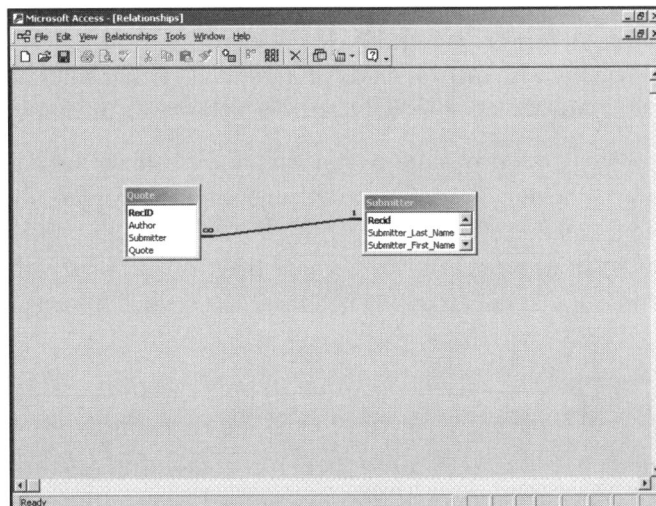

Figure 6.7

Relationships between tables allow you to join the tables to extract relevant information.

Many types of relationships can be defined between two tables. These are advanced database design concepts and thus outside the scope of this book. However, if you look at Figure 6.8, you will see how the relationship between the Submitter column in the Quote table and the RecID column in the Submitter table is defined.

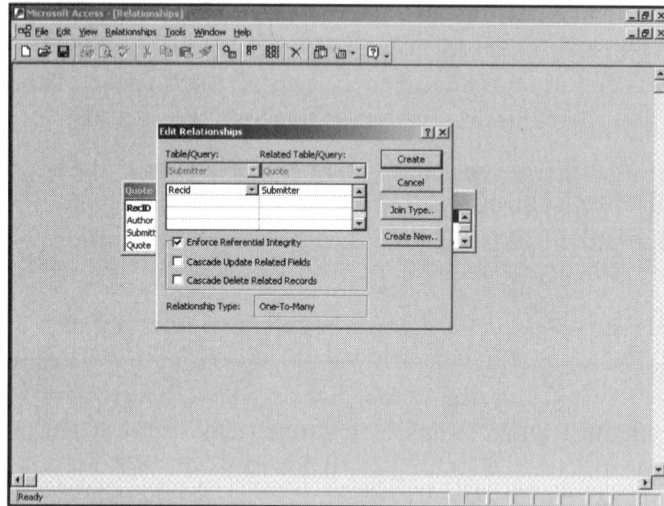

Figure 6.8

How a relationship is defined between two tables in an MS Access database

Take a look at a practical example where this type of function is useful. Suppose you want to know the name of the person who submitted the quote in the Quote table attributed to Winston Churchill. Certainly, this information is not in either the Quote or the Submitter table alone, but it is in both tables. If you were to query the Quote table to get the value in the Submitter column for the rows where the Author is Winston Churchill, you would see that the value in this column is a 2. Then, if you queried the Submitter column to see what the value is in the Submitter_Last_Name column where the RecID had a 2 in it, you would see the value is Colliver.

Working with Records and Recordsets

Records are synonymous with rows in RDBMS terminology. You will find just as many people using the word "record" as those that use the word "row." Recordsets, however, are not synonymous with anything else.

A *recordset* contains the results of a query in a temporary holding area that resides somewhere in the memory of the computer that is holding the database. In our example in Figure 6.4, a recordset containing the results of a query that asked for all the rows where the Author is Mark Twain would contain three rows. Recordsets are a useful element in Dreamweaver UltraDev because they let you work with a smaller set of data for subsequent database transactions if that data is stored in a recordset created from a query.

NOTE: *The specific location in memory that the recordset is stored is completely irrelevant to you, because the safekeeping of this is one of the functions of the RDBMS product. You create and reference the recordset, but the placement and location of it are managed by the RDBMS.*

Understanding Schemas, Catalogs, and Clusters

A database *schema* (pronounced "skee-ma") describes the structure of a database system. In a relational database, the schema defines the tables, the fields in each table, and the relationships between the fields and the tables.

Database schemas are generally stored in a data dictionary. Although a schema is defined in textual database language, the term is often used to refer to a graphical depiction of the database structure.

The data dictionary or system catalog can be considered the heart of the system—the system catalog. It may be regarded as a database in its own right (a system database as opposed to a user database). The data dictionary contains data about data (metadata), such as descriptions of other objects in the system, rather than simply "raw data." In particular, all the various schemas and mappings (external, conceptual, and so on) are physically stored in this dictionary. The dictionary also includes information on what programs and/or end users can use what data. It should also be possible to query the data dictionary so that, for example, you are able to determine which programs and/or users are likely to be affected by some proposed change to the system.

Before you can do anything, you must initialize a database storage area on disk, which you can refer to as a *database cluster*. A database cluster is a collection of databases that will be accessible through a single instance of a running database server. After initialization, a database cluster will contain one database.

Understanding the Structured Query Language (SQL)

SQL (pronounced "sequel") is a language designed for accessing and manipulating data within a database. Dreamweaver UltraDev supports the access of data stored in databases using SQL. Each provider of RDBMS products (such as Oracle, Microsoft, Sybase, and so on) has its own unique dialect of SQL. However, all RDBMS products support a common set of commands.

NOTE: *You must understand the syntax of the RDBMS product your data is stored in to write syntactically correct SQL statements. The examples supplied in this section of Lesson 6 are basic enough to be commonly used on most RDBMS systems.*

The SQL language is not case-sensitive. However, for clarity, the examples that follow in this section have the SQL code portion of the command string capitalized, and the data portion of the command string in lowercase.

Table 6.1 summarizes the four major SQL keywords and their uses.

Table 6.1 The four major SQL keywords

Keyword	Usage
SELECT	Retrieve data from a database
INSERT	Insert new data in an existing database
UPDATE	Modify data stored in a database
DELETE	Remove data or entire tables from a database

Using the SELECT Statement

Suppose you want to retrieve all the data in the Quote table. You would need to execute the following SELECT query (remember that words in uppercase represent the SQL keywords):

```
SELECT * FROM quote;
```

This query would return the entire table, as shown in Figure 6.9.

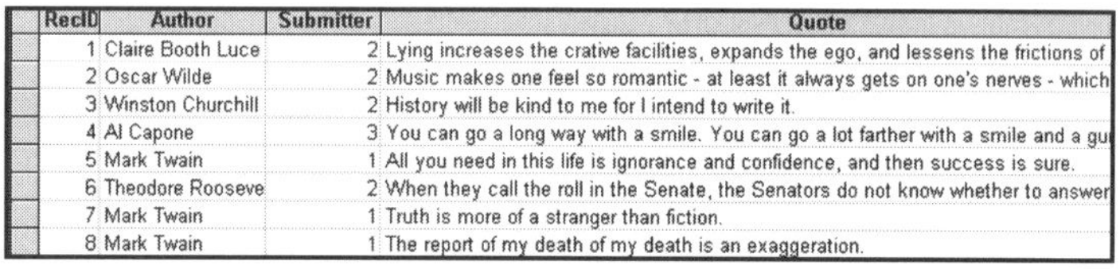

Figure 6.9

Results of the SELECT * FROM quote; query

RecID	Author	Submitter	Quote
1	Claire Booth Luce	2	Lying increases the crative facilities, expands the ego, and lessens the frictions of
2	Oscar Wilde	2	Music makes one feel so romantic - at least it always gets on one's nerves - which
3	Winston Churchill	2	History will be kind to me for I intend to write it.
4	Al Capone	3	You can go a long way with a smile. You can go a lot farther with a smile and a gu
5	Mark Twain	1	All you need in this life is ignorance and confidence, and then success is sure.
6	Theodore Rooseve	2	When they call the roll in the Senate, the Senators do not know whether to answer
7	Mark Twain	1	Truth is more of a stranger than fiction.
8	Mark Twain	1	The report of my death of my death is an exaggeration.

Several components comprise a SQL query. The first word always represents the action the SQL statement will perform. This is the verb. The word that follows the SQL pronoun FROM is the table from which you want to extract the data.

In the preceding query, the asterisk (*) specifies that you want to see all of the columns in the table. You can also perform a query to return specific columns. You do this by specifying the names of the columns you want extracted, each separated by a column, after the SQL verb SELECT.

Suppose that you want to see just the names of the authors and submitters who have quotes stored in the database. You would do this by writing a query that looks like this:

```
SELECT AUTHOR, SUBMITTER FROM quote;
```

The results of this query would look like Table 6.2.

Table 6.2 Results of query extracting only the AUTHOR and SUBMITTER

Author	Submitter
Claire Booth Luce	2
Oscar Wilde	2
Winston Churchill	2
Al Capone	3
Mark Twain	1
Theodore Roosevelt	2
Mark Twain	1
Mark Twain	1

You can enter qualifying criteria on the SELECT statement. For example, if you want to know who the authors are for all the quotes submitted by Submitter 2, you could write the following SQL statement:

```
SELECT Author FROM quote WHERE Submitter = 2;
```

The results of this query would look like Table 6.3.

Table 6.3 Results of query extracting AUTHOR when SUBMITTER = 2

Author
Claire Booth Luce
Oscar Wilde
Winston Churchill
Theodore Roosevelt

Note that we have introduced a new SQL keyword, WHERE. The WHERE clause is important for displaying a specific record.

NOTE: *You could have written a query to extract the SUBMITTER(s) for the author Mark Twain. This would be written:*

```
SELECT Submitter FROM quote WHERE Author = 'Mark Twain'
```

Note the use of the single quotes to surround the text. This is a SQL convention to signify a text string in a search statement. This query would create a result set containing three rows of data, one row for each of the three quotes in the table attributable to Mark Twain.

Another useful keyword in writing a SQL statement to extract data is the UNIQUE clause. This clause is useful if you want to identify the number of unique occurrences of a particular search string that exist in a table. For example, consider the following SQL statement:

```
SELECT UNIQUE Author FROM Quote;
```

This query would return the result set shown in Table 6.4.

Table 6.4 Results of query extracting unique AUTHORs

Author
Claire Booth Luce
Oscar Wilde
Winston Churchill
Theodore Roosevelt

The INSERT Statement

The SQL INSERT statement allows you to add new data to your database, and is heavily used in a Web application. In your example application, you would use this statement to add quotes to the Quote table, and to add the names of submitters to the Submitter table.

Suppose that you want to add a new quote to the Quote table from an existing submitter. You would write the following SQL query:

```
INSERT INTO quote (Author, Submitter, Quote) VALUES ('Al Capone', 3, 'Somebody
give me 32-inch Louisville Slugger!');
```

You use the word "query" when discussing SQL statements to describe any type of SQL statement, not just ones written to extract data from a database. SQL writers even refer to the SQL statements written to delete data from a database as a SQL query.

In the preceding query, the INSERT verb comes first, followed by the SQL pronoun INTO, followed by the name of the table into which data is to be inserted. Following this are the (optional) names of the columns that you wish to insert data into. Then, the SQL keyword VALUES lets the RDBMS know that the values that follow are to be inserted into the table. A comma must separate each value.

You did not insert a value into the RecID column because this column is defined as being AUTONUMBER. A column that is an AUTONUMBER column automatically increments each time a new row is added.

Because we are submitting values for every column in the table, we did not need to supply the names of the columns that contain data. We must do this only if we are inserting data in a table for some of the columns. In other words, we could have written the preceding query in an abbreviated form with the following query:

```
INSERT INTO quote VALUES ('Al Capone', 3, 'Somebody give me 32-inch Louisville
Slugger!');
```

When this query executes, the data in the table will look like Figure 6.10.

Figure 6.10

The Quote table after the INSERT statement

RecID	Author	Submitter	Quote
1	Claire Booth Luce	2	Lying increases the crative facilities, expands the ego, and lessens the frictions of
2	Oscar Wilde	2	Music makes one feel so romantic - at least it always gets on one's nerves - which
3	Winston Churchill	2	History will be kind to me for I intend to write it.
4	Al Capone	3	You can go a long way with a smile. You can go a lot farther with a smile and a gu
5	Mark Twain	1	All you need in this life is ignorance and confidence, and then success is sure.
6	Theodore Rooseve	2	When they call the roll in the Senate, the Senators do not know whether to answer
7	Mark Twain	1	Truth is more of a stranger than fiction.
8	Mark Twain	1	The report of my death of my death is an exaggeration.
9	Al Capone	3	Somebody give me a 32-inch Louisville Slugger

In an INSERT statement, the values must follow the same order that is specified for the columns in the INSERT statement. But, the INSERT statement does not have to follow the same order that the columns are defined as within the table. Therefore, we could have accomplished exactly the same results using the following query:

```
INSERT INTO quote (Submitter, Quote, Author) VALUES (3,'Somebody give me 32-
inch Louisville Slugger!', 'Al Capone');
```

Using the UPDATE Statement

The UPDATE statement lets you modify the values of existing data in a database. The UPDATE statement relies heavily on the WHERE clause, because the WHERE clause is the mechanism that you use to describe exactly which row(s) of data to change. Suppose that you want to change the author of the quote whose RecID is 6 from Theodore Roosevelt to Teddy Roosevelt. You would write the following query to do so:

```
UPDATE quote SET Author = 'Teddy Roosevelt' WHERE Recid = 6;
```

Note that the Update query begins with the SQL verb UPDATE, followed by the name of the table to update. Then, the adverb SET and the phrase that follows specifies how the data is to change. Finally, what follows the WHERE clause describes the rows in the table that are to be changed.

After executing this query, the Quote table would look like Figure 6.11.

Figure 6.11

The Quote table after updating

RecID	Author	Submitter	Quote
1	Claire Booth Luce	2	Lying increases the crative facilities, expands the ego, and lessens the frictions of
2	Oscar Wilde	2	Music makes one feel so romantic - at least it always gets on one's nerves - which
3	Winston Churchill	2	History will be kind to me for I intend to write it.
4	Al Capone	3	You can go a long way with a smile. You can go a lot farther with a smile and a gu
5	Mark Twain	1	All you need in this life is ignorance and confidence, and then success is sure.
6	Theodore Rooseve	2	When they call the roll in the Senate, the Senators do not know whether to answer
7	Mark Twain	1	Truth is more of a stranger than fiction.
8	Mark Twain	1	The report of my death of my death is an exaggeration.
9	Al Capone	3	Somebody give me a 32-inch Louisville Slugger

NOTE: *An UPDATE statement can be written to update one row in a table or multiple rows concurrently. This is a very powerful statement and should be tested thoroughly before being used to update production data. For example, the following statement would actually update three rows in the table, not just one:*

```
UPDATE quote SET Submitter = 3 WHERE Author = 'Mark Twain';
```

Using the DELETE Statement

The DELETE statement lets you remove data from a database. Using the DELETE statement, you can delete a single row or the entire contents of a table.

Assume you want to delete the row of data added earlier with the INSERT statement, the quote of Al Capone that was added. You could do this with the following statement:

```
DELETE FROM quote WHERE Recid = 9;
```

Note that this query begins with the SQL verb DELETE. The second keyword identifies the name of the table we are going to be deleting data from, in this case the Quote table. The WHERE clause lets the RDBMS know that you intend on deleting a specific row in the table.

After executing the query, the table would look like Figure 6.12.

Figure 6.12

The Quote table following the DELETE statement

RecID	Author	Submitter	Quote
1	Claire Booth Luce	2	Lying increases the crative facilities, expands the ego, and lessens the frictions of
2	Oscar Wilde	2	Music makes one feel so romantic - at least it always gets on one's nerves - which
3	Winston Churchill	2	History will be kind to me for I intend to write it.
4	Al Capone	3	You can go a long way with a smile. You can go a lot farther with a smile and a gu
5	Mark Twain	1	All you need in this life is ignorance and confidence, and then success is sure.
6	Theodore Rooseve	2	When they call the roll in the Senate, the Senators do not know whether to answer
7	Mark Twain	1	Truth is more of a stranger than fiction.
8	Mark Twain	1	The report of my death of my death is an exaggeration.
(mber)		0	

Notice that the data for the second quote of Al Capone is gone. The query we wrote allowed us to remove the one row of data.

NOTE: *The DELETE SQL statement is another very powerful SQL command. For example, if we had written the query as follows, we would have deleted two rows of data, not the one that we intended to delete:*

```
DELETE FROM quote WHERE Author = 'Al Capone';
```

What You Must Know

This lesson introduced you to database architectures and terminology. An understanding of databases is critical if you're going to exploit the capabilities of UltraDev. You learned that the most common type of database in Web applications is a relational database. You also learned about SQL, which is the language used to access data stored in a relational database. In Lesson 7, "ODBC, JDBC, and the UltraDev Languages," you will learn Open Database Connectivity (ODBC) and Java Database Connectivity (JDBC). You will also learn how to connect to a database engine that exists on your computer on your network.

Before you continue to Lesson 7, make sure you understand the following key concepts:

◆ The most popular type of database for Web sites is the relational database, which is one of three main types of database architectures.

◆ A relational database has many different types of components.

◆ A relational database is comprised of tables, rows, columns, and attributes.

◆ A database schema describes the layout of the data contained within the database, and the relationship between data components.

◆ Structured Query Language (SQL) is the language used to interact with relational databases.

◆ There are three parts to any SQL statement, with various types of actions you can perform on data in a database using SQL.

Lesson 7

ODBC, JDBC, and the UltraDev Languages

In Lesson 6, "Understanding Database Basics," you learned about relational databases and how to write SQL statements to perform the four major actions you'll be doing while working with a database on your Web site. In this lesson you will learn about Open Database Connectivity (ODBC) and Java Database Connectivity (JDBC). You will learn how to connect to a database engine that exists on your computer on your network. By the time you finish this lesson, you will understand the following key concepts:

◆ Open Database Connectivity is the open standard developed to link an application to a database.

◆ Java Database Connectivity is the open standard developed to link Java code to an existing database.

◆ There are strengths and weaknesses of ODBC and JDBC, and you will develop an understanding of when to use which method.

◆ There are three different server platforms supported by UltraDev.

Understanding the Database Connection

Web sites can be built to access data stored in a variety of different databases. Although how a Web site connects to each of these different types of databases varies slightly from one to the next, the basic processes remain the same. One of these consistent processes, regardless of the type of database your Web site will be accessing, is creating the database connection.

> **NOTE:** *It is assumed that you will be building a Web site that attaches to a database that has already been created for you. Creating a database on a server is outside of the scope of this book. If you are tasked with the responsibility of creating a database, you should consider reading about this in one of the many good books available that deal with this subject.*

Understanding Database Connectivity Definitions

Before you can delve deeper into the relationship between Dreamweaver UltraDev and the database that stores the data so important to a Web site, you need to understand a few key terms and acronyms, which are presented in Table 7.1.

Table 7.1   Key definitions used throughout this lesson

Term or Acronym	Definition
ADO	*ActiveX Data Objects,* Microsoft's newest high-level interface for data objects. ADO is designed to eventually replace DAO (*Data Access Objects*) and RDO (*Remote Data Objects*). Unlike RDO and DAO, which are designed only for accessing relational databases, ADO is more general and can be used to access all sorts of different types of data, including Web pages, spreadsheets, and other types of documents.
API	*Application programming interface,* a set of routines, protocols, and tools for building software applications. A good API makes it easier to develop a program by providing all the building blocks. A programmer or Web developer puts the blocks together.
ASP	A specification for a dynamically created Web page with an *.ASP* extension (ASP stands for Active Server Pages) that utilizes ActiveX scripting—usually VBScript or JavaScript code. When a browser requests an ASP page, the Web server generates a page with HTML code and sends it back to the browser. So ASP pages are similar to CGI scripts, but they enable Visual Basic programmers to work with familiar tools.
CGI	*Common Gateway Interface,* a specification for transferring information between a Web server and a CGI program. A CGI program is any program designed to accept and return data that conforms to the CGI specification. The program could be written in any programming language, including C, Perl, Java, or Visual Basic.

(continued)

Table 7.1 *(continued)*

Term or Acronym	Definition
CFML	*ColdFusion Markup Language*, a range of HTML tags added specifically to the ColdFusion development environment that extends the utility and function of HTML.
Driver	A driver acts as a translator between the device and the programs that use the device. Each device has its own set of specialized commands that only its driver knows. In contrast, most programs access devices by using generic commands. The driver, therefore, accepts generic commands from a program and then translates them into specialized commands for the device.
Javasoft	The business unit of Sun Microsystems that is responsible for Java technology.
JDBC	*Java Database Connectivity*, a Java API that enables Java programs to execute SQL statements. This allows Java programs to interact with any SQL-compliant database. Because nearly all RDBMs support SQL, and because Java itself runs on most platforms, JDBC makes it possible to write a single database application that can run on different platforms and interact with different RDBMs. JDBC is similar to ODBC, but is designed specifically for Java programs, whereas ODBC is language-independent.
JSP	*JavaServer Pages*, a server-side technology that is an extension to the Java servlet technology developed by Sun as an alternative to Microsoft's ASP (*Active Server Pages*). JSP has dynamic scripting capability that works in tandem with HTML code, separating the page logic from the static elements—the actual design and display of the page. Embedded in the HTML page, the Java source code and its extensions help make the HTML more functional, being used in dynamic database queries, for example. JSP is not restricted to any specific platform or server.
ODBC	*Open Database Connectivity*, a standard database access method developed by Microsoft. The goal of ODBC is to make it possible to access any data from any application, regardless of which DBMS is handling the data. ODBC manages this by inserting a middle layer, called a database driver, between an application and the DBMS. The purpose of this layer is to translate the application's data queries and commands that the DBMS understands. For this to work, both the application and the DBMS must be *ODBC-compliant*—that is, the application must be capable of issuing ODBC commands and the DBMS must be capable of responding to them.

Working with Open Database Connectivity

As presented in the preceding table, ODBC is an API that lets developers interface a program with a database. When writing code to interact with a database, you usually have to add code specific to the database containing the data. For example, if you were connecting your Web site to an Oracle database, and not using ODBC to do it, then the database calls you write would have to be written specifically for an Oracle database. Using ODBC, you write generic code to access the database, and the ODBC driver you use converts the generic SQL to database-specific SQL.

When you write SQL using generic SQL commands, the ODBC manager figures out how to contend with the type of database you are targeting. Regardless of the database type you are using, all of your calls will be to the ODBC API. All that you must have installed is the ODBC driver for your database.

Using ODBC has one major disadvantage and two main advantages. The major disadvantage is performance. When the ODBC driver interprets the generic SQL into database-specific SQL, the conversion requires a certain amount of CPU time, which translates directly to a loss in performance. The advantages of working with ODBC include:

◆ You do not need to learn database-specific SQL to interface your programs to the target database.

◆ Usually you can change from one database to another without having to rewrite any SQL code. All you must do is to configure a new ODBC driver specific for the new target database.

Using the Current ODBC Version

Since ODBC's inception, there have been a few different versions of the ODBC API released by Microsoft Corporation. The current version is 3.5.

Typically, when you install ODBC on your machine (if you have a 32-bit version of a Windows operating system on your machine, you probably have ODBC installed), you are installing the ODBC Manager. To verify the version of ODBC Manager on your machine, do the following:

1. Click on the Start button and you will see the Windows Programs list.

2. From the Windows Programs list, click on the menu item that reads Settings and you will see a pop-up menu list of programs accessible from the Settings menu.

3. From the list of Settings menu items, click on the Control Panel menu item, and the Control Panel will start.

4. On the Control Panel, locate the icon or menu item that reads ODBC Data Sources. (If you are using Windows NT, the icon or menu item will be Data Sources [ODBC].) If you do not see this icon, then you do not have the ODBC Manager installed. If you do see this icon, double-click on it and you will see the ODBC Data Source Administrator dialog box.

5. On the ODBC Data Source Administrator, click on the About tab. Your window should look very similar to what you see in Figure 7.1. As you can see in Figure 7.1, the ODBC Driver Manager on my machine is highlighted, with the version installed on my machine directly to the right of the description. The version of the ODBC Driver Manager on your machine is directly to the right of the description.

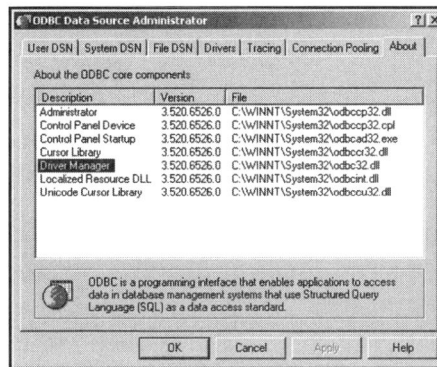

Figure 7.1

The About tab on the ODBC Data Source Administrator shows the current version of the ODBC Driver Manager installed on your machine.

ODBC version 3.5 is completely backwards-compatible. This means that when using an ODBC 3.5 driver manager:

◆ An ODBC 2.*x* application works with an ODBC 3.0 driver or an ODBC 2.*x* driver.

◆ An ODBC 3.0 application works with an ODBC 3.0 driver.

◆ An ODBC 3.0 application works with an ODBC 2.*x* driver as long as the application uses only ODBC 2.*x* features.

Getting ODBC

There are a number of places to get ODBC. For example:

♦ To get a copy for the Windows platform, go to Microsoft's ODBC home page at www.microsoft.com/data/odbc/default.htm.

♦ To get a copy for the Unix platform, go to the home page of the unixODBC project at www.unixodbc.org/. This group's goals are to develop and promote a Linux implementation of ODBC.

♦ If your workstation has an Alpha processor, you can get a copy of the ODBC Driver Manager from ftp://www.roth.net/pub/ntperl/odbc/alpha/.

♦ Brian Jepson is an IT specialist who has a Web site devoted to expanding the use of ODBC and Web technologies. You can get a free copy of an ODBC Manager from his site at www.jepstone.net/FreeODBC/.

♦ Also on Brian Jepson's site is a free ODBC Driver Manager for the Macintosh. The URL to get this is www.jepstone.net/directory/index.cgi/Databases/APIs/ODBC/Macintosh.

Using Javasoft's JDBC

Java Database Connectivity is similar to ODBC in that it provides seamless access to databases from a program. The main difference is that JDBC provides this access to programs written in Java and JavaScript code.

JDBC is a wrapper to let you feed SQL requests to a database server. The interface is less than elegant, and certainly less elegant than the ODBC interface. This loss in elegance stems from how JDBC came about. It originated by gluing ODBC onto SQL, and then hurriedly grafting Java/JDBC onto ODBC. JDBC does not in the least look like the database interface designed for Java. However, the developers at Macromedia developed their interface of creating a JDBC connection to a database to be as elegant as creating an ODBC interface. You will see how to create both a JDBC and an ODBC connection from within UltraDev in Lesson 16.

Working with JDBC Drivers

Four different types of JDBC drivers are available. These are summarized in Table 7.2.

Table 7.2   The four types of JDBC drivers

Type	Description
ODBC Bridge	Use this driver to hook into a database you already own that does not yet directly support JDBC. Nearly every SQL database supports the JDBC ODBC Bridge. Java supports it by loading JDBC drivers into the clients that emulate ODBC protocol. Because of the extra layers of protocols that your code and data must proceed through, the extra overhead creates a performance hit.
Native API, Native Code	This driver is the best solution if performance is critical. The JDBC driver is written partly in Java and partly in native code. It speaks the native protocol of the SQL database you are using. This is an efficient solution, but suffers from the problem that it must be installed on every client.
Net Protocol, Pure Java	This driver is the most flexible solution, especially in large and widely distributed Web sites. The JDBC driver is written in 100 percent Java, which means it can be safely loaded on the fly into any Java-compatible Web browser.
Native Protocol, Pure Java	This driver is the most efficient way to distribute a Web site from a single server. The JDBC driver is written in 100 percent Java. The driver is DBMS vendor–specific and interacts directly with SQL Server. This directness is efficient, but if you need to attach to several vendors' SQL databases, you need to load several JDBC drivers into the clients' machines.

Finding JDBC Resources

There is a veritable panacea of useful resources available on the Web to help you with JDBC if you're new to it. Table 7.3 lists just a few.

Table 7.3   Useful JDBC resources

Link	Description
www.cs.odu.edu/~cs745/presentations/jdbc/jdbc1	A useful PowerPoint slide presentation that gives a very nice high-level overview, and also includes slides with many useful links.
www.javasoft.com/products/jdk/1.1/docs/guide/ jdbc/getstart/introTOC.doc.html	A very thorough and well-written presentation of material that gives you more information about Java than what you'll probably ever want to know.

(continued)

Table 7.3 *(continued)*

Link	Description
www.cs.odu.edu/~cs745/presentations/jdbc/page1.html	These pages provide some useful Java programs that should provide a good foundation of understanding of the types of things you can do with the language. You can also use some of the code as examples if you decide to learn to write Java code yourself.
www.cs.odu.edu/~cs745/presentations/jdbc/page0.html	These pages provide good examples and reference material on how to use JDBC with Java servlets.

Using the UltraDev ODBC/JDBC Connectivity Model

In this section you will take a close look at the UltraDev database connectivity model and understand how it works. With this as a background, creating and maintaining an actual database connection will be easier to understand.

UltraDev lets you connect to a database using one of four different methods. These methods, in decreasing order of popularity, are as follows:

◆ ADO (ODBC)

◆ JDBC

◆ ADO (Connection String)

◆ Cold Fusion Data Source Name

In Figure 7.2, you see the UltraDev database connectivity model. Although this lesson calls it the UltraDev database connectivity model, the diagram defines the connectivity model used by any Web site accessing a database via an ODBC or JDBC connection.

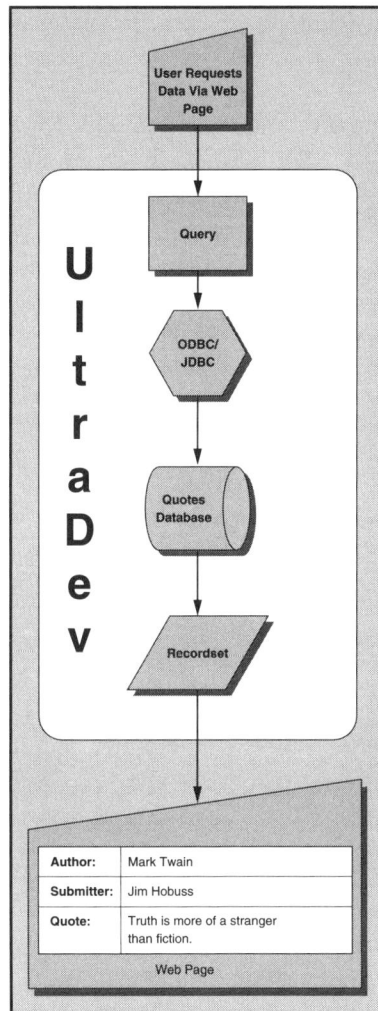

Figure 7.2

The UltraDev database connectivity model

In the topmost symbol on Figure 7.2, you see that *all* access to data is initiated by a user request initiated on a Web page. This may be a user clicking on a Submit button or a Go button, pressing the Enter key, or executing one of a slew of other types of actions. From this action, the code behind the Web page (written by a Web developer, such as yourself) is written to format a SQL query to the database to access data that is needed to satisfy the user's request.

The query is then sent from UltraDev, where an established ODBC or JDBC connection translates the query into a specific syntax required by the RDBMS to which the Web site is attached. Once this translation (which occurs via a driver supplied by either your RDBMS vendor or a third-party product) occurs, the SQL query is sent to the RDBMS for database access.

Once the RDBMS processes the query, and if that query is a SELECT statement, a recordset is created by the RDBMS that it sends back to UltraDev. If the SQL statement is not a SELECT statement, then no recordset is created. In place of a recordset, the RDBMS returns what is called a return code that UltraDev can then interpret to determine the success or failure of the SQL query.

In the event a recordset is returned by the RDBMS, the code written by the Web developer will massage the data contained in the recordset and format it for display on a Web page. In the event the RDBMS sends a return code in place of a recordset, then code written by the Web developer should be written to interpret the code and display (if appropriate) a message to the user.

Once this is done, the cycle could begin again with the user changing the data appearing on the page or requesting a new set of data to view on a Web page. However, changing or requesting new data should be done before clicking on a Submit or a Go button, pressing the Enter key, or performing one of a slew of other types of actions.

Selecting a Development Language and Server Platform

When you first establish your site, you need to make decisions on what language(s) you will be using to write custom code, as well as the database server that these pages will be communicating with. Dreamweaver Ultra-Dev lets you develop Web sites in four different languages to be deployed on three different server platforms. The four languages are:

- VBScript

- JavaScript

- Java

- ColdFusion Markup Language

The three different server platforms are:

- Active Server Pages

- JavaServer Pages

- ColdFusion Markup Language

The following sections introduce you to the three server platforms.

NOTE: *I have chosen to use VBScript in an ASP environment for the examples throughout this book. If you know JavaScript or Java better than VBScript, you should be able to make the translations easily enough.*

Using Active Server Pages

As you would expect, because ASP supports VBScript (a Microsoft-developed language), Microsoft developed ASP. ASP represents a group of technologies that can be used from within a wide variety of programming languages. It is symbolized by the presence of programming code embedded within the HTML page and intertwined with the HTML code.

ASP is an extremely adaptable development environment that offers a wide range of features and flexibility. VBScript is more widely used as the programming language within ASP, but many people also write code using JavaScript. VBScript is an easy language to understand and to learn to write code in, but it is also inefficient in execution. A more efficiently executed language, JavaScript, is also a bit more difficult to learn to write. If you have a background in C or C++, you should find learning JavaScript more rewarding than learning VBScript.

One of the biggest drawbacks to using ASP as a server technology is that it is very proprietary (after all, it was developed by Microsoft), meaning it was developed to run only on a Windows 32-bit operating system. Fortunately, though, a product available from Chili!Soft called Chilisoft lets you add an ASP environment to several Unix-based systems, including Solaris and Linux. You can read more about the product, or download an evaluation copy of it, from www.chilisoft.com.

If you are running a Windows operating system, but it's not Windows NT (I'm using Windows 98 on this machine), you're in luck. Microsoft has written and made available free of charge a product called Personal Web Server (PWS). Although the product is very slow and therefore should not be considered for a production site, it is a viable alternative if you're not using a Windows NT system and don't have access to a Windows NT server. Follow these directions to install a copy of PWS on your machine if you're running Windows 98:

1. Insert your Windows 98 CD-ROM in your CD-ROM drive.

2. Within Windows, click on the Start menu and select Run. Windows will display the Run dialog box.

3. Within the Run dialog box Open field, type: **x:\add-ons\pws\setup.exe**, where **x** is the letter of your CD-ROM drive, and then click on the OK button.

4. Follow the directions in Personal Web Server Setup.

Using Java Server Pages

JSP is another embedded programming technology (similar to ASP) that is based on the Java programming language. The technology is based on servlets. Servlets are pieces of Java code that are compiled and used to perform Web page tasks such as generating an HTML page or processing input from a Web page. They were initially created to address the need for a Java-based method of writing the equivalent of CGI programs within the Java programming language.

One of the best aspects of JSP is that it is based in Java. What this means is that you truly have platform independence with JSP. In this context, platform independence means that Java code written for a Microsoft Windows platform will execute without modification on a Unix workstation. Any Web server that supports JavaServer Pages can run a JSP page without any code modification whatsoever. So, if you're already a Java programmer, writing JSP code is a very easy thing to do. You just need to learn the HTML that wraps around the Java code.

Although this all sounds wonderful, bear in mind that if you don't know the Java programming language, the learning curve to become proficient in it is steep, especially if you don't already have experience using another object-oriented language such as C++.

Using ColdFusion

ColdFusion is a programming environment that has a growing legion of advocates. It is not a true programming language as much as it is a development environment. In fact, it looks more like an extended version of HTML that includes database access, with new tags, than a programming language. Creating HTML pages that include database access is not much more complicated than writing HTML code for nondatabase access pages.

There are drawbacks to a ColdFusion server environment, though. The first one is that it sometimes takes seasoned programmers a little while to grasp the concept of writing code in it. For example, there are no For ... Next loops in ColdFusion. These are replaced by special tags, such as <LOOP> ... </LOOP>. Another limitation of ColdFusion is that these extra tags can (and often do) decrease the performance of your Web site while the application server translates the tag pairs to meaningful instructions. And, as is the case with ASP pages, ColdFusion is not platform-independent. You can, however, purchase versions of the technology to run on Windows, HP-UX, Linux, and Solaris Unix.

Until March 2001, ColdFusion was sold and supported by a company called Allaire (www.allaire.com). In January 2001, Macromedia, Inc., announced its acquisition of Allaire, which was concluded on March 20, 2001, bringing ColdFusion into the fold of products sold and supported by Macromedia.

What You Must Know

In this lesson, you learned about ODBC and JDBC. You learned how to connect to a database engine that exists on your computer on your network. In Lesson 8, "Setting Up an UltraDev Site," you will learn how to establish your basic folder structure with UltraDev for your site, including establishing a database connection.

Before you continue to Lesson 8, make sure you understand the following key concepts:

◆ ODBC is the open standard developed to link an application to a database.

◆ JDBC is the open standard developed to link Java code to an existing database.

◆ There are strengths and weaknesses to both ODBC and JDBC, and you know when to use which method.

◆ Four main server platforms are supported by UltraDev: Active Server Pages (VBScript), ASP (JavaScript), JavaServer Pages, and ColdFusion Markup Language.

Part II

Getting Started Using Dreamweaver UltraDev

Lesson 8

Setting Up an UltraDev Site

In Lesson 7, "ODBC, JDBC, and the UltraDev Languages" you learned about the four main server platforms supported by UltraDev: Active Server Pages (VBScript), ASP (JavaScript), Java Server Pages, and Cold Fusion Markup Language. In this lesson, you will learn about some of the design considerations specific to a Web site as well as how to set up an UltraDev site. By the time you finish this lesson, you will understand the following key concepts:

◆ Before you start building your Web using UltraDev, you must first design your site's layout and structure.

◆ UltraDev lets you create local and remote sites. A local site runs on your "local" personal computer. A remote site runs on a server that resides across a network.

◆ To create a local site within UltraDev, you create a folder (and optional sub-folders) that contain the components and objects that comprise the site.

◆ To create a remote site using UltraDev, you must specify the location of the application server that will host your site.

Start by Planning Your Site, and Then Design It

In my 23-year career as a professional building computer systems for companies, the last five years of which have been spent building Web sites, I have never before seen such a fanatical frenzy to get the builders of these sites to be productive. The technical architects, business analysts, creative analysts, software engineers, developers, and project managers who are building Web sites are working under tremendous pressure to build and launch sites just as soon as humanly possible. One of the casualties of this frenetic pace is sound site planning and design.

Unfortunately, when planning for a Web site is not done effectively, the Web site is ineffective. And for an e-commerce Web site, an ineffective site design ultimately yields a site that is not going to be visited. Just as in the retail world, the phrase "location, location, location" is critical, in the world of Web sites, "planning, planning, planning" is critical. Many people make the mistake of thinking that really cool graphics, or a wiz-bang animation on each page, will make the site appear on everyone's top 100 Web site list, but this is not true.

Planning of your Web site is critical, for these reasons:

◆ Planning reduces the amount of time you need to develop the site.

◆ Proper planning creates a uniform look and feel to each page on the site.

◆ By planning the user interface, you make a visitor's navigation of the site easier and more intuitive.

◆ Through proper planning, you reduce maintenance time and expense after you launch the site.

◆ Proper planning normally allows you to launch the site quicker.

Planning Considerations

As shown in Figure 8.1, you must address four primary considerations before you begin to design your site.

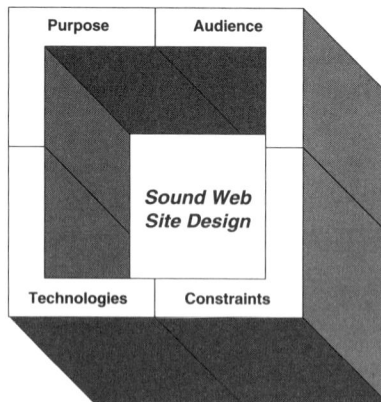

Figure 8.1

You must consider each of these four factors when planning your site.

Planning Your Site's Purpose

The first point of consideration when planning your site is to define the site's purpose:

◆ Is the site for personal use (such as to display family photos, personal biographies, and so on)?

◆ Is the site for individual business use (to display résumé and professional affiliations, side-line business from your primary source of employment, and so on)?

◆ Is the site for business-to-consumer (B2C) nontransactional use (explains who the company is, what it's selling, how to contact it)?

◆ Is the site for B2C transactional use (sells products, displays the status of orders, provides a help desk, and so on)?

◆ Is the site for business-to-business (B2B) transactional use (allows inventory checking and fulfillment, order placement, order tracking, and so on)?

Before you design and construct a site, you must have a clear understanding of your site's purpose. You must know what message you are trying to communicate to the site's visitors.

If you can articulate the purpose of your site in one sentence, you are well on your way to describing an effective purpose for the site. An example of a poorly written purpose statement is "To have the coolest Web site with the most awesome graphics." Table 8.1 gives some examples of well-written purpose statements.

Table 8.1   Well-written purpose statements

Type of Site	Purpose Statement
Personal	To chronicle the design, construction, and launching of my 36-foot sailboat named Dianegans for family and friends.
Individual business	To post my résumé and describe my professional accomplishments for potential employers.
B2C nontransactional	To describe what a company does, and what its products are, to potential customers and investors.
B2C transactional	To provide a full description of a company's products and a shopping cart function to allow for online order placement and order tracking by customers.
B2B transactional	To provide a place for a company's subcontractors to see when specific products are due and to automatically replenish inventory items.

NOTE: *If you are having a hard time defining the purpose of your site in one sentence, perhaps it is because you are trying to put too much function in one site. Consider creating two or more sites. It is not uncommon for companies (and even very Web-efficient individuals) to create multiple Web sites with each site having a different purpose.*

Defining Your Audience

When you examine Table 8.1, you should notice that each purpose statement includes the target audience in the statement. This is not accidental. Who the site is created for is a critically important item to understand when planning your site. If you don't know the reason why people will be visiting your site, and who these people are, you should not build the site, because you undoubtedly will be disappointed with the number of visits you get.

To help you better understand the process of identifying your audience, consider a couple of sites that I worked on. As you look at these two sites, pay close attention to how the information on the site pages changes as well as how the navigation changes, based on the audience.

The first site you should look at is one I managed the development work for at www.philbingroup.com. This site was built for a small industrial company located in Portland, Oregon. The owner of the company wanted a site built both for customers (mostly businesses, but the company did get some business from individual consumers) to learn what Philbin Manufacturing is, and to serve as a portal into the company's catalog of products. The company consciously decided not to build a facility into the site to allow for ordering of products. Now, take a look at another site I worked on at www.hamptonaffiliates.com. This site was built for a medium-sized lumber company located in Portland, Oregon. The company wanted this site to describe who it is and what it sells, but also for business customers to be able to check on the status of orders. Notice that the home page has a login function, which gives users access to the order status pages for qualified customers.

Recognizing Site Constraints

Three constraints affect each and every Web site development project:

- ◆ Resources (people, technical, and architectural)

- ◆ Budget

- ◆ Schedule

How well you manage and balance each of these three resources affects how successful you are in building the site. If you do not balance and manage each of these three constraints well, your Web site project will be in jeopardy. Consider the following example.

Assume you have a requirement given by management to build a corporate B2B Web site in no more than two months—your schedule. Management has budgeted $50,000 to build the site—your budget. Management has also assigned one developer, one business analyst, one project manager, and one creative analyst to the project, and they have told you to build the site to a minimum specification of Internet Explorer or Netscape Communicator browser version 4.0 with a browser resolution of 800 × 600 pixels—your resources. Perhaps all of this sounds good to you initially, but as you begin to dig deeper, you find that to give management the site they want, you need three months instead of two months to do it. However, with an additional developer, you can give them the site they want within two months.

Since most of us work for income, the second developer will cost about $15,000 for the two months, blowing your budget of $50,000. You now have a dilemma on your hands. You can give management the site they desire with the resources and budget they have allotted to you, but not within the two-month timeframe specified. Or, you can give management the site they want on the schedule they desire, but not with the resources or budget they have allotted.

This type of situation is common to almost all Web site projects. Unfortunately, there is no easy solution or resolution. Communication and effective presentation of the true situation to management is helpful. Unfortunately, you may find yourself in a situation where management will not budge on any of the three constraints and you are left with an impossible situation.

Considering Available Technologies

The fourth planning consideration is the technological constraints that exist in not only the environment where the Web site will be deployed, but the development environment as well.

Table 8.2 presents some of the important issues that need to be addressed in planning your site.

Table 8.2   Technological considerations of the target audience

Consideration	Importance
Browser	As you will see later in this book, not all browsers are created equal. The way Web pages look in a Netscape Communicator version 4.5 browser may be different from how the same page looks in a Internet Explorer version 4.5 browser. You need to understand the type of browser your site visitor will be using in order to design and build the site effectively.
Screen resolution	Unless a company has a standard that all employees are required to abide by, visitors to your site will be accessing your site with different screen resolutions. Two of the more common screen resolutions are 800×600 and 1024×768. These numbers represent how many pixels are in each inch of screen space. Therefore, a screen resolution of 800×600 has 800 pixels per horizontal inch, and 600 pixels per vertical inch. Thus, a screen with 1024×768 pixels has a higher screen resolution than one with 800×600 pixels. You need to know the screen resolution of your target audience, as well as how to build a site that incorporates these differences.
Connection speed	Believe it or not, some people still connect to the Internet with 300Mbps (megabits per second) modems. Others connect using a high-speed T3 connection that moves data 500 times faster than a 30 bps modem. You need to know and understand the speed at which your users will connect to your site in order to design it well. For example, you don't want to include a lot of graphics and animations (these typically require large amounts of disk space) if the majority of people visiting your site will be connecting using a 300Mbps modem.

Understanding Design Considerations

All well-designed Web sites begin with a storyboard. A *storyboard* is a visual representation and description of how each page relates to each other page on a Web site, as well as a representation and description of each page. How each page relates and interfaces with each other page determines how visitors navigate around your site.

After you determine a design model to use, then you can begin the task of laying out what each page on the site is to do. When you have this figured out, then you can create the storyboard.

The following three design alternatives are the most common and widely used.

Using a Hierarchical Design

Figure 8.2 depicts a typical hierarchical representation of the relationship between the pages on a site.

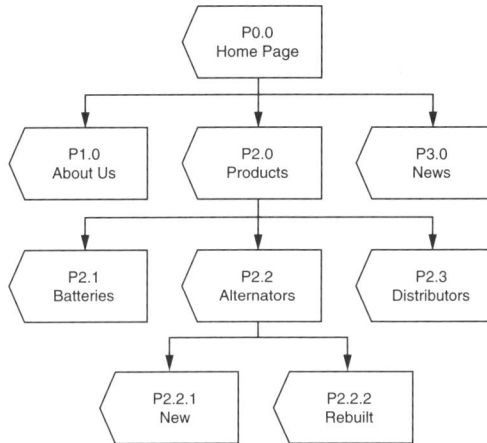

Figure 8.2

A hierarchical Web site design allows for moving to deeper levels of granularity as you move through the site.

Within Figure 8.2, you will notice a few characteristics unique to this design model:

◆ The hierarchical design model is a top-down approach. A page on a Web site (referred to here as a parent page) can have subordinate pages (referred to here as child pages) that relate in some way to the parent page. In a hierarchical design model, a parent may have no child pages or it may have a large number of child pages. A child page can then become a parent page if it has subordinate pages to it.

◆ A page-naming convention of $Pn^1.n^2$ is used, where n^1 is the parent page number, and n^2 is the relative page number.

◆ Each branch from the Home Page (P0.0) takes the user to a main branch in the site. Each branch from there is to a lower level of detail that relates to the main branch.

◆ Visitors have a clear sense of where they are on the site, because they know exactly how they got to where they are. Frequently, Web designers place a navigation bar at the top of each page that shows the names of the different pages that were navigated through to get to where they are. For example, this navigation bar might look like the following for a person on the P2.2.2 Rebuilt page on the site depicted in Figure 8.2: Home Page → Products → Alternators.

Using a Linear Design

Figure 8.3 represents the linear design model used in site design. It is characterized by a very lock-step approach to the design of a site.

Figure 8.3

A linear design of a Web site provides a rigorous and lock-step approach to controlling site navigation.

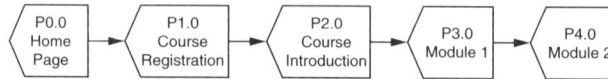

The linear design approach is useful if you want to control the navigation a user is allowed to take on a site. A Web-based training course is an example of this. In this scenario, you may not want a person taking a course on your Web site to take lesson 2 before they have viewed and passed lesson 1.

Within Figure 8.3, you will notice a few characteristics unique to this model:

♦ A linear design model is very rigid and disciplined in terms of what the user can do when on a site page.

♦ A page-naming convention of $Pn^1.n^2$ is used, where n^1 is the parent page number, and n^2 is the relative page number.

♦ Each branch from the Home Page (P0.0) takes the user to a main branch in the site that represents an entirely unique topic.

Using a Wheel Design

Figure 8.4 represents a typical wheel design for a Web site.

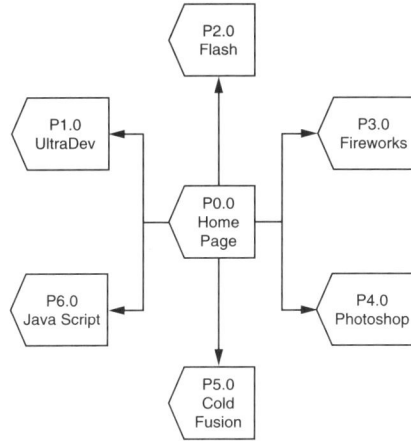

Figure 8.4

The wheel design of a Web site allows for quick navigation to very-high-level subject areas, which allows for the capability to quickly return to the home page.

The wheel design approach is useful if you need quick access to any key page on the site with equally quick jumps back to the Home Page.

Within Figure 8.4, you will notice a few characteristics unique to this model:

◆ A wheel design model allows for key subject areas to be easily separated from each other.

◆ A page-naming convention of $Pn^1.n^2$ is used, where n^1 is the parent page number, and n^2 is the relative page number.

◆ The Web's hyperlink structure makes navigation between the home page and subordinate pages very easy.

NOTE: *You are not locked in to building your site using one design model exclusively. For example, you could use a linear design approach to control the logging in and security validation process, and then use the wheel design approach to allow the user to pick one training course over the others, and, finally, use the linear design approach to control the viewing of lessons.*

Defining a Site in UltraDev

After you have the basic design of your site complete, you are ready to begin building your Web site. The first step in doing this is to define the site so that UltraDev knows where the different files that comprise the site are located. Before you can do this, though, you must understand a few things about how UltraDev handles object addresses and links.

Understanding UltraDev Addressing

On a Web site, frequently many components comprise each page. The following are some of these components:

◆ Text

◆ Pictures

◆ Audio files

◆ Animations

◆ Links to other pages

UltraDev uses three main methods to keep track of the various site and page components. You need to understand each of these three methods and decide which one to use on your site when you begin to build the site, and then stick to the decision as the site is built. Failure to do so often results in pages that do not have all the components they need, links to pages that are broken, and ultimately unhappy site visitors.

Understanding Absolute Addressing

An absolute address is the full Universal Resource Locator (URL) for the object, including its type of protocol, domain name, path, and file name. These components of a URL are depicted in Figure 8.5.

Figure 8.5

The basic components of a URL

```
http://www.philbingroup.com/home/graphics/logo.jpg
```
Type of protocol   Domain name   Path   File name

You usually would *not* use absolute addressing to link components on a Web site if the components reside on the same server. However, you would use absolute addressing to link components that reside on different servers. These are the main reasons why you would not use absolute addressing to link components on your UltraDev pages:

◆ Typing in the full URL for each item linked on a page takes a lot of extra keystrokes.

◆ If any item changes its location on the target server, then you will get "Broken Link" messages on your site.

Using Document-Relative Addressing

A *document-relative address* is an address that relates to the address of the current page. It is similar to absolute addressing but allows you to exclude one or more elements of the absolute URL.

The key element to understand about document-relative addressing is that the URL for a component that is included on a Web page is relative to the address of the document page itself. For example, assume you have a Web page whose full Web page URL is:

www.philbingroup.com/home/main.html

Now, assume there is a graphical button on this page, and that this button is located in a directory and is named as specified here:

www.philbingroup.com/home/graphics/gobutton.jpg

Using document-relative addressing, the following is the address for this button that you'd specify to UltraDev:

. . . graphics/gobutton.jpg

You can also specify an address and name for a component or object appearing on a Web page that is in a directory that is hierarchically above the current document directory. You do this by specifying two dots and a slash (../) for each directory above the current directory. So, assume in the design of your site you decide to place all graphics for your site in a directory named as follows:

www.philbingroup.com/images/

Using document-relative addressing, the address you'd specify for the gobutton.jpg file would be as follows:

. . . /images/gobutton.jpg

This type of link instructs UltraDev to move up the directory structure one directory from the current location (www.philbingroup.com/home/) and then look in a subdirectory from there called images for a file named gobutton.jpg.

Using Site-Relative Addressing

Site-relative addressing is similar to document-relative addressing with one important distinction: site-relative addressing leaves off the protocol and server segments of the URL but retains the path.

The format for a site-relative address begins with a slash (/). The slash signifies that the path that follows is relative to the site host directory.

NOTE: *The site host directory is the main directory for a Web site that is designated as being publicly accessible. You will see in a later section of this lesson how you specify this when you create a site in UltraDev.*

Using our example of the gobutton.jpg file, assume that the site host directory is called www.philbingroup.com/site. Using this as a reference, and assuming that all the site's static graphical elements are in a subdirectory to the host directory called /Static/Images, you would specify the following as the address to the button using site-relative addressing:

/Static/Images/gobutton.jpg

Setting Up a New Site in UltraDev

Now that you've learned about some of the important design considerations specific to your site and have developed an understanding of how UltraDev uses different types of addressing to keep track of where site components are located, you can define your site.

To begin the process of setting up a local site folder on your machine, click on the Site menu to display the Site submenu items. From the list of Site submenu items, click on the submenu item named New Site. You will see a dialog box that looks very much like Figure 8.6.

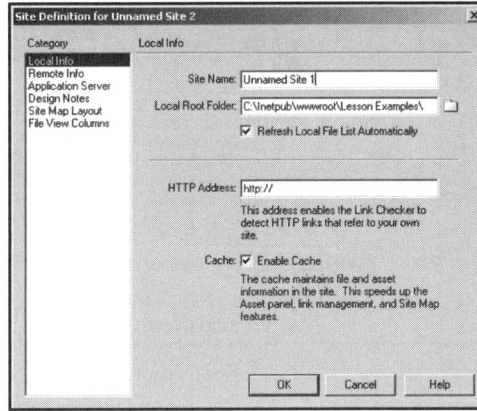

Figure 8.6

The Site Definition dialog box is where you define the attributes for a new site.

The left column of this dialog box, titled Category, has the following items listed as categories:

◆ Local Info

◆ Remote Info

◆ Application Server

◆ Design Notes

◆ Site Map Layout

◆ File View Columns

As you click on each of these categories, the layout of information on the right side of the window changes, allowing you to specify details specific to each category.

The following sections describe each of these categories and the elements specific to each category.

Understanding Local Info

Figure 8.6 shows the Site Definition window with the Local Info category selected. Setting up a local site in UltraDev means that you can use UltraDev with FTP to upload your site to a remote or shared Web server, automatically track and maintain your links, and collaboratively share files.

The local site is the site structure that you set up on your computer to contain all of your folders, site components, and files. The local root folder should be the folder that you create specifically to contain all the components (in the root folder and subfolders, of course) for that site.

Table 8.3 describes the elements that appear on the Site Definition window that are specific to the Local Info category.

Table 8.3 Elements of the Local Info category

Page Element	Description
Site Name	The name you want to give to your site. This is a free-form text field and can be anything you like because it is for reference purposes only.
Local Root Folder	The folder on your local disk where the site files, templates, and library items will be stored. Document- or site-relative addresses are resolved to the address you specify here. You can either click on the folder icon to browse your hard drive for the folder, or enter a path and folder name in the associated text box.
Refresh Local File List Automatically	Indicates whether or not to automatically refresh the local file list every time you copy files to your machine. If you select this option (by clicking on it to place a check mark in the box), the Local Info pane of the Site Definition window updates automatically whenever files specific to your site are copied into the site. If you deselect this option (by clicking on it to remove the check mark from the box), performance of UltraDev will increase. If you do deselect this option, you can manually refresh the Local Pane only by clicking on the View menu and then clicking on the Refresh Local submenu item.
HTTP Address	Specifies the HTTP address that your completed Web site will use. This is specified here so that UltraDev can verify and resolve links you specify on your Web pages that use absolute addressing.
Cache	Indicates whether or not to create a cache on your machine to improve performance. If you select this option (by clicking on it to place a check mark in the box), performance of UltraDev on your machine will improve. (Frankly, I do not know of a reason why you would *not* want this option checked, unless you were using a machine that had very limited memory.)

Understanding Remote Info

Figure 8.7 shows the Site Definition window with the Remote Info category selected. You use the Remote Info category to add or change associated remote server information and Check In/Check Out preferences.

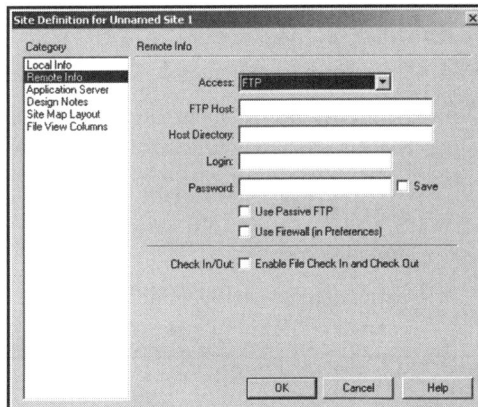

Figure 8.7

The Site Definition window with the Remote Info category selected

Your window may not look like what you see in Figure 8.7. In fact, your window probably only has one item, Access, on the window, with a drop-down list box that has the word None in it. This is okay. When you click on the Access drop-down list box, you see the following items in the list:

◆ None

◆ FTP

◆ Local/Network

◆ SourceSafe Database

◆ WebDAV

Table 8.4 lists and describes each of these options.

Table 8.4 Access methods and their definitions

Access Method	Description
None	If you are not moving your site to a remote server (for example, your site will execute off of the machine you are using for development), select this option.
FTP	Select this option if you are using File Transfer Protocol to move the files from your development machine to a remote server.
Local/Network	Select this option if you are copying the files from your development machine to a remote server using native Copy commands.
SourceSafe Database	Select this option if you are using SourceSafe (a Microsoft product) as a repository to store all of your Web site components before staging to a production server.
WebDAV	Select this option if you are using WebDAV as a repository to store all of your Web site components before staging to a production server.

If you are using SourceSafe or WebDAV for staging areas, then you should consult the documentation accompanying those products for an understanding of how to set the parameters that appear on this window. If you select FTP or Local/Network, then the information in the table below is pertinent to you.

Table 8.5 describes the elements on the Site Definition window that are specific to the Remote Info category when the FTP access option is specified.

Table 8.5 Elements of the Remote Info category when FTP access is selected

Page Element	Description
FTP Host	The FTP host name of the computer that will contain the production Web site, such as ftp.philbingroup.com.
Host Directory	The name of the host directory at the remote machine where you store documents visible to the public.
Login	The login name used to connect to the FTP server.
Password	The login password used to connect to the FTP server.
Save	If this box is checked, UltraDev saves the login name and password.
Use Passive FTP	If you are using a passive FTP site, click on this option to place a check mark in the box.
Use Firewall	If you are connecting to the remote server from behind a firewall, click on this option to place a check mark in the box.
Check In/Out	If you are using UltraDev's Check In/Out facility, click on this option to place a check mark in the box.

NOTE: *If a team of developers and designers is creating the Web site, the Check In/Out feature is particularly useful. With this option enabled, UltraDev places a check mark next to the file name in the remote directory pane of the Site window for all team members to see when a file is checked out and being used by another team member.*

Table 8.6 describes the elements on the Site Definition window that are specific to the Remote Info category when the Local/Network access option is specified.

Table 8.6 Elements of the Remote Info category when Local/Network access is selected

Page Element	Description
Remote Folder	The name of the folder on the network machine (or possibly a different folder name on the development machine) that is to house the site components. To identify the folder, either click on the folder icon and use the browse window that opens to select the folder name, or type the folder name in the adjacent text box.
Refresh Remote File	If the file list for the remote folder is to be refreshed automatically, click on this option to place a check mark in the box.
Check In/Out	If you are using UltraDev's Check In/Out facility, click on this option to place a check mark in the box.

Understanding the Application Server

Figure 8.8 shows the Site Definition window with the Application Server category selected. You use this window to tell UltraDev what server technology you're using, so that it knows what type of server-side scripts to insert into your pages. If you have a server with Microsoft's Active Server Pages specification, then UltraDev inserts either VBScript or JavaScript scripts into your pages. If you have a server with Sun's JavaServer Pages specification, UltraDev inserts Java code into your pages. And if you're using a ColdFusion server, UltraDev inserts the necessary ColdFusion tags and scripts into the pages.

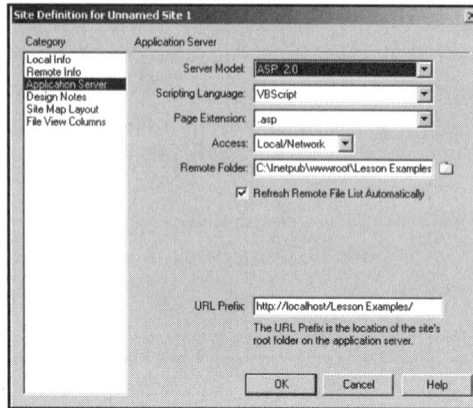

Figure 8.8

The Site Definition window with the Application Server category selected

Your window may not look like what you see in Figure 8.8. In fact, your window probably has only the None item selected in the Server Model drop-down list box. However, if you click on the Server Model drop-down list box arrow, you'll see the following items listed:

◆ ASP 2.0

◆ ColdFusion 4.0

◆ JSP 1.0

Table 8.7 describes the elements on the Site Definition window that are specific to the Application Server category when the ASP, ColdFusion, or JSP server model option is specified.

Table 8.7   Elements of the Application Server category when a server model of ASP, ColdFusion, or JSP is selected

Page Element	Description
Scripting Language	If ASP is selected as the Server Model, the options in this drop-down list box are VBScript or JavaScript. If you select ColdFusion as the Server Model, the option in this drop-down list box is CFML. And if you select JSP as the Server Model, the option in this drop-down list box is Java.
Page Extension	If ASP is selected as the Server Model, the options in this drop-down list box are .asp, .htm, and .html. If ColdFusion is selected as the Server Model, the option in this drop-down list box is .cfm. And if you select JSP as the Server Model, the option in this drop-down list box is .jav.

Table 8.7 (*continued*)

Page Element	Description
Access	The method that the server site will be accessed from UltraDev. The options are None, FTP, and Local/Network.
Remote Folder	The name of the folder on the network machine (or possibly a different folder name on the development machine) that is to house the site components. To identify the folder, either click on the folder icon and use the browse window that opens to select the folder name, or type the folder name in the adjacent text box.
Refresh Remote File	If the file list for the remote folder is to be refreshed automatically, click on this option to place a check mark in the box.
URL Prefix	The location of the site's root folder on the application server.

Design Notes

Figure 8.9 shows the Site Definition window with the Design Notes category selected. You use this window to tell UltraDev that you want it to reserve space to place and maintain design notes associated with site components.

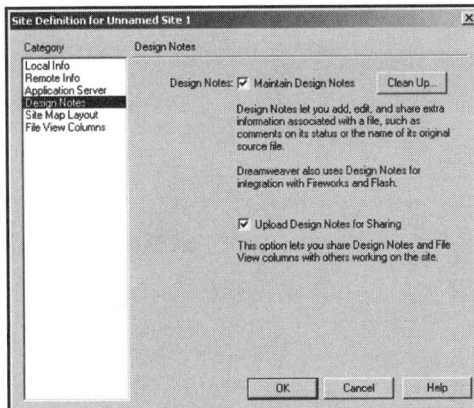

Figure 8.9

The Site Definition window with the Design Notes category selected

Table 8.8 describes the elements on the Site Definition window that are specific to the Design Notes category.

Table 8.8   Elements of the Design Notes category

Page Element	Description
Design Notes	Placing a check mark in this box by clicking on it lets you store comment information specific to site components.
Clean Up	Clicking on this button removes all design notes that are associated with site components that no longer exist. This situation can occur if you create a site component, such as a page, add design notes to the page, and subsequently delete the page.
Upload Design Notes For Sharing	Placing a check mark in this box by clicking on it lets you share design notes with other people working on the site. If this option is not checked, then design notes can only be viewable by the person who originally created them.

Defining Your Site Map Layout

Figure 8.10 shows the Site Definition window with the Site Map Layout category selected. You use this window to customize the appearance of your site map. You can specify the home page, the number of columns displayed, and whether to show hidden and dependent files.

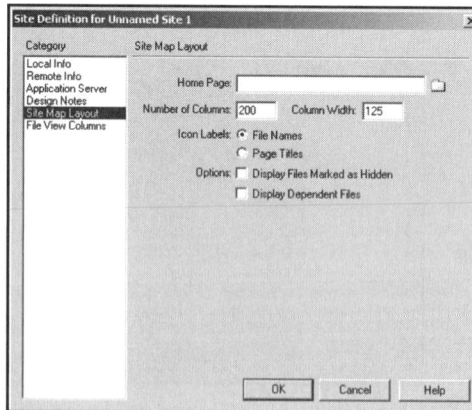

Figure 8.10

The Site Definition window with the Site Map Layout category selected

Table 8.9 describes the elements on the Site Definition window that are specific to the Site Map Layout category.

Table 8.9   Elements of the Site Map Layout category

Page Element	Description
Home Page	The name of the folder that contains the home page. To identify the folder, either click on the folder icon and use the browse window that opens to select the folder name, or type the folder name in the adjacent text box. UltraDev searches for a file named index.html or index.htm in this folder and displays a prompt to select a home page when you open the site if one is not found.
Number Of Columns	The number of pages to display per row in the site map window.
Column Width	The width in pixels of the site map columns.
Icon Labels: File Names	Specify whether the name displayed with the document icons in the site map represents a file name.
Icon Labels: Page Titles	Specify whether the name displayed with the document icons in the site map represents a page title.
Options: Display Files Marked As Hidden	When checked, this option tells UltraDev to display HTML files that are marked as hidden in the site map. When this option is not checked, UltraDev will not display hidden files in the site map.
Options: Display Dependent Files	When checked, this option tells UltraDev to show all dependent files (for example, images and other non-HTML components) in the site's hierarchy. When this option is not checked, UltraDev will not display dependent files in the site map.

File View Columns

Figure 8.11 shows the Site Definition window with the File View Columns category selected. You use this window to customize the appearance of your site map. You can specify the home page, the number of columns displayed, and whether to show hidden and dependent files.

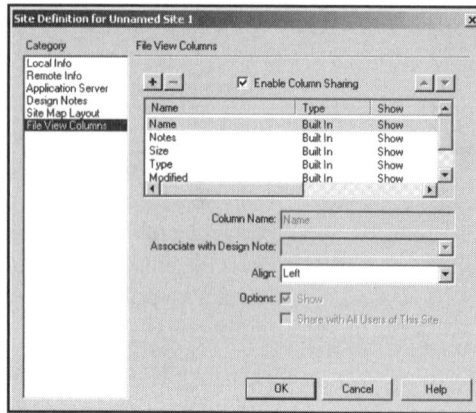

Figure 8.11

The Site Definition window with the File View Columns category selected

Table 8.10 describes the elements on the Site Definition window that are specific to the File View Columns category.

Table 8.10　Elements of the File View Columns category

Page Element	Description
Column Name list box	Shows the names of the columns that appear in the site map definition.
Column Name	Lets you specify the name of the column to be added to the site map. If you click on a row in the Column Name list box, the name of the column in that row populates this text box and you can change its attributes as they relate to the site map.
Associate With Design Note	A drop-down list box allowing you to associate a design note with a column. You can select a design note to apply to the column from multiple design notes, if there happens to be more than one design note for the column.
Align	A drop-down list box with three options (left, center, and right) that let you specify how the column selected displays in the site map.
Show Option	Shows the selected column in the site map if this check box is checked. Uncheck this check box if you do not want the column to show in the site map.
Share With Other Users	Lets you share the definition of this column in the site map with other users if the check box is checked. To make the column showing in the site map specific to your view of the site map, uncheck this check box.

What You Must Know

In this lesson, you learned about some of the considerations specific to designing a Web site, as well as how to set up an UltraDev site. In Lesson 9, "Laying the Groundwork for an Application," you learn how to organize your files for a Web site, create a Web page with text, and use page separators.

Before you continue to Lesson 9, make sure you understand the following key concepts:

◆ Your first step to a successful Web site is a successful site design.

◆ Within UltraDev, you create a local site (one that runs on your computer) by creating a folder (and optional sub-folders), to contain the site components.

◆ To create a remote site with UltraDev, you must specify the location of the application server that will host your site.

◆ Using relative addressing (as opposed to absolute path addressing), you make your site easier to modify and maintain.

Lesson 9

Laying the Groundwork
for an Application

In Lesson 8, "Setting Up an UltraDev Site," you learned about the design considerations specific to a Web site. You also learned how to use UltraDev to set up a new Web site. In this lesson, you will begin to learn how to use the UltraDev interface to work with site pages. Specifically, you will create a site with text on pages that you type in and copy in from an external file. By the time you finish this lesson, you will understand the following key concepts:

◆ Using UltraDev, creating a new Web page in an existing site is easy.

◆ UltraDev gives you powerful capabilities to insert text on site pages.

◆ Within UltraDev, you can quickly paste text that resides in an external file into a Web site page.

◆ Using page separators helps you manage your site.

◆ You can define and use a browser to preview your work.

Working with Pages

UltraDev gives you powerful and easy-to-use features for working with Web pages. To start, take a look at the submenu bar, shown in Figure 9.1.

Figure 9.1

The submenu bar gives easy access to commonly used components.

Table 9.1 provides a brief description of the function of each of the buttons on the submenu bar.

Table 9.1   The submenu bar

Button	Description
Show Code View	Displays the HTML code for the current page.
Show Code And Design View	Displays the HTML code in the top pane and the graphical representation for the current page in the bottom pane.
Show Design View	Displays the graphical representation of the current page in the bottom pane.
Show Live Data	Displays the recordset of data, if the page references data.
Title	Lets you change the title of the page.
File Management	Allows access to various file management facilities, such as Get, Check Out, Put, Check In, Undo Check Out, Design Notes, and Locate In Site.
Preview/Debug In Browser	Lets you preview the page in one or more predefined browsers. Also allows you to enter debug mode in one or more predefined browsers. You can define target browser types in this menu item.
Undo	Allows you to undo the last-made change.
Reference	Allows access to reference material specific to the location on the page where the cursor is located. As you place your cursor on different locations in the page, clicking the Reference button takes you to that specific location in the UltraDev reference material.
Code Navigation	If you are in Code or Code and Design View, this option gives you access to debugging tools that let you set and unset breakpoints in the code.
View Options	Provides access to various options that control the view of the page, dependent on the way you are viewing the page. If you are viewing the page in Code View, Code and Design View, or Design View, the View Options submenu items change accordingly.

With these subnavigation buttons, you can quickly work with the content and view or manipulate the HTML code that appears on a page.

Creating a New Page and Setting Page Properties

Within UltraDev, you create a new page on an existing site by performing the following steps:

1. Within the Menu bar, click on the File Menu item. UltraDev displays the File submenu.

2. Within the File submenu, click on New. UltraDev responds by creating a new, empty page in the Document window.

NOTE: *You will see a submenu item under the New submenu item titled New From Template. This is a feature in UltraDev that lets you create a new page and apply specific styles and preferences as stored in a template file. Lesson 23, "Speeding Up Your Web Site Development by Reusing Elements," discusses styles and preferences in detail.*

If you have made changes to an existing page before you perform the previous steps, UltraDev will ask you if you want to save your changes before it creates a new page. Now that UltraDev has created a new page, you are ready to manipulate some of the properties on the page.

To modify any of the page properties, as shown in Figure 9.2, perform the following steps:

1. Within the Menu bar, click on the Modify menu item. UltraDev displays the Modify submenu.

2. Within the Modify submenu, click on the Page Properties submenu item. You will see the Page Properties window, as shown in Figure 9.2.

3. After you have made changes to any of the attributes in the Page Properties window, click on the OK button, the Apply button, or the Cancel button. Clicking on OK applies the changes specified and closes the Page Properties window. Clicking on Apply applies the changes specified and keeps the Page Properties window open. Clicking on Cancel closes the Page

Figure 9.2

The Page Properties window allows you to modify many of the attributes of a Web page appearing on your site.

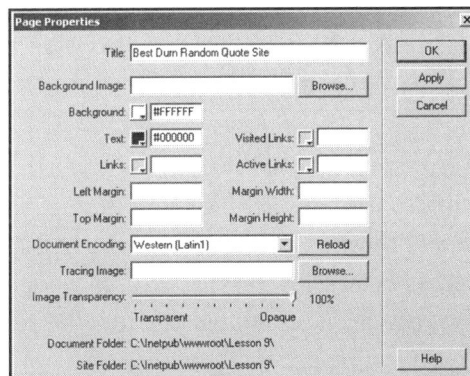

Properties window without applying any of the changes made since the window was first opened and you last clicked the Apply button.

Table 9.2 provides a brief description of the function of each of the buttons and controls that appears in the Page Properties window.

Table 9.2   The Page Properties window

Button or Control	Description
Title	Specifies the title of the Web page that appears in the title bar of the Document window and most browser windows. The Web page title is what gets saved to the browser bookmarks or favorites lists, so it is worthwhile to spend time thinking of a meaningful name.
Background Image	Specifies the background image for the Web page.
Background	Specifies the background color for the Web page.
Text	Specifies the default color for text appearing on the Web page.
Links	Specifies the default color for links appearing on the Web page.
Left Margin	Specifies the left margin for text, tables, or images appearing on the Web page.
Top Margin	Specifies the top margin for text, tables, or images appearing on the Web page.
Document Encoding	Specifies the encoding used for characters appearing on the Web page.
Tracing Image	Specifies an image to use as a guideline for copying a design. The image specified is used for reference only and does not display on the Web page.
Image Transparency	Specifies the transparency of the tracing image used on the Web page. This ranges from completely transparent to completely opaque.
Visited Links	Specifies the default color for visited links that appear on the Web page.
Active Links	Specifies the default color for active links that appear on the Web page.
Margin Width	Specifies the width of the page margin in the body tag.
Margin Height	Specifies the height of the page margin in the body tag.

NOTE: *The Margin Width and Margin Height attributes in the Page Properties window are applicable to Netscape Navigator only. Microsoft Internet Explorer ignores these values and uses the Left Margin and Top Margin instead. To provide cross-browser compatibility, provide margin values for both browsers instead of just one browser, unless you are 100 percent positive that users of only one browser type will be accessing your site.*

Entering and Centering Text on a Page

To add text to a page, simply start typing on the page that appears in the Document window—it is that easy. Manipulating text that appears on a page is almost as easy. To manipulate text, select the text you want to manipulate by holding the left mouse button down while you drag the mouse cursor across the text. Release the left mouse button after you have highlighted all the text you desire. You will probably see the Property Inspector (shown in Figure 9.3) in your Document window. If you do not, click on the Window menu and choose Properties.

NOTE: *Notice the shortcut key that appears next to the Properties submenu item (Ctrl+F3). By holding down the Ctrl key while pressing the F3 key, you can toggle the display of the Property Inspector on and off.*

Figure 9.3

The alignment icons in the Property Inspector control the placement of text appearing on a Web page.

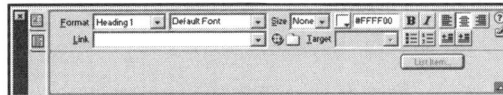

After you highlight the text to manipulate and the Property Inspector appears in the Document window, you can perform one of a number of functions that alter its appearance and location on the Web page. For example, to center the text on the Web page, click on the icon that is labeled in Figure 9.3 as Align Center. A full description of each of the controls and attributes that is on the PropertyIinspector for text appears in Table 9.3.

Table 9.3   The Property Inspector window for text

Button or Control	Description
Format	Specifies a block style to the text. Heading styles are used to apply a standardized hierarchical structure to the formatted text.
Default Font	Specifies a font face to the selected text.
Size	Specifies the font size of the selected text. The size is either a specific font size of 1 through 7 or a relative font size of plus or minus 1 through plus or minus 7 relative to the base font size, which is 3.

(continued)

Table 9.3 *(continued)*

Button or Control	Description
Text Color	Specifies the font color of the selected text as it appears on a Web page. You can make this selection in one of two ways. First, you can select a browser-safe color by clicking on the color box with your mouse and picking one of the colors that appear there. Or, you can specify a hexadecimal value (for example #FF0000) in the adjacent text field.
Bold and Italic	Specify whether the selected text will appear in a bold and/or italicized font face.
Link	Makes the selected text a hyperlink to a specified URL. You can click on the folder icon to select another page on your site, or you can type the URL to another page in the text box.
Target	Specifies the frame or window that the linked page should load. If you are using frames in the page (see Lesson 13, "Controlling Page Layout"), the names of all the frames for the current document appear in the list.
Unordered List	Turns the selected text into an item in a bulleted list.
Ordered List	Turns the selected text into an item in a numbered list.
Indent	Indents the selected text.
Outdent	Outdents the selected text.

Pasting Text from an External File

As you create pages, there are times when, to reduce typing, you will want to insert text from an external file into a page on your site. To copy text from one file and paste the text into a Web page using UltraDev, perform the following steps:

1. Open the document that contains the text you want to copy, using a program you are comfortable with (such as Notepad, Microsoft Word, and so on).

2. Within the document, select the text to be copied. There are multiple ways to select text. One is simply to hold down the left mouse button while you drag the cursor of your mouse across the text you desire.

3. Copy the selected text to the Clipboard by holding down the Ctrl key and pressing the C key. (You can also select the Edit menu Copy option.)

4. Within UltraDev, click your mouse at the location on the page that appears in the Document window where you want the copied text to appear.

5. Within the UltraDev Menu bar, select the Edit menu Paste as Text option. You will see the text that you copied from your source document appear on the Web page in the Document window.

NOTE: *Instead of using the menu items in UltraDev to paste the copied text onto your Web page, you could also use key combinations to do the same thing. In Windows, press and hold down the Ctrl key while pressing the V key. On a Macintosh, press and hold down the Ctrl and Shift keys while pressing the V key. Within the Lesson 9 folder on the CD-ROM that accompanies this book, you will find a file called InsertedText.txt within the Lesson Examples directory. You can use this file to practice copying and pasting text into a Web page.*

Apply Text Formatting to Inserted Text

At this point, you have inserted text onto your Web page. But, the text is probably not formatted the way you would like it to appear. To change the format of some text, perform these steps:

1. If you copied and pasted the text that resides within the InsertedText.txt file (located on the CD-ROM that accompanies this book) onto the Add A Quote page, select the text string that reads: *On this page, you can enter quotes into our database. Please perform a query before you do this to make sure the quote doesn't yet exist.*

2. Select the text by holding the left mouse button down while you drag the cursor of your mouse across the text to be manipulated. Release the left mouse button when all of the text to be manipulated is highlighted. You should see the Property Inspector in the Document window. If you do not, follow the instructions described earlier in this lesson to display it.

3. Click on the Format drop-down list box. UltraDev will display a list of predefined formatting options. Click on the Heading 3 item within the list. When you do this, you should see the size of the font decrease.

4. Next, click on the Text Font drop-down list. UltraDev will display a list of predefined fonts. You should see a font titled Arial, Helvetica. Select this font face by clicking on the font name. UltraDev, in turn, will change the appearance of your text to match the font.

5. Click on the Text Color box. UltraDev will display a two-dimensional array of colors. Click on one of the colors that appears bright red. UltraDev, in turn, will apply the color to your text.

That is all there is to manipulating text within UltraDev. You have successfully inserted, pasted, and formatted text that appears on your Web page. Your page should look very similar to Figure 9.4

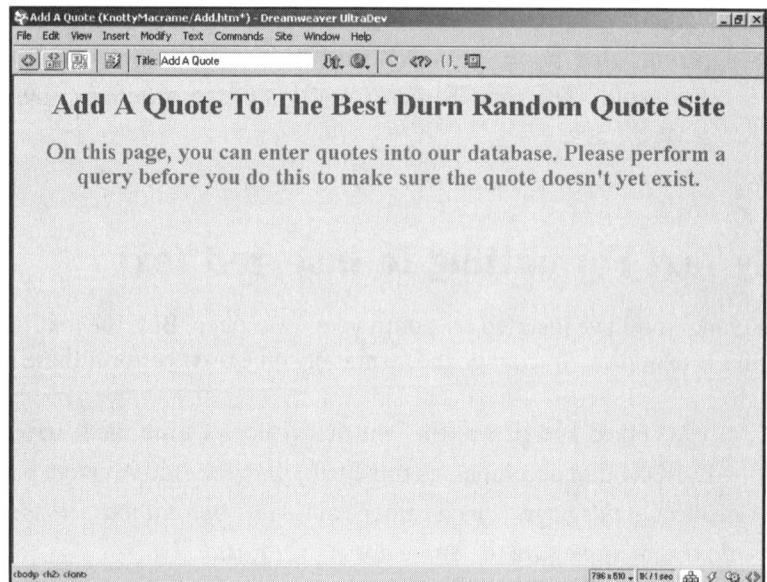

Figure 9.4

This is what your Web page should look like up to this point in the lesson.

Adding a Page Separator

A page separator is any graphical element that helps the person viewing the page to recognize logical divisions on the page. For example, you may want to use a page separator between heading and detail lines on a page. To insert a page separator, perform these steps:

1. Place your cursor at the location on the page where you want to insert a page separator and click on that spot.

2. As shown in Figure 9.5, you should see the Objects palette. If you do not see this on your Document window, select the Window menu Object option.

3. Also as shown in Figure 9.5, you should see that the horizontal rule icon is circled. Click on this icon. UltraDev, in turn, will insert a horizontal line on your Web page at the insertion spot.

Figure 9.5

The Objects palette has an icon to place a page separator on your Web page.

Modifying Attributes of a Page Separator

Just as you have the ability to modify the appearance of text on a Web page using a Property Inspector for text, UltraDev gives you a Property Inspector for a page separator. If the Property Inspector is not displayed on your Document window, you can active it by performing these steps:

1. Select the horizontal rule by clicking on the rule. UltraDev, in turn, will highlight the rule within the Document window.

2. Click on the Window menu and choose Properties. UltraDev will display the Property inspector shown in Figure 9.6.

3. After you see the Property Inspector for the page separator, you can manipulate any of the attributes as described in Table 9.4.

Figure 9.6

The Property Inspector window for the page separator

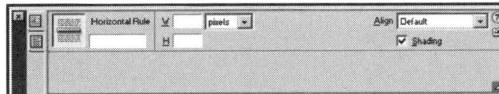

Table 9.4   The controls and objects on the Property Inspector window for the page separator

Button or Control	Description
W (Width)	Specifies the width of the page separator in either pixels or as a percentage of the page size.
Pixels or Page Size	Specifies whether the page separator width is specified in pixels or as a percentage of the total page width.
Align	Specifies the alignment of the page separator, with the choices being Default, Left, Center, or Right. This attribute is only applicable if the width of the page separator is less than the full-page width.
Name	Specifies the name of the page separator. In most cases, you will not name the page separators. However, it is possible to manipulate any of the attributes of the page separator via program code, and if you choose to do this, you need to identify the page separator by name.
H (Height)	Specifies the height of the page separator in either pixels or as a percentage of the page size.
Shading	Specifies whether the page separator is drawn with shading. To draw the page separator with shading, click the check box to place a check mark in it.

Saving Your Work

UltraDev is a What You See Is What You Get (WYSIWYG) tool, meaning the way things appear on the Web page in your Document window is very close to how they will appear in a Web browser. However, as you will learn, the more you use UltraDev to build Web sites, not all browsers display HTML and objects the same way. Because of this, you will want to save your work and view it in a browser periodically. To save your work done in this lesson so far, perform the following steps:

1. Select the File menu Save option. UltraDev, in turn, will display the Save dialog box.

2. Within the Save dialog box File Name text box, type the file name you want to use to identify this Web page. As you can see in Figure 9.7, I saved the page with a name of *AddAQuote*.

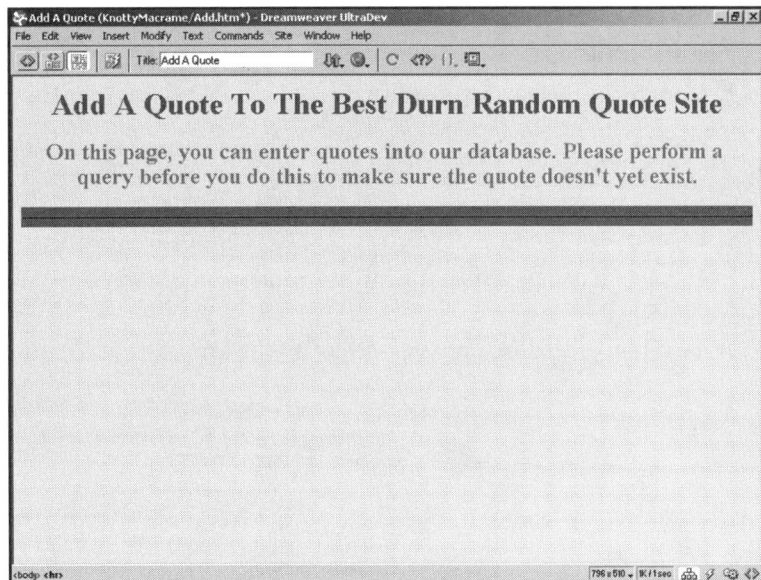

Figure 9.7

The AddAQuote.html page as created in this lesson

That is it. You have created a new Web page, inserted and formatted text, copied and formatted text, and saved your work. Now, you can learn how to view the Web page in a browser.

Previewing a Page in a Browser

You can define up to 20 different browsers to be used for previewing purposes in UltraDev. With the overwhelming popularity of Microsoft Internet Explorer and Netscape Navigator, I generally have these two defined for every site I build.

When you install UltraDev, the setup program tries to locate the different browsers you already have installed on your machine. You can see what browsers UltraDev currently recognizes on your machine by selecting the File menu Preview option. UltraDev, in turn, will display a dialog box that displays the browsers installed on your system, along with an item at the bottom of the list that says Edit Browser List. If you must set up a new browser, perform these steps:

1. Click on the Edit Browser List. UltraDev will display the Preferences window with the Preview in Browser category already selected.

2. Within the Preferences window, click on the plus (+) icon next to the Browsers text. UltraDev, in turn, will display the Add Browser window.

3. Within the Add Browser window, click on the Browse button to browse your hard drive for the executable file of the browser you want to add. You will see a File List dialog box in which you can locate and select this executable.

4. Within the Name text box, specify the name for this browser.

5. Click on either the Primary Browser or Secondary Browser default check box. You can see an example of a completed Add Browser window in Figure 9.8.

6. Repeat this procedure until you select all the browsers you require.

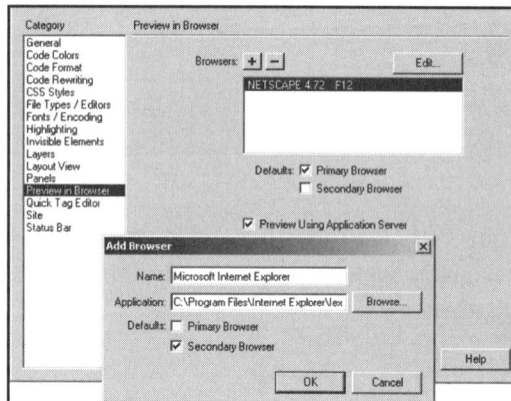

Figure 9.8

The Add Browser window identifying the Microsoft Internet Explorer as a browser type

NOTE: *UltraDev uses a keyboard shortcut of Ctrl+F12 to test the current page in the Document window with the default primary browser. It is for this reason that the browser you specify as the primary browser is important.*

What You Must Know

In this lesson, you learned how to use the UltraDev interface to work with site pages. Specifically, you learned how to create a site with text on pages that you typed in and copied in from an external file. In Lesson 10, "Using Graphics and Multimedia on a Page," you will learn how to incorporate graphical and multimedia elements on your site pages. Before you continue to Lesson 10, make sure you understand the following key concepts:

◆ To create a new page in an existing site, use the File menu New option.

◆ To paste text from an external file, first select the text you desire and copy it to the Clipboard. Then, within UltraDev, use the Edit menu Paste Text option to insert the text within your page.

◆ Using page separators, you can organize the appearance of items on a page.

◆ To define a browser for use within UltraDev, use the File menu Preview option.

Lesson 10

Using Graphics and Multimedia on a Page

In Lesson 9, "Laying the Groundwork for an Application," you learned how to use the UltraDev interface to work with pages within a Web site. You also learned how to insert and manipulate text on a Web page. In this lesson, you will learn how to work with graphics and multimedia on a Web page. Specifically, you will add and manipulate images and other multimedia on your Web pages. By the time you finish this lesson, you will understand the following key concepts:

♦ You can easily add an image to a Web page in UltraDev.

♦ Within a Web page, a rollover image is an image that changes when the user's mouse hovers over it. You will learn how to insert a rollover image.

♦ In addition to letting you add text and graphics to a Web page, UltraDev also lets you place audio files on a page.

♦ Macromedia Flash is a software program designers use to create animations. Using UltraDev, you can easily place Flash components within a Web page.

♦ Java is a programming language programmers use to create a wide range of Web-based applications. Using UltraDev, you can easily place a Java applet (a Web-based program) within a Web page.

Working with Images

Almost every program you can buy to work with computer graphics has its own proprietary format for storing the images on your hard drive. However, there are three formats that are almost universally accepted as standards, which Table 10.1 describes.

Table 10.1   The three types of graphic formats for your Web pages

Format	Description
JPEG (JPG)	Developed by the Joint Photographic Experts Group (JPEG) to store photographic data. The JPEG format offers millions of colors at 24-bit resolution per screen pixel.
GIF	Known as the Graphic Interchange Format, the GIF standard was developed by CompuServe in the late 1980s. GIF images are bitmapped images, which means the format maps each pixel to a specific color. A GIF image can have a maximum of 256 unique colors. Line drawings and screen art are ideal types of graphics to be stored using GIF.
PNG	Also known as Portable Network Graphics, the PNG format combines the best of JPEG and GIF by providing an interlace scheme for storing colors that offers almost the high-density color storage as in JPEG, but takes up little more storage space per image than a GIF image.

NOTE: *One of the nagging problems encountered by people creating graphics viewable on both PC and Macintosh platforms is that images created on a PC appear brighter on a Macintosh, and images created on a Macintosh appear darker on a PC. The PNG format solves this problem by including gamma correction capabilities in the file that alter the image depending on the computer used by the viewer.*

Inserting an Image on a Page

Within the Index.html page of the site you have been creating for this book, there are four GIF files of flames underneath the page heading, with nothing underneath these four images. You will now place a graphic of a horizontal bar underneath these four images, by performing these steps:

1. Within UltraDev, place the cursor at the location on the Web page where you want to insert the image. You will notice the insert point blinking on the Web page.

2. Click on the title bar of the Objects palette to activate the palette. If you do not see the Objects palette on your page, you may have closed it. To reopen the Objects palette, click on the Window menu and then choose Objects.

3. Within the Objects palette, click on the Insert Image icon, which is shown circled in Figure 10.1. UltraDev, in turn, will display the Select Image Source window, as shown in Figure 10.2, which lets you locate and specify the location of the graphic to insert.

Figure 10.1

The Objects palette contains the icon that gives access to the Select Image Source window.

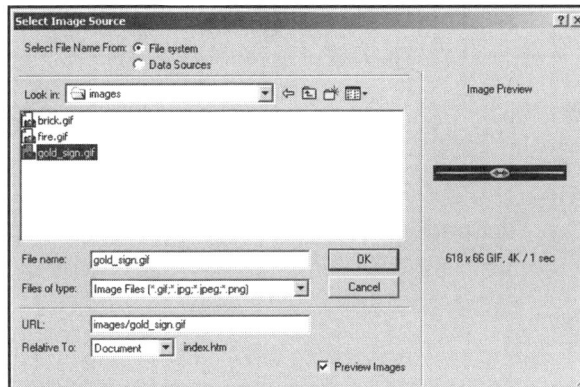

Figure 10.2

The Select Image Source window allows you to locate and specify the graphic to place on the Web page.

4. Within the Select Image Source window, locate and specify the graphic you want to insert onto your Web page and then click on the OK button.

Table 10.2 gives you a brief description of some of the controls and objects that appear on the Select Image Source window.

Table 10.2 The Select Image Source window controls and objects

Control or Object	Description
Look in drop-down list box	Lets you locate and select the graphic of interest.
File list	Displays the contents of the folder selected in the Look in drop-down list box with the file extensions matching those specified in the Files of type drop-down list box.
File name	A text box showing the name of the file in the file list area that you select by clicking on it.
Files of type drop-down list box	Lets you select one of a number of combinations of predefined file types for filtering the contents of the selected folder that display in the file list area.
URL	The URL of the graphic selected.
Relative to list box	Lets you specify the location of the selected graphics file relative to either the Document that contains the graphic or the Site Root.
Preview Images check box	When checked, the graphic you select by clicking on it once will display on the right side of the Select Image Source window.

NOTE: *If you are selecting a graphic that is not in the Site folder, UltraDev will ask if you want to copy it into the Site folder. You should answer Yes to the question to ensure that the graphic is always available. If you answer No to the question, and if the graphic or the folder the graphic is in somehow gets deleted or renamed, your site will no longer display the graphic.*

As shown in Figure 10.3, the image you just inserted is now visible in the Document window. When you select the image (by clicking on it), the Property Inspector changes to display attributes specific to the image.

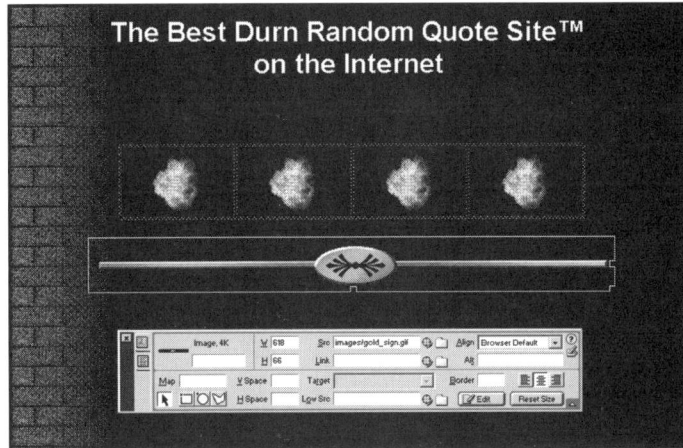

Figure 10.3

The image on your Web page, with the Property Inspector visible

Within UltraDev, the resize handles for a graphic become visible when you click on the graphic. These handles are handy for changing the vertical, horizontal, or vertical *and* horizontal size of the graphic. If you want to change the size of the image while maintaining its *aspect ratio* (the dimension along one scale in relation to the dimension along the other scale), press and hold down the Shift key while you use your mouse to drag one of the resize handles to a new location. If you make a mistake while sizing an object and you want to revert to the actual dimensions for the graphic, simply click on the Reset Size button on the Property Inspector.

Aligning an Image with Text

Within UltraDev, you can align an image that appears on a page relative to the page itself, or relative to other objects that appear on the page. To align an image relative to the page it appears on, perform the following steps:

1. Click on the image that you want to position relative to the page.

2. Within the Property Inspector, click on one of the three icons (align left, align center, or align right) that matches how you want the graphic to appear relative to the Web page.

Table 10.3 describes the 10 alignment options available to you to align the image selected relative to other components on the Web page.

Table 10.3   *Options in the Property Inspector for aligning the image relative to other page objects*

Alignment Option	Description
Browser Default	Usually aligns to the baseline, but this is dependent on the browser.
Baseline	Aligns the bottom of the image with the bottom of the selected object.
Top	Aligns the top of the image with the selected object.
Middle	Aligns the middle of the image with the selected object.
Bottom	Aligns the bottom of the image with the selected object.
TextTop	Aligns the image with the highest text selected.
Absolute Middle	Aligns the middle of the image with the middle of the selected text.
Absolute Bottom	Aligns the bottom of the image with the bottom of the selected text.
Left	Aligns the image to the left of the selected object.
Right	Aligns the image to the right of the selected object.

Specifying Alternate Text for a Graphic

When your site contains large graphics or when people view your site Web page using a slow connection, the user spends considerable time looking at an unsightly page while waiting for the graphics to load. As a Web developer, you cannot do much to speed the connections people use when viewing your site, but, by specifying alternate text for the graphic, you can make the experience slightly more pleasant while they wait for your graphics to load.

As previously shown in Figure 10.3, the Property Inspector provides a text box labeled Alt for graphics objects. If you type text within this box, the browser will display the text on the user's screen while the browser waits to load the corresponding graphic. When you specify such "alternative text," be descriptive with the words you choose. Your description should help the user anticipate your image.

Understanding Graphic Rollovers

Within a Web page, a *rollover* is an effect that occurs when a user's mouse pointer crosses over an object. Usually, a rollover is the presentation of a slightly different graphic from the graphic appearing on the page when the mouse pointer is not crossing over it. Rollovers are a very popular type of graphic used on most Web sites. They add "life" and "pop" to the pages they appear on.

NOTE: *The words "life" and "pop" are used in Web site design to mean special things. The word "life" means the amount of activity or movement that occurs on the page. The word "pop" means the suddenness or movement that appears on the page. The more pop there is on a page, the more sudden movement there is. Using these terms, the Index.html page in our sample site has plenty of life by now, but not a whole lot of pop.*

In the past, designers created rollover effects using a combination of HTML and JavaScript. With UltraDev, you can create some interesting rollover effects without having to write a line of HTML code or JavaScript. To include a rollover image on a Web page, perform the following steps:

1. Within UltraDev, place your mouse cursor on the location in your Web page where you want to insert the rollover image, and click your mouse button once.

2. Within the Objects palette, click on the icon representing Insert Rollover Image, which is shown circled in Figure 10.4. When you click on this icon, UltraDev will display the Insert Rollover Image window, as shown in Figure 10.5.

Figure 10.4

The Objects palette with the Insert Rollover Image icon framed

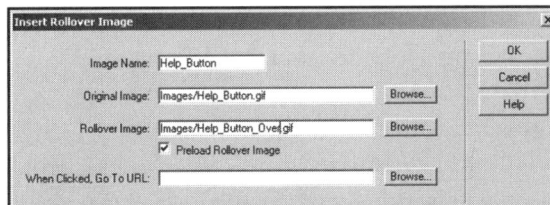

Figure 10.5

The Insert Rollover Image window with the various page elements completed

3. If you desire (it is not required), you can enter a name for the image in the Image Name text box.

4. Within the Original Image text box, supply the name of the image that will be viewed when the mouse pointer is not over the object. If needed, you can click on the Browse button next to the Original Image text box to open a File dialog box that lets you select the original image.

5. Within the Rollover Image text box, supply the name of the image that will be viewed when the mouse pointer is over the object. If needed, you can click on the Browse button next to the Rollover Image text box to open a File dialog box that allows you to select the original image.

6. To direct the browser to load the rollover image into the viewer's computer when the page first loads (this is highly recommended to speed the performance of the rollover effect), place a check mark in the Preload Rollover Image check box by clicking on the box.

7. If you want the viewer to see a different page when he or she clicks on the original image, specify the page's URL within the When Clicked, Go To URL text box.

NOTE: *It is highly recommended, although not required, that the rollover image be the same dimension as the original image. This make the rollover effect more aesthetic.*

Creating a Navigation Bar with Rollovers

There are two types of navigation bars that you can place on your site, if you decide to use a navigation bar at all: a text-only navigation bar and a graphical navigation bar with rollovers. To decide what type of navigation bar would work best for your site, consider the following:

◆ How much graphical complexity do you want on your site?

◆ How will site visitors be connecting to the Internet?

◆ How comfortable are you working with complex graphical elements?

The answers to these questions will help you to determine which of the two types of navigation bars you place on your site.

Using a Text-Only Navigation Bar

You will use a text-only navigation barwhen you want to provide a navigation bar that is simple and straight-forward, with little visual elaboration. Or, you might select a text-only navigation bar if you expect visitors to your site to be using low-speed modems, or browsers that do not support JavaScript.

A text-only navigation bar is something you already have the skills to create. It is a row of text links arranged horizontally or vertically on a page that does not require any work in an image-editing or illustration program. Each text link is associated with another page on the site via a hotlink. It is minimal in file size and downloads almost instantaneously regardless of your visitor's Internet connection configuration. In addition, text-only navigation bars are fully visible and functional in nongraphical browsers.

There are still quite a few sites on the Internet that have text-only navigation bars. Two good examples are www.primalinux.com and primagamedev.com.

Using a Graphical Navigation Bar with Rollovers

You will use a graphical navigation bar with rolloverswhen you want your site to have graphical navigation features that give it a distinctive appearance and provide enhanced visual cues to help visitors find what they are looking for. You would also choose a graphical navigation bar if you expect your visitors to have high-speed modems or even faster connections for downloading moderate-sized graphics without difficulty.

To create a navigation bar with rollovers, perform the following steps:

1. Within UltraDev, place your mouse cursor on the location in your Web page where you want to insert the navigation bar, and click your mouse button once.

2. Within the Objects palette, click on the icon representing Insert Navigation Bar Image, which is shown circled in Figure 10.6. UltraDev, in turn, will display the Insert Navigation Bar window, as shown in Figure 10.7.

Figure 10.6

The Objects palette with the Insert Navigation Bar icon framed

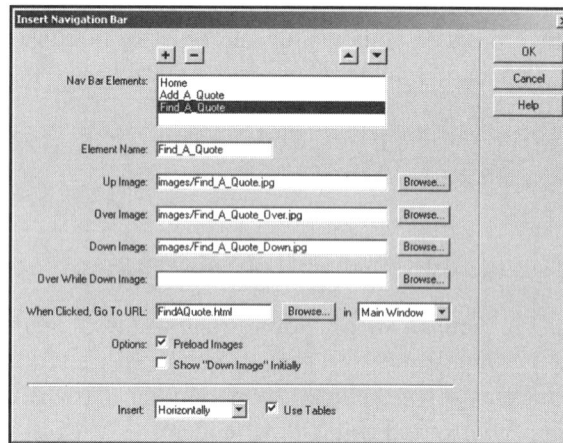

Figure 10.7

The Insert Navigation Bar window with the various page elements completed

3. When UltraDev first displays the Insert Navigation Bar window, there is an initial unnamed element in the list of Nav Bar Elements. Within the Element Name text box, you can option-ally change the name of the first navigational bar element to something meaningful and descriptive to you, remembering that spaces are not allowed.

4. Within the Element Name text box, click on the Browse button next to the Up Image text box. UltraDev will display the File Locate window that lets you locate an image your site will display when the mouse pointer is not over the image and when it is not clicked.

5. This step is optional, but gives your site pop. Click on the Browse button that appears next to the Over Image text box. UltraDev, in turn, will display the File Locate window that lets you locate the image your site will display when the mouse pointer is over the image.

6. This step is also optional, but gives your site even more pop. Click on the Browse button that appears next to the Down Image text box. UltraDev, in turn, will display a File Locate window that lets you locate an image your site will display when the user has clicked on the navigational bar graphic.

7. Within the When Clicked, Go To URL text box, specify a URL or page name that the user should go to when the navigational bar graphic is clicked.

8. Next, you will add additional navigation buttons by clicking on the add (+) button. To remove a navigation button, click your mouse once in the Nav Bar Elements window, and then click on the minus (–) button.

9. Optionally, you can reorder the navigation bar graphics by clicking on the item to be reordered in the Nav Bar Elements box, and then clicking on either the up or down arrow button to move the selected item up or down one location, respectively.

10. Notice the Insert drop-down list box at the bottom of the Insert Navigation Bar window. The two options that appear in this drop-down list box are Vertically and Horizontally. Whichever option you select will directly determine whether your navigation bar appears vertically or horizontally on the page.

Adding Sound to Your Web Page

Using UltraDev, you can add audio (sound) files to your site in a way similar to how you add graphics. Although audio files can add pop to your site, be careful using them when you are not sure that your site visitors have a sound card and speakers. You can add audio files a number of different places. For example, you can add a sound file to play when:

◆ A page first displays

◆ A visitor clicks on a control

◆ A certain visitor-triggered event occurs, such as entering an invalid amount in a text box

Creating a Link to Audio Files

To start, you will take a look at how you add a sound file that plays when a visitor clicks his or her mouse on a control. For this example, you will play a sound file when a visitor clicks on the Help button that you added to the page earlier in this lesson. To direct your site to play the sound file with the event, perform these steps:

1. Within UltraDev, right-click on the image of the Help graphic. UltraDev, in turn, will display a pop-up menu.

2. Within the pop-up menu, select Properties. UltraDev will display the Property Inspector for the Help graphic.

3. Because you are going to link a sound file that plays when a visitor clicks on the Help graphic, you are really creating a hyperlink for the Help graphic that corresponds to the audio file. Therefore, you must associate the sound file with the graphic as a link. Click on the icon of the folder that appears next to the Link text box. UltraDev, in turn, will display the Select File window.

4. Within the Select File window, locate the file named Help, and click on the file name one time to select the file. Then, click on the OK button to close the Select File window.

5. Within the Property Inspector Link text box, you should see the file name Help.wav for the Help graphic, as shown Figure 10.8.

Figure 10.8

The Property Inspector after associating a sound file as a link with a graphic

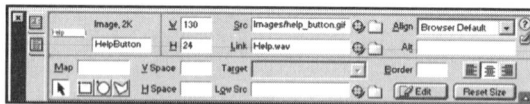

That is it! You have just associated a sound file as a link to a user clicking on the Help graphic. To test it out and make sure it works as expected, you must view your site in a browser. To do that, you can click on the File menu and then the Preview In Browser submenu item, as described earlier. A quicker way to preview a site in a browser window is to click the shortcut keys. In this case, the shortcut key to view the site in a browser window is the F12 key. UltraDev, in turn, will launch the primary browser. If you have defined a secondary browser, you can press and hold down the Ctrl key while you press the F12 key to view the site within the secondary browser.

An Exercise in Adding Text and Linking Audio Files

If you examine Figure 10.9, you will notice that I have added some text lines to the home page.

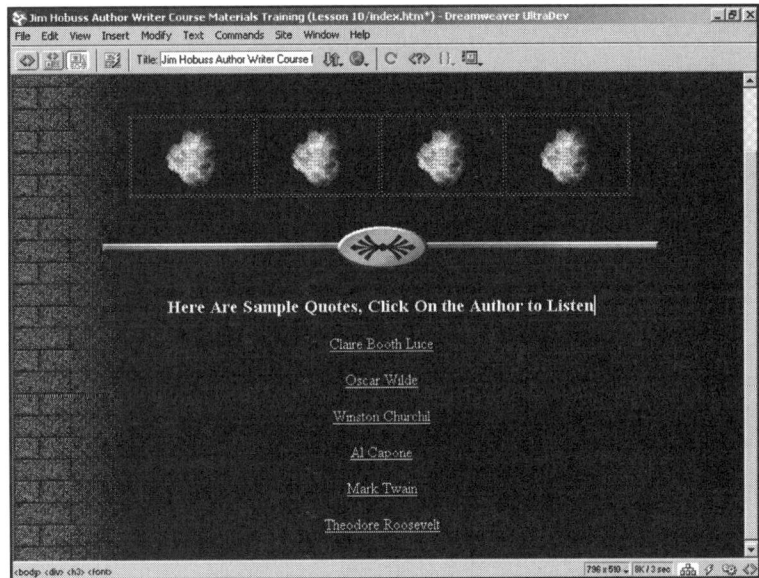

Figure 10.9

The index.html page with linked text to audio files of quotes

In this case, the page links each person's name that appears as an author of a quote to a quote attributable to that person. To add these lines and attributes to your site, perform the following steps:

1. Within the page, position the cursor directly under the graphic of the horizontal bar by clicking your mouse at that location.

2. To change the font settings such that the next line that you type uses the Arial font with a yellow color, click on the Text menu item to display the Text menu list.

3. Within the Text menu list, click on the Font option. UltraDev, in turn, will display a list of fonts.

4. Within the font list, click on the Arial font.

5. To change the font color, click on the Text menu and choose Color. UltraDev, in turn, will display the Color palette.

6. Within the Color palette, click on the small square containing a yellow color (which is located on the first row, and second column).

7. Using your keyboard, type these words: Here Are Sample Quotes, Click On The Author To Listen. Press the Enter key to position your cursor on the next line.

8. Using your keyboard, type the names of the various quote authors, as shown in Figure 10.9, pressing the Enter key after each one.

Next, you will link each of the author names you entered in the previous step to an audio file. By default, Ultra-Dev changes the color of linked text to a deep blue. In this case, visitors to your site will not be able to see the blue text against the black background, so you need to change the color of linked text to yellow, by performing these steps:

1. Click on the Modify menu and choose Page Properties. UltraDev, in turn, will display the Page Properties window.

2. Within the Page Properties window, you will see a line of text that reads Links. Directly to the right of this line is a small square that, when you click on it, will bring up a Color palette. Directly to the right of the Color palette is a small text box in which you can type the hexadecimal number for any given number. The hexadecimal number for bright yellow is #FFFF00. Type this value, including the pound sign (#), into this text box. Then, click on the OK button.

After you click on the OK button in step 3, the color of the text for the names of the authors does not change, because you have not made the author names links to the audio files yet. To add an audio file to the text line that reads Claire Booth Luce, perform these steps:

1. Within your page, right-click on the name Claire Booth Luce. UltraDev, in turn, will display the Attributes window pop-up window.

2. Within the Attributes window, click on the Make Link option. UltraDev will display the Select File window.

3. Within the Select File window, locate the file ClaireBoothLuce.wav. (This is a file included on the CD-ROM accompanying this book.) Click on the file and then click the OK button to finish associating this file name with the selected text.

NOTE: *The names of the audio files for the various authors on the page all follow the same naming convention. That convention is the name of the author as it appears on the page, minus the spaces between each name, with the file extension of .wav. Therefore, the name of the audio file for Oscar Wilde is OscarWilde.wav.*

Using Flash to Create Animated Objects

Macromedia Flash and Director have become the standards for Web animations. And beginning with UltraDev version 4, Macromedia has made it easier to add a variety of flash components to your Web site. Flash objects are so popular to put on Web pages because they are small in size and frequently stunning in appearance. A shown in Figure 10.10, there are three types of Flash objects that you can put on a page, as represented by icons on the Objects palette:

◆ Flash Animations

◆ Flash Buttons

◆ Flash Text

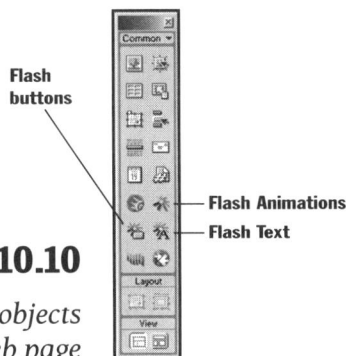

Figure 10.10

The three type of Flash objects that can be put on a Web page

The following sections discuss each of these three types of Flash objects.

Using Flash Animations

You insert a Flash animation onto a page the same way that you insert an audio file:

1. Within UltraDev, click your mouse at the location on the page where you want the Flash animation to appear.

2. Within the Objects palette, click on the Flash Animations icon to display the Select File window.

3. Use the controls on the Select File window to select, by clicking your mouse, the Flash file that you want to display on the page. As shown in Figure 10.11, I have selected a Flash file mrnonpotato.swf, which I have also included on the CD-ROM accompanying this book.

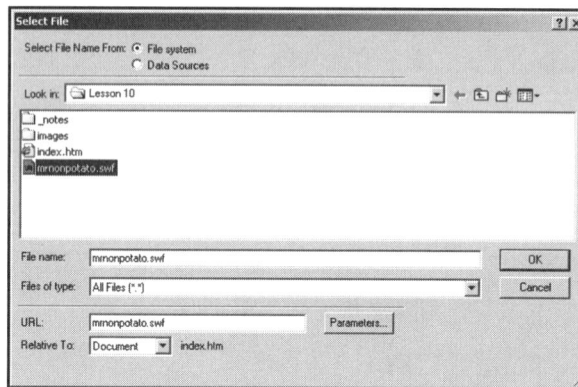

Figure 10.11

The Select File window with the mrnonpotato.swf Flash animation selected

4. Within your Web page, you will see a rectangular box that marks the size of the Flash animation. You can click your mouse inside the rectangular box to activate the image handles, which you can then drag using your mouse to resize the image.

Using Flash Buttons

A Flash button is a graphical button with text appearing on it that changes colors or shapes as an animation. In prior versions of UltraDev, you had to use Macromedia Flash to create Flash buttons that you then incorporated into your pages as a Flash animation, as described in the previous section. Beginning with UltraDev version 4, the process of using Flash buttons has become much simpler. Many people use a series of Flash buttons to create a Navigation bar across the top or left side of the page. To add a Flash button to your page, perform the following steps:

1. Within UltraDev, click your mouse near the location on the page where you want the Flash button to appear.

2. Within the Objects palette, click on the Flash Button icon (shown previously in Figure 10.10). UltraDev, in turn, will launch the Insert Flash Button window, shown in Figure 10.12, that you can use to configure the behavior of the Flash button. Notice that the Sample section of this window shows how each Flash button selection looks.

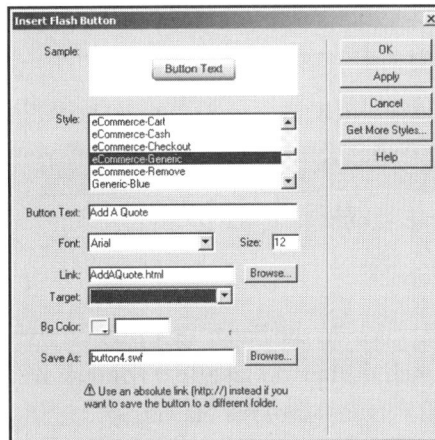

Figure 10.12

The Insert Flash Button window allows you to create and manipulate a Flash button.

3. Within the Insert Flash Button window, click on the different items as you scroll down the Style drop-down list box. Keep an eye on the Sample section of the window, until you find a Flash button style you like.

4. After you find a style you like, position the cursor in the text box next to the words Button Text, and type the text that you want to appear on the face of the button.

5. Within the Font, Size, and Bg Color controls, specify the attributes you desire for your button.

6. To create a link that the browser activates when the visitor clicks his or her mouse on the Flash button, specify the link target address in the Link text box.

7. Within the Save As text box, you can specify a name for the Flash button. This is not *required,* because UltraDev will assign a name and keep track of the name automatically if you do not specify one.

8. Finally, click on the OK button and you will see the Flash button appear on the page.

NOTE: *After the Flash button is on your page, you can adjust the size of it the same way that you adjust the size of the Flash animation. You do this by clicking anywhere inside the Flash button, and grabbing and moving one of the resize handles.*

Using Flash Text

Within a Web page, Flash text operates much the same way as Flash buttons. Using Flash text, you can add very high-quality vector text to your Web pages. To add Flash text to your page, perform the following steps:

1. Within UltraDev, click your mouse near the location on the page where you want the Flash text to appear.

2. Within the Objects palette, click on the Flash Text icon (shown previously in Figure 10.10). UltraDev, in turn, will launch the Insert Flash Text window, as shown in Figure 10.13, which you can use to configure the behavior of the Flash text.

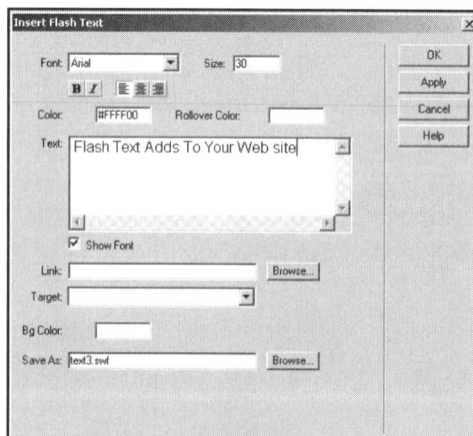

Figure 10.13

Flash text adds high-resolution vector text to your Web pages.

3. The Flash text controls are very similar to the controls on a word processor, meaning you can select and manipulate the Font, Size, Color, and Style (Bold or Italic). Using the controls, assign the font attributes you desire.

4. You can link the Flash text to a different Web page (or different location on the same Web page) by specifying the linked address in the Link text box.

5. You can also select a background color for the Flash text. You will probably want to select a background color that matches the background color of the section of the Web page on which it will appear.

6. Within the Save As text box, you can specify a name for the Flash text. This is *not* required, because UltraDev will assign a name and keep track of the name automatically if you do not specify one.

7. Finally, click on the OK button and you will see the Flash text appear on the page.

Using Java Applets

Java is a programming language developed by Sun Microsystems that is very popular for developing cross-platform code. *Cross-platform* means that a given piece of Java code will run in a Netscape browser on a Macintosh exactly the same, and without any code modifications whatsoever, as it will run in a Microsoft Internet Explorer browser on a PC. A Java applet is a small self-contained program that runs within a Web page. The code for Java applets usually resides within the HTML page. UltraDev gives you the ability to include Java applets within the pages on your Web site.

If you do not know how to write Java code, do not worry, because an abundance of already-written Java and Java applet code is available for free, or nearly free, on the Internet.

NOTE: *The CD-ROM that accompanies this book contains a Java applet named Scrolling Text Applet in the Lesson 10 folder. This applet was written by Patrick O'Brien of Sirius Computer Consultants and is distributed free of charge. Its function is to scroll any amount of text on a Web page for a really cool animation effect.*

To include a Java applet on your Web page, perform the following steps:

1. Within UltraDev, click your mouse near the location on the page where you want the Java applet to appear.

2. Within the Objects palette, click on the down arrow to display a list of different types of palettes. Within the palette list, click on Special, shown in Figure 10.14.

Figure 10.14

The Special Objects palette is one of many different groupings on the Objects palette.

3. Within the Special palette, click on the Insert Applet icon. UltraDev, in turn, will display the Insert Applet dialog box.

4. Within the Insert Applet dialog box, locate the file that corresponds to the Java applet you want to insert in your page and then click on the OK button. UltraDev, in turn, will display an applet placeholder on your Web page.

5. Within the Applet Property Inspector, shown in Figure 10.15, the name of the applet source file appears in the Code text box. You can adjust the height and width of the applet object by specifying values in the H and W text boxes.

Figure 10.15

The Applet Property Inspector allows you to modify attributes of the Java applet.

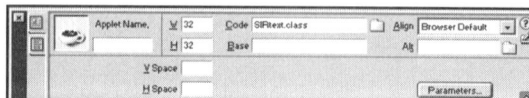

6. Many applets, such as the Scrolling Text Applet previously described, require code to be written to specify certain behaviors. You would write this code into a text file, save the text file, and then reference the text file containing the code in the specifications of your applet in UltraDev. For example, a file named SIRtextHelp.html, located in the Lesson 10 folder on the companion CD-ROM, describes the parameters and values needed by the applet to behave appropriately. You must specify the name of the text file containing the applet code within the Base text box.

7. You enter any custom attributes for the applet by clicking on the Parameters button. Ultra-Dev, in turn, will display the Parameters window, within which you can add these attributes.

And that is all there is to adding a Java applet to your Web pages. Normally, the most sensitive part of adding a Java applet to a Web page is specifying the applet code correctly. Be careful of this as you write your own Java applets, but be even more careful of this as you include Java applets written by others in your Web pages.

What You Must Know

In this lesson, you learned how to work with graphics and multimedia on a Web page. Specifically, you learned how to add and manipulate images and other multimedia on your Web pages. In Lesson 11, "Understanding File Links," you will learn how to link your Web pages to other Web pages and controls. Before you continue to Lesson 11, make sure you understand the following key concepts:

◆ UltraDev makes it easy for you to add a variety of image types to your Web page.

◆ Rollovers add "pop" to your Web pages. Using UltraDev, building and integrating rollovers into your Web pages is easy.

◆ Using UltraDev, sound files are easy to add to your pages in a number of different ways.

◆ Flash components come in three flavors: Flash animations, Flash buttons, and Flash text. Using the UltraDev Objects palette, you can quickly insert Flash components on a page.

◆ Java applets are easy to incorporate into your site and can be done without writing a line of Java code, given you are able to find the correct (and a freely distributable) applet on the Web.

Lesson 11

Understanding File Links

In Lesson 10, "Using Graphics and Multimedia on a Page," you learned how to work with graphics and multimedia on a Web page. Specifically, you learned how to add and manipulate images and other multimedia on your Web pages. In this lesson, you will learn how to work with different types of links on your Web pages. As you will learn, by using relative links that specify the location of a file "relative" to the HTML document, you make your Web pages easier to move from one location to another. Understanding links is essential to your success in creating Web pages. If your page contains errant links, the browser or users will not find the files you specify. By the time you finish this lesson, you will understand the following key concepts:

◆ Within an HTML file, you can specify the location of a file using either a relative or absolute link.

◆ An *absolute* link specifies all the information the browser needs to locate a file, such as the computer name, directory paths, and the file name, such as www.some_server.com/path/sub-path/filename.gif.

◆ A *relative* link specifies a file's location relative to the location of the HTML file, such as ../images/filename.gif.

◆ Within UltraDev, placing a hyperlink to a page is a very simple process that involves just a few mouse clicks.

◆ Within HTML, page *anchors* let you specify a link to another spot in the same page

◆ Using the Point-To-File icon within UltraDev is a fast way to specify links within a Web page.

◆ An image map is a graphic that takes the visitor to different pages, depending on what spot in the graphic the visitor clicks. Image maps are useful when you need to isolate different links within the same graphic.

Understanding Paths: The Roadmap to the Web

Within a Web page, a *path* is an address you specify to the browser that indicates where the browser can find an object or file, either on the local computer or on some other computer across the Web. As you create Web page, you will use two types of paths: absolute and relative paths.

A great way to comprehend absolute and relative addresses is to think of the address of your house. Assume you live in a house whose address is:

3149 SE 182nd Avenue
Portland, Oregon   97236

This address information succinctly describes a location that anyone can find with a map. This is an example of an *absolute* address. It provides you with all the information you need to find the location.

Now, assume I do not know exactly where you live, but that you tell me you live three doors south of a gasoline station that we both know about. In this case, you would describe your address "relative" to an address (or location) that we both know. This is an example of a relative address.

Table 11.1 gives some examples of absolute and relative address of objects or files located on your computer and on the Web.

Table 11.1   Absolute and relative addresses of different files on your computer and the Web

File or Object Name	Absolute or Relative
C:\WINNT\COMMAND.SYS	Absolute address, because it specifies the file's complete address (including the disk drive, subdirectory, and file name).
IOMEM.SYS in the Windows System directory	Relative address, because it specifies the name of a file stored in a directory, but does not fully describe the location of the directory.
www.teleport.com/index.html	Absolute address, because the path fully qualifies the location of the file on the Web.
../../resume.htm	Relative address, because the path specifies the location of a file as being two folders above the current directory.

When you specify file locations on the Web, you use an entity called a URL (*Uniform Resource Locator*). Just as there is conformity in how you specify your home address (you start with the street address, followed by the street name, followed by the city, followed by the state you live in, and then your ZIP code), there is certain syntax that you use to specify absolute addresses in URLs. Figure 11.1 illustrates the parts of a URL.

Figure 11.1

An absolute URL consists of many predefined components.

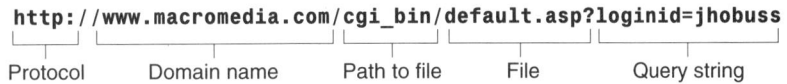

```
http://www.macromedia.com/cgi_bin/default.asp?loginid=jhobuss
```
Protocol   Domain name   Path to file   File   Query string

Table 11.2 describes the components of a URL. Bear in mind that there are quite a few derivations of how URLs are specified, but the information here is primarily applicable to how UltraDev uses URLs.

Table 11.2   The main components of a URL

Component	Description
Protocol	Describes the type of information or format for the data contained at the page. The two main options for types of protocols are *http* and *ftp*.
Domain name	The name of the Web server containing the file. Each server on the Web has its own unique domain name, such as www.primapub.com.
Path to file	The name of a directory or subdirectory on the server that contains the specified file.
File	The name of the program, file, or Web page.
Query string	An optional component that sends information from the visitor's browser to a program running on the server.

NOTE: *UltraDev uses both absolute and relative paths as it manages the locations of the various components in your site. When possible, you should use relative addresses, because in most cases, when you move the Web site directory structure from the development machine to the production machine, the directory names will change. For example, you may have a directory named QUOTESITE, with two subdirectories named PAGES and IMAGES on the development machine. If you use relative addressing and change the name of the home directory on the production server from QUOTESITE (as it was known on the development machine) to QUOTES, but keep the subdirectory names the same, your site should work without modification. However, if you use absolute addressing, you have to go in and change the names of every reference from QUOTESITE to QUOTES.*

Creating Hyperlinks on Your Web Site

In Lesson 10, you learned how to create a hyperlink without really describing what you were doing.

In this section, you will learn how to describe and create a hyperlink. To illustrate this process, you will create a Flash button on the home page and create a link to another page, which the browser will load when the visitor clicks on the button. To add the button to your page, perform these steps:

1. Within UltraDev, click at the bottom on the page where you want the Flash button to appear.

2. Within the Objects palette, click on the Flash Button icon, as shown in Figure 11.2. Flash, in turn, launches the Insert Flash Button window, shown in Figure 11.3, that you use to configure the behavior of the Flash button. Notice that the Sample section of this window shows how each of the Flash button selections looks.

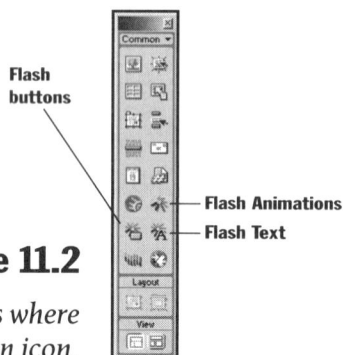

Figure 11.2

The Objects palette is where you find the Flash Button icon.

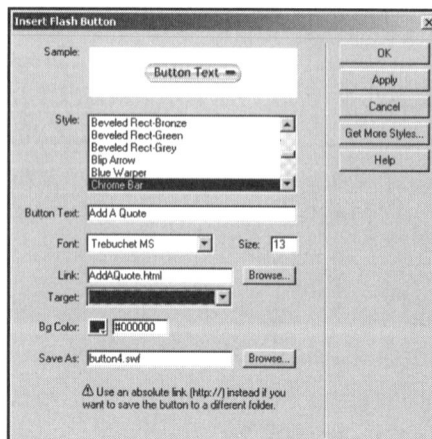

Figure 11.3

Configure the Insert Flash Button window to look as you see it here, including the link to the file named AddAQuote.html.

3. Within the Insert Flash Button window, select a button and configure it such that the Insert Flash Button window looks like Figure 11.3.

4. Within the Insert Flash Button dialog box, click your mouse on the Browse button that appears next to the Link text box. Within the File List window, locate the file AddAQuote. html. Click on the file name and then click the OK button to select the file and automatically close the window.

5. Finally, within the File List window, click on the OK button. UltraDev, in turn, will display the Flash button on your page.

As shown in Figure 11.4, you have created a relative address to the linked file in the Insert Flash Button window. You know that the link is a relative address because you have not included the domain name or directory that contains this file.

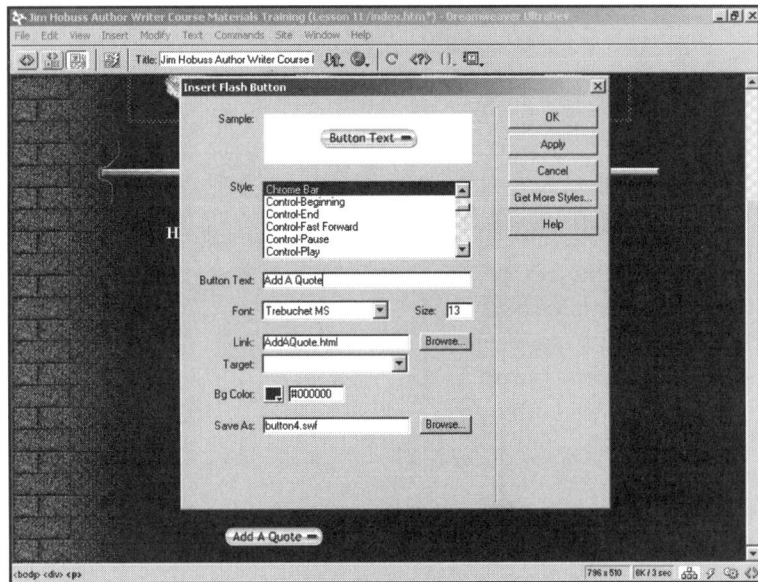

Figure 11.4

A relative link exists on the Add A Quote button to the AddAQuote.html document.

Using Named Anchors to Specify a Location on the Current Web Page

Occasionally, you will have so much textual information to place on a Web page that the page really becomes too long for your visitors to navigate. For example, many business and commerce sites include a legal notice page that is sometimes very long. In cases such as this, you can use *named anchors* to make navigation through the page much easier.

A named anchor works much the same as a hyperlink in that when a visitor clicks on the anchor, the browser takes the visitor to a new location in the site. A named anchor differs from a hyperlink in that the new location is a specific location on the same page that contains the named anchor, not a different page.

Figure 11.5, for example, illustrates a legal notice page for the Best Durn Random Quote Site On The Net. The page itself is quite long, so the site uses named anchors within the page. At the top of the page is the text that contains all the named anchor links, and below these links is the actual text.

Figure 11.5

Named anchors work very similarly to hyperlinks, except that the visitor never leaves the page that contains the named anchor.

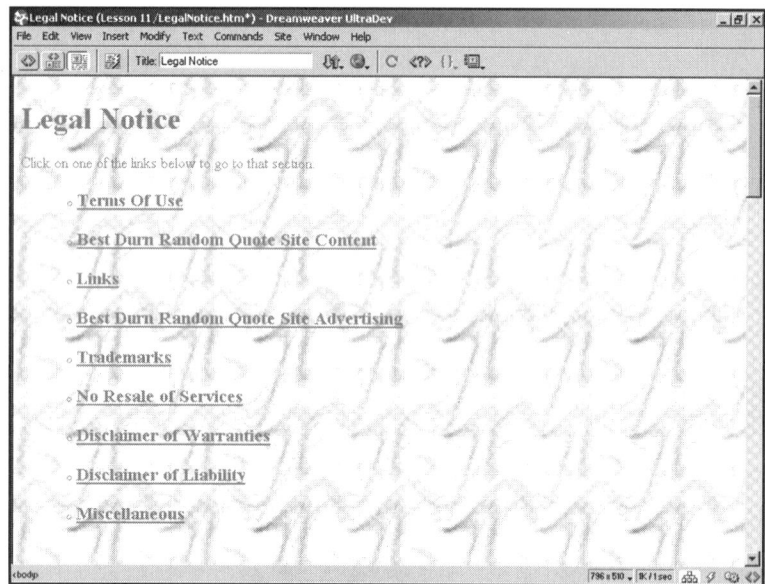

Creating a Named Anchor

Using UltraDev, creating a named anchor within a page is a simple two-step process. The first step is to add a named anchor that defines the location to which the user will jump. The second step is to create a hyperlink to the named anchor.

To add a named anchor that defines the location to which the user will jump, perform these steps:

1. Within the page, click at the location on the page where you want to place the named anchor. In the previous sample site, I scrolled down the LegalNotice.html page, past the bulleted list, to the section containing a paragraph of text where the heading is Terms Of Use.

2. Select the Insert menu Invisible Tags option and choose named anchor. UltraDev, in turn, will display the Insert Named Anchor window, as shown in Figure 11.6.

Figure 11.6

The Insert Named Anchor window is where you complete the first step in creating a named anchor.

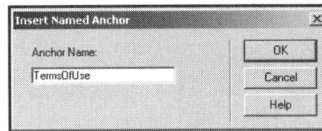

3. Within the Insert Named Anchor window Anchor Name text box, type a meaningful name for the named anchor. For the LegalNotice.html page, I used the section-heading name, with the spaces removed, TermsOfUse.

4. Within the Insert Named Anchor window, click on the OK button to close the window.

The second step to create the named anchor is one you have already performed, and that is to create a hyperlink. There is one slight twist to the process, though, and that is in the name that you give to the hyperlinked text. To reference a named anchor, you must precede the name with a pound sign (#). For example, to reference TermsOfUse, you assign the name #TermsOfUse to the hyperlinked text. The pound sign tells UltraDev (and eventually a user's browser) that the hyperlinked text is a named anchor.

To create the hyperlinked text to a named anchor, perform these steps:

1. Within the Web page, use your mouse to select the text that you will link to the named anchor. In the previous example, select the text Terms Of Use.

2. Within the Properties Inspector window's Link text box, shown in Figure 11.7, enter the name of the named anchor, which in this case is #TermsOfUse.

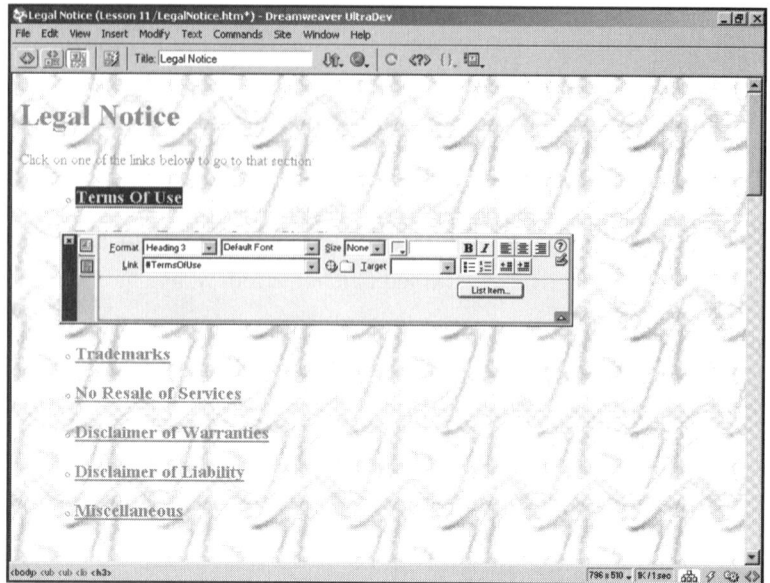

Figure 11.7

Enter the name of the named anchor in the Link text box of the Properties Inspector window for the hyperlinked text.

NOTE: You can link to a Named Anchor that exists on a page that is different from the page that contains the hyperlink. The syntax you would use in the Link box of the Properties Inspector window for a named anchor that exists on a different site is: /www.pacificinterpresters.com/pages/ legalnotice#TermsOfUse. If the named anchor is on a different page in the same site, and if that page resides in the same directory as the page containing the hyperlinked text, you could use the syntax legalnotice#TermsOfUse.

Using the Point-To-File Icon to Work with Named Anchors

The Property Inspector window, shown in Figure 11.8, includes a small icon called Point-To-File that resides between the Link drop-down list box and the Link select-folder icon. Using your mouse, you can drag the icon to a named anchor or file located in a Web site to create a reference to that named anchor or file.

Figure 11.8

Using your mouse, you can drag the Point-To-File icon to a named anchor or file in a Web site to establish a hyperlink.

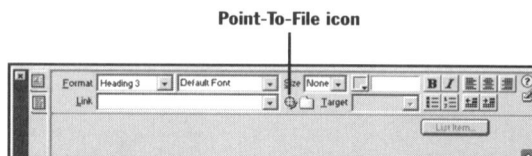

Point-To-File icon

The Point-To-File icon is a useful tool if you have a large number of named anchors in your site, or if you have a site with named anchors that are quite long and you do not want to risk a typo. The way you use the Point-To-File icon is as follows:

1. Within the page, use your mouse to select the text that you will link to the named anchor. In the previous example, you selected the phrase Terms Of Use.

2. Within your document window, scroll to a location where you can see the named anchor. Then, using your mouse, drag the Point-To-File icon to the selected text.

3. Release the mouse button. UltraDev, in turn, will display the name of the named anchor in the Link text box of the Properties Inspector window.

Using the Mailto Link

UltraDev includes an easy-to-use component, the mailto link, that lets site visitors quickly format, generate, and send e-mail to any e-mail address you want. To create a mailto link on a page, perform these steps:

1. Within the Web page, click at the location where you want to insert the mailto link.

2. Select the Insert menu Email Link option. UltraDev, in turn, will display the Insert Mail Link window, shown in Figure 11.9.

Figure 11.9

The mailto link allows you to quickly add an e-mail contact point for your site visitors.

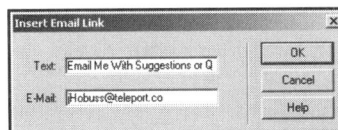

3. Within the Insert Email Link window Text section, type the text that you want UltraDev to place on your page, for the mailto link's hyperlinked text.

4. Within the Insert Email Link window E-Mail section, type the e-mail address to which you want the browser to send the message when the visitor executes the mailto link.

5. Within the Insert Email Link window, click on the OK button to place this link on the Web page.

NOTE: *You can also use the mailto link on text that already appears on the page. You do this by selecting the text that you want hyperlinked to the mailto link facility, and then following Step 3 in the preceding steps. When you do this, you will see the text that is selected appear in the Text section of the Insert Email Link window, and you can continue on with Steps 5 and 6.*

Using Image Maps to Link Locations Within an Image to a URL

Within a Web page, an alternative way to provide navigation is to use an image map. An image map defines areas of a single image that will become links to other pages when the visitor clicks on the defined areas.

Image maps are useful not only for site navigation, but also whenever you have a graphic that represents different pages that you want to let visitors access on your site. Another beneficial use for image maps is that they are frequently faster for a user's browser to load than are individual graphics that a site might use for buttons.

To create an image map on a site page, you must first insert the image. Then, you map locations within the image to specific links. To insert an image within a page, perform the following steps:

1. Within the page, click at the location where you want to insert the image.

2. Select the Insert menu Image option. UltraDev, in turn, will display the Select Image Source window.

3. Within the Select Image Source window, locate and select the image you want to insert on your Web page, and then click OK.

In Figure 11.10, for example, you will see an image that you can use to create an image map. You will also see the Image Property Inspector.

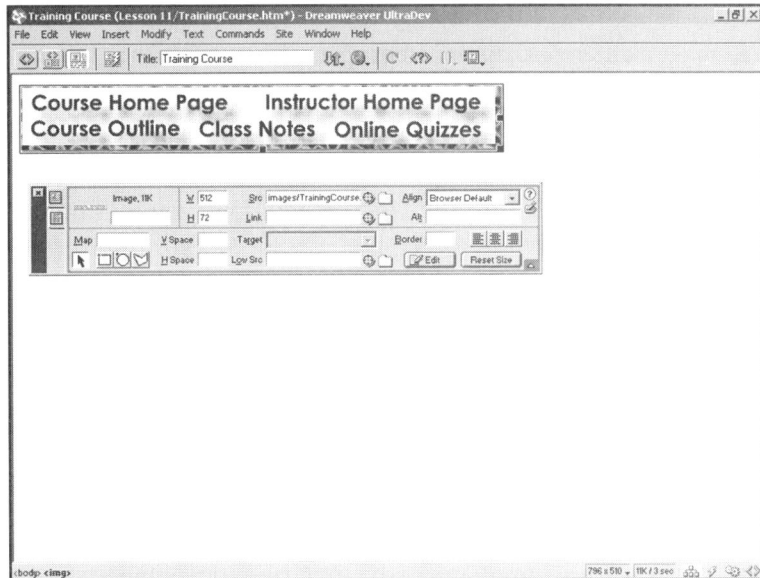

Figure 11.10

The image about to be made into an image map, along with the Image Property Inspector

To create an image map from the image you just inserted onto a page, perform these steps:

1. Within the Property Inspector window Map text box, type a meaningful name for the image you just inserted onto the page.

2. Within the lower-left corner the Property Inspector window, you will notice three drawing icons. These three icons, immediately to the right of the pointer icon, are Rectangle, Circle, and Polygon. Using your mouse, select one of these icons that most closely matches the area on the image that you want to make into a *hot spot*—the area that corresponds to a specific link.

3. Using a drawing tool, position the cursor on the image and drag the mouse pointer across the area you want to use for the hot spot.

4. Release the mouse button. UltraDev will display the Hotspot window.

5. Within the Hotspot window, provide a name of a page (or the name of a named anchor preceded with a pound sign).

6. At the bottom of the Hotspot window, you will see the three drawing icons. If you need to make a different shape for a hot spot, use your mouse to select another drawing tool by clicking on the appropriate icon. Or, you can continue to use the same drawing tool just used. In either case, repeat Step 3 until you have created all the hot spots desired on the image map.

NOTE: *Within the Hotspot window, you will notice a text box labeled Alt. Whatever text you type in this area of the Hotspot window will appear as a tool tip when visitors move their mouse cursor over that particular hot spot. Therefore, care should be taken to select appropriate, meaningful, yet abbreviated descriptions for this helpful component.*

What You Must Know

In this lesson, you learned how to work with different types of links on your Web pages. Specifically, you learned how to create and use hyperlinks, anchors, the mailto link, and hot spots. In Lesson 12, "Using Lists and Tables," you will learn how to create a table, and then import data into that table using UltraDev. Before you continue to Lesson 12, make sure you understand the following key concepts:

◆ To specify a file location within an HTML file, you can use either a relative or absolute link.

◆ Absolute links specify all the information the browser needs to locate a file, such as the computer name, directory path, and file name, such as www.some_server.com/path/subpath/filename.gif.

◆ Relative links specify a file's location relative to the location of the HTML file, such as ../images/filename.gif.

◆ Within HTML, page anchors let you specify a link to another spot in the same page. To name a page anchor, you precede the name using a pound sign (#).

◆ Within UltraDev, the Point-To-File icon provides a fast way to specify links within a Web page.

◆ An image map defines areas within an image that you want to link to specific URLs. Using UltraDev, you can quickly define image maps within a graphic.

Lesson 12

Using Lists and Tables

In Lesson 11, "Understanding File Links," you learned how to work with different types of links on your Web pages. Specifically, you learned how to create and use hyperlinks, named anchors, the mailto link, and hot spots within an image. In this lesson, you will learn how to work with various types of lists and tables in UltraDev. By the time you finish this lesson, you will understand the following key concepts:

♦ Within UltraDev, you can quickly create bulleted and numbered lists.

♦ Within a Web page, tables give you a lot of control over how a browser displays data and text.

♦ UltraDev makes importing and exporting data to and from tables a point-and-click process.

♦ To improve a table's appearance, UltraDev makes it easy for you to colorize a table for visual impact.

Working with Lists

Lists serve a valuable purpose in publications, Web pages included. Using a list, you can quickly present a topic's points, or catalog the properties of an object. Within a Web page, lists provide a visual improvement over the basic paragraph and heading text. Table 12.1 presents the three basic list types that this lesson covers: bulleted, numbered, and definition lists.

Table 12.1   The UltraDev list types, useful for presenting a topic's points and highlights

List Type	Attributes
Bulleted (unordered) list	Each textual element preceded by a bullet. Used when the sequence of items listed is unimportant. Each list item is indented from the bullet.
Numbered (ordered) list	A sequential number precedes each list item. Used when the sequence of items listed is important. The primary benefit to using a numbered list, as opposed to a bulleted list, is that numbers automatically generate as you add items to the list.
Definition list	A form of list that does not use bullets or numbers as leading characters. These are commonly used in glossaries and FAQ pages where you have a list of terms or descriptors that are followed by their description or explanation.

Creating an Unordered List

As discussed, a bulleted, or unordered, list contains entries whose order is not important. Within the list, a bullet precedes each entry. To create an unordered list from scratch while working on an UltraDev page, perform the following steps:

1. Within the page, click at the location where you want to begin the unordered list, and click your left mouse button.

2. Within the Text palette, shown in Figure 12.1, click on the Unordered List icon. UltraDev will insert a bullet on your Web page.

3. Type the first item in your list, and press the Enter key.

4. Type successive list items, pressing the Enter key after each item.

5. After you type the list items, click on the Text palette Unordered List icon.

NOTE: *If you prefer not to use the Text palette, you can also activate the Unordered List feature by clicking on the Text menu List item and choosing Unordered List.*

Figure 12.1

The Text palette is where you specify unordered and ordered lists.

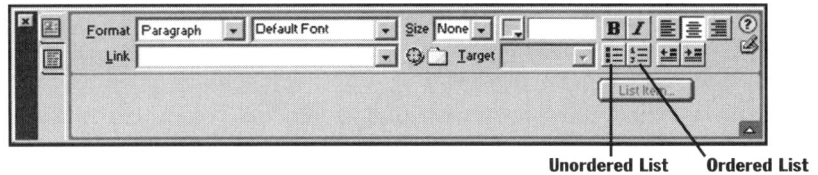

Unordered List   Ordered List

The method just described assumes that you will be creating the items in your unordered list as you type the items. Sometimes, however, you will want to turn lines of existing text into an unordered list. After you have text typed into a Web page, you can quickly and easily turn those text lines into an unordered list.

To turn existing lines of text into an unordered list, perform these steps:

1. Highlight the lines of text that you want to turn into an unordered list by dragging your mouse pointer over the text lines.

2. Click on the Text palette Unordered List button.

Editing an Unordered List

As you work, there will be times when you must change items in the unordered list. To edit an unordered list, perform these steps:

◆ If you want to add a new item at the end of an existing list of unordered list items, click at the end of the last character of the last list item. Then, press the Enter key. UltraDev will display a new bullet below the last list item. Type the new list item you desire.

◆ If you want to insert a new item within an existing list, click at the end of the last character of the item directly above the new item to be inserted and press the Enter key. UltraDev will insert a new bullet below the last list item. Type the new list item you desire.

◆ If you want to insert a new item at the very top of an existing list, click at the beginning of the first item in the existing list and then press the Enter key. UltraDev will display a new bullet above the first list item. Type the new list item you desire.

NOTE: *To turn off the Unordered List feature, you can either click the Unordered List icon on the Text palette or press the Enter key twice.*

Understanding List Tags

As you create a Web page, there may be times when you will want to manipulate by hand the HTML or programming code that UltraDev creates and formats for you. There are some nice ways to do this in the UltraDev interface.

Figure 12.2 shows a button bar on the Document window. Within the button bar, you will see three labeled icons, which Table 12.2 describes. By selecting these buttons, you can change the way UltraDev displays the page's HTML and programming code.

Table 12.2   UltraDev's ways to look at your Web page

Button	Description
Show Code View	Changes the layout of the Document window so that the entire frame displays the HTML and programming code on the Web page near where the mouse cursor is located.
Show Code And Design View	Changes the layout of the Document window so that the top pane displays the HTML and programming code of the Web page near where the mouse cursor is located, while the bottom pane gives you the WYSIWYG view of the Web page.
Show Design View	Changes the layout of the Document window so that the entire frame displays the WYSIWYG view of the Web page.

Figure 12.2

The menu bar showing the three icons that control the layout of the Document window

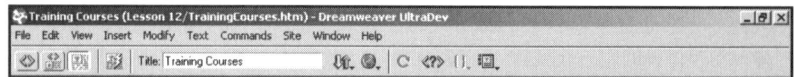

Changing Bullet Symbols

Unfortunately, HTML specifications do not provide for a wide variety of symbols for bullets on Web pages. However, you do have a few options other than the solid circle. To change the bullet style used for an unordered list, perform these steps:

1. Click anywhere inside the unordered list.

2. Within the List Properties Inspector, click on the List Item button to see the List Properties window, shown in Figure 12.3.

Figure 12.3

You can select different styles of bullets on the List Properties window.

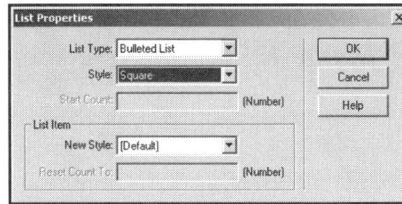

3. Within the List Properties window, click on the Style drop-down list box. UltraDev, in turn, will display the options available to you for a new bullet. Click on the option you desire and then click the OK button.

NOTE: *Most Web developers do not use the filled-in circles or squares provided by HTML specifications for bullets on their pages. Rather, they use graphics to represent the bullet with the text associated with that bullet to the right of it. This takes extra work in laying out the page but creates a much more appealing view of the page. You will learn how to lay out a page this way later in this lesson using tables. You can also modify the symbol used for bullets by using cascading style sheets, which are covered in Lesson 13, "Controlling Page Layout."*

Creating an Ordered List

As you have learned, an ordered list precedes each entry with a number. UltraDev gives you the ability to select from a wider variety of bullet styles for ordered lists than for unordered lists, but you lose the ability to further customize the leading character using cascading style sheets. Many of the steps you performed to create and modify an unordered list are the same for creating and modifying an ordered list.

To create an ordered list from scratch, while working on an UltraDev page, perform these steps:

1. Within the Web page, click at the location where you want to begin the ordered list.

2. Within the Text palette, previously shown in Figure 12.1, click on the Ordered List icon. UltraDev will insert a bullet on your Web page.

3. Type the first item in your list, and press the Enter key.

4. Type successive list items, pressing the Enter key after each item.

5. After you have created the list of items, click on the Ordered List icon.

NOTE: *If you prefer not to use the Text palette, you could also activate the Ordered List feature by selecting the Text menu List option and choosing Ordered List.*

The method just described assumes that you will be creating the items in your ordered list as you type the items. Sometimes, however, you will want to turn lines of existing text into an ordered list. Once you have text typed into a Web page, you can quickly and easily turn those text lines into an ordered list. To turn existing lines of text into an ordered list, perform these steps:

1. Highlight the lines of text that you want to turn into an ordered list by dragging your mouse pointer over the text lines.

2. Within the Text palette, click on the Ordered List button.

To edit an ordered list, perform the steps previously presented for editing an unordered list.

Creating a Definition List

Definition lists are a special type of list that do not use a leading character of any kind. They are particularly useful for glossaries or definition pages. To create a definition list from scratch, while working on an UltraDev page, perform these steps:

1. Within the page, click at the location where you want to begin the definition list.

2. Select the Text menu List option and choose Definition List.

3. Type the first item in your list, and press the Enter key. You will notice a slight indentation on the next line. This indentation exists to relate the second line to the text you just typed.

4. Type the associated line and press the Enter key. You will notice a new line that is no longer indented.

5. Repeat Steps 3 and 4 until you complete your list.

To edit a definition list, perform the steps previously presented for editing an unordered list.

Using Tables to Organize Data

Within a Web page, tables are a powerful tool available to you to format and display data in a meaningful and logical way. Tables not only are used to present data in a traditional row and column format, but combined with merging cells, they also present a method to format a page that gives you a lot more control than what you have seen so far. How you use tables in UltraDev is very similar to how you use tables in word-processing applications.

Creating a Table

Creating a table on a Web page is a very simple process. To place a table on a Web page using UltraDev, perform these steps:

1. Within the Web page, click at the location where you want to insert the table.

2. Within the Objects palette, click on the Insert Table icon, shown in Figure 12.4. UltraDev, in turn, will display the Insert Table window, shown in Figure 12.5.

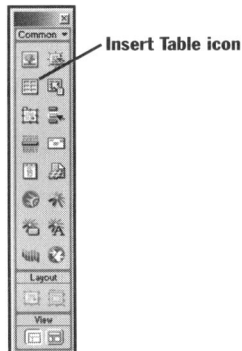

Figure 12.4

The Insert Table icon on the Objects palette allows you to place a table on your Web page.

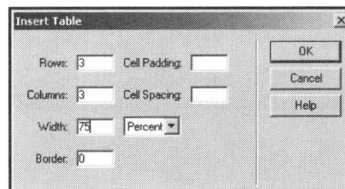

Figure 12.5

The Insert Table window allows you to specify, among other attributes, the number of rows and columns in the table.

3. Within the Insert Table window, accept the default values for rows and columns, or change them to match the requirements, as you know them. Within this window, you can also modify the width of the table and border size.

4. In the Cell Padding text box, specify the number of pixels between the cell content and cell boundary. The default padding is 1 pixel.

5. In the Cell Spacing text box, specify the number of pixels between each table cell. The default spacing is 2 pixels. Enter 0 for no spacing.

6. In the Width text box, specify the width of the table as a number of pixels or as a percentage of the browser window.

7. In the Border text box, specify the pixel width of the table border. Enter 0 if you don't want a border on the table.

8. Click on the OK button. UltraDev, in turn, will insert the table into your Web page.

Setting Table Properties

Within UltraDev, you can modify a large number of the properties of the table by using the Table Property Inspector, shown in Figure 12.6. The Table Property Inspector is also where you modify the properties of a column, row, or individual cell.

Figure 12.6

The Table Property Inspector allows you to modify table, column, row, and cell properties. In this figure, the specific attributes for a row are displayed and presented for modification.

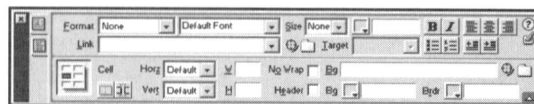

The following gives a description of how you modify many of the table properties.

To name the table, perform these steps:

1. Click on one of the four corners. UltraDev will display the Table Property Inspector window.

2. Within the Table Property Inspector window Table Name text box, type the table name you desire.

To select table layout options, perform these steps:

1. Click on one of the four corners. UltraDev will display the Table Property Inspector window.

2. Within the Table Property Inspector window Rows and Columns text boxes, type the new number of rows or columns for the table.

3. Within the Table Property Inspector window W and H text boxes, type the width and height of the table in either pixels or as a percentage of the browser window.

4. Within the Table Property Inspector window Align drop-down list box, specify how you want the table to align elements of the same paragraph. If you click Left, the table is aligned to the left of other elements in the paragraph. If you click Right, the table is aligned to the right of other elements in the paragraph. If you click Center, the table is centered in relation to other elements in the paragraph.

5. Within the Table Property Inspector window, you can click on the Clear Column Widths and Clear Row Heights buttons to reset all the columns and rows to the default width and height.

6. Within the Table Property Inspector window, you can click on the Convert Table Widths To Pixels button to convert the table width from a percentage of the browser window to a fixed width, as specified in pixels.

7. Within the Table Property Inspector window, you can click on the Convert Table Widths To Percent button to convert the table width from a fixed width to a percentage of the browser window.

To set cell padding and spacing, perform these steps:

1. Click on one of the four corners. UltraDev will display the Table Property Inspector window.

2. Within the Table Property Inspector window CellPad text box, specify the number of pixels between the cell content and the boundary of the cell.

3. Within the Table Property Inspector window CellSpace text box, specify the number of pixels between each cell in the table.

To set the borders or background image for the table, perform these steps:

1. Click on one of the four corners. UltraDev will display the Table Property Inspector window.

2. Within the Table Property Inspector window Border text box, specify the width of the table border in pixels. If you are using the table to control the layout of the page, specify a border width of 0, which gives the table no visible borders.

3. To change the color of the borders of the table, click the Table Property Inspector window Brdr Color icon and select a color for the border of the entire table.

4. To change the background color for the table, click the Table Property Inspector window Bg Color icon and select a color for the background of the entire table.

5. To change the background image for the table, click the Table Property Inspector window Bg Image icon and select an image from the File List window for the entire table.

Setting Column, Row, and Cell Properties

When you create tables within UltraDev, you can select any combination of cells (rows and columns) and then use the Table Property Inspector, shown in Figure 12.6, to modify their appearance. The following gives a description of how you would modify many of the column, row, and cell properties.

To format a column, row, cell, or group of cells, do the following:

1. Drag your mouse over the cells you want to modify, to select those cells. UltraDev displays the cells that are selected by placing a black border inside the selected cells.

2. Within the Table Property Inspector window, use the Horizontal drop-down list box to specify the horizontal alignment of a column's, row's, or cell's contents. You can align the contents to the left, center, right, or to the browser's default.

3. Within the Table Property Inspector window, use the Vertical drop-down list box to specify the vertical alignment of a column's, row's, or cell's contents. You can align the contents to the top, middle, bottom, baseline, or to the browser's default.

4. Within the Table Property Inspector window, use the W (for width) or H (for height) text boxes to specify, in pixels, the width or height of selected cells. You can also modify the display of this attribute by specifying the value as a percentage by typing a percent sign (%) after the number specified in these text boxes.

5. Within the Table Property Inspector window, you can set a background color for a column, row, or cell(s) by clicking on the Bg icon to display the color palette, where you then select the preferred color. You can also specify the hexadecimal value of the color, if you know it, in the text box directly to the right of the Bg icon.

6. Within the Table Property Inspector window, you can set a background image for a column, row, or cell(s) by clicking on the Bg folder icon to display the File List window, where you select the image.

7. Within the Table Property Inspector window, you can set a color for the borders of the selected column, row, or cell(s) by clicking on the Brdr icon to display the color palette, where you then select the preferred color. You can also specify the hexadecimal value of the color, if you know it, in the text box directly to the right of the Brdr icon.

8. Within the Table Property Inspector window, you can merge the adjacent cells into one cell by clicking on the Merge Cells icon.

9. Within the Table Property Inspector window, you can split a selected cell into two or more cells, arranged as either rows or columns, by clicking on the Split Cells icon. When you click

on this icon, you will see the Split Cell window, shown in Figure 12.7. Select the number of rows or columns you want to split the selected cell into, and click OK. If you want to split a single cell into multiple rows *and* multiple columns, you can accomplish this by repeating the Split Cell process.

Figure 12.7

The Split Cell window allows you to split a cell into multiple rows or columns.

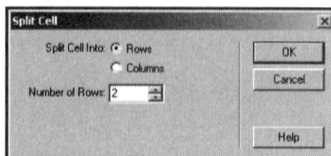

10. Within the Table Property Inspector window, click on the No Wrap check box to place a check mark in it. When this is checked, text placed in that cell will cause the cell to widen as text is entered that exceeds the width of the cell.

11. Within the Table Property Inspector window, click on the Header check box to place a check mark in it. When this is checked, the text contents of selected cell(s) will appear in bold and centered, by default.

Adding Data to a Table

To add data to a table, perform these steps:

1. Click in the table cell where you want to add data.

2. Within the cell, type the text you desire.

3. Press the Tab button to move the cursor to the next cell in the table.

Adding a Graphic to a Table

To insert a graphic into a cell of a table, perform these steps:

1. Click in the table cell where you want to add the graphic.

2. Within the Objects palette, click on the Insert Image icon. UltraDev, in turn, will display the Select Image Source window, shown in Figure 12.8.

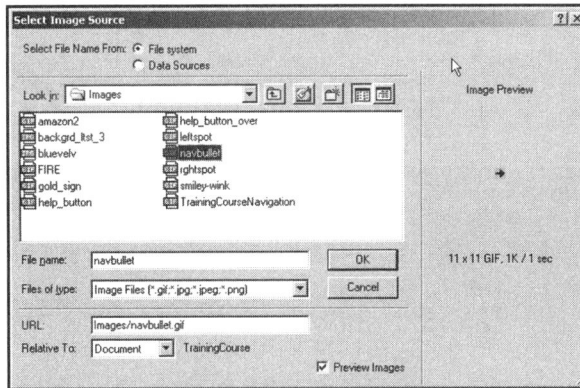

Figure 12.8

The Select Image Source window is where you select the image to insert into a table's cell.

3. Within the Select Image Source window, choose the image you want to insert and click on the OK button. UltraDev will display your image within the table.

NOTE: *Frequently, you will use this method to insert a graphical bullet in cells directly adjacent to cells containing text. This is how Web developers create pages of listed items using attractive bullets.*

To see the type of impact tables can have on the way pages are laid out, take a look at Figure 12.9 and Figure 12.10. Figure 12.9 shows how the Index.html page looks when the audio links are centered in the middle of the page. But, when we place these same links in a table, and include a graphical button for each link, the page looks much more pleasant, as shown in Figure 12.10.

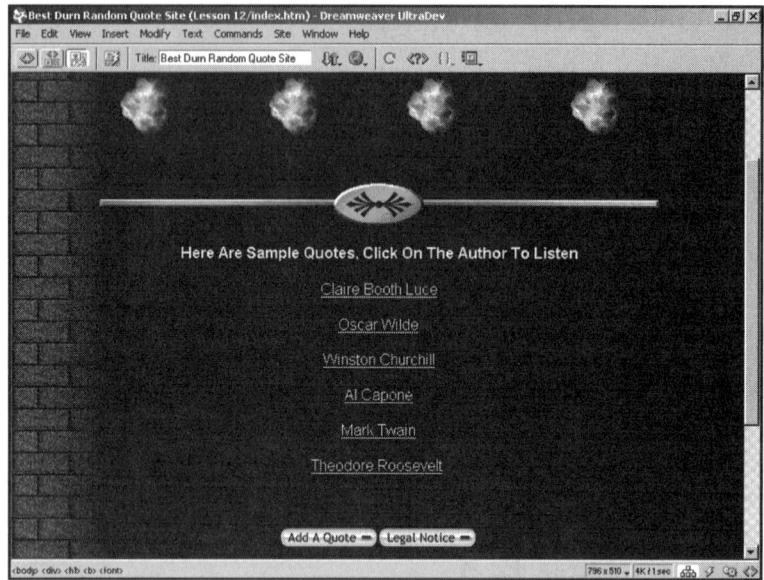

Figure 12.9

The Index.html page with the audio links centered in the page

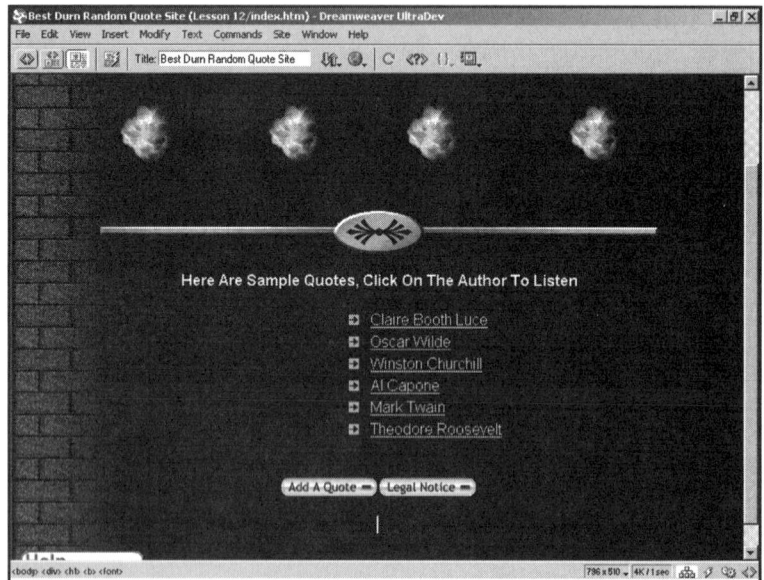

Figure 12.10

The Index.html page with the audio links embedded in a borderless table with graphical buttons next to each link

Sorting Table Data

Frequently, you will want to display table data in an organized, sequential manner. You could certainly input the data into the table in the order it is to be presented. However, sometimes it is not convenient or timely to do this. In instances such as this, you can let UltraDev sort the data in the table for you. To sort data in a table using UltraDev, perform these steps:

1. Click on one of the four corners of the table. UltraDev will select the table, displaying a black border around the outside of the table.

2. Select the Command menu Sort Table option. UltraDev, in turn, will display the Sort Table window, shown in Figure 12.11.

Figure 12.11

The Sort Table window allows you to specify sort criteria for data in a table, and to initiate the sort process.

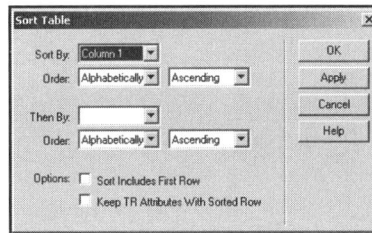

3. Within the Sort Table window, use the Sort By drop-down list box to select the column upon which you want UltraDev to sort your table, by clicking on the column's name.

4. Within the Sort Table window Order drop-down list box, select whether you want the data in the identified column sorted alphabetically or numerically.

5. Within the Sort Table window Ascending drop-down list box, select the sort order you want the data sorted in: ascending or descending.

6. Below the Sort Table window Primary Sort Attributes section, you have the ability to specify a secondary sort to occur within the primary sort. For example, if the data contains a large number of first and last names for people, you may want to conduct a secondary sort of first names within the primary sort of last names. In this way, John Smith would appear before Susan Smith.

7. If the first row of the table is a header row, do not place a check mark in the box that reads Sort Includes First Row. If the first row is *not* a header row, then you want to include the data in the first row in the sort, and you should place a check mark in this control

8. Within the Sort Table window, clicking on the check box next to the Keep TR Attributes With Sorted Row text lets you keep table row attributes with the row after the sort. This will preserve the formatting of your table if you have formatted it specific to the data in certain cells.

9. Click the OK button to begin the sort.

NOTE: *If you realize you made a mistake after you sort the contents of a table, you can undo the sort by clicking on the Edit menu, and then clicking on the Undo Sort submenu item.*

Nesting One Table Within Another Table

UltraDev gives you the ability to create and use a table within the cell of an existing table, which gives you tremendous control over the layout of the elements that appear on a page. You will find as you use UltraDev to build Web sites that you will be increasingly relying on nested tables to control the layout of a page.

To create a nested table on a page, perform these steps:

1. Within the Web page, click at the location where you want to place the table.

2. Within the Objects palette, click on the Insert Table icon. UltraDev will display the Insert Table window.

3. Within the Insert Table window, accept the default values for rows and columns, or change them to match the requirements, as you know them. Within this window, you can also modify the width of the table and border size.

4. Within your new table, click within the cell within which you want to nest a new table.

5. Within the Objects palette, click on the Insert Table icon. UltraDev will display the Insert Table window.

6. Within the Insert Table window, accept the default values for rows and columns, or change them to match the requirements, as you know them.

7. Click on the OK button.

Using UltraDev's Preset Table Formats

As you create tables within a Web page, you can take advantage of a number of predefined table formats Ultra-Dev provides for you. Most of these predefined formats have colors associated with rows or column headings that make the table quite aesthetic. The preset tables also affect the alignment and border size of the table.

To select and use one of UltraDev's preset table formats, perform these steps:

1. Within your Web page, click at the location where you want to place the table.

2. Select the Command menu Format Table option. UltraDev, in turn, will display the Format Table window, as shown in Figure 12.12.

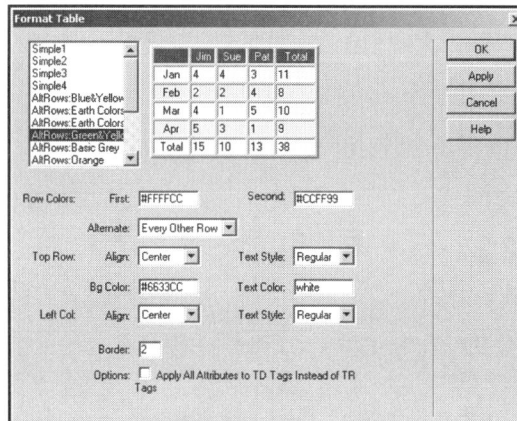

Figure 12.12

The Format Table window allows you to specify a preset format for your table.

3. Within the Format Table window, use the scrolling menu to select the format you desire. Within the table to the right of the scrolling menu, UltraDev will display a representation of how the table will look on your page.

4. Within the Format Table window, modify any of the color or display attributes for the selected table format by clicking with your mouse. After you're done, click on the OK button to insert the specified table on your Web page.

Importing Data into a Table

UltraDev has a facility that you should become very familiar with if you are going to be using tables to display data, the Import Data facility. Using the Import Data component, you can import existing data and create an UltraDev table. This existing data could be data created by another application, such as a word processing or spreadsheet program.

It may take a little practice for you to master the technique of importing data, but the time invested to do this will be time recouped many times over by you (or someone else) not having to retype scores of data to get it to appear on a Web page.

To import a tabular data file, perform these steps:

1. Make sure the data you are going to import has been saved in a delimited text file format. UltraDev will not read native Word (*.doc) or Excel (*.xls) files. So, you (or someone else) must go into the proper program and save the data as a comma- or tab-delimited file.

2. Within UltraDev, select the File menu Import option and choose Import Tabular Data. UltraDev, in turn, will display the Import Table Data window, shown in Figure 12.13.

Figure 12.13

The Import Table Data window allows you to specify where the source data file is located as well as some of the attributes for how the table will appear on the Web page.

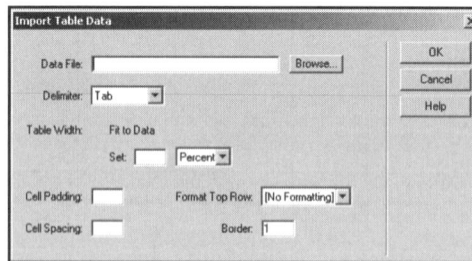

3. Within the Import Table Data window, click on the Browse button and then select the file you want to import.

4. Using the Import Table Data window Delimiter drop-down list box, select the delimiter format that corresponds to the one used to separate the data elements on the source data file.

5. For the Table Width area of the window, you have an option here. You could select Fit To Data to create a table that adjusts itself to the longest text string in each column. Or, you could select Set to specify either a table width that is a percentage of the browser window or one that is a certain number of pixels.

6. The table formatting options that appear at the bottom of the window control the cell padding, cell spacing, formatting of the top row of data, and width of the border. These options are the same as the ones of the same name that are on the Format Table window.

7. Click on the OK button to begin importing the data.

NOTE: *There are many more options available on the Format Table window than what appears on the Import Table Data window. After you import the data and create the table, you certainly can manipulate the format of the table as you've already seen earlier in this lesson.*

Exporting Data from a Table

Just as you can import data into UltraDev, you can also export data from an UltraDev table for use by another application. Between importing or exporting data, you will probably do a lot more importing than exporting, but it is useful to know how to export data.

To export data from an UltraDev table, perform these steps:

1. Select the table to export data from by clicking on any of the four corners of the table. UltraDev will highlight the table by displaying a black border outside the table.

2. Select the File menu Export option and choose Export Table. UltraDev, in turn, will display the Export Table window, shown in Figure 12.14.

Figure 12.14

The Export Table window allows you to specify a data file to be created for use on a Windows-, Mac-, or Unix-based machine.

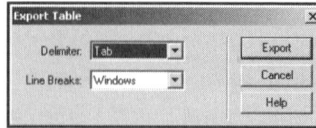

3. Within the Export Table window, select the type of delimiter you want UltraDev to place between each column of data by clicking on and then selecting a choice from the Delimiter drop-down list box.

4. Using the Line Breaks drop-down list box, select the appropriate line break style used by the operating system of the machine that will be using the data file created from this export process. In other words, if you are running the export process on a Windows machine, but using the created file as input to a process running on a Unix machine, then you should select Unix from the Line Breaks drop-down list box.

5. Click on the Export button to initiate the create process. You will see the Export Table As window that allows you to specify a name and location for the exported file. Supply this information and click the OK button to create the export file.

What You Must Know

In this lesson, you learned to work with various types of lists and tables in UltraDev. Specifically, you learned how to create different types of lists, how to create and change the appearance of tables, and how to import data to and export data from a Web page. Before you continue to Lesson 13, "Controlling Page Layout," make sure you understand the following key concepts:

◆ Various list types—bulleted, numbered, and definition lists—are easy to create in UltraDev and are useful when presenting a topic's key points.

◆ Creating tables in UltraDev gives you a lot of control over how data and text are displayed on a page.

◆ UltraDev allows to you import data into a table from various types of applications, such as spreadsheets and word-processing documents. Alternatively, you can export table data from UltraDev for use by other applications.

◆ Using UltraDev's predefined table formats, you can create visually appealing tables quickly.

Lesson 13

Controlling Page Layout

In Lesson 12, "Using Lists and Tables," you learned how to use various types of lists and tables in your site. In this lesson, you will learn how to work with layers, which make it easier for you to place objects on your page, and cascading style sheets, with which you can assign attributes to objects, such as headings, paragraph text, and table data, so that your pages maintain a consistent look and feel. By the time you finish this lesson, you will understand the following key concepts:

◆ Dynamic HTML (DHTML) extends HTML by allowing you to build Web sites that dynamically change between site visits.

◆ Within UltraDev, layers let you control the placement of text and objects on a page. Using layers, you can place objects on top of one another.

◆ A cascading style sheet (CSS) gives you the ability to apply a uniform look and feel to different pages on a Web site. Using a cascading style sheet, you assign attributes to objects that appear within your page, such as headers, text, tables, and so on. To later change an object's appearance, you can change the object's attributes within the style sheet.

Understanding Dynamic HTML

Dynamic HTML is a recent extension to the HTML specification that lets you, a Web-page developer, have much greater control over the placement and the look and feel of objects on a Web page. Using DHTML facilities, you can precisely place any object on a Web page and accurately control how that object looks in a Web browser. Well, that is the promise of DHTML. The reality, however, is that Netscape and Microsoft have provided support for divergent models of the DHTML extensions. This divergence between Microsoft's view and Netscape's view of DHTML often creates havoc for Web developers. Fortunately, the programmers who created UltraDev recognize the differences between the Netscape and Microsoft DHTML support models and accommodate both in UltraDev.

In general, DHTML is a combination of five different components, which Table 13.1 describes.

Table 13.1   The major architectural components of DHTML

Component	Description
Absolute positioning	You can position objects on a Web page with pixel-perfect precision.
Cascading style sheets	Lets you build Web pages with elements that have a consistent look and feel.
Data binding	Data from a server-based database is linked to a table or form on a Web page, which allows for dynamic updating of the data appearing on the page.
Downloadable fonts	Moving closer to typography, you can now embed specific fonts in a Web page.
Dynamic content	This facility lets you build Web pages that have content added, modified, or deleted dynamically.

In this lesson, you will see how to control the absolute positioning of the objects that appear on a page, as well as how to use cascading style sheets. In subsequent lessons, you will learn how to accommodate the other three elements of DHTML.

Understanding Layers

Within UltraDev, think of a layer as a container on your Web page that holds various objects. Using layers, you have much greater control over the layout and appearance of elements on the page. HTML specifications were added to support layers with the purpose of giving Web developers a similar degree of flexibility over the design of pages as traditional print-page designers have enjoyed.

Layers let you stack one object on top of the other, overlap one object with another, completely hide an object from view, and even move objects across the screen, mimicking the appearance of an animation.

A disadvantage worthy of consideration when using layers is that both the Internet Explorer and Netscape Navigator browsers began to include support beginning with version 4.0. This means that any visitors to your site who are using a browser prior to version 4.0 will not see the pages you create in the manner you desire.

Setting Layer Preferences

Within the Layers category of the UltraDev Preferences dialog box, shown in Figure 13.1, you can establish design preferences you want UltraDev to employ for the layers you create.

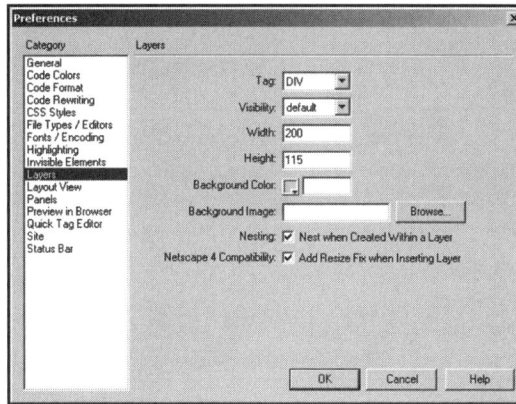

Figure 13.1

The Layers category of UltraDev Preferences is where you establish default attributes for the use of layers in your site.

To modify the layer preferences within UltraDev, perform these steps:

1. Select the Edit menu Preferences option. UltraDev, in turn, will display the Preferences window.

2. Within the Preferences window, click on the Layers category.

Table 13.2 describes the controls on the Preferences window that are specific to the Layers category.

Table 13.2   Components of the Layers category on the Preferences window

Window Component	Description
Tag	Establishes the default HTML tag used when creating a layer. Options are DIV (the default), span, layer, and ilayer. You should only use layer or ilayer when you are sure the visitors to your site will be using a Netscape 4.x browser. Otherwise, use DIV or span. The DIV tag gives structure to block-level content in a page. If you need a container for arbitrary content, use the span tag.
Visibility	Specifies whether layers are visible by default.
Width	Sets the default width for layers added to a page.
Height	Sets the default height for layers added to a page.
Background Color	Sets the default background color. You can do this by selecting a color from a color grid by clicking on the square icon, or if you know the hexadecimal value for the color, you can specify it in the adjacent text box.

(continued)

Table 13.2 (continued)

Window Component	Description
Background Image	Specifies the background image. You can either supply the file name or open a File list box by clicking on the Browse button.
Nesting	When this check box is checked, you can nest a layer within a layer. If this box is not checked, you will not be able to nest layers.
Netscape 4 Compatibility	When this check box is checked, UltraDev automatically inserts JavaScript into the <HEAD> content of the HTML to fix a known limitation encountered by visitors using Netscape 4.*x*.

NOTE: *You can temporarily reverse the behavior of the Nesting check box layer preferences by holding the Alt (Windows) or Option (Mac) key down while drawing a layer.*

Inserting a Layer Object

UltraDev uses the same technique for inserting and drawing layers as most page-layout programs, such as PageMaker and QuarkXPress. To insert a layer as an object in UltraDev, perform these steps:

1. Within the Objects palette, click on the Insert Layer icon, as shown in Figure 13.2.

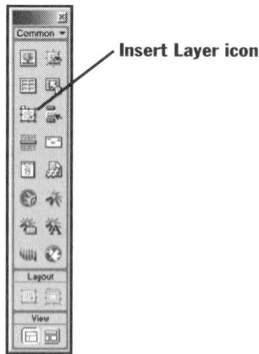

Figure 13.2

The Objects palette with the Insert Layers icon identified

2. Within your Document window, click near the location where you want to locate one of the layer's four corners. Drag your mouse cursor across the Document window until you have created a layer of about the dimensions that you desire.

3. Release the mouse button. UltraDev will draw the layer within your Document window.

Moving and Sizing a Layer Object

As shown in Figure 13.3, there are two types of objects that appear on a new layer. One type is a selection handle, and the other type are sizing handles. If you click outside of the layer, you will notice that the selection handle and sizing handles disappear. However, if you click anywhere inside the layer, the selection handle will reappear. If you click on the selection handle itself, the sizing handles reappear. You can also click at any time on the outside border of the layer to display the selection handle and the sizing handles.

Figure 13.3

A layer with the selection handle and sizing handles visible

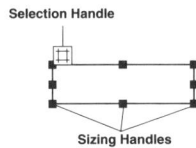

Selection Handle

Sizing Handles

To move a layer within UltraDev, perform the following steps:

1. Click inside the layer you want to move. UltraDev, in turn, will display the selection handle.

2. Using your mouse, drag the layer to the location within your Document window where you want to place the layer.

3. Release the mouse button.

To size a layer, perform these steps:

1. Click inside the layer you want to move. UltraDev, in turn, will display the selection handle.

2. Using your mouse, drag a sizing handle to resize the layer.

3. Release the mouse button.

NOTE: *If you grab and hold one of the sizing handles in the four corners of the layer, you can adjust both the vertical and horizontal sides of the layer at the same time.*

Using the Layer Property Inspector

Within UltraDev, you can use the Layer Property Inspector, shown in Figure 13.4, to modify almost any of the properties of a layer. Table 13.3 briefly describes the layer attributes you can modify within the Layer Property Inspector.

Figure 13.4

The Layer Property Inspector allows you to adjust all the visual elements of a layer.

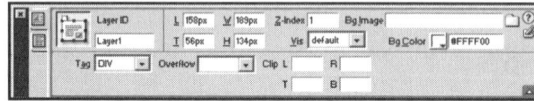

Table 13.3   The attributes of the Layer Property Inspector you can modify

Attribute	Description
BgColor	The background color of the layer.
BgImage	The background image of the layer.
Clip (Top, Bottom, Left, Right)	The measurements for the displayable section of the layer. If no measurements are provided, the entire layer is visible.
H (Height)	The vertical dimension of the layer.
L (Left)	The distance to the left of the layer from the origin point.
Name	The name for the layer.
Overflow (Visible, Scroll, Hidden, Auto)	Specifies how text is to be handled in the event that more text is in the layer than what can be displayed given the drawn dimensions of the layer.
T (Top)	The distance to the top of the layer from the origin point.
Tag (Span, DIV, Layer, Ilayer)	Specifies the type of HTML tag used for the layer.
Vis (Default, Inherit, Visible, Hidden)	Specifies if a layer is visible on the Web page.
W (Width)	The horizontal dimension of the layer.
Z-Index	Stacking order of the layer in relation to other layers on the page. Higher numbers are closer to the top.

Understanding the Layer Stacking Order

As you have learned in this lesson, UltraDev gives you tremendous control over the placement of objects on the page using layers. You also have the ability to overlap layers, and to control the priority in which overlapped layers are viewed.

UltraDev uses the term "z-index" to specify the stacking order of layers in relation to other layers on a page. The layer with the highest z-index is the one on top. In other words, consider a layer with a z-index of 1 that overlaps in the document window a layer with a z-index of 2. When a user views that Web page in a browser, the layer with the z-index of 2 will show in front of the layer with the z-index of 1. You can modify the z-index value for any layer by using the Layers window, as shown in Figure 13.5.

Figure 13.5

The Layers window allows you to adjust the z-index of the layers on a page.

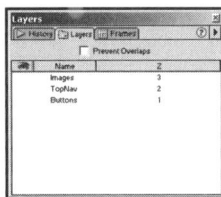

As discussed in Table 13.3, you can and should provide a name for each layer using the Layer Property Inspector. By assigning layer names, it will be much easier for you to work with the z-index of the layers that appear in the Layers window.

To adjust the layer stacking order of layers on a Web page, perform these steps:

1. Select the Window menu Layers option. UltraDev, in turn, will display the Layers window.

2. Click on the layer whose z-index you want to change. UltraDev will display that layer's name and z-index value in a bold font within the Layers window.

3. Click on the z-index value for the layer you desire, type a new z-index value, and press Enter.

Understanding Layer Visibility

UltraDev gives you the ability to show and hide layers within the document window, so you can see how the page will look under different conditions. To change the visibility of a layer, perform these steps:

1. Select the Window menu Layers option. UltraDev, in turn, will display the Layers window.

2. Within the row of the layer you want to change, click on the eye icon to set the desired visibility. An open eye means the layer is visible. A closed eye means the layer is invisible. If there is no eye, the layer inherits its visibility from its parent.

Using Cascading Style Sheets to Control Object Attributes

Cascading style sheets (CSS) let you define an object with a given set of properties, and then use that object on different pages in your site. Using CSS, for example, you can specify the attributes for a header, text, a navigation bar, a color palette, borders around tables, and so on.

A major benefit to using CSS is the ability to update attributes quickly and to have your changes automatically reflected on all pages where the style sheet is used. Another benefit is the time savings you achieve when you reuse the objects you define using the style sheets.

Within a Web page, you identify cascading styles by using a name or by using an HTML tag. As such, you can change an attribute of a style and instantly see the change reflected in all of the text that is affected by that style.

Creating a Custom Style

Before you can use a style as a cascading style sheet, you must define the style to UltraDev. Then, your style is accessible as an object on any page you create. To create a custom style, perform these steps:

1. Select the Window menu CSS Styles option. UltraDev, in turn, will display the CSS Styles window, as shown in Figure 13.6.

Figure 13.6

The CSS Styles window

2. Within the CSS Styles window, click on the New Style button. UltraDev will display the New Style window, as shown in Figure 13.7.

Figure 13.7

The New Style window is where you provide a name for the style and specify what style sheet the new style is a part of.

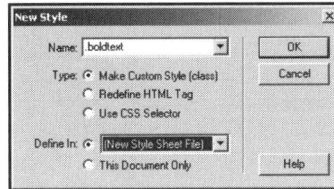

3. Within the New Style window, click on the Make Custom Style (class) radio button, and make sure (New Style Sheet File) is selected in the Define In drop-down list box.

4. Within the Name drop-down box, type a name for the style. All custom names should begin with a period (.). As shown in Figure 13.7, the current style is .boldText.

5. Click on the OK button. UltraDev will display the Save Style Sheet File As window for the .boldText style, as shown in Figure 13.8.

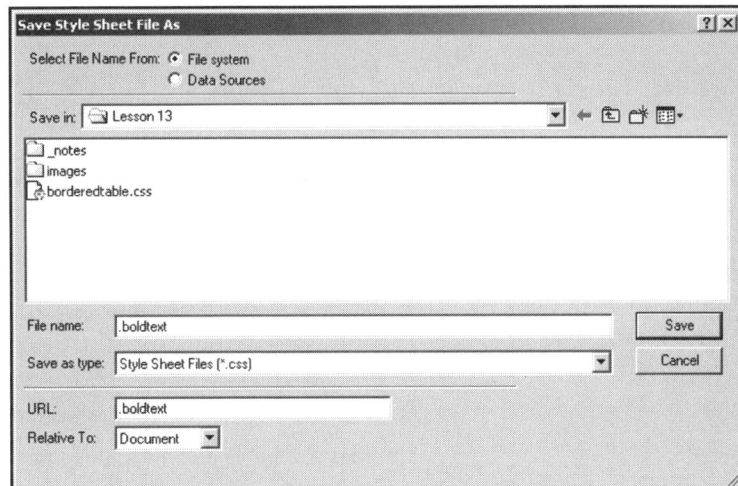

Figure 13.8

The Save Style Sheet File As window allows you to provide a file name for the newly created style sheet.

6. As you can see in Figure 13.8, I use a file-naming convention for the style sheet where the file name is the same name as the style. So, I am creating a style sheet for the .boldText style with the file name of .boldText.css. After you supply a file name for the style sheet, click on the OK button. UltraDev, in turn, will display the Style Definition window, as shown in Figure 13.9.

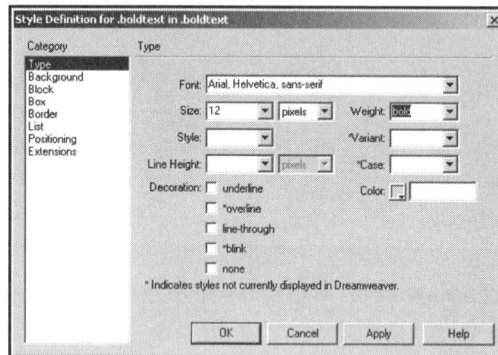

Figure 13.9

The Style Definition window is where you define the specific attributes for the style.

7. Within the Style Definition window, specify the attributes for the style by clicking on one or more of the eight categories, and then supplying the definition parameters in the controls to the right of the window. Notice that the layout of the window changes depending on the category selected. Table 13.4 lists the type of information specified for each of these eight categories.

Table 13.4   The eight categories of style settings

Category	Definition
Type	Specifies font characteristics such as size, weight, style, and so on. These can be applied to text, or to objects that contain text.
Background	Specifies background characteristics such as image and color. These can be applied to any style or object (such as tables, pages, and so on) that have a background.
Block	Specifies characteristics for paragraphs.
Box	Specifies characteristics for margins that are applied to objects.
Border	Specifies attributes that are applied to objects that have borders, such as tables, images, layers, and so on.
List	Specifies list attributes such as bullet type, color, and so on.
Positioning	Specifies layer attributes such as visibility and z-index.
Extensions	Specifies attributes specific to Internet Explorer 4.x.

NOTE: *To see a very thorough definition for what each of the controls does for each of the eight categories in the Style Definition window, click on the Help button and UltraDev will launch a browser window with the definitions preloaded.*

8. Click on the OK button and you will see your newly created style in the CSS Styles window.

NOTE: *Take a close look at the title bar of the Style Definition window, shown in Figure 13.9, which says: Style Definition for .boldText in boldText.css. As this implies, you can create multiple styles to be contained within one style sheet. How you do this is very simple. Look at the New Style window, shown in Figure 13.7. In the Define In drop-down list box, you can specify which cascading style sheet file you want to place the new style in. As a rule of thumb, I place all font-specific styles in a CSS named Fonts.css.*

Applying a Style to an Object

After you create a style, applying a style contained in a style sheet is a very simple process:

1. Within the document window, select the object or text that you want to define the style to, using the method appropriate for the object. In other words, if you want to select a layer, click on one of the four corners of the layer. If you want to select text, highlight the text by dragging your cursor over it while holding down the left mouse button.

2. If the CSS Styles window is not visible on the document window, activate it by holding down the Shift button and pressing F11.

3. Within the CSS Styles window, click on the name of the style that you want to apply to the selected object or text. You should see the text or object change appearance according to the style selected.

Attaching Styles to Multiple Pages

After you create a style and save it in a CSS, the style is created and saved for the page that was active in the document window. This is fine for that page, but what if you want to use the same style in different pages?

Fortunately, UltraDev gives you a strong capability to use styles throughout your site by attaching the styles created on one page to other pages in the site. To use the styles for one page within other pages, perform these steps:

1. Within the Document window, display the page to which you want to apply the style.

2. If the CSS Styles window is not visible in the Document window, press and hold the Shift button while pressing the F11 button and you will see it.

3. Within the CSS Styles window, click on the Attach Style Sheet button on the bottom of the window. UltraDev, in turn, will display the Select Style Sheet File window, as shown in Figure 13.10.

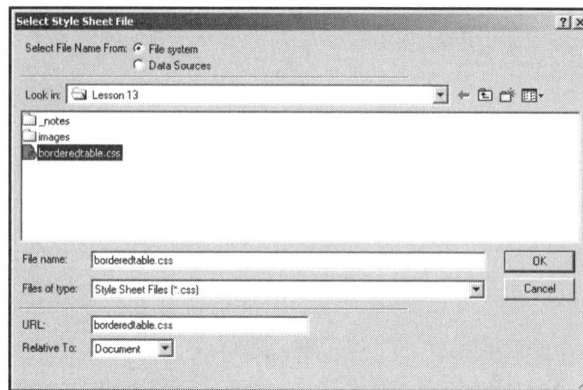

Figure 13.10

You can attach styles defined for different pages to the current page using the Attach Style Sheet window.

4. Within the Attach Style Sheet window, select the style that you want to attach by clicking on the style's name, and then click on the OK button. UltraDev, in turn, will display the style within the CSS Styles window.

What You Must Know

In this lesson, you learned to work with UltraDev facilities that give you more control over the layout of information on the pages you create, as well as how that information appears. Specifically, you learned how to create layers, and use cascading style sheets. Before you continue to Lesson 14, "Scripting and UltraDev Actions," make sure you understand the following key concepts:

◆ Layers are a great way to control the placement of objects on a Web page.

◆ UltraDev gives you a very clean interface to insert and manipulate layers on a Web page.

◆ Cascading style sheets define attributes for objects that appear on your Web page, and they can create a consistent look and feel to each page on the site.

Lesson 14

Scripting and UltraDev Actions

In Lesson 13, "Controlling Page Layout," you learned how to use layers and cascading style sheets to control, with great precision, the layout of text and controls on your page, as well as the consistency in the look and feel of the site. In this lesson, you will learn how to work with scripted functions and behaviors.

By the time you finish this lesson, you will understand the following key concepts:

◆ Using scripted functions and behaviors, you can build interactivity in your site by causing events to trigger based on a visitor's actions.

◆ A scripted function is a function pre-defined and re-used as needed by you, the developer.

◆ Within UltraDev, a behavior is a facility that causes a Web page to perform a certain action based on a stimulus. Creating a behavior is a lot simpler than you may think and can be done without any coding.

◆ Within UltraDev, timelines give you a way to move graphics or text on a Web page without using Flash or Fireworks.

Understanding Behaviors and Scripted Functionality

In UltraDev, a *behavior* is a facility that causes a Web page to perform a certain action based on a stimulus (normally a user operation, such as a mouse click). In short, a behavior is an action that is triggered by a specific event.

Whereas the action is defined by JavaScript code, which is often generated by UltraDev, the event is a trigger captured by the visitor's browser. Table 14.1 lists some of the more common events.

Table 14.1   *Some of the more common events used to trigger behaviors*

Event	Description
OnBlur	Triggered when an object on a page loses focus
OnClick	Triggered when the visitor clicks on the object
OnFocus	Triggered when the object is made active
OnMouseDown	Triggered when the visitor presses the mouse button
OnMouseUp	Triggered when the visitor releases the mouse button

Events trigger actions that cause behaviors to occur. Some of the events are discussed in Table 14.1. Actions are the JavaScript code that causes certain behaviors. Table 14.2 lists some of the UltraDev behaviors.

NOTE: *Although UltraDev ships with about 25 behaviors, third-party developers have created additional behaviors that you can install into your copy of UltraDev. In Lesson 26, "Customizing Dreamweaver UltraDev," you will see how to download and incorporate these behaviors into your Web pages.*

Table 14.2   *Some of the more common UltraDev behaviors triggered by an event*

Behavior	Description
Call JavaScript	Causes a specified snippet of JavaScript code to execute
Change Property	Changes the properties of a specified object
Drag Layer	Makes a layer draggable and defines a target where it will be dragged
Go To URL	Loads a predefined URL into the browser and transfers to that URL
Set Nav Bar Image	Changes the image appearing in a Nav bar
Play Sound	Plays a sound
Play Timeline	Begins the execution of a timeline
Popup Message	Causes a pop-up window to display with a predetermined message
Set Text Of Frame	Places text into a frame
Stop Timeline	Stops the execution of a timeline
Swap Image	Swaps a prespecified image source for another image source
Swap Image Restore	Returns the image source to its original value
Validate Form	Causes data entered on a form to be validated

A Few Observations About Behaviors

There are a few constructs that you must bear in mind when considering how to use behaviors in your Web site:

♦ You attach behaviors to objects in your Web page. After you attach the behavior to the object, UltraDev opens a dialog box appropriate for the behavior you select. Within the dialog box, you identify the characteristics of the behavior as well as the event that will trigger the behavior. UltraDev, in turn, will insert the necessary JavaScript code in your page.

♦ You can attach to objects only certain behaviors that make sense. UltraDev will not let you attach a behavior to an object that is not appropriate.

♦ UltraDev does let you attach multiple behaviors to an object, each triggered by an event. Each event can trigger multiple actions.

♦ Different browsers recognize events differently. If a specific event does not work in a given browser, the user will either see nothing or may get a JavaScript error generated by their browser.

The following sections give you some examples of how you make behaviors work.

Using a Behavior to Show and Hide Layers

As you can see in Figure 14.1, I have added a line of text at the bottom of the index.html page of our site that reads: Hide Fireballs. As the text implies, the line's purpose is to hide the fireballs from view when the user clicks on the text.

To begin, you will place the fireball graphics inside the cells of a table, and then place the table inside a layer. The behavior you want to create is to have the layer that contains the fireballs hide when the user clicks on the Hide Fireballs text. As an option, you could have designed this process such that the text changed from Hide Fireball to Show Fireball, depending on the visibility of the layer containing the fireballs.

To create the desired behavior when the Hide Fireball link is clicked on, perform these steps:

1. Within your page, highlight the text for which you want to create the behavior by dragging the mouse over the text.

2. If the Property Inspector is not displayed in the document window, press the Ctrl+F3 keyboard combination to display it.

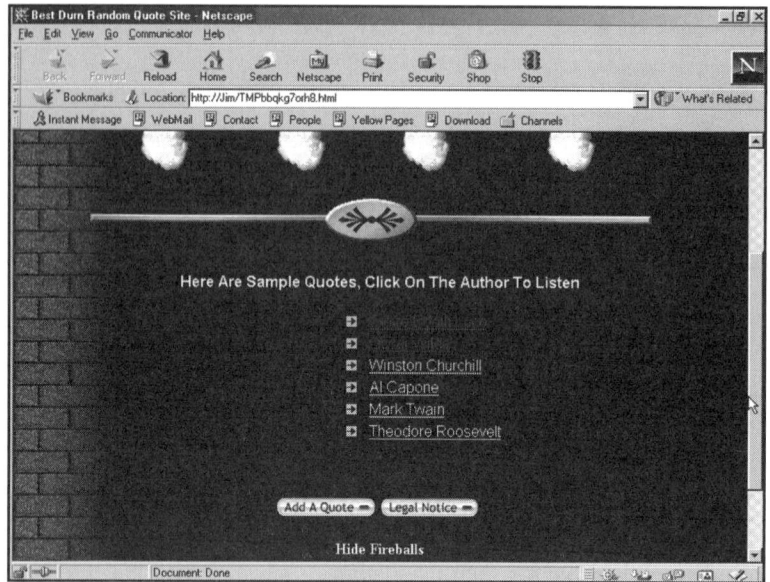

Figure 14.1

The text "Hide Fireballs" appears at the bottom of the page.

3. Within the Property Inspector, type a link name or a pound sign (#). This is a reserved link name in UltraDev that doesn't go anywhere. It is, in essence, a NULL link.

4. Open the Behavior Inspector, if it is not already open, by pressing Shift+F3. The title of the Inspector should read: `Behaviors - <p> Actions.` If the title does not show this text, double-click on the text that reads Hide Fireballs.

5. Within the Behavior Inspector window, click on the plus (+) sign to display the behaviors that are modifiable for the selected text. Then, click on the Show Events For menu item. UltraDev, in turn, will display a list of available browser types. Within the list, select 4.0 and Later Browsers.

6. Within the Behavior Inspector window, click again to display the behaviors that are modifiable for the selected text. Then, click on the Show-Hide Layers item to display the Show-Hide Layers window, as shown in Figure 14.2. You will notice two named layers in the Named Layers box: one named Fireballs and one named Layer1.

Figure 14.2

The Show-Hide Layers window shows all of the layers defined for the page currently in the Document window.

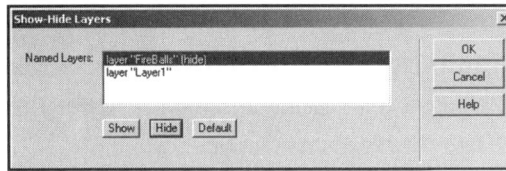

7. Within the Show-Hide Layers window, click on the layer named Fireballs to highlight it in the center box. You'll notice three buttons at the bottom of the window: Show, Hide, and Default. By clicking on each of these buttons, you change the behavior of the selected layer. Click the Hide button until the item in the center box reads: layer "FireBalls" (hide). Click OK. UltraDev will display the Behaviors Inspector with the Action of Show-Hide Layers specified.

8. Within the Behaviors Inspector, click on the down arrow for this event to see a list of the different events that you can select to trigger the behavior you just specified.

9. Within the list, click on the behavior named OnClick.

You have created a behavior that is triggered by an event.

Creating a New Browser Window and Playing a WAV File

Next, you can add a couple of behaviors that one event will trigger. The event will be someone clicking on the hotlink that reads Al Capone. The two behaviors are

◆ A new browser window will open with a picture of Al Capone displayed, sized just right to show no more than just the picture.

◆ An audio file will begin playing of the quote attributable to Al Capone.

To create these two behaviors, perform these steps:

1. Within your page, drag your mouse to highlight the text (Al Capone).

2. If the Property Inspector is not displayed in the document window, press Ctrl+F3 to display it.

3. Within the Property Inspector, change the name of the link from *AlCapone.wav* to *#*.

4. Open the Behavior Inspector, if it is not already open, by pressing Shift+F3. You should see the title of the Inspector read: Behaviors – <p> Actions. If it does not display this text, double-click on the text that reads Al Capone.

5. Within the Behavior Inspector window, click on the plus sign (+) to display the behaviors that are modifiable for the selected text.

6. Within the list of behaviors that are selectable, click on the item that reads Open Browser Window. UltraDev, in turn, will display the Open Browser Window dialog box.

7. Within the Open Browser Window dialog box, fill in the controls so they match Figure 14.3. Do not forget to specify a Window Width of 172 pixels and a Window Height of 225 pixels. Click OK.

Figure 14.3

Configure the Open Browser Window dialog box so it looks like this.

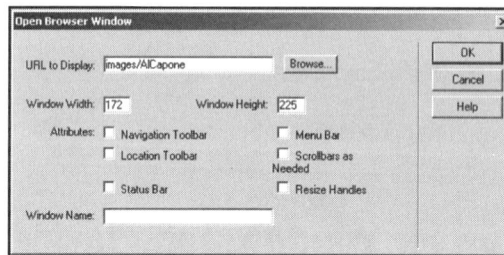

8. Within the Behavior Inspector window, click on the down arrow to the left of the Open BrowserWindow string. UltraDev will display a list of available events.

9. Within the list of available events, click on the event named OnClick.

10. Because you want to add a second behavior to an event on the Al Capone text string hyperlink, click on the plus sign (+) again within the Behavior Inspector window to display the behaviors that are modifiable for the selected text.

11. Within the list of selectable behaviors, click on the item that reads Play Sound. UltraDev, in turn, will display the Play Sound window.

12. Within the Play Sound window, click on the Browse button to display the Select File window.

13. The audio file you want to play is not located in the Images subdirectory (which was copied from the CD-ROM accompanying this book), so click up one level in the directory structure. Then, click on the file named AlCapone.wav, and then click on OK. UltraDev will display the file name in the Play Sound window.

14. Within the window, click on the OK button to return to the Behavior Inspector.

15. Within the Behavior Inspector window, click on the down arrow that appears to the left of the PlaySound string to display a list of available events.

This completes the process of adding two behaviors to one event.

Using Timelines to Simulate Animation

Using UltraDev timelines, you gain the ability to add motion in relation to time to pages in your site, without relying on any external plug-ins. This is a powerful capability that adds plenty of pop and sizzle to your site.

The technique that UltraDev uses with timelines is to change the properties of layers over time. You achieve movement by changing the location of one or more layers, including left and top positions, over time. UltraDev also gives you the ability to change the visibility attributes of those layers over time. There are three primary roles of timelines:

◆ Timelines can alter a layer's position, dimension, and visibility.

◆ Timelines can change the source of an image that appears on a Web page, and cause an image of the same height and width to display in the same location.

◆ All UltraDev behaviors can be triggered from any frame in a timeline.

NOTE: *To illustrate the material in this section of the lesson, I added a button to the index.html page and labeled it Credits. Clicking on this button takes you to a credits.html page where I have created a timeline that illustrates all of the material described in the remainder of this lesson.*

Attending Timeline Boot Camp

Before you should use timelines on your site, you need to be aware of a few fundamental considerations:

◆ Timelines refresh at a rate of about 15 frames per second (fps). This is about half of the refresh rate for video.

◆ The actual fps rate for an animation is determined by many things, such as the speed of the machine the visitor is using, the connection speed to the Internet, and the video card the visitor is using.

◆ Events can start anywhere along the timeline, meaning an event does not need to start at the first frame.

◆ To use timelines, a visitor must be using a version 4.*x* browser or higher.

◆ Objects that move along a timeline must reside within a layer. Timelines accomplish movements of objects by adjusting the properties of layers.

◆ You can include multiple animations within one timeline, although no two animations can affect the same layer at the same time. Therefore, you can have two animations running at the same time on the same page, but each animation must be affecting different layers.

If you are going to create and use timelines in UltraDev, you need to become familiar with the Timelines Inspector, shown in Figure 14.4.

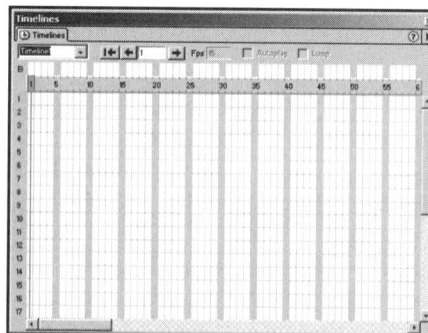

Figure 14.4

The Timelines Inspector is the tool that allows you to create and manipulate animations.

Within the Timelines Inspector, you will see a number of different sections, which Table 14.3 describes.

Table 14.3   The major components of the Timelines Inspector

Component	Description
Timeline Frames	Displays the names of the different timelines associated with the page. The name of the timeline visible in the drop-down list box is the one that is displayed in the Timelines Inspector.
Behavior Channel	Shows the placement of any behaviors attached to specific frames of the timeline.
Playback Head	Shows the location in the timeline playback sequence that is most active in the Timelines Inspector.
Animation Channels	Shows the animations for any included layers and images.
Command Buttons	Provides access to various controls that are used to change position in the timeline sequence.
Frames	Displays the frames in the timeline sequence. This scale, taken into consideration with the Playback Head, gives you an indication of where the playback sequenced is in relation to the entire timeline.

Record an Animation Path

The first step in creating a timeline on a page is to create a layer, and place something (such as text, a graphic, or a table) inside the layer. Then, you can animate the layer. In Lesson 13, you learned how to create layers. Assuming you have a layer with some text in it, you can animate the layer by performing these steps:

1. Position the layer on the page where you want the animation to start, by using your mouse to drag the layer to the location you desire.

2. If the Timeline Properties window is not already open, open it by pressing the Shift+F9 keyboard combination.

3. Within the Timeline Properties panel, make sure the Playback Head is on track 1 to begin recording. If the Playback Head is not on track 1, click on the Playback Head and slide it across to track 1.

4. Select the Modify menu Timeline option and choose Record Path of Layer. You will not see anything different on your Document window at this time, but be careful that you do not accidentally move any of the layers.

5. Click on the layer handle and then drag your mouse to slide the layer across the document window, as you want the layer to move during the animation. You will notice, as you slide the layer, that UltraDev leaves a solid, thick line to mark the trail of the animated layer, as shown in Figure 14.5.

Figure 14.5

As you slide the layer across the Document window, UltraDev draws a dotted line to mark its path.

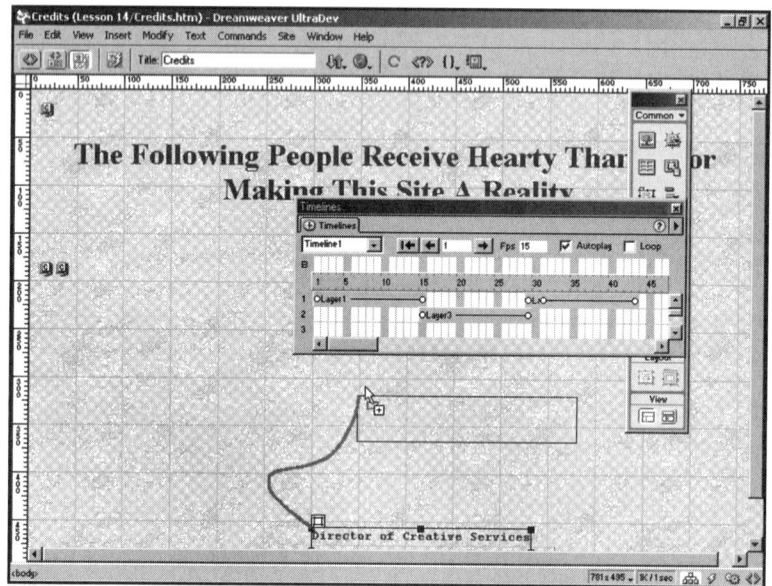

6. After the layer is at the end of the animation, release the mouse button. You will notice that the thick, solid line marking the trail changes to a solid line, as shown in Figure 14.6.

Figure 14.6

When you release the mouse button, the dotted line changes to a solid line, marking the permanent location of the path.

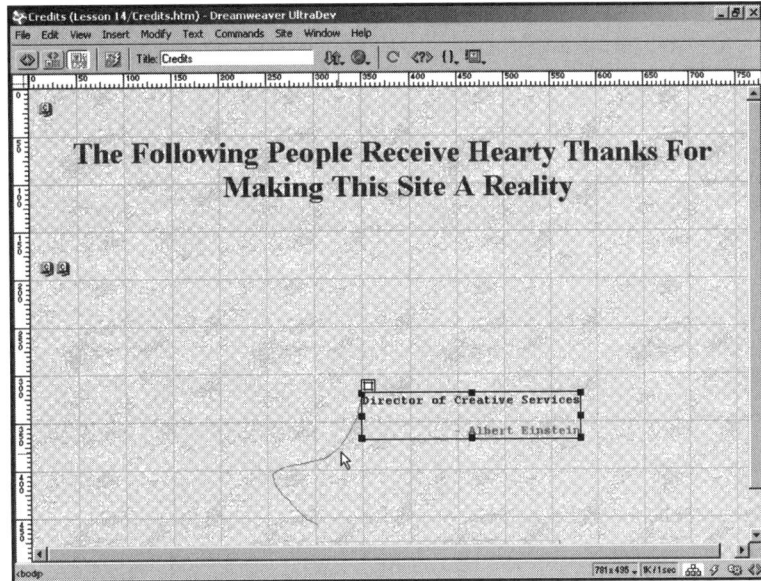

That is all there is to creating a basic UltraDev animation.

> **NOTE:** *Notice the two check boxes on the Timelines Inspector, shown in Figure 14.4, labeled Autoplay and Loop. As their names imply, when a check is placed in either the Autoplay or Loop check boxes, the animation automatically plays when the page is first displayed and continues looping if the Loop check box is checked. I usually have the Autoplay check box checked, because I want the animation to display when the visitor first sees the page, but I do not check the Loop check box, because a looping animation usually becomes quite annoying.*

Modifying Timeline Behaviors

As you learned earlier in this lesson, you can modify behaviors of many of the objects you can place on a Web page, and this includes layers appearing in timelines. The types of behaviors that you can modify for a layer in a timeline are shown in Figure 14.7.

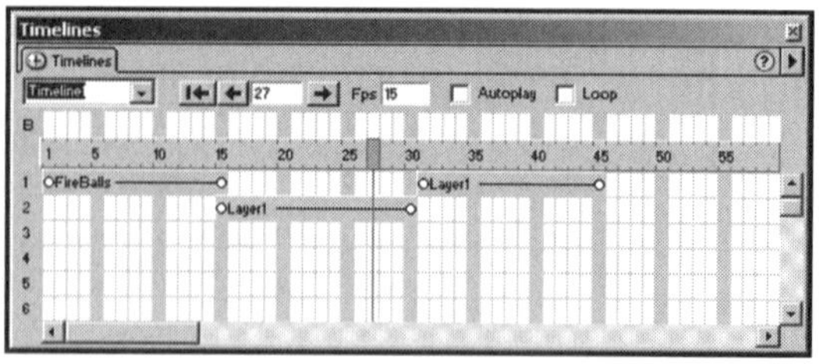

Figure 14.7

You can modify all of these behaviors for a layer object in a timeline.

You modify a behavior of an object in a timeline by first selecting the timeline frame in which the object is to have its behavior modified, by double-clicking in the timeline frame along the Behavior Channel. In other words, if you want to modify the behavior of a layer while in animation in behavior channel 5, for instance, you would double-click in the fifth rectangular box to the right of the bold letter B on the Timelines Inspector.

When you do this, the Behavior Inspector will display. Then, you create behaviors just as you learned how to do earlier in this lesson. For example, if you want to have a layer hide (disappear) on the sixth timeline frame, but reappear on the seventh timeline frame, you would perform these steps:

1. Within the timeline, double-click on the sixth frame directly to the right of the Behavior Channel indicator (B), which will launch the Behavior Inspector.

2. Within the Behavior Inspector, click on the plus sign (+) to open the behaviors menu list, similar to that previously shown in Figure 14.7.

3. Within the menu list, click on the Show-Hide Layers menu item to launch the Show-Hide Layers window, as previously shown in Figure 14.2.

4. Within the Show-Hide Layers window, click on the Hide button. UltraDev, in turn, will place the Hide attribute on the layer.

5. Click on the OK button to close the window and save your changes.

So, you have hidden the layer when it is in the sixth timeline layer, but unless you show the layer in either the seventh or subsequent layer, its animation will stay hidden. In other words, a behavior that you set on a layer in an animation stays in effect (until it is changed), even while the animation continues. To remedy this situation, you could go in and set the Show attribute for the same layer on the seventh timeline frame.

Adding Layers to a Timeline

So far in this lesson, you have created a timeline with one layer animating in it. UltraDev gives you the ability to have multiple layers performing multiple behaviors within the same timeline. As if this were not enough flexibility, you can also add multiple timelines on the same Web page.

To add additional layers to an existing timeline, perform these steps:

1. Within the Document window, click on the layer handle that you want to add to the timeline, and drag it to the next available channel on the Timelines Inspector. As shown in Figure 14.8, three layers are included in that timeline. Release the mouse button and you will see the layer added to the channel in the Timelines Inspector.

2. You can extend or contract the animation time of the layer just added by grabbing either end of the animation bar with your mouse and sliding it in or out.

3. You can also adjust the play time of the layer just added by clicking with your mouse anywhere inside the timeline channel and sliding it to the left or the right.

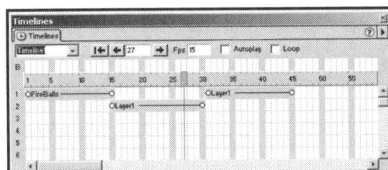

Figure 14.8

This Timelines Inspector has a layer in each of three channels.

Understanding Keyframes

A *keyframe* is a single frame in an animation in which you can define behaviors. This is important because it gives you the ability to do so much more with timelines than move a layer from point A to point B in either a straight or a wavy line. You can even do more than adjust the behaviors, as shown earlier. By using keyframes, you can change many of the attributes for the object itself. UltraDev only lets you do this in keyframes, so you must add keyframes along the timeline path where you decide you want to change some attribute about the object (you can even change the object itself in a keyframe).

The easiest way to add a keyframe to a timeline path is to hold down the Ctrl key while you click on the timeline frame that you want to establish as a keyframe. When you do this, you will see that a small, open circle is placed on the timeline at the timeline frame.

After you have added a keyframe to a timeline path, you can then modify the object's attribute(s).

Changing Animation Speed

Within the Timelines Inspector, directly to the right of the command buttons, is a text box with a number in it. This number represents the frames per second your animation *should* play in the users' browsers. I emphasize the word *should* because you probably cannot be sure of the configuration of the machines people who visit your site will be using. Therefore, you don't know whether someone visiting the site has a really fast machine with a really fast Internet connection, or a really slow machine on a 1,200bps modem.

However, UltraDev does give you the ability to adjust the playback frequency by typing a new number in the Fps text box. It is best to experiment with the value you place in the Fps text box to determine the optimal playback frequency.

NOTE: *There is a maximum limit that you can specify the playback frequency to be in the Fps text box. Unfortunately, you almost undoubtedly don't know what that is because it is very machine-dependent for your site visitors. However, UltraDev compensates for this by allowing you to enter an Fps value that exceeds a machine's capability and thus renders the animation on that machine's browser at the maximum capacity for that machine.*

What You Must Know

In this lesson, you learned about scripted functions and events that cause behaviors to occur based on visitor interaction with your site. Specifically, you learned how to create scripted functions and behaviors, as well as timelines. Before you continue to Lesson 15, "Collecting User Data on Forms," make sure you understand the following key concepts:

◆ Within UltraDev, a behavior is a scripted function that is triggered when the site visitor performs a certain action. UltraDev behaviors let you add interactivity to your Web site.

◆ Although behaviors and scripted functions are usually accomplished by writing JavaScript code, UltraDev gives you the ability to create them without writing any JavaScript code.

◆ The UltraDev Timeline facility lets you create animations by applying a few key concepts.

Lesson 15

Collecting User Data on Forms

In Lesson 14, "Scripting and UltraDev Actions," you learned how to work with scripted functions, behaviors, and timelines. Most Web sites, regardless of their content, eventually must get information from the user. In this lesson, you will learn how to create a form and collect user input. By the time you finish this lesson, you will understand the following key concepts:

♦ Within a Web page, you can use a form to collect user input and to display output to a user.

♦ Within a form, you can place various controls that perform a specific purpose. You might use one control to prompt the user for his or her name, and a second type of control to prompt the user to select a Yes or No answer.

♦ After a user completes a form, the user normally clicks on a Submit button to send the information the form contains to a server.

♦ Using forms, you can direct a Web page to perform certain actions based on data input by a visitor.

Understanding Forms

Within a Web site, forms let you build interactivity into pages by supplying the visitor with a way to input data, and, consequently, a way to view data that matches a certain criteria supplied by the visitor.

UltraDev provides a very nice implementation of forms, and coupled with database access, provides as much of the look and feel (and functionality) of a true online transaction processing (OLTP) system as you would find in a traditional client/server-based implementation.

Whereas the objects you have used so far to build pages on your site have focused on design and presentation, forms provide the visitor the ability to pass information to the Web site. Within a Web site, there are many uses for forms, some of which include the following:

◆ Creating a guest book within which you record information about your site's visitors

◆ Implementing online surveys

◆ Providing a way for visitors to request information

◆ Collecting order information

In this lesson, you will use Forms on your Web site to enter a new quote into a database and to retrieve a quote that someone else has supplied.

Creating a Form

Within UltraDev, a form is a container that holds other objects. As shown in Figure 15.1, objects within a form may include these:

◆ Text fields

◆ Command buttons

◆ Check boxes

◆ Radio buttons

◆ List menus

◆ File fields

◆ Image fields

◆ Hidden fields

◆ Jump menus

Figure 15.1

The Forms panel in the Objects palette shows the various objects that can be placed in a form.

To add a form to a Web site, perform these steps:

1. Within the Web page upon which you want to place the form, click at the location where you want the form to reside.

2. If the Objects palette is not showing, press the Ctrl-F2 keyboard combination.

3. Within the Objects palette, click on the Form icon. UltraDev, in turn, will display a dotted red line at the cursor location, as shown in Figure 15.2

NOTE: *All form controls that appear on a Web page must appear within the form object. Otherwise, you will not be able to receive the data input in the form controls by the visitor. You can insert other objects, such as text, tables, layers, and graphics, inside the form object. The use of tables (or layers) is highly recommended to control the aesthetics of the page.*

To select a form for editing, click on any edge of the form. As you can see in Figure 15.3, the Property Inspector for the form contains only three elements, which Table 15.1 describes.

Figure 15.2

The dotted red line marks the insertion point for the form.

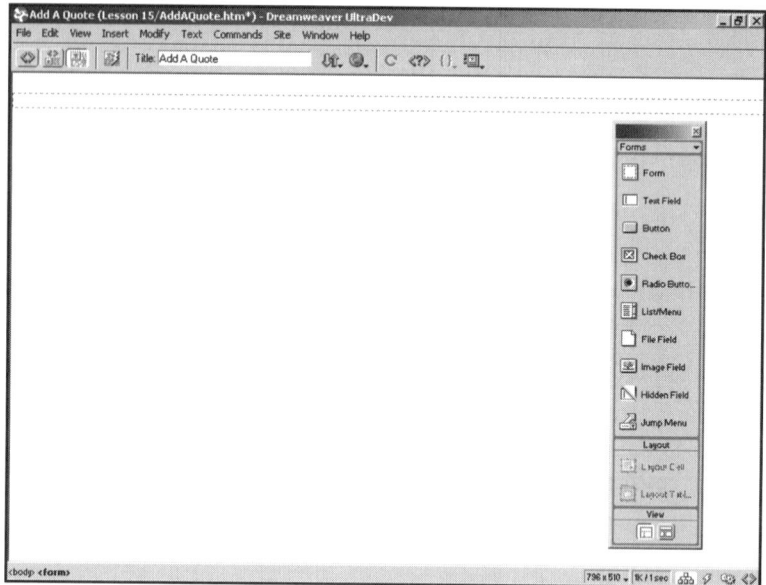

Figure 15.3

The Property Inspector for a form

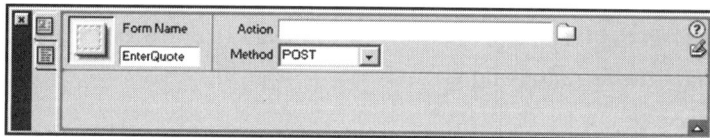

Table 15.1   The three objects on the Property Inspector for the form

Object Name	Description
Form Name	An optional field that holds a unique name (for the entire site) of the form.
Method	The method that page will use to send or receive the form's data: POST and GET. The POST method sends the form values back to the server. The GET method sends the form values to the server by using values appended to the URL.
Action	Specifies the path of the URL where the processing script or application that processes the form data resides. You can either click on the Folder icon and then navigate to the correct folder, or type the path to the URL containing a CGI script.

NOTE: *Do not choose the GET method if your form is going to display or accept a large amount of characters of data, because current HTML standards only allow for a URL with a maximum of 8,192 characters. The GET method appends the data going back to the Web server at the end of the URL, so this is a consideration.*

Adding Text and Text Fields to a Form

As you can see in Figure 15.4, I have added a table to the form control, with the table having seven rows and six columns. Within the cells of the table, I'll show you how to add text.

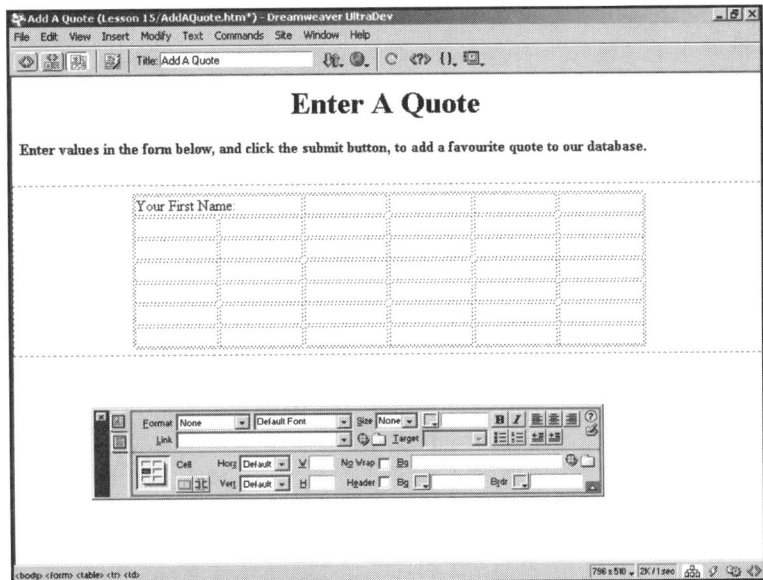

Figure 15.4

A table inside a form is a wonderful way to control the layout of controls on the form.

Prior to entering the text that you see in the figure, the two cells were merged into one so that when the text flowed, it wouldn't wrap. To merge two or more cells in a table, perform these steps:

1. Within the table, drag your mouse across the cells that you want to merge. UltraDev will display a thin black border inside the selected cells.

2. If the Table Property Inspector is not visible, press Ctrl+F3.

3. Within the Table Property Inspector, click on the Merge Cells icon. UltraDev will merge the selected cells into one cell.

To place text inside a form, perform these steps:

1. Within the form, click your mouse at the location where you want the text to appear.

2. Type the text you desire.

3. Using the Table Property Inspector, modify any of the text attributes you desire. If the Table Property Inspector is not visible, press Ctrl+F3.

Text fields appear on Web pages as three-dimensional rectangular boxes that accept keyboard input. A text field is usually one line, but may be several lines if lengthy information is required. To create a text field inside a form, perform these steps:

1. Within the form, click your mouse at the location where you want the text field to appear.

2. If the Objects palette is not visible, press Ctrl+F2.

3. Within the Objects palette, click on the Text Field icon. UltraDev, in turn, will place a text field control on the form, as shown in Figure 15.5.

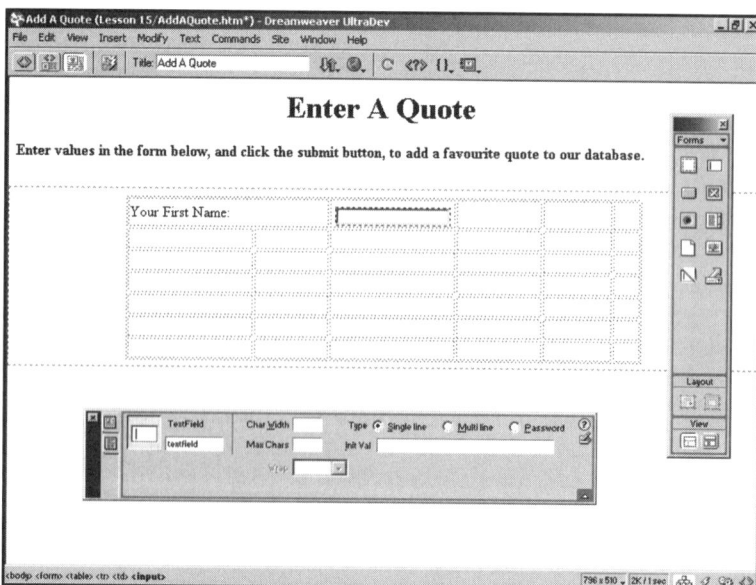

Figure 15.5

The text field is the rectangular box that appears on the form. The Text Field Property Inspector allows you to customize the text field.

Modifying Text Field Attributes

UltraDev gives you the ability to modify many of the attributes of text fields. For example, you can make a text field support multiple-line input. You can also designate a text field as containing password data, so that asterisks (*) appear in place of the typed characters. You can also specify a maximum number of characters that the text field will accept from a visitor.

Within UltraDev, you use the Text Field Property Inspector, shown in Figure 15.5, to modify the attributes for a text field. Table 15.2 describes each of the controls that appear on the Text Field Property Inspector.

Table 15.2   The Text Field Property Inspector controls

Control Name	Description
TextField	The name of the text field. UltraDev assigns a name to this field, but also allows you to change it. The name for each text field must be unique.
Char Width	Lets you specify the maximum number of characters visible on the form when viewed in a browser. In essence, this attribute controls how wide the text field is.
Max Chars	Lets you specify the maximum number of characters that the field will allow as input from the visitor.
Wrap	Disabled if the Single line or Password radio button is selected. When the Multiline radio button is selected, lets you select one of four methods with which to wrap text in the text field.
Init Val	Lets you specify an initial value to display to the visitor in the text field. For example, if you want the visitor to enter their home phone number in a particular format, you could specify that format as (###)###-####.
Type Radio Buttons	Lets you specify one of three different configurations for the text field. Single line provides a single line. Multiline provides a multiline area for input. Password provides a single line, but asterisks (*) replace any characters typed on the page by the visitor.

NOTE: *If you select the Multiline radio button, the Max Chars attribute is replaced with the Num Lines attribute. The Num Lines attribute specifies the maximum number of lines of text that the visitor will be allowed to enter.*

Figure 15.6 gives an example of what the Enter A Quote page looks like after all text associated with text fields has been input.

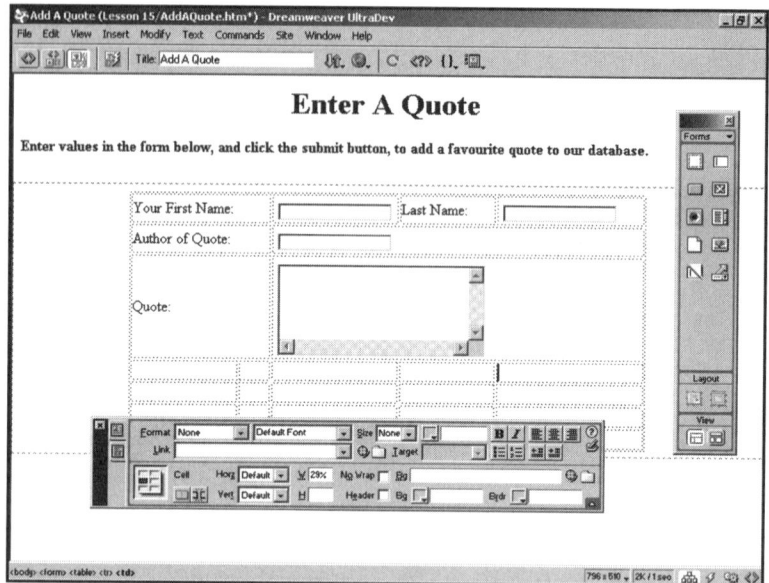

Figure 15.6

The Enter A Quote page with the text associated with text fields placed within cells of a table, with the table inserted in a form.

Adding Radio Buttons to a Form

Within a Web page, radio buttons provide a way to collect visitor input when you want to give the visitor only a single correct choice. For example, radio buttons are frequently used to specify a gender. People are either male or female, and some questions require either a Yes or No response.

You can also group radio buttons so that only one radio button can be selected at a time. To create a radio button group, perform these steps:

1. Within your form, click your mouse at the location where you want to place the radio button.

2. Within the Objects palette, click on the Radio Button object. UltraDev, in turn, will insert a radio button. If you do not see the Radio Button Property Inspector, press Ctrl+F3. UltraDev will display the Radio Button Property Inspector, as shown in Figure 15.7.

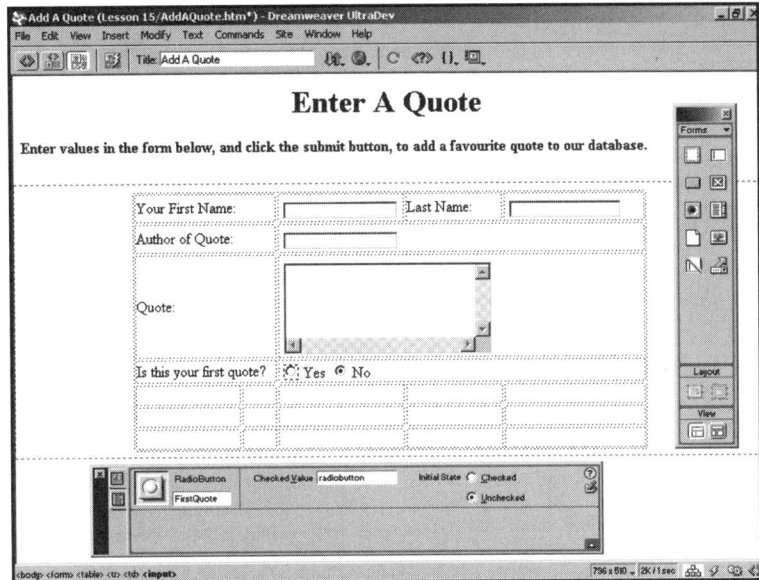

Figure 15.7

The Radio Button Property Inspector is where you adjust the properties for the radio button. By specifying a RadioButton name, and then using that same RadioButton name for other radio buttons, you can create a radio button group.

3. Within the RadioButton name box, type a name for the radio button. If you want to create a radio button group (which is a collection of radio buttons relating to the same object), the name you specify in this box will be the same name you specify for the other radio buttons in the radio button group.

4. Within the Checked Value field, type the value you want sent to the server-side application or processing script when a user selects this radio button. For example, you might type **FirstTime** in the Checked Value field to indicate that a visitor chose that this is their first quote.

5. Within the Initial State radio button (which, I might add, is an excellent example of how radio buttons should work), click whether you want the initial state of the radio button to be checked or unchecked. Only one radio button in a radio button group can be checked.

6. Repeat Steps 1 through 5 for each radio button in the radio button group.

Adding Check Boxes to a Form

Within a Web page, check boxes provide a way to collect visitor input when you want to give the user the ability to make multiple selections. Check boxes differ from radio buttons in that you cannot group check boxes. Check boxes provide a useful way to elicit visitor input when the visitor can select multiple correct options.

To place a check box on a form, perform these steps:

1. Within the form, click at the location where you want to place the check box.

2. Within the Objects palette, click on the Check Box object. UltraDev, in turn, will insert a check box at the insertion point. If the Check Box Property Inspector, shown in Figure 15.8, is not visible, press Ctrl+F3.

Figure 15.8

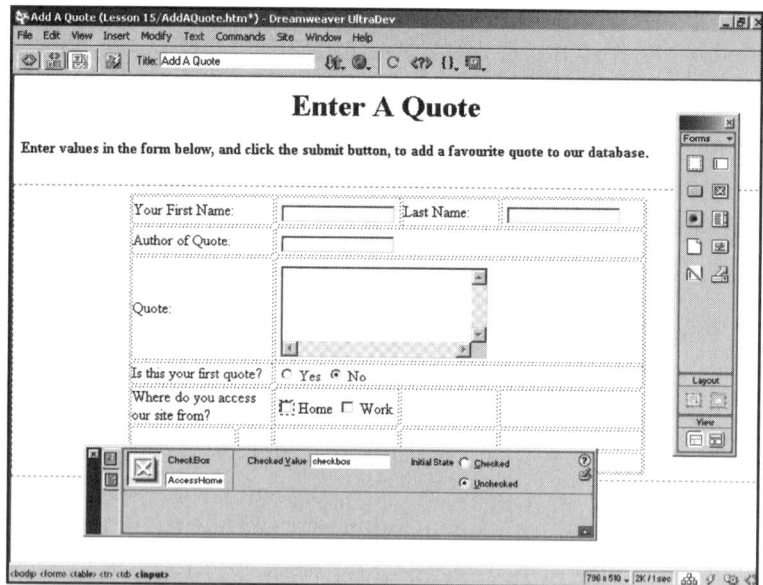

The Check Box Property Inspector is where you adjust the properties for the check box. Check boxes cannot be grouped together in the same way as radio buttons.

3. Within the CheckBox name box, type a name for the check box.

4. Within the Checked Value field, type the value you want sent to the server-side application or processing script when a user selects this check box. For example, you might type **HomeUse** in the Checked Value field to indicate that a visitor chose that they access the site from home.

5. Within the Initial State radio button, click whether you want the initial state of the check box to be checked or unchecked.

Adding a Menu or List Boxes to a Form

Within a Web page, a menu and list boxes provide a great way to show the visitor a variety of selections to choose from, and give them the option of choosing one, or more than one, of the selections. For example, if you want to show the visitor a list of a variety of places where they might have heard of your site, show the list in a list box and give them the opportunity to select one or more of the items in the list. This is a much-preferred way over having the user type their response in a text field, because their answer is prone to typographical errors if they type it, as opposed to selecting an item from a list.

NOTE: *Menus show the visitor one line when the control displays on a Web page, but then expands to more lines when the visitor clicks on the control. The display of the multiple lines can overlay other objects that appear on the page. Lists show the visitor as many lines as you specify and do not expand when the visitor clicks on the control. Lists therefore frequently take more room on a page to display because they do not have the ability to "shrink" to a one-line display.*

To place a menu or list box on a form, perform these steps:

1. Within the form, click your mouse at the location where you want the menu or list box to appear.

2. Within the Object palette, click on the List/Menu object. UltraDev, in turn, will insert a menu or list box at the insertion point. If the List/Menu Property Inspector, shown in Figure 15.9, is not visible, press Ctrl+F3.

3. Within the List/Menu name box, type a name for the menu or list box.

4. Within the Type radio group, specify whether this is a menu or a list. This indicates whether the object is a pop-up menu or a scrolling list. For a list, you can set the height (the number of items displayed at once) and indicate whether the visitor can select multiple items from the list.

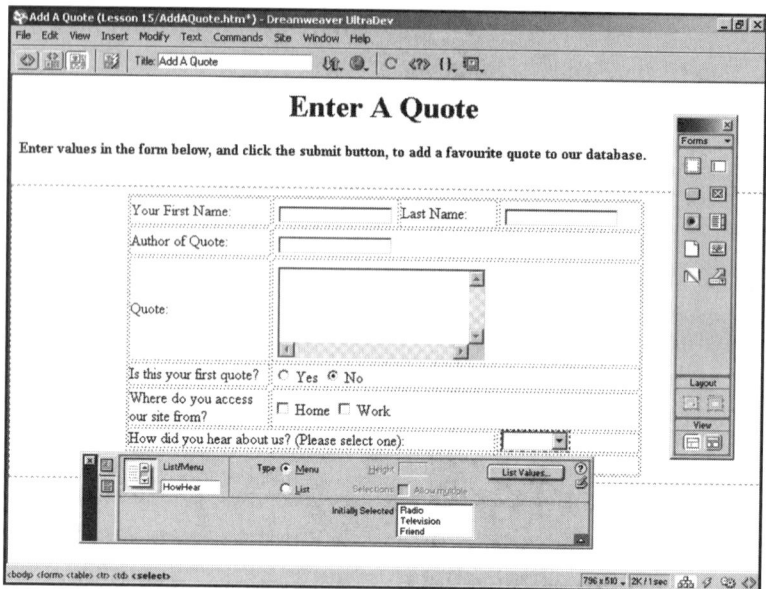

Figure 15.9

The List/Menu Property Inspector is where you adjust the properties for the menu or list box.

5. Within the Height text box (if you select the List Type radio button), you can specify how many items appear in the list box at a time.

6. Within the Selections check box, check the box if you want the visitor to be able to select multiple items in the menu or list.

7. Click on the List Values button to modify the items that display in the menu or list. When you do this, you will see the List Values window, shown in Figure 15.10.

Figure 15.10

The List Values window is where you specify the items that appear in the list or menu, as well as the values that will be sent from the page to the Web server when a visitor clicks on an item.

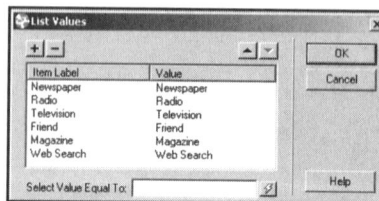

8. Within the List Values window, type under the column heading Item Label the name of an item as it will display in the menu or list. Press the Tab key and enter in the Value column a value that will be sent to the Web server when a visitor selects that item. The value typed in the Value column should not contain spaces or special characters.

NOTE: *You cannot control the width of the menu or list directly, because the control will automatically size itself to display all of the characters in the widest value entered under the Item Label column on the List Values window.*

9. Click on the plus sign (+) on the List Values window to add an item between two other items, and use the minus sign (−) to remove a value in the List Values window. Then, click on the OK button.

10. Within the Initially Selected list box, click on the List Item that you want the visitor to see when they first see the page.

NOTE: *If you supply a blank value under the Item Label and Value columns for an item in the List Values window, you can prevent a situation from occurring where the visitor hasn't selected an item from the list but nonetheless sends the default value to the Web server.*

Adding Submit and Reset Buttons to a Form

Within UltraDev, you can add Submit and Reset buttons to a form from the Form panel of the Objects palette. These buttons have predefined functions. The Submit button triggers the page to send to the Web server the data input on the form by the visitor. The Reset button clears the input supplied by the visitor from the form, making the fields appear as they did when the visitor first viewed them.

To place a Submit or Reset button on a form, perform these steps:

1. Within the form, click your mouse at the location where you want to place the Submit or Reset button.

2. Within the Objects palette, click on the Button object. UltraDev will insert a button within the form. If the Button Property Inspector, shown in Figure 15.11, is not visible, press Ctrl+F3.

Figure 15.11

The Button Property Inspector is where you adjust the properties for the button.

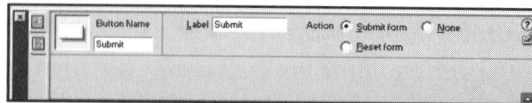

3. Within the ButtonName name box, type a name for the button.

4. Within the Label text box, supply the text that will appear on the button.

5. Within the three Action radio buttons, select the one that matches the function of the button. Selecting None means that neither a submit nor reset action will occur when the button is clicked.

Adding an Image Field to a Form

As you place buttons on a form, UltraDev does not limit you to the buttons on the Objects palette. By combining what you know about adding behaviors to an image of a button, you can add custom bullets to your forms with specific behaviors when the visitor clicks them. To add a Submit or Reset button to a form, perform these steps:

1. Within your form, click at the location where you want the button to appear.

2. Within the Objects palette, click on the Image Field object. UltraDev will display the Select Image Source window, as shown in Figure 15.12. You will use this window to select the image to insert on the form.

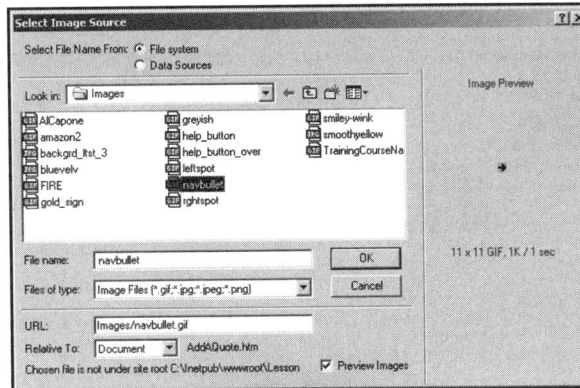

Figure 15.12

Select the image to be placed on the form using the Select Image Source window.

3. Within the Select Image Source window, choose the image you desire and then click on the OK button. UltraDev, in turn, will display the Image Source Property Inspector, shown in Figure 15.13.

Figure 15.13

The Image Source Property Inspector is where you adjust the properties for the image.

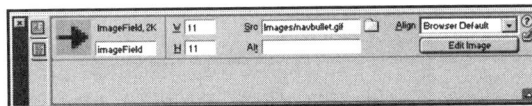

4. Within the ImageField text box, supply a name for the image field.

5. Within the W (Width) and H (Height) text boxes, accept the default dimension attributes for the selected image, or change the attribute as needed.

6. Within the Alt text box, you can provide a text message that is displayed when the visitor's mouse passes over the image on the form.

7. Within the Align drop-down list box, select an alignment option for the image in the form.

When you use an image field on a form, you want a certain event to trigger when the visitor clicks on the image. You do this by coding a script behavior to be executed on the onClick event. You learned how to do this in Lesson 14 by using the Behavior Inspector.

NOTE: *You can also add a Flash text to a button to a form, and associate a behavior to it when a specific event occurs, as you learned in Lesson 14. This is a quick way to build a form with some very nice looking buttons.*

Adding a Jump Menu to a Form

Within a Web page, jump menus let a visitor quickly link to other Web sites, or to other pages in the current site. Sites often use jump menus for links to other sites, e-mail links, images, or any other object that a browser can display. To place a jump menu on a form, perform these steps:

1. Within the form, click your mouse at the location where you want the jump menu.

2. Within the Objects palette, click on the Jump Menu object. UltraDev will insert a jump menu within your form. If the Jump Menu Property Inspector, shown in Figure 15.14, is not visible, press Ctrl+F3.

Figure 15.14

The Jump Menu Property Inspector is where you adjust the properties for the jump menu.

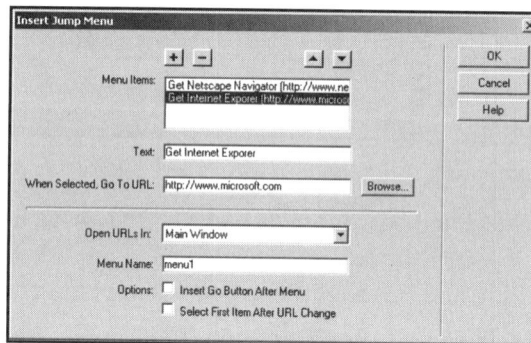

3. To create an item that the visitor sees on the form, type it in the Text field of the Insert Jump Menu window.

4. To create the link that is navigated to when the visitor clicks on the text specified in Step 3, select the file either by clicking on the Browse button and then selecting the page to link to, or by typing in the URL for the linked-to page. You'll notice that I have used the latter method in Figure 15.14.

NOTE: *Page names that you specify in the When Selected, Go To URL text box need to be correctly URL-encoded. This means that spaces and special characters are not allowed. In other words, if you link the text to a page named* Add A Quote.htm, *this should be entered in the text box as* **Add%20A%20Quote.htm**. *You'll notice that the hexadecimal (correct URL encoding) equivalent of a space character is a %20.*

5. Within the Open URLs In drop-down list box, select Main Window if you want the linked-to site to open in the main window, or select the name of a frame to open the linked-to site in.

6. Click on the Insert Go Button After Menu check box to add a Go button instead of a menu selection prompt.

7. To reset the menu selection to the top item in the list after every jump is executed, click on the Select First Item After URL Change check box.

8. Click on the plus (+) icon to add another menu item to the list and repeat Steps 3 through 7.

9. Click on the minus (−) icon to remove a menu item from the list.

10. Click on the OK button.

NOTE: *A technique I use to create a meaningful and descriptive jump menu is to make the text for the first item* Choose One, *without specifying a link. I also click in the check box that reads Select First Item After URL Change. Since you never want to give the user the ability to select this item, the lack of a specification for a link will prevent this item from being selected. And, with the Select First Item After URL Change check box checked, this item will reappear after the visitor has clicked on an item.*

Using Hidden Fields and File Fields

UltraDev gives you a couple of different special-purpose form fields that are used in very specific circumstances. The hidden field is useful for passing values of variables to application programs. A file field lets a visitor attach a file to the form being submitted.

To place a hidden field on a form, perform these steps:

1. Within the form, click at the location where you want to place the hidden field.

2. Within the Objects palette, click on the Hidden Field object. UltraDev will insert a hidden field within your form. If the Hidden Field Property Inspector, shown in Figure 15.15, is not visible, press Ctrl+F3.

Figure 15.15

The Hidden Field Property Inspector is where you specify a value passed to your application program running on the Web server.

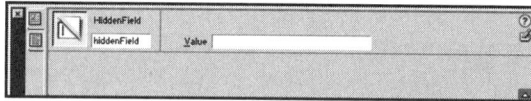

3. Within the HiddenField name text box, type a name for the hidden field. This is the name that the application program running on the Web server will search for to extract the passed value.

4. Type the value that is passed to the application program in the Value text box.

File fields are used less frequently than hidden fields. However, UltraDev provides you a very nice interface to provide this functionality on your site.

When you insert a file field on a form, UltraDev places a text box with a Browse button at the insertion point. When the visitor clicks on the Browse button, they see a File List window in which they select the name of a file to be sent from their machine to the Web server. Once the file is selected, its name will then appear in the text box adjacent to the Browser button.

To place a file field on a form, perform these steps:

1. Within your form, click at the location where you want to place the file field.

2. Within the Objects palette, click on the File Field object. UltraDev will insert a file field within your form. If the File Field Property Inspector, shown in Figure 15.16, is not visible, press Ctrl+F3.

Figure 15.16

The File Field Property Inspector is where you specify parameters describing the look and function of the file field control.

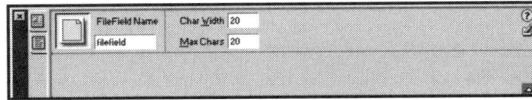

3. Within the FileField Name name text box, type a name for the file field.

4. Within the Char Width text box, type a value that represents the maximum number of characters that will display at any one time in the selection text box. The box will hold more data than what is specified in this control, but only the number of characters specified here will display at any one time.

5. Within the Max Chars text box, type a value that represents the maximum number of characters allowed in a file name. No more characters than what is specified here will be accepted.

Sending and Receiving Form Data

Providing a means for the visitor to enter or view data via a form is only half the process to building interaction into your Web site. The other half of the process is to describe the processes that occur to validate form data, and to set up a page to submit a CGI script. You want to make sure information sent to the Web server is complete and in the right format before it is sent. And you want to set up a page to submit a CGI script to inform the Web server how to process the data it receives from the Web page.

Validating Form Data

There are two events that occur for which you can specify that the data input by a visitor is to be validated. Both of these events are established by using behaviors, as described in Lesson 14. One of these events is the onClick event that is triggered when the user clicks on the Submit button. The other is the onBlur event that is triggered when the visitor's cursor leaves the control that is validated. Which one of these two methods is used is very much a matter of personal preference.

To validate a form, using either of the two methods just described, perform these steps:

1. Click on the Submit button (for the onClick event) or on the text field in the form (for the onBlur event).

2. Open the Behavior Inspector by pressing Shift+F3.

3. Click on the plus icon (+) on the Behavior Inspector to view the different events for which a behavior can be specified.

4. Within the Events list of the Behavior Inspector, click on the item that reads Validate Form, and you will see the Validate Form window, shown in Figure 15.17. Within this window, you will see a list of all the text field names on the form.

Figure 15.17

The Validate Form window is where you specify the validation criteria to apply to the various text boxes on a form.

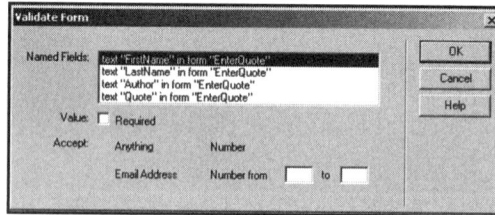

NOTE: *If you are validating the entire form on the onClick event, you will create validation criteria for every text field that requires validation. If you are validating each text field individually on the onBlur event, you will set up validation settings for only the field you clicked on to launch the Behavior Inspector.*

5. Click in the Value Required check box if the text field must have data entered.

NOTE: *A standard convention used to indicate that a text field is required is to place an asterisk (*) next to the label.*

6. Click on the Anything radio button if the visitor needs to enter data in any format in the text field.

7. Click on the Number radio button if the visitor should only enter numeric data.

8. Click on the Email Address radio button if the visitor needs to enter an e-mail address. The e-mail address is not verified for accuracy, as the edit only checks for an at sign (@).

9. Click on the Number from radio button, and enter a low and high range in the two adjacent boxes, if the visitor is required to enter numeric data in a certain range.

10. Click on the OK button when the Validate Form window is complete.

11. On the Behavior Inspector, click on the down-arrow icon under the Events column heading to change the event that triggers the specified behavior. The options are onBlur, onClick, onFocus, onMouseDown, and onMouseUp.

Figure 15.18 shows the message that is displayed when a visitor breaks one of the validation rules. In this example, an author was not specified for the quote. Incidentally, the author for this particular quote is Will Rogers.

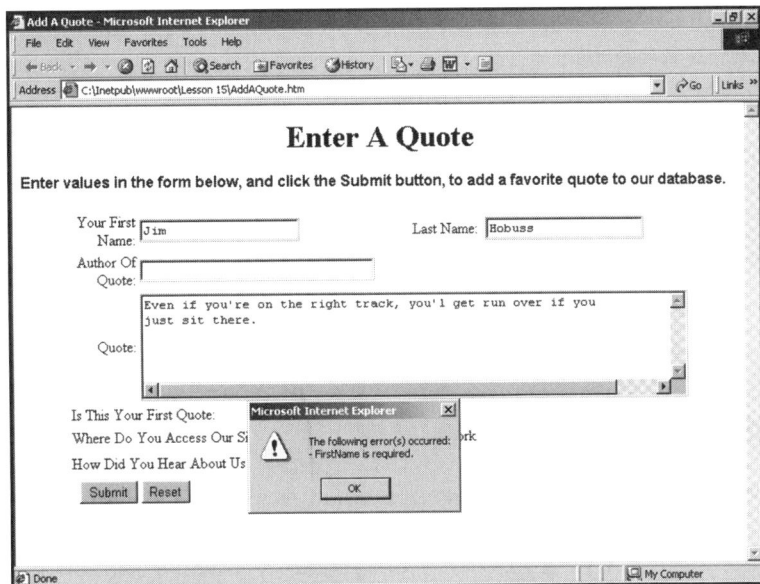

Figure 15.18

An example of a message displayed to visitors when a validation rule is broken.

Receiving Form Data

Perhaps the most popular method used to accept form data from a Web page is by using a Common Gateway Interface (CGI) program that runs on the Web server, or on a machine attached to the Web server, called an application server. CGI programs are most frequently written in a language such as Perl, but the reality is that almost any language, from COBOL to VBScript, can be used to write a CGI program.

NOTE: *Writing and executing CGI programs is outside the scope of this book. These are usually written by programmers, because Web developers don't always have the skill set needed to write them.*

When using CGI programs, data sent from the Web page is parsed and then sent to the CGI program as an input data stream. Parsing is the process of separating each data element into a *name-value* pair. The *name* portion of the pair is the name of the control, and the *value* portion of the pair is the actual data value entered by the visitor. You will recall from what you read earlier in this lesson that each control allows you to specify a name for the control. The name you specify becomes the name portion of the name-value pair when it is sent to the Web server. For example, a text field will have a name-value pair of the name of the text field and the value entered by the visitor. A radio button group will send the name of the radio button group along with the value of the button that was selected.

The following are two incredibly rich Web sources for information about CGI scripts, as well as for many sample scripts:

- ◆ Freescripts **www.freescripts.com**

- ◆ Matt's Scripts **www.worldwidemart.com/scripts/**

What You Must Know

In this lesson, you learned about forms and how to use them on your Web pages. Specifically, you learned how to create and use forms with various types of controls on them to send and react to data entered on forms. In Lesson 16, "Setting Up for Database Interaction," you will learn how to establish a connection between your UltraDev site and the data in the database the site accesses.

Before you continue with Lesson 16, make sure you understand the following key concepts:

- ◆ Within a Web page, forms not only display data to the site visitor, but also accept data the user inputs.

◆ A form normally contains several different types of controls.

◆ A text field lets visitors enter strings of alphanumeric data.

◆ A radio button lets visitors select one item, as represented in the radio button, from a selection of items.

◆ A radio group is the collection of radio buttons that share a common object.

◆ A check box lets the visitor select whether an option is active (or true) or not.

◆ Using a menu or list box, a site provides visitors with the ability to select one or more entities from a list of predefined entities.

Part III

Using Database Access Components of Dreamweaver UltraDev

Lesson 16

Setting Up for Database Interaction

In Lesson 15, "Collecting User Data on Forms," you learned how to create and use a form to collect user data. Specifically, you learned how to create a form and collect user input. In this lesson, you will learn how to establish a connection between UltraDev and a database. By the time you finish this lesson, you will understand the following key concepts:

♦ The first step in accessing a database from within a Web page is to connect to the database.

♦ UltraDev can communicate with various types of databases, which include ADO, ODBC, JDBC, and ColdFusion.

♦ To build a connection between a Web site and a database, you use a comfortable and easy-to-use interface built in UltraDev.

♦ To test the connection from UltraDev to a database, you use a easy-to-use function within the UltraDev interface.

Understanding the Database Connection

Building dynamic Web sites almost always entails incorporating database access of some sort. That access could be for the purpose of doing any of the following:

♦ To extract data from a database for viewing on a Web page

♦ To extract data from a database for application of business rules or logic (for example, password verification)

♦ To update data stored in a database with data supplied by a visitor

♦ To insert new data in a database

♦ To delete data from a database

You will learn in this and subsequent lessons how to accomplish all of these functions using UltraDev. Before a Web page can use a database, the page must connect to the database.

Identifying an Application Server

Although you can have multiple database connections in one Web site, this practice does not occur frequently. It is more common to have multiple data sources associated with one site. Before you can identify a data source or a database connection, you must identify the application server to UltraDev. An *application server* is a component in a Web site's architecture that processes the requests received from Web pages for data and routes that request to the appropriate data source.

The first step in establishing a database connection is to define and describe the application server to UltraDev. An example of where this is done is shown in Figure 16.1.

Figure 16.1

The Application Server panel of the Site Definition window is where you define the location and type of application server your site is using.

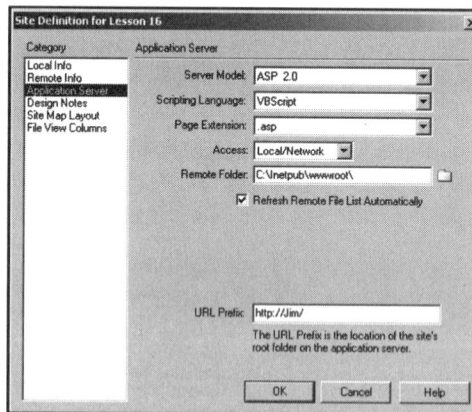

Within the Site Definition window, you define the following attributes specific to the application server:

♦ Server Model (such as ASP 2.0, JSP 1.0., or ColdFusion 4.0)

♦ Scripting Language (such as JavaScript or VBScript)

♦ Page Extension (such as ASP, JSP, HTM, HTML, or CSP)

♦ Access (such as FTP or Local/Network)

♦ Remote Folder

♦ URL Prefix

To launch the Site Definition window, shown in Figure 16.1, and view the Application Server panel, perform these steps:

1. Within UltraDev, select the Site menu Define Sites option to display the Define Sites window.

2. Within the Define Sites window, click on the site name you desire. Then, click on the Edit button. UltraDev will display the Site Definition window.

3. Within the Site Definition window, click on Application Server in the Category list. Ultra-Dev, in turn, will display the Application Server definition window, shown in Figure 16.1.

Figure 16.2

The Define Sites window is where you work with the definitions for various sites known to UltraDev.

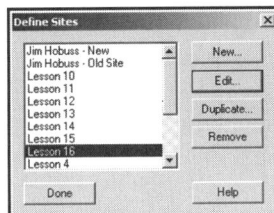

NOTE *The URL Prefix text box on the Site Definition window is where you specify the directory location of the root directory for the site. Since I am using Microsoft Personal Web Server as my application server, and because the name of my machine is "Jim," you see that the URL prefix for my machine is: http://Jim/.*

After you define your Web site using the correct server model for your environment, you can define a database connection. The type of database connection you define is highly dependent on the data access method specific to the architectural configuration of your server. The three choices are described in Table 16.1.

Table 16.1   The three different data access methods supported by UltraDev

Access Method	Description
ADO/ODBC	ADO (Application Data Object) is the latest specification from Microsoft to connect to data sources. ODBC (Open Database Connectivity) is a specification adopted by most RDBMS vendors for accessing their databases from external programs. You use an ADO/ODBC access method when you are using the ASP Server model.
JDBC	JDBC (Java Database Connectivity) is a method for connecting to data sources if you're using a JSP server setup, and because it is Java-based, it is fully platform-independent.
ColdFusion	A data source defined in the ColdFusion product that adheres to the ColdFusion model for server connectivity.

Creating the Database Connection

Creating a database connection in UltraDev follows a very clean setup process. It is highly dependent on the access method you are using on your server. Therefore, the three subsections that follow explain, in turn, how to create a database connection for each of the three access methods described in Table 16.1.

Regardless of the type of access method you are using on your application server, you begin the process of creating a database connection the same way:

1. Select the Modify menu Connections option. UltraDev, in turn, will display the Connections window, shown in Figure 16.3.

Figure 16.3

The Connections window is where you create or modify a database connection.

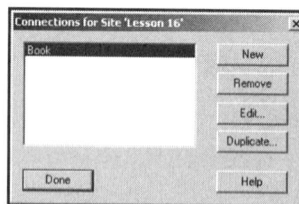

2. Within the Connections window, click on the New button to start a new database definition.

3. Depending on the server model defined, you will follow one of the processes described in the following three subsections.

NOTE: *You could also click on the Edit button on the Connections window after first clicking on a connection name to edit that connection. Or, you could click on the Delete button on the Connections window after clicking on a connection name to delete that connection.*

Using the ADO/ODBC Access Method

Using an ODBC access method in an UltraDev application requires that you first establish an ODBC connection outside of UltraDev. Within a Microsoft Windows environment, a program called ODBC Administrator, located in the Control Panel, is used to set this up. Accessing this program is outside the scope of this book, but for the sake of continuity, assume that I have created an ODBC connection in the ODBC Administrator and named it Lesson.

When you click on the New button on the Connections window, you will see a submenu with two choices: Custom Connection String and Data Source Name (DSN). You must choose one of these two options to continue. Which option you choose is dependent on how much flexibility you want in choosing the location of the database and other parameters without having to define those parameters in the ODBC data source definition on your machine. To use the more friendly but less flexible method to define an ADO/ODBC access method, use the method described next; otherwise, use the method described following the next one.

To create an ADO/ODBC connection type accessing a Data Source Name (DSN), complete the Data Source Name (DSN) window, shown in Figure 16.4, using the information in Table 16.2 as a guideline.

Figure 16.4

The Data Source Name (DSN) window allows you to specify a predefined ODBC data source.

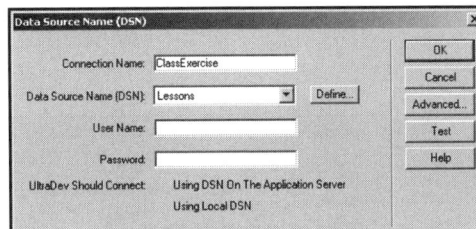

Table 16.2   The text boxes and controls in the Data Source Name (DSN) window

Control Name	Description
Connection Name	The name of the connection that you provide. Use a descriptive name here, because the name you choose here displays as the name for the connection in the Connections window. Macromedia suggests you precede the Connection Name with the prefix string **conn.**
Data Source Name (DSN)	The name of the data source as created using the ODBC Administrator. You can either click on the down arrow to display a list of ODBC DSNs, or click on the Define button to create a definition for a new Data Source Name.
User Name	The username passed to the database to establish a connection with the database. If the database you are connecting to does not require a username, leave this field blank.
Password	The password that is passed to the database to establish a connection with the database. If the database you are connecting to does not require a password, leave this field blank.
UltraDev Should Connect	Instructs UltraDev to connect to the database using a DSN on the application server, or one that is stored locally. Click on the Using Local DSN radio button if the DSN you are using is located on the local machine; otherwise, click on the Using DSN On The Application Server radio button.

To create an ADO/ODBC connection type using a Custom Connect String, complete the Custom Connection String window as seen in Figure 16.5, using the information in Table 16.3 as a guideline.

Figure 16.5

The Custom Connection String window allows you to connect to a database without requiring an ODBC DSN to be predefined.

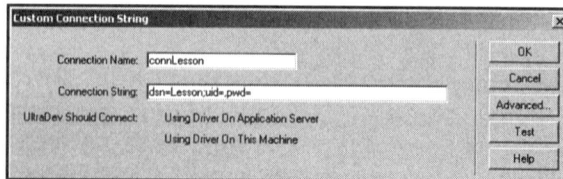

Table 16.3   The text boxes and controls in the Custom Connection String window

Control Name	Description
Connection Name	The name of the connection that you provide. Use a descriptive name here, because the name you choose here displays as the name for the connection in the Connections window. Macromedia suggests you precede the Connection Name with the prefix string **conn**.
Connection String	The format for this string varies, depending on whether a DSN is known or not. If a DSN is known, you only need to specify the name of the DSN, and optionally a UserID and Password to access the database. If a DSN is not known, more information is needed. You must specify the type of database and the type of driver used to access the database. For example, a DSN-less connection string to access a Microsoft Access database might look like: `DRIVER={Microsoft Access Driver (*.mdb)};DBQ=c:\inetpub\wwwroot\lesson.mdb`.
UltraDev Should Connect	Instructs UltraDev to connect to the database using a driver on the application server, or one that is stored locally. Click on the Using Driver On This Machine radio button if the driver you are using is located on the local machine; otherwise, click on the Using Driver On The Application Server radio button.

Using JDBC Connections

A *Java DataBase Connection (JDBC)* is used to connect a Web page with Java code to a database. If you choose JSP as your server platform, you must establish a JDBC connection. When you click on the New button on the Connections window, you will see a submenu with seven choices: Inet Driver (SQL Server), Oracle Thin Driver (Oracle), Sun JDBC-ODBC Driver (ODBC Databases), Custom JDBC Connection, IBM DB2 App Driver (DB2), IBM DB2 Net Driver (DB2), and MySQL Driver (MySQL). You must choose one of these options to continue. Which option you choose is dependent on the type of database you are establishing the JDBC connection to connect to.

When you select one of the seven types of databases, you will see a window that looks very similar to Figure 16.6. Complete this window as necessary, using the information in Table 16.4 as a guide.

Figure 16.6

JDBC drivers require a bit more knowledge on how to use them, but provide complete cross-platform scalability.

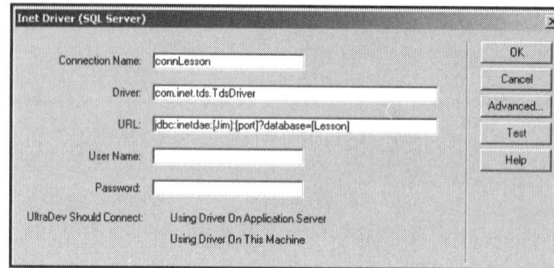

Table 16.4   The text boxes and controls in the JDBC Connections window

Control Name	Description
Connection Name	The name of the connection that you provide. Use a descriptive name here, because the name you choose here displays as the name for the connection in the Connections window. Macromedia suggests you precede the Connection Name with the prefix string **conn**.
Driver	The name of the driver used to access the database. Consult the documentation that accompanied the database server for a description of the possible drivers, as well as the exact syntax for specifying the driver.
URL	A text string to set where and how the database connection is made. Because this is very specific to the database, consult the documentation accompanying the database for the exact syntax of this.
User Name	The username passed to the database to establish a connection with the database. If the database you are connecting to does not require a username, leave this field blank.
Password	The password that is passed to the database to establish a connection with the database. If the database you are connecting to does not require a password, leave this field blank.
UltraDev Should Connect	Instructs UltraDev to connect to the database using a driver on the application server, or one that is stored locally. Click on the Using Driver On This Machine radio button if the driver you are using is located on the local machine; otherwise, click on the Using Driver On The Application Server radio button.

Using ColdFusion Connections

A *ColdFusion Connection* is used to connect a Web page with ColdFusion code to a database. ColdFusion connections, in terms of how they are created, are more similar to ADO/ODBC connections than to JDBC connections. When you click on the New button on the Connections window, you will see a window that looks very similar to Figure 16.7. Complete this window as necessary, using the information in Table 16.5 as a guide.

Figure 16.7

ColdFusion requires you to use a ColdFusion DSN when the definition is created.

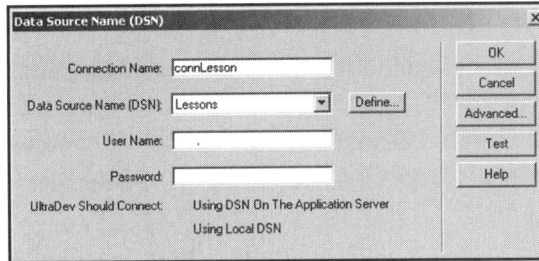

Table 16.5   The text boxes and controls in the ColdFusion Connections window

Control Name	Description
Connection Name	The name of the connection that you provide. Use a descriptive name here, because the name you choose here displays as the name for the connection in the Connections window. Macromedia suggests you precede the Connection Name with the prefix string **conn**.
Data Source Name (DSN)	The name of the ColdFusion DSN used to define the ColdFusion database.
User Name	The username passed to the database to establish a connection with the database. If the database you are connecting to does not require a username, leave this field blank.
Password	The password that is passed to the database to establish a connection with the database. If the database you are connecting to does not require a password, leave this field blank.
UltraDev Should Connect	Instructs UltraDev to connect to the database using a DSN on the application server, or one that is stored locally. Click on the Using DSN On This Machine radio button if the DSN you are using is located on the local machine; otherwise, click on the Using DSN On The Application Server radio button.

Testing the Connection

After you create a connection, you should test the connection. You can test the connection as a final step to creating it, or you can test it at any time later.

To test the connection, perform these steps:

1. Select the Modify menu Connections options. UltraDev will display the Connections window.

2. Within the Connections window, click on the name of the connection that you want to test.

3. Click on the Edit button. UltraDev will display the Connect Window appropriate for the connection type (such as ADO/ODBC, JDBC, or ColdFusion) you have established.

4. Within the Connect window, click on the Test button. If you have properly defined the connection, UltraDev will display a window similar to that shown in Figure 16.8. If the test is unsuccessful, you will see a message describing the nature of the problem.

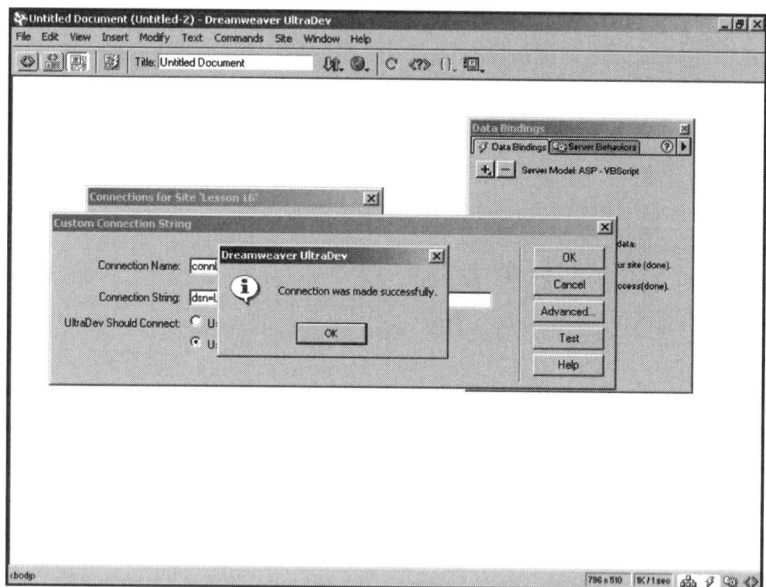

Figure 16.8

Testing a connection should result in the display of a confirmation window.

If your test was unsuccessful, perform these steps to diagnose the problem:

1. Verify the Connection settings you supplied on the Connections window.

2. If you are accessing the database using a driver, verify the existence of the driver either on your machine (if you have defined it as being locally accessible) or on the server.

3. Verify the UserID and Password you supplied are correct.

4. Verify the database server allows remote access if you are accessing a database on a remote machine.

If performing all of these tests does not fix the problem, contact your network administration support person for assistance.

Running a Test Query

When you test the connection, you verify that UltraDev can establish a connection to the database. But, you still do not know that you can actually retrieve data from the database. To get that level of assurance, you must execute a test query.

To run a test query, perform these steps:

1. Select the Window menu Server Behaviors option. UltraDev, in turn, will display the Server Behaviors window, shown in Figure 16.9.

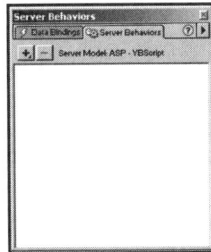

Figure 16.9

The Server Behaviors window is where you create the query to run against the database you connected with.

2. Within the Server Behaviors window, click on the plus sign (+) icon. UltraDev will display a list of the different types of Server Behaviors you can create.

Figure 16.10

The Recordset window is where you specify the parameters needed to run the test query.

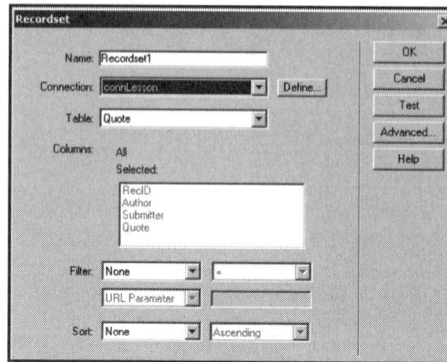

3. Within the Server Behaviors list, click on the Recordset (Query) menu item. UltraDev will display the Recordset window, shown in Figure 16.10.

4. Within the Connection drop-down list, select the name of the connection that you want to test by clicking on the down arrow and then clicking on the appropriate connection name.

5. Using the Table drop-down list, click on the down arrow and then click on the table that you want to run your query against.

6. Although at this point you can specify additional criteria against which to test a query, it is not necessary to define anything further to run a test query. So, at this point, click on the Test button. You should see a results page similar to Figure 16.11.

Figure 16.11

The Test SQL Statement window shows the results of a test query.

If you receive an error message when you click on the Test button, or if your query returns no rows in the result set, you have a problem (unless, of course, the table you ran the query against has no data in it!). Contact your network administration support person for assistance.

What You Must Know

In this lesson, you learned about database connections and connecting an UltraDev Web site to a database. In Lesson 17, "UltraDev Dynamic Data Access Tools," you will learn more about UltraDev's tools that allow dynamic data access.

Before you continue to Lesson 17, make sure you understand the following key concepts:

◆ Before a Web site can perform database operations, the site must connect to a database.

◆ Using UltraDev, you can connect a Web page to any ODBC-compliant database.

◆ UltraDev offers a clean interface to connect a Web site to a database.

◆ UltraDev provides built-in support for ADO, ODBC, JDBC, and ColdFusion.

Lesson 17

UltraDev Dynamic Data Access Tools

I n Lesson 16, "Setting Up for Database Interaction," you learned how to create and use a database connection. Specifically, you learned how to connect to databases using one of three methods, and then how to test the connection to be sure it is configured properly. In this lesson, you will learn more about UltraDev's tools that allow dynamic data access. By the time you finish this lesson, you will understand the following key concepts:

♦ The terminology UltraDev uses to describe the process of connecting to databases, making queries, and displaying the results of queries.

♦ The Recordset (Query) behavior describes all the records returned when a database query is executed.

♦ The Insert Record behavior inserts a new record into a database.

♦ The Update Record behavior updates an existing record in a database.

♦ The Delete Record behavior deletes an existing record in a database.

♦ The Command behavior executes a stored procedure or straight HTML and returns a recordset.

Understanding Web Databases

Many people think that databases accessed by a Web site are managed by a relational database management system (RDBMS) that is specifically designed for Web databases. This is not true.

Other people think that a database designed and developed for a desktop application or interface is not accessible by a Web site. This is not true.

Still other people think that a database designed and developed for a desktop application must be redesigned if it is to be accessed by a Web site. This is not true.

In fact, I have managed many Web site development projects where the Web site accesses data stored in a database created many months (and in some cases, years) before a Web site accessing that data was ever envisioned.

Understanding Database Connections

As you learned in Lesson 16, database connections are used in UltraDev to build the link between the UltraDev Web site and the data accessed by that Web site. It is best to think of a connection in UltraDev as the conduit that connects the database with the Web site.

Database connections are stored with the site, and accessible by any machine accessing the Web site. This means that when you copy the site from a development machine to a production server, the database connections are copied as well.

Understanding Server Behaviors

After your page establishes a database connection, your page can take advantage of server behaviors to perform specific database tasks. Server behaviors use database connections to facilitate an action occurring on a Web or database server.

An understanding of how server behaviors work in relation to visitors seeing information on a Web page and clicking certain controls is beneficial. Here's how they work:

1. You create an HTML page that feeds data from a form on the page to the database.

2. You define a server behavior to describe how that data is to interact with the database. Frequently used server behaviors are Insert, Update, and Delete. The function of each is exactly as its name implies.

3. An event triggered by a visitor doing something on the page containing the server behavior initiates the execution of the server behavior.

4. The server behavior redirects the visitor's browser to another Web page.

5. The visitor browses the new Web page, fills out a form on the page, and clicks on a button on the page.

6. The form submits the data back to the same page that contains the server behavior, which that page then executes.

7. Upon execution of the server behavior, the visitor is redirected to another page or Web site.

Within UltraDev, you access server behaviors from the Servers palette, which you can display by pressing the Ctrl+F9 keyboard combination. If you click on the plus sign (+) icon within the Servers palette, UltraDev will display server behaviors described in Table 17.1. The server behaviors highlighted in bold in the table are presented in this lesson, and the ones in normal font are presented in Lesson 18.

Table 17.1 Server behaviors and their meanings

Server Behavior	Description
Recordset (Query)	Describes all the records returned after a database query is executed.
Insert Record	Inserts a record in a database.
Update Record	Updates an existing record in a database.
Delete Record	Deletes a record from a database.
Command	Executes a stored procedure or straight HTML and returns a recordset.
Repeat Region	Displays multiple records within a recordset. You can display as many records as are available, or limit the number displayed.
Show Region	Conditionally displays (shows) a region on the Web page based on the contents of a recordset.
Move To Record	Provides navigation within an existing recordset.
Go To Detail Page	Goes to a specific detail page in the recordset.
Go To Related Page	Goes to a related page in the recordset.
User Authentication	Restricts Web page access to a specified group of people.
Dynamic Elements	Employs a drag-and-drop interface to move data elements from the Data Bindings tab to a control on a Web page.

NOTE: *Of the server behaviors listed in Table 17.1, five are used the majority of the time: Recordsets, Insert Record, Update Record, Delete Record, and Command. Mastering these five server behaviors will give you the power to perform most functions needed to build database access into a Web site. It is these five that are presented in this lesson.*

The following sections describe the first five of these server behaviors and how they are used.

Using the Recordset (Query) Server Behavior

As you learned in Lesson 16 when you tested the database connection, the Recordset (Query) server behavior extracts a recordset from a database. A Recordset is simply a collection of records that satisfies a query.

You create a Recordset (Query) by supplying the SQL code (via a point-and-click interface) and then letting that SQL code execute against the database. The data retrieved from the SQL query is the recordset.

When a Recordset is created as a result of a query coded by the developer, only the first row of data is accessible by the Web site. You can move through the Recordset by using additional server behaviors, though.

There are two ways you can create a Recordset (Query) in UltraDev. The first is to use a basic interface, and the other is to use an advanced interface. The basic interface is shown in Figure 17.1.

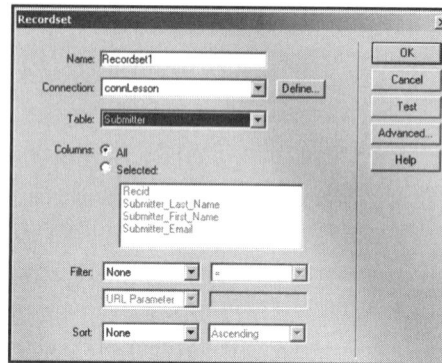

Figure 17.1

The basic interface to the Recordset (Query) server behavior.

You use the basic interface to select a group of records from a database table with as few restrictions and conditions as possible. You can also use the basic interface to perform filtering and sorting on the result set. Filtering allows you to restrict the recordset created to rows of data that match a certain criteria. Sorting allows you to return the recordset to the Web site in a determined and specific sort order.

By clicking on the Advanced button, you display the advanced interface to the Recordset (Query) server behavior, as shown in Figure 17.2.

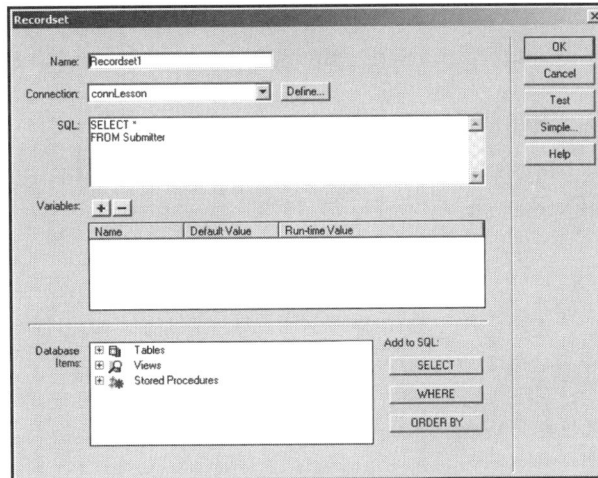

Figure 17.2

The advanced interface to the Recordset (Query) server behavior.

To define an advanced Recordset (Query) from the advanced Recordset (Query) window, perform these steps:

1. Within the Name text box, enter a name for this Recordset (Query). A common practice is to prefix the names of queries with the characters *rs*.

2. Within the Connection drop-down list box, select a connection name by first clicking on the down arrow, and then clicking on the connection name.

3. Within the SQL box, type the SQL statement. To reduce the amount of typing, you can use the Database Items tree at the bottom of the window. The way you use this is to click on the plus sign (+) next to the database component you want to expand, and then select the database component by clicking on it. After you select the database component, click on the SELECT, WHERE, or ORDER BY button to place a database item, with its associated action, in the SQL box.

4. If you have typed the names of variables in the SQL statement, define the values for these variables in the Variables section of the window. You do this by clicking on the plus sign next to the word Variable, and then entering the variable's name, default value taken when there is no run-time value set for the variable, and the run-time value for the variable. The run-time value for the variable is usually a server object that holds a value sent by a browser.

5. Click on the Test button to verify the SQL statement created returns a satisfactory recordset. If it does not, modify the SQL statement in the SQL text area. If it does, click on the OK button.

6. Clicking on the OK button adds the recordset to the list of available data sources in the Data Bindings panel, as shown in Figure 17.3.

Figure 17.3

After a Recordset (Query) is defined, it is added to the list of available data sources in the Data Bindings panel.

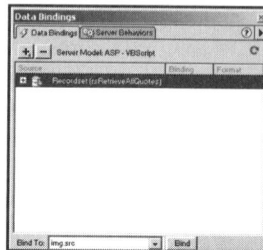

Using the Insert Record Server Behavior

The Insert Record server behavior adds data to a database. This data must come from a form on a Web page.

Before data can be inserted into a database, you must define a form. The Insert Record server behavior is triggered from input on the form. As shown in Figure 17.4, the trigger is usually a visitor clicking on a button.

Figure 17.4

A Submit button with the text changed to read "Insert Record" is often used to trigger an Insert Record server behavior.

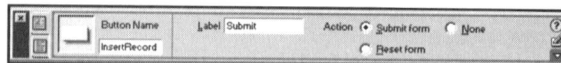

To define an Insert Record server behavior, perform these steps:

1. Within the Document window, click on the control on the form that is to trigger the server behavior.

2. Within the Server Behaviors palette, click on the Insert Record server behavior. UltraDev will display the Insert Record window, as shown in Figure 17.5.

Figure 17.5

The Insert Record server behavior creates a new row of data in the database from information contained on a Web page form.

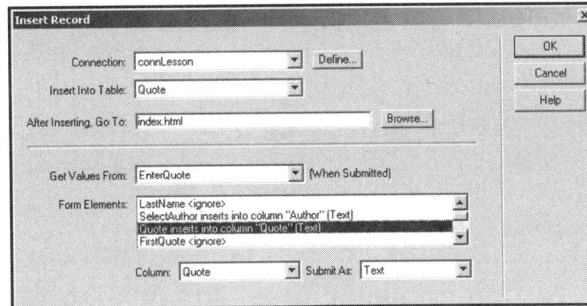

3. Within the Connection drop-down list, select the connection for this server behavior.

4. In the Insert Into Table drop-down list, select the table in the database that data is to be inserted into when this server behavior executes.

5. Within the After Inserting, Go To text box, type the URL that the visitor is to see when the server behavior finishes executing. You could also click on the Browse button to use a point-and-click interface to select the page to navigate to.

6. Within the Get Values From drop-down list, select the name of the form that the data to be inserted into the database comes from.

7. Within the Form Elements list, specify what each object on your form will update in the database table by selecting a form object in the list, and then choosing a table column from the Column pop-up menu and a data type from the Submit As pop-up menu. The data type is the kind of data the column in your database is expecting (text, numeric, Boolean check box).

8. Repeat Step 7 for each form object in the Form Elements list.

9. Click on the OK button.

Using the Update Record Server Behavior

The Update Record server behavior updates data currently existing in a database. As is the case with the Insert Record server behavior, the data used in the Update Record server behavior must come from a form on a Web page. Before data can be updated in a database, you must define a form. The Update Record server behavior is triggered from input on the form. Frequently, this trigger is a visitor clicking on a button, similar to what is described in the previous section for the Insert Record server behavior.

To define an Update Record server behavior, perform these steps:

1. Within the Document window, select the control on the form that is to trigger the server behavior by clicking on it.

2. Within the Server Behaviors palette, click on the Update Record server behavior. UltraDev, in turn, will display the Update Record window, as shown in Figure 17.6.

Figure 17.6

The Update Record server behavior changes existing data in the database by using data input by a visitor on a form in a Web page.

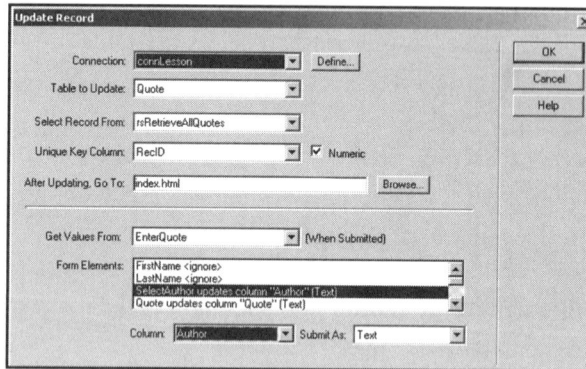

3. Within the Connection drop-down list, select the connection for this server behavior.

4. Within the Table to Update drop-down list, select the table in the database that data is to be updated in when this server behavior executes.

5. Using the Select Record From drop-down list, select the name of the Recordset (Query) that contains the record displayed in the form on the Web page.

6. Within the Unique Key Column drop-down list box, select a key column to identify the correct record in the database to update. This is usually a record ID, often referred to as a *RecID*. Click on the Numeric check box if the key column accepts only numeric values.

7. Within the After Updating, Go To text box, type the URL that the visitor is to see when the server behavior finishes executing. You could also click on the Browse button to use a point-and-click interface to select the page to navigate to.

8. Using the Get Values From drop-down list, select the name of the form that the data to be updated in the database comes from.

9. Within the Form Elements list, specify what each object on your form will update in the database table by selecting a form object in the list, and then choosing a table column from the Column pop-up menu and a data type from the Submit As pop-up menu. The data type is the kind of data the column in your database is expecting (text, numeric, Boolean check box).

10. Repeat Step 9 for each form object in the Form Elements list.

11. Click on the OK button.

Using the Delete Record Server Behavior

The Delete Record server behavior deletes data currently existing in a database. As is the case with the Insert Record and Update Record server behaviors, the data used to identify which record is to be deleted in the Delete Record server behavior must come from a form on a Web page. Before data can be deleted in a database, you must define a form. The Delete Record server behavior is triggered from input on the form. Frequently, this trigger is a visitor clicking on a button, similar to what is described in the previous section for the Update Record server behavior.

To define a Delete Record server behavior, perform these steps:

1. Within the Document window, select the control on the form that is to trigger the server behavior by clicking on it.

2. Within the Server Behaviors palette, click on the Delete Record server behavior. UltraDev will display the Delete Record window, as shown in Figure 17.7.

3. Using the Connection drop-down list, select the connection for this server behavior.

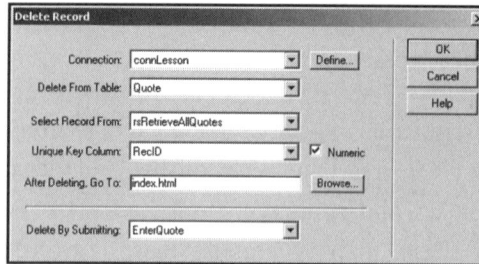

Figure 17.7

The Delete Record server behavior removes data in a database.

4. Using the Delete From Table drop-down list, select the table in the database that data is to be deleted from when this server behavior executes.

5. Using the Select Record From drop-down list, select the name of the Recordset (Query) that contains the record displayed in the form on the Web page.

6. Within the Unique Key Column drop-down list, select a key column to identify the correct record in the database to delete. This is usually a record ID, often referred to as a *RecID*. Click on the Numeric check box if the key column accepts only numeric values.

7. In the After Deleting, Go To text box, type the URL that the visitor is to see when the server behavior finishes executing. You could also click on the Browse button to use a point-and-click interface to select the page to navigate to.

8. Using the Delete By Submitting drop-down list, specify the HTML form with the control triggering the Delete Record behavior that sends the delete command to the server.

9. Click on the OK button.

Using the Command Server Behavior

The Command server behavior lets you execute a stored procedure (or HTML) and returns a Recordset, if necessary. A stored procedure is a small piece of program code stored on a server that performs a specific task. The defining attribute of the Command server behavior is that it allows you to tie the behavior to UltraDev variables.

You can use UltraDev variables in the same way that you can use Recordsets, as previously described. Specifically, you can use session data, cookies, or any other data elements that you want inside the body of the command.

To define a Command server behavior, perform these steps:

1. Within the Document window, click on the control on the form that is to trigger the server behavior.

2. Within the Server Behaviors palette, click on the Command server behavior. UltraDev, in turn, will display the Command window, as shown in Figure 17.8.

3. Within the Name text box, type a name that this behavior will be named.

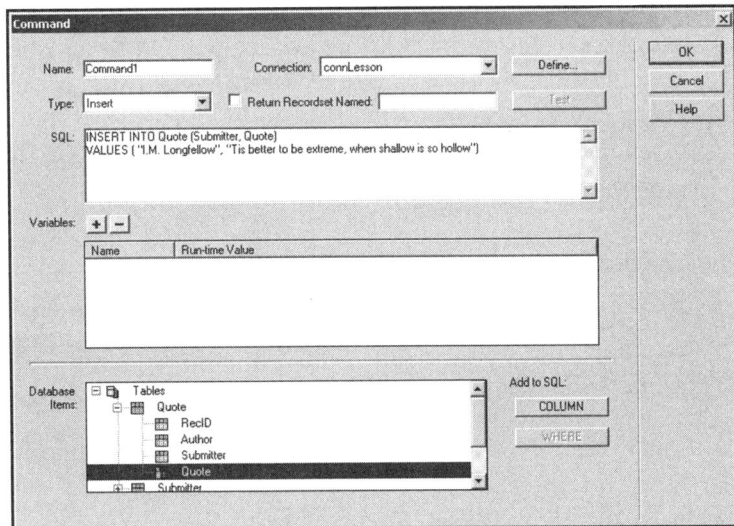

Figure 17.8

The Command server behavior is used to execute a stored procedure or straight HTML.

4. Using the Type drop-down list, select the type of command. The options are None, Stored Procedure, Insert, Update, and Delete.

5. Click in the Return Recordset Named check box, and type a name for the recordset in the adjacent text box, if the Command server behavior is to return a recordset.

6. Within the SQL text box, type (or supply the missing values) for the SQL that is to execute when the Command server behavior executes.

7. If the command processes variables, click the plus sign (+) icon and enter the variable name and run-time value for the variable.

8. In the Database Items tree structure, you can point and click on objects in the database to add to the SQL text box.

9. Click on the OK button.

What You Must Know

In this lesson, you learned more about UltraDev's tools that allow dynamic access to data. In Lesson 18, "Advanced Server Behaviors," you will learn how to place objects on your page that let the server perform key database operations. Before you continue with Lesson 18, make sure you understand the following key concepts:

◆ UltraDev uses a specific set of terminology to connect to databases and to use the data retrieved from those databases.

◆ Server behaviors supply access to effectively use UltraDev's database access facilities.

◆ Using the Recordset (Query) server behavior, your page can describe all the records returned when a database query is executed.

◆ Using the Insert Record server behavior, your page can easily insert a new record into a database.

◆ Using the Update Record server behavior, your page can update an existing record in a database.

◆ Using the Delete Record server behavior, your page can delete an existing record in a database.

◆ Using the Command server behavior, your page can execute a stored procedure or straight HTML and return a recordset.

Lesson 18

Advanced Server Behaviors

In Lesson 17, "UltraDev Dynamic Data Access Tools," you learned how to use the five most common of UltraDev's server behaviors that are specific to data access. Specifically, you learned how to create a Recordset (Query), insert a record, update a record, delete a record, and execute a customer command. In this lesson, you will learn more about UltraDev's server behaviors that allow dynamic data access. By the time you finish this lesson, you will understand the following key concepts:

◆ Within UltraDev, the Repeat and Show Region server behaviors let you display multiple records within a recordset on a page.

◆ The Move To server behavior provides navigation within an existing recordset.

◆ The Go To Detail Page and Go To Related Page server behaviors let you go to a specific detail page or a related page in the recordset, respectively.

◆ The Dynamic Elements server behavior lets you use a drag-and-drop interface to populate various form controls with data.

◆ The User Authentication server behavior enables you to restrict Web page access.

Understanding Server Behaviors

Table 18.1 presents the full range of server behaviors you can access from the Servers palette. The server behaviors in normal font in the table were presented in Lesson 17, and the ones highlighted in bold are presented in this lesson.

Table 18.1   Server behaviors and their meanings

Server Behavior	Description
Insert Record	Inserts a record in a database.
Update Record	Updates an existing record in a database.
Delete Record	Deletes a record from a database.
Recordset (Query)	Describes all the records returned after a database query is executed.
Command	Executes a stored procedure or straight HTML and returns a recordset.
Repeat Region	Displays multiple records within a recordset. You can display as many records as are available, or limit the number displayed.
Show Region	Conditionally displays (shows) a region on the Web page based on the contents of a recordset.
Move To Record	Provides navigation within an existing recordset.
Go To Detail Page	Goes to a specific detail page in the recordset.
Go To Related Page	Goes to a related page in the recordset.
User Authentication	Restricts Web page access to a specified group of people.
Dynamic Elements	Employs a drag-and-drop interface to move data elements from the Data Bindings tab to a control on a Web page.

NOTE: *To access the Server Behaviors palette, press and hold down the Ctrl key and then press the F9 key.*

The following sections describe the remainder of the server behaviors and how they are used.

Understanding the Repeat Region Server Behavior

The Recordset (Query) server behavior creates a recordset that satisfies the query parameters, but unless you specify a Repeat Region server behavior, you will not be able to display multiple records on a Web page. The Repeat Region server behavior is used to display multiple records on a Web page. To define a Repeat Region server behavior, perform these steps:

1. Within the Document window, select a region on the Web page that is to contain the repeating region. This can be a table, a table row, or a paragraph of text.

2. Within the Server Behaviors palette, click on the Repeat Region server behavior. UltraDev will display the Command window, as shown in Figure 18.1.

Figure 18.1

The Repeat Region server behavior is used to display multiple rows of data on a Web page.

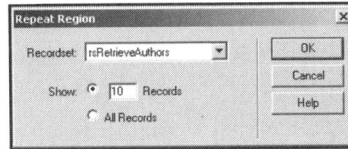

3. Within the Recordset drop-down list, select the name of the recordset containing the data to display in the repeating region.

4. Within the Show radio button group, click on either the All Records or the *number* Records radio button. If you click on the *number* Records radio button, type a number for the number of records to display in the repeated region.

5. Click on the OK button.

NOTE: *If you specify a number of records that is less than the total number of records that will be retrieved from the recordset, you should add navigation elements to the Web page that allow the user to scroll backward or forward through the recordset.*

Understanding the Show Region Server Behavior

The Show Region server behavior displays a region within a document based on the satisfaction of a condition. The behavior is triggered by the contents of a recordset.

An example of how you could use the Show Region server behavior is a Web page that lets the user scroll through a recordset. You could, for example, place a Next button on the page that the visitor clicks on to view the next group of records (using the Repeat Region server behavior just presented). When the last row of data from the recordset is displayed on the page, you should not display the Next button, because clicking on it by the visitor would be pointless. You would define a Show Region server behavior to cause this behavior.

To define a Show Region server behavior, perform these steps:

1. Within the Document window, select a control or region on the Web page that controls the region.

2. Within the Server Behaviors palette, click on the Show Region server behavior. UltraDev will display a menu of options: Show Region If Recordset Is Empty, Show Region If Recordset Is Not Empty, Show Region If First Record, Show Region If Not First Record, Show Region If Last Record, and Show Region If Not Last Record. Select one of these menu items and you will see a window that looks similar to Figure 18.2.

Figure 18.2

The Show Region server behavior is used to control when regions of data are displayed.

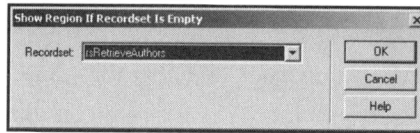

3. Within the Recordset drop-down list, select the name of the recordset containing the data to control the display.

4. Click on the OK button.

Using the Move To Record Server Behavior

The Move To Record server behavior controls the records that are displayed from a recordset. Sites often use the Move To Record server behavior in conjunction with the Repeat Region server behavior. The reason for this is that if you limit the number of rows of data that display on a page using the Repeat Region server behavior, you also need a mechanism to move around among the repeated regions.

There are a number of options to choose from when you use the Move To Record server behavior, as described in Table 18.2.

Table 18.2 Options available in the Move To Record server behavior

Behavior Option	Description
Move To First Record	Moves to the very first record in the recordset
Move To Previous Record	Moves to the previous record in the recordset
Move To Next Record	Moves to the next record in the recordset
Move To Last Record	Moves to the very last record in the recordset
Move To Specific Record	Moves to a specific record in the recordset based on the relative number of the record in the recordset

To define a Move To Record server behavior, perform these steps:

1. Within the Document window, select a control or region on the Web page that controls the region.

2. Within the Server Behaviors palette, click on the Move To Record server behavior. UltraDev will display a menu of options, previously described in Table 18.2. Select one of these menu items and you will see a window that looks similar to Figure 18.3.

Figure 18.3

The Move To Record server behavior is used to navigate through the records in a recordset.

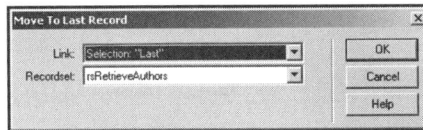

3. Within the Link drop-down box, select the linked text that contains the server behavior. You can also supply the text for a new link in the control if you currently don't have one defined on the page.

4. Within the Recordset drop-down list box, select the recordset that you want this server behavior to act upon.

5. Click on the OK button.

Using the Dynamic Elements Server Behavior

The Dynamic Elements server behavior controls the display of records from a recordset in one of five different types of controls appearing on a page. There are a number of options to choose from when you click on the Dynamic Elements server behavior, all of which are described in Table 18.3.

Table 18.3 Options available in the Dynamic Elements server behavior

Behavior Option	Description
Dynamic Text	Inserts a value from a recordset into the document
Dynamic List/Menu	Populates a menu or selection list with items from the recordset
Dynamic Text Field	Inserts a field from a recordset into a text field
Dynamic Check Box	Determines if a check box should be checked based on the value of a data element in a recordset
Dynamic Radio	Determines if a radio button should be on or off based on the value of a data element in a recordset

To define a Dynamic Element server behavior, perform these steps:

1. Within a Document window, select a control or region on the Web page that controls the region.

2. Within the Server Behaviors palette, click on the Dynamic Elements server behavior. Ultra-Dev will display a menu of options, previously described in Table 18.3. Select one of these menu items and you will see a window tailored to the type of Dynamic Elements selected. If you select the Dynamic List/Menu menu item, the window will look similar to Figure 18.4.

Figure 18.4

The Dynamic Elements server behavior is used to place data in various types of controls.

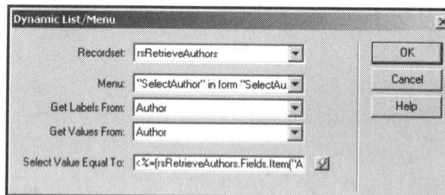

3. Within the Recordset drop-down list, select the recordset containing the information to populate in the control.

4. In the Get Labels From drop-down list, select the field that contains the labels for the menu items.

5. Within the Get Values From drop-down list box, select the field that contains the values for the menu items.

6. If you want a particular menu item to be selected when the page opens in a browser or when a record is displayed, enter a value in the Select Value Equal To text box.

7. Click on the OK button.

Using the Go To Detail Page Server Behavior

Occasionally, within a site, you will have the need to create a master-detail relationship between two pages. For example, consider a Web page that displays a list of records from a recordset. You want to give the visitor the ability to update any of the displayed records. To indicate their desire to update a record, the user clicks on the row of data, and then on a button, which ultimately launches a secondary page with the selected row of data displayed on the page. In this scenario, the Web page that displays the rows of source data is called the master page, and the page that displays the selected row and gives the visitor the ability to update the data is called the detail page.

Before you can use the Go To Detail Page server behavior, you must build a master-detail page set. To do that, you need to accomplish the following:

◆ Create a master page and define a recordset for the master page.

◆ Display records from the recordset on the master page.

◆ Pass the ID of the record the user selects on the master page to the detail page.

◆ Define a recordset for the detail page that holds the detail data, and then bind the recordset to the page.

◆ Either define a recordset filter for the detail page to extract the record matching the ID passed from the master page, or add a Move To Specific Record server behavior.

NOTE: *Defining a recordset filter on the detail page is more efficient than extracting a record matching the ID passed from the master page, because the filtered recordset will contain only one record.*

To display the records on the master page, perform these steps:

1. Create a page layout with a form to display multiple records.

2. Create a repeating region to display more than one record at a time.

To open a detail page and pass a URL parameter that contains the ID of the record the user clicked on the master page, do the following on the master page:

1. Within the Document window, select the dynamic content that will function as a link in the repeated region.

2. Within the Server Behaviors palette, click on the Go To Detail Page server behavior. Ultra-Dev will display a window that looks similar to Figure 18.5.

Figure 18.5

The Go To Detail Page server behavior is used to relate a selected record on a master page with a record on a detail page.

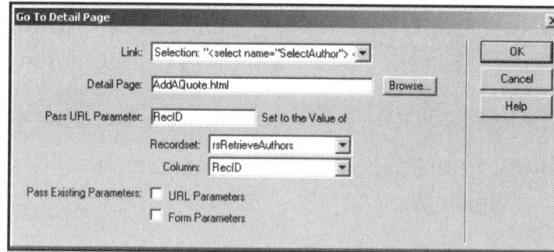

3. Within the Detail Page text box, identify the name of the page that will be the detail page. You can optionally click on the Browse button to use a point-and-click interface to accomplish this.

4. Using the controls on the bottom of the window, specify the information you want to pass to the detail page by selecting a recordset and a column from the recordset from the Recordset and Column drop-down list boxes.

5. Click on the OK button.

Next, switch to the detail page and perform these steps:

1. Within the Data Bindings panel of the Server Behaviors Inspector, click on the plus sign (+) icon. UltraDev will display a pop-up menu.

2. Within the pop-up menu, click on Recordset (Query) and the Recordset (Query) window will display.

3. Within the Recordset (Query) window, type a name for the recordset in the text box, and then choose a connection and database table that provides access to the recordset.

4. Within the Column object, select the name of the column(s) to include in the recordset.

5. If you are using a recordset filter to locate the correct record as passed from the master page, leave the Recordset dialog box empty and click on the Filter button to define a filter.

6. If you are using the Move To Specific Record server behavior, click on the OK button to close the window. Otherwise, add the Move To Specific Record server behavior, as presented earlier in this lesson.

Using the Go To Related Page Server Behavior

Within a site, you use the Go To Related Page server behavior to transfer parameters that exist on a page, or anything else submitted on a page, to another page. To define a Go To Related Page server behavior, perform these steps:

1. Within the Document window, select a region on the Web page that is to contain the server behavior.

2. Within the Server Behaviors palette, click on the Go To Related Page server behavior. Ultra-Dev, in turn, will display the Go To Related Page window, as shown in Figure 18.6.

Figure 18.6

The Go To Related Page server behavior is used to pass parameters from one page to another.

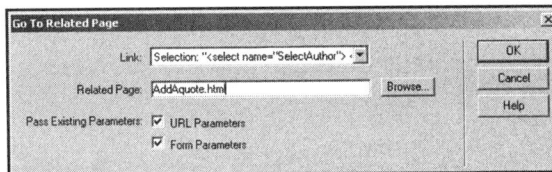

3. Within the Related Page drop-down list box, specify the URL for the page to transfer data to. You could optionally click on the Browse button to use a point-and-click interface.

4. Within the Pass Existing Parameters check boxes, check the URL Parameters check box if you are passing parameters with the URL (you use this method if you are using the GET

method). If you are passing parameters directly from the HTML form, check the Form Parameters check box (you use this method if you are using the POST method).

5. Click on the OK button.

Understanding User Authentication

Many sites do not restrict access to pages on the site. In these cases, there is no need for user authentication. However, many sites have a need to restrict access to pages on the site to certain users. Prior to version 4 of UltraDev, this required a substantial amount of coding in a language such as JavaScript.

Macromedia responded to requests from its user community to provide a clean way to implement restricting access to pages in a site developed with UltraDev by incorporating User Authentication. By using this facility, you can do the following:

♦ Log a user in to a site

♦ Restrict access to a page to certain users

♦ Log a user out of the site

♦ Check for a new username

The developers at Macromedia created an interface to this facility that is clean. All the information specific to a visitor's authority to enter and access a site is contained in a database table containing usernames and passwords in text format. UltraDev maintains the information about a user's access to a site in a session variable called MM_Username. After a user successfully logs in to a site, this session variable is set and referenced throughout the site. The following sections describe each of the four user authentication capabilities.

Using the Log In User to a Site Server Behavior

If your site has a need to restrict access to certain users, then you probably have a Log In page. Within the Log In page, you will place the Log In User To A Site server behavior. After a user logs in to the site (and triggers this server behavior), the MM_Username session variable is set and the user has access to any page in the site where they are not restricted because of a Restrict Access To Page server behavior. To use the Log In User server behavior, perform these steps:

1. Make sure the Log In page for your site is in the Document window.

2. Within the Server Behaviors palette, click on the User Authentication server behavior. Ultra-Dev will display a menu of options.

3. Within the menu, click on the Log In User option. UltraDev, in turn, will display the Log In User window, shown in Figure 18.7.

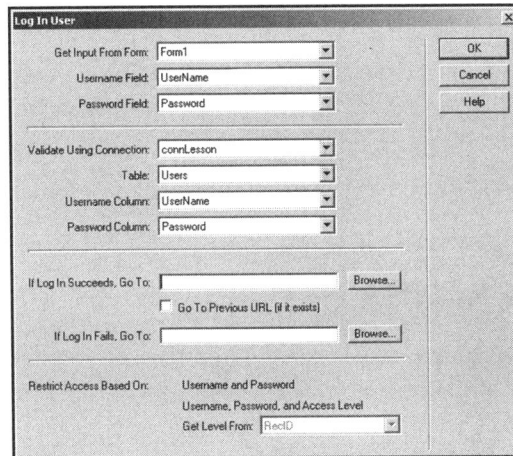

Figure 18.7

The Log In User window is where you configure user authentication to your site.

4. Within the Get Input From Form drop-down list, supply the name of the form that contains the data specific to the user.

5. Within the Username Field drop-down list, click on the name of the control containing the username.

6. Within the Password Field drop-down list, click on the name of the control containing the password.

7. Using the Validate Using Connection drop-down list, click on the name of the connection you want to use to connect the site to your database.

8. Using the Table drop-down list, click on the name of the table containing the validation data.

9. Within the Username Column drop-down list box, click on the name of the column in the table that contains the username to validate.

10. Within the Password Column drop-down list box, click on the name of the column in the table that contains the password to validate.

11. Using the If Log In Fails, Go To text box, specify the name of the page to go to if the login process fails. You can click on the Browse button to use a point-and-click interface to select this page.

12. By clicking on the appropriate radio button, specify whether to grant access to the page based on username and password alone, or based on the authorization level contained in the database as well.

13. Click on the OK button.

Using the Restrict Access To Page Server Behavior

After you have placed the Log In User server behavior on the Log In page, you can use the Restrict Access To Page server behavior to check whether or not the user has successfully logged in before allowing them to view a page. You simply place this server behavior on every page in your site in which you want to implement this type of control.

To use the Restrict Access To Page server behavior, perform these steps:

1. Open the page within which you want to place the Restrict Access To Page server behavior within the Document window.

2. Within the Server Behaviors palette, click on the User Authentication server behavior. UltraDev will display a menu of options.

3. Within the menu, select the Restrict Access To Page option. UltraDev will display the Restrict Access To Page window, as shown in Figure 18.8.

Figure 18.8

The Restrict Access To Page window is used to control access to the page to users who have successfully logged on.

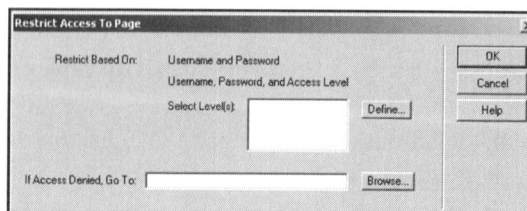

4. Within the Restrict Access To Page window, click on the Username and Password radio button if you want to verify user access based on their username and password.

5. Click on the Username, Password, and Access Level radio button if you want to verify user access based on their username, password, and access level.

6. In the Select Level(s) box, click on the access level you want to restrict access to the page to. If none are listed, or if the access level you desire is not listed, click on the Define button and create one.

7. In the If Access Denied, Go To text box, specify the name of the page to go to if user access fails. You can click on the Browse button to use a point-and-click interface to select this page.

8. Click on the OK button.

Using the Log Out User Server Behavior

You ordinarily do not need to provide this capability on your site. A user either will not be able to successfully log in to your site, or will close their browser window (or enter a URL to a site completely different from yours), which effectively logs the user out of the site.

However, some sites do provide a logout feature. Other sites provide a feature that allows a visitor to log in using different user IDs. In these scenarios, you want to use the Log Out User server behavior.

To use the Log Out User server behavior, perform these steps:

1. Open the page within which you want to place the Restrict Access To Page server behavior within the Document window.

2. Within the Server Behaviors palette, click on the User Authentication server behavior. Ultra-Dev will display a menu of options.

3. Within the menu, select the Log Out User option. UltraDev will display the Log Out User window, as shown in Figure 18.9.

Figure 18.9

The Log Out User window is where you specify when a user logout occurs.

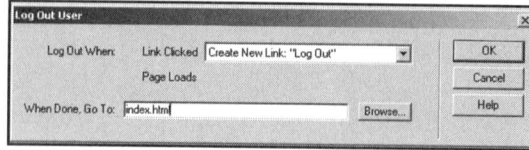

4. Within the Log Out User window, click on the Log Out When Link Clicked radio button, and then click on the related drop-down list box and select the link that triggers the log out function, if the logout event is triggered by clicking on a link.

5. Click on the Log Out When Page Loads radio button to trigger a user's logging out of the site when the page this server behavior is on first loads.

6. Within the When Done, Go To text box, specify the name of the page to go to when the user is logged out. You can click on the Browse button to use a point-and-click interface to select this page.

7. Click on the OK button.

Using the Check New Username Server Behavior

You may provide on your site the capability that allows users to pick their own usernames. The problem with this is that users may want to pick a username that has already been chosen. To eliminate this situation, you can use the Check New Username server behavior to verify that a username picked by a site visitor is unique.

To use the Check New Username server behavior, perform these steps:

1. Open the page within which you want to place the Check New Username server behavior in the Document window.

2. Within the Server Behaviors palette, click on the User Authentication server behavior. Ultra-Dev will display a menu of options.

3. Within the menu, select the Check New Username option. UltraDev, in turn, will display the Check New Username window, as shown in Figure 18.10.

Figure 18.10

The Check New Username window is used to verify that the username supplied as a new username by a visitor has not been taken.

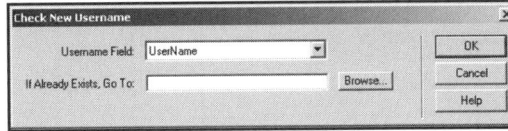

4. Within the Check New Username window, click on the Username Field drop-down list box to select the name of the database field that contains the usernames as stored in the database.

5. In the If Already Exists, Go To text box, specify the name of the page to go to if the user selected a name already in use. You can click on the Browse button to use a point-and-click interface to select this page.

6. Click on the OK button.

What You Must Know

In this lesson, you learned more about UltraDev's tools that allow dynamic access to data. In Lesson 19, "Building Interactive Pages That Have Database Access," you will learn how to build interactivity into your Web pages by using database access.

Before you continue with Lesson 19, make sure you understand the following key concepts:

♦ Within a Web page, you can use the Repeat Region and Show Region server behaviors to display multiple records within a recordset on a page.

♦ The Move To Record server behavior provides you with a way to navigate within an existing recordset.

♦ The Go To Detail Page and Go To Related Page server behaviors let you go to a specific detail page or related page in the recordset, respectively.

◆ Using the Dynamic Elements Behavior, you can employ a drag-and-drop interface to populate various form controls with data.

◆ The User Authentication server behaviors let you restrict Web page access.

Lesson 19

Building Interactive Pages That Have Database Access

In Lesson 18, "Advanced Server Behaviors," you learned how to use the remainder of the server behaviors that provide access to data. Specifically, you learned how to use the Repeat Region, Show Region, Move To Record, Go To Detail Page, Go To Related Page, and User Authentication server behaviors.

In this lesson, you will learn how to pull data from live databases and use that data to build a highly interactive Web site. By the time you finish this lesson, you will understand the following key concepts:

◆ Recordsets are the rows of data returned from a query made against a database. Using Ultra-Dev, you can easily define and work with recordsets.

◆ A results list lets you display the results of a query on a Web page.

◆ UltraDev provides a number of facilities that let a visitor navigate through a Recordset.

◆ Within a Web site, you can use detail pages to view specific columns of a record in a Recordset.

◆ Within a Web site, the master page displays the results of a query made against a database, while a detail page is used to view specific columns of a record contained within a Recordset.

◆ To navigate through a Recordset, you can link a master page with a detail page.

Starting with Dynamic Content

Before you can display any data on a Web page that is to have dynamic content, you must extract data and display it on a Web page. In Lesson 17, "UltraDev Dynamic Data Access Tools," you learned that you use a Recordset (Query) server behavior to extract data from a database.

Defining a Recordset (Query)

To begin the process of adding dynamic content to your Web site, you must first build a query to extract data from a Microsoft Access database. To define a Recordset (Query), perform these steps:

1. Within the Document window, select the File menu New option. UltraDev, in turn, will open a new page.

2. Within the new page, set the properties shown in Figure 19.1.

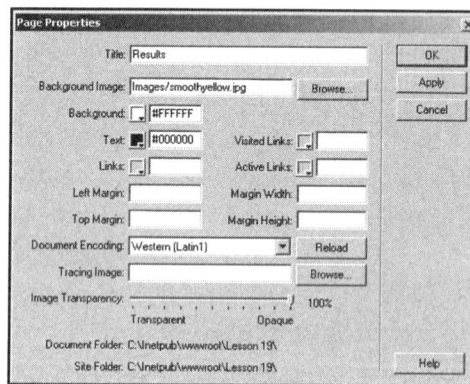

Figure 19.1

Establish page properties for the Results page as shown here.

3. Open the Server Behaviors window by pressing the Ctrl+F9 keyboard combination.

4. Within the Server Behaviors window, click on the plus sign (+) icon to open the Server Behaviors list.

5. Within the Server Behaviors list, select the Recordset (Query) option. UltraDev, in turn, will open the Recordset (Query) window.

6. To continue, you will work in the window's Advanced view. If you're not looking at the Advanced view, click on the Advanced button.

7. Within the Name text box, enter a name for this Recordset (Query). In this case, use **rsGetShortDescriptions**.

8. Within the Connection drop-down list, select the connLesson connection.

9. Next, you will use a query that was previously written and stored by me in the MS Access database as the source for the data in this Recordset (Query). To do this, click on Views in the Database Items portion of the window. UltraDev will expand the section.

10. Within the section, click on the query named qryGetQuotesAndNames, and then click on the SELECT button. UltraDev will display the following within the page's SQL window:

    SELECT *

    FROM qryGetQuotesAndNames

11. Within the Database Items window, click on the column named Author, and then click on the ORDER BY button. Your window should now appear as shown in Figure 19.2.

Figure 19.2

The Advanced (SQL) server behavior window describing the use of an MS Access Query.

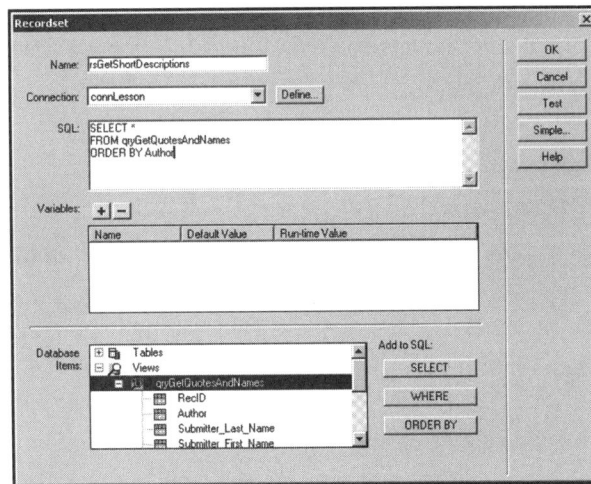

12. Click on the Test button to verify the SQL statement returns a satisfactory recordset. When you do this, the result set should look like that shown Figure 19.3. If it does not, modify the SQL statement in the SQL text area. If it does, click on the OK button.

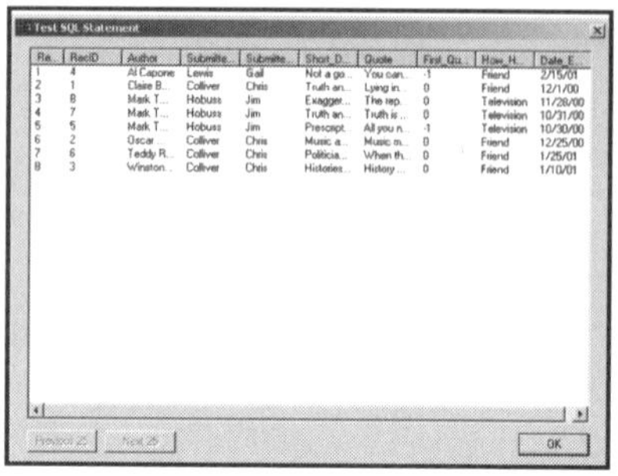

Figure 19.3

The result window when you test the new Recordset (Query) should look like this.

13. Click on the OK button to add the recordset to the list of available data sources in the Data Bindings panel.

Inserting and Viewing Dynamic Content

UltraDev has a nice component that lets you view data while you are working in Design mode. Using this facility, you have the ability to see roughly what your page will look like in a browser, when the page is full of data, while you're designing it.

To insert dynamic content on a Web page, perform these steps:

1. Within the Document window, type the phrase **The quote of the day is:**.

2. Within the Server Behaviors window, click on the Data Bindings tab. UltraDev will display the data bindings.

3. Click on the plus sign (+) that appears next to the rsGetShortDescriptions query name to expand the list of all the data elements available in this recordset.

4. Click on the column named Quote, to highlight it. Next, click on the Insert button that is at the bottom of the Data Bindings tab. UltraDev, in turn, will insert the column name in your document window, similar to what you see in Figure 19.4.

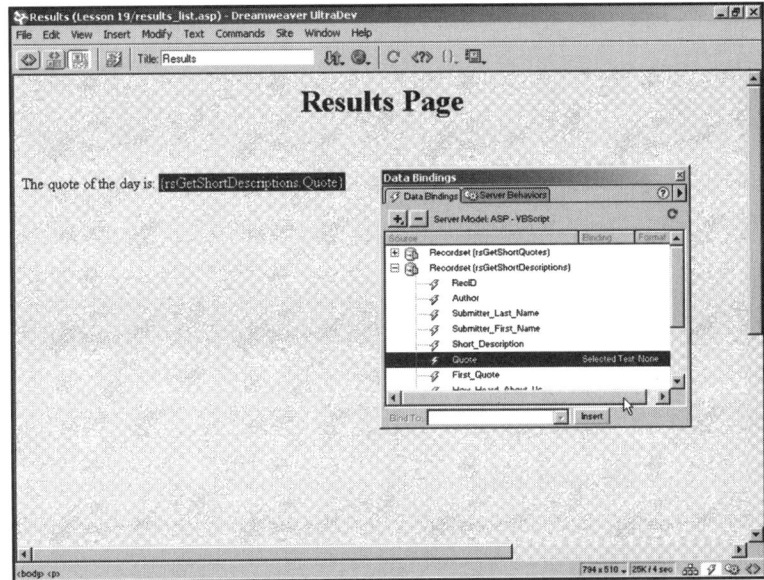

Figure 19.4

The Document window showing the Data Bindings tab, with the Query column inserted into the Web page.

NOTE: *Instead of clicking on the column name and then clicking on the Insert button to place a column into a Web page, you could also click on the column name in the Data Bindings tab and drag and drop it on the page where you want it located.*

To view dynamic content on a Web page, select the View menu Live Data option. UltraDev will display the first record in the rsGetShortDescriptions recordset, as shown in Figure 19.5.

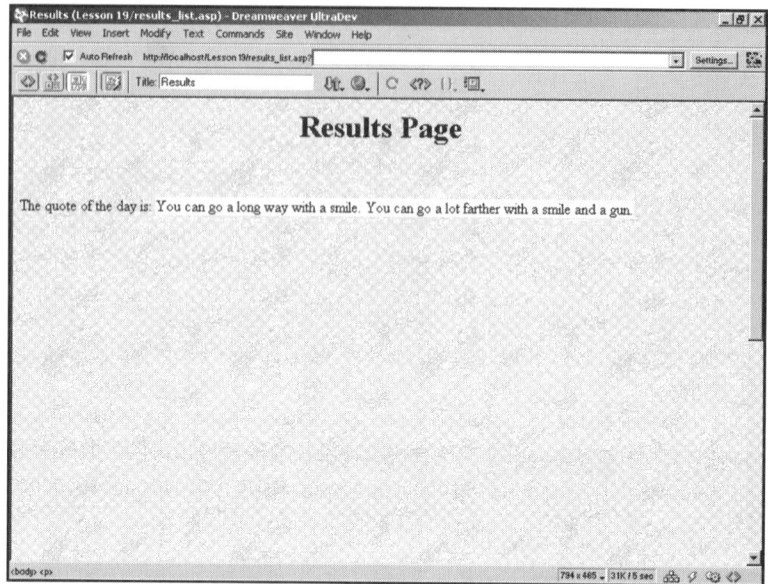

Figure 19.5

The Document window showing live data

Using Results Lists

Results lists contain the entire set of rows retrieved from a query against a database. You display a results list on a master page, and then allow the user to see certain columns of data that are specific to a selected row which resides on the master page on the detail page.

To save you time, I have created a page named Results_List_Begin.asp that contains some objects and controls already placed on the page, as shown in Figure 19.6. By the time you complete the page in this lesson, the page will look like Figure 19.7.

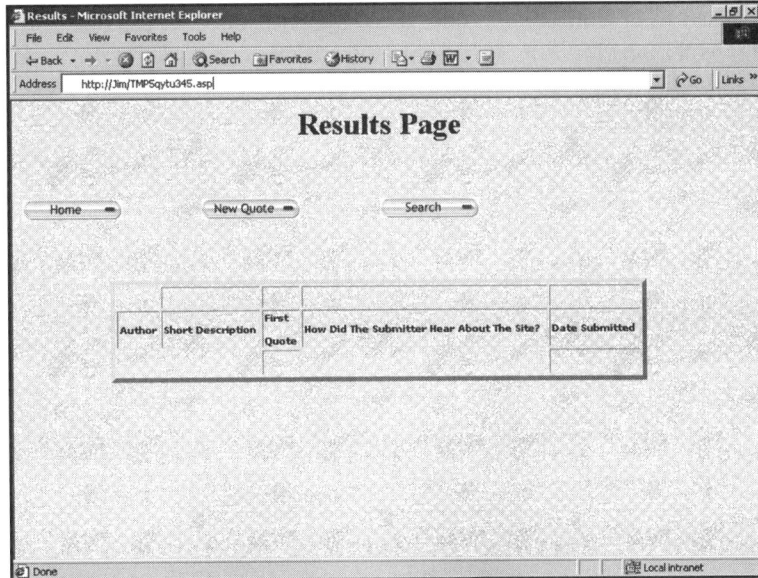

Figure 19.6

Use the Results_List_Begin.asp page as a starting point. You'll add the dynamic page components in this lesson.

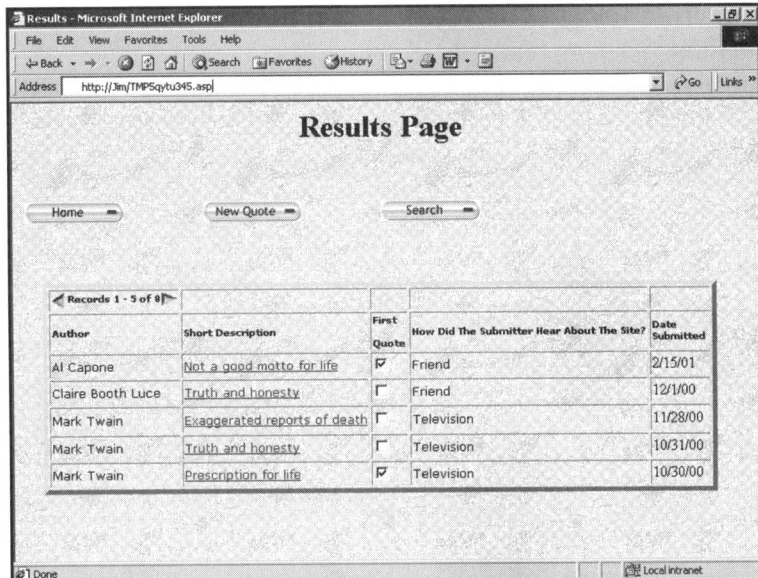

Figure 19.7

When done with this lesson, the Results List page will look like this.

As discussed in Lesson 18, populate the table embedded in the form on the ASP page with the data elements from the rsGetShortDescriptions recordset, as listed in Table 19.1. When you get done, your page should look similar to Figure 19.8.

Table 19.1   The table in the form is populated with these data elements from the rsGetShortDescriptions recordset

Column Heading	rsGetShortDescriptions Column Name
Author	Author
Short Description	Short_Description
First Quote	First_Quote
How Did The Submitter Hear About The Site	How_Heard_About_Us
Date Submitted	Date_Entered

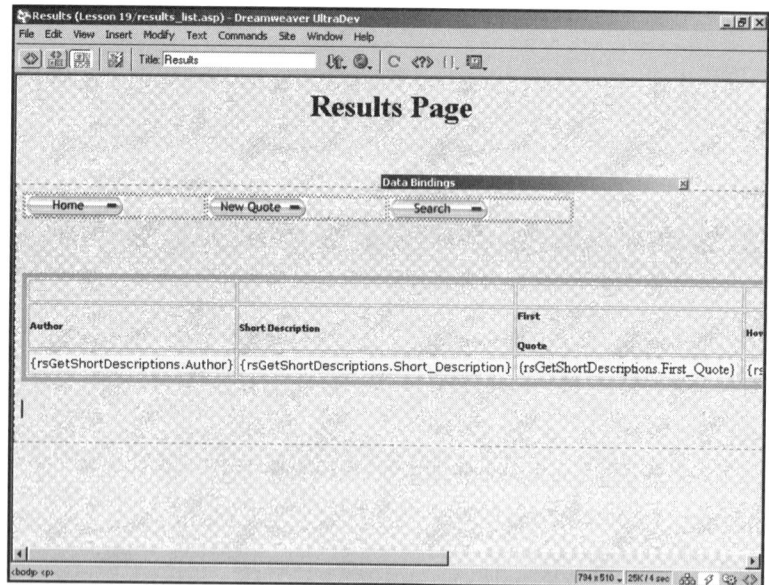

Figure 19.8

The Results_List_Begin.asp page after being populated with data elements from the rsGetShortDescriptions recordset.

NOTE: *The UltraDev placeholders that you see in the table cells expand the width of the cells. This is for usability purposes to assist you in working in the Document window. When the page is viewed in a browser window, the expansion of the cell widths will be based on the properties assigned to the cells. If you view the page in Live Data mode, it will look more like how you'd expect it to look in a browser, as shown in Figure 19.9.*

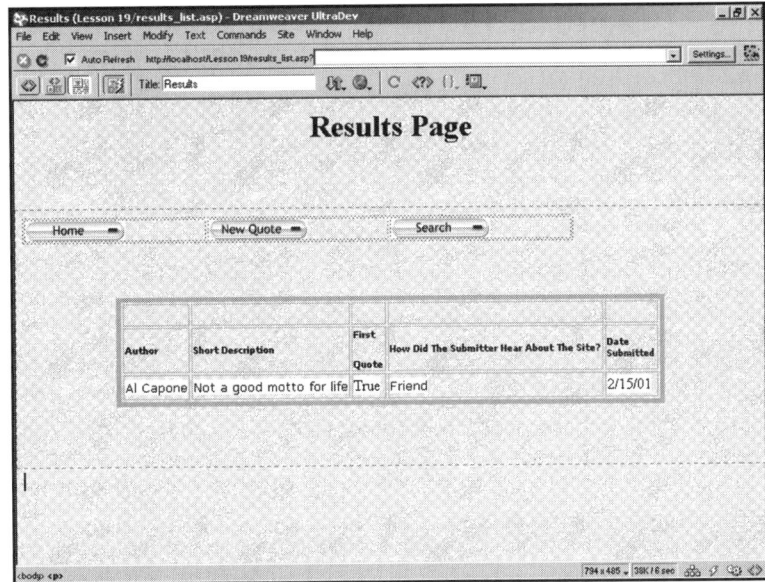

Figure 19.9

Viewing the page in Live Data mode allows you to see the page, with the dynamic data, as it will be viewed in a browser, with a single row of data inserted into the page from the recordset.

Displaying Multiple Records on a Page

Recall the Repeat Region server behavior discussed in Lesson 18, the one that returns multiple records in a recordset to a page. You will use that behavior now to populate the table with five rows of data at a time.

To add the Repeat Region server behavior to the table, perform these steps:

1. Select the entire row in the table on the form. This can be tricky. To do this, position your mouse pointer along the left border of the leftmost cell in the row that you want to select. UltraDev will turn the mouse pointer into an arrow. Click to select the row. You will know the entire row is selected when you see a border inside each of the cells in the row.

2. Open the Server Behaviors window by pressing the Ctrl+F9 key combination.

3. Within the Server Behaviors window, click on the plus sign (+) icon to open the Server Behaviors list.

4. Within the Server Behaviors list, click on the Repeat Region menu item. UltraDev, in turn, will display the Repeat Region window, as shown in Figure 19.10.

Figure 19.10

The Repeat Region server behavior provides the ability to display multiple records in a recordset on a page.

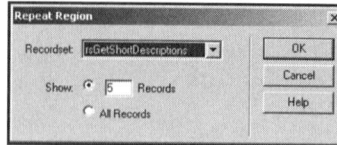

5. Within the Repeat Region window, specify that five records should be repeated by clicking on the Show radio button and entering the number 5 in the adjacent text box.

6. Click on the OK button. UltraDev will display a tab icon, similar to that shown in Figure 19.11, above the first cell in the row that has the Repeated Region Server Behavior.

Figure 19.11

The icon above the first cell in the repeated row shows you that this row has a Repeat Region Server Behavior associated with it.

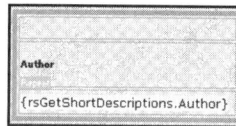

You will now be able to view the results of the addition of the Repeat Region server behavior by viewing the page in Live Data mode. When you do so, the page will look similar to that shown in Figure 19.12.

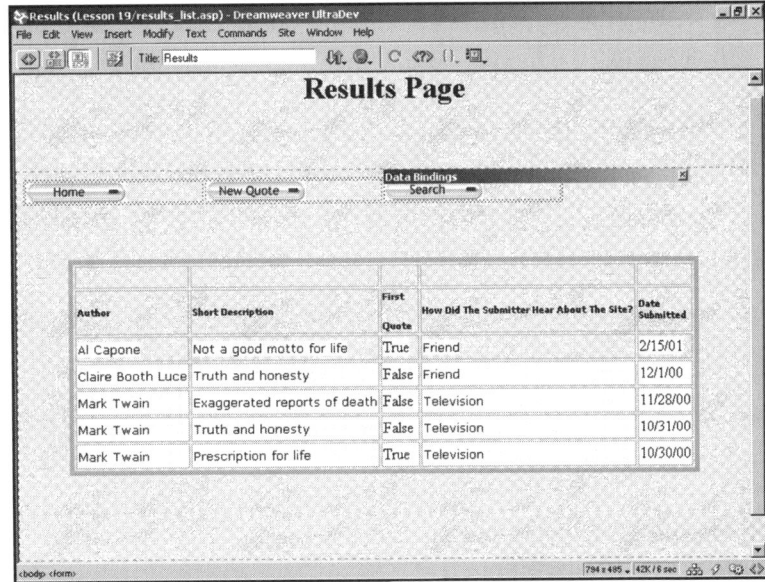

Figure 19.12

The Repeat Region server behavior viewed in Live Data mode.

Using a Check Box Bound to a Data Source

Currently, the information displayed under the column heading First Quote is not a check box, which is usually the control you use when data can either be Yes or No, or True or False.

To add a check box to a form that is bound to a data source, perform these steps:

1. Click in the cell underneath the First Quote heading that reads {*rsGetShortDescriptions. First_Quote*}. UltraDev will highlight the cell.

2. Press the Delete key to delete this data element.

3. Make sure the cursor remains in this cell (it might have shifted over to the cell to the right), and click on the check box icon on the Forms pane of the Objects palette. UltraDev will display a check box in the cell that was just vacant.

4. Click on the plus sign (+) icon to open the Server Behaviors list.

5. Within the Server Behaviors menu list, select the Dynamic Elements option and then choose Dynamic Check Box. UltraDev will display the Dynamic Check Box window.

6. Within the Dynamic Check Box window, click the data sources icon (this is the one that looks like a lightning bolt). UltraDev will open the Dynamic Data window.

7. Within the Dynamic Data window, click on the data element named First_Quote to identify the column in the recordset that will control the display of the check box. When you select this data element, the Dynamic Data window will look like Figure 19.13.

Figure 19.13

The Dynamic Data window with the First_Quote column identified as the data source.

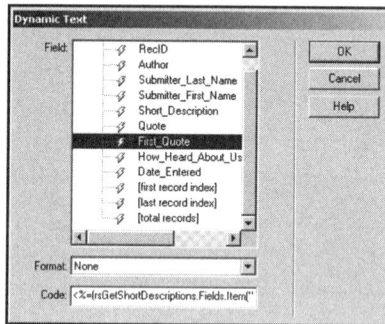

8. Click on the OK button to return to the Dynamic Check Box window.

9. Within the Equal To text box, type the word **True** to indicate that the check box is to appear checked when the value in the First_Quote column is equal to True. When you do this, the Dynamic Check Box window should look like Figure 19.14.

Figure 19.14

The Dynamic Check Box window allows you to configure the behavior of the dynamic check box.

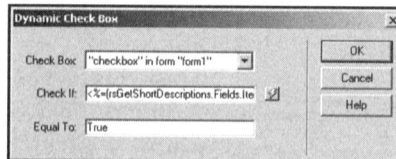

10. Click on the OK button to finish creating this behavior.

Navigating Through a Recordset

As you learned when you created the Repeat Region server behavior, you are only displaying five records at a time on the page. You may be wondering what happens when there are more than five records in the database, as is the case with the Random.mdb database. The answer is that you must add navigational elements to the page that let the visitor scroll through the recordset.

To add navigation through a recordset on a Web page, perform these steps:

1. Within the Recordset, add the following text to the cell in the first row of the first column: **Quotes a – b of c**. The table should now look like Figure 19.15.

Figure 19.15

You're going to add record navigation in the first cell of the table.

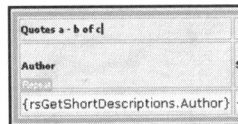

2. Using your mouse, highlight the letter *a* that follows the word Quotes. Within the Data Bindings tab of the Server Behaviors window, expand the recordset named rsGetShortDescriptions and click on the item named (first record index). UltraDev will highlight the item.

3. Click on the Insert button at the bottom of the Server Behaviors window, and you will note the changes shown in Figure 19.16.

Figure 19.16

The first element of the recordset navigation is in place.

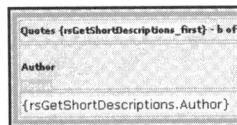

4. Using your mouse, highlight the letter *b* that follows the dash (–) sign. Within the Data Bindings tab, click on the item named (last record index).UltraDev will highlight the item.

5. Click on the Insert button at the bottom of the Server Behaviors window.

6. Using your mouse, highlight the letter *c* that follows the word of. Within the Data Bindings tab of the Server Behaviors window, click on the item named (total records). UltraDev will highlight the item.

7. Click on the Insert button at the bottom of the Server Behaviors window.

8. If you view the page in Live Data mode at this point, it will look similar to Figure 19.17.

Figure 19.17

Now you give the visitors a visual queue of what records they're looking at in the entire recordset.

Within a Web page, giving the visitors a way to know what records in the entire recordset they are looking at is good, but you should also give them a graphical way to move through the recordset.

To add the graphical elements that allow navigation through the recordset, perform these steps:

1. Click your mouse directly in front of the word Quote.

2. Select the Insert menu Image option. UltraDev, in turn, will display the Select Image Source window.

3. Within the window, navigate in the file list portion of the window into the Images subdirectory and double-click on the image named LeftGreenArrow.gif. UltraDev will place the image of a left-pointing green arrow to the left of the word Quote.

4. Press the spacebar once to put a space between the graphic and the word Quote.

5. Click your mouse directly behind the tag for the Total Quotes at the end of the cell.

6. Press the spacebar once to put a space between the graphic and the tag.

7. Select the Insert menu Image item. UltraDev will display the Select Image Source window.

8. Within the window, navigate in the file list portion of the window into the Images subdirectory and double-click on the image named RightGreenArrow.gif. UltraDev will place the image of a right-pointing green arrow to the left of the word Quotes.

9. Click on each of these images and resize them to be roughly 1.5 times the size of the text. After you are done, this portion of the page should look similar to Figure 19.18 when viewed in Live Data mode.

Figure 19.18

This is what the page should look like in Live Data mode with the navigation graphics.

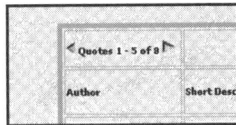

Now that you have added the graphical elements to the page, all that is left to do is to add a server behavior to each of the two images.

To add the Server Behaviors to the images that control the navigation, do the following:

1. Click on the first image, the one named LeftGreenArrow.gif. Next, click on the plus sign (+) icon to open the Server Behaviors list.

2. Within the Server Behaviors list, select the Move To Record option and choose Move To Previous Record. UltraDev will display the Move To Previous Record window with the name of the graphic already inserted in the Link text box, and the rsGetShortDescriptions recordset name already inserted in the Recordset drop-down list box, as shown in Figure 19.19. If this is not the case, make the modifications necessary.

Figure 19.19

The Move To Previous Record associates the linked control with the recordset to be navigated.

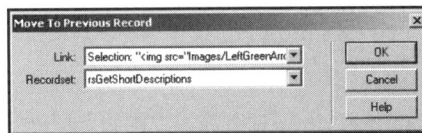

3. Click on the OK button.

4. Click on the second image, the one named RightGreenArrow.gif. Next, click on the plus sign (+) icon to open the Server Behaviors list.

5. Within the Server Behaviors list, select the Move To Record option and choose Move To Next Record. UltraDev will display the Move To Next Record window with the name of the graphic already inserted in the Link text box, and the rsGetShortDescriptions recordset name already inserted in the Recordset drop-down list box. If this is not the case, make the modifications necessary.

6. Click on the OK button.

When you are done with these modifications and you view your page in a browser, it should look like Figure 19.20.

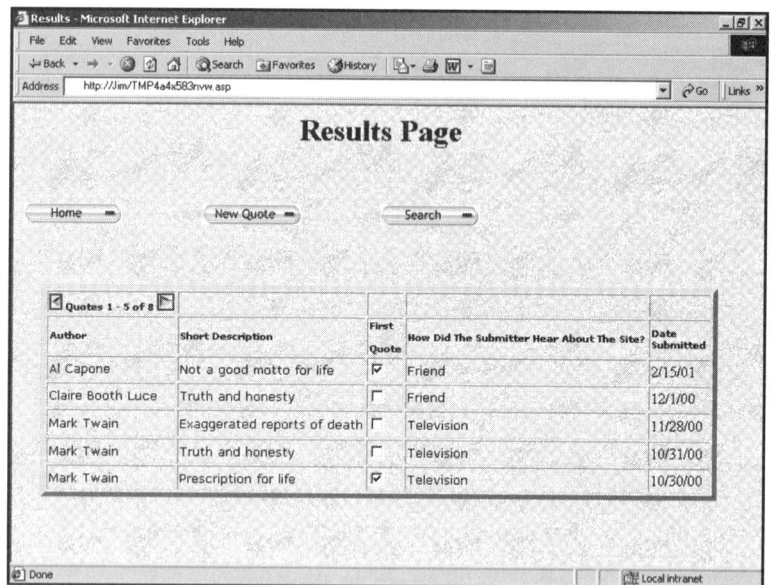

Figure 19.20

The Results page with repeating groups and navigation controls

Using Master-Detail Pages

The work you have done so far in this lesson has been to construct a master page of the data in your database. To give the visitor the ability to select one of the records on the master page and view the details of that record, or see additional information specific to that record, you must build a detail page and link the two pages together.

I have created a detail page for you, named Detail_Page.asp, and placed it in the Lesson 19 folder. An image of this page, in Live Data mode, is shown in Figure 19.21.

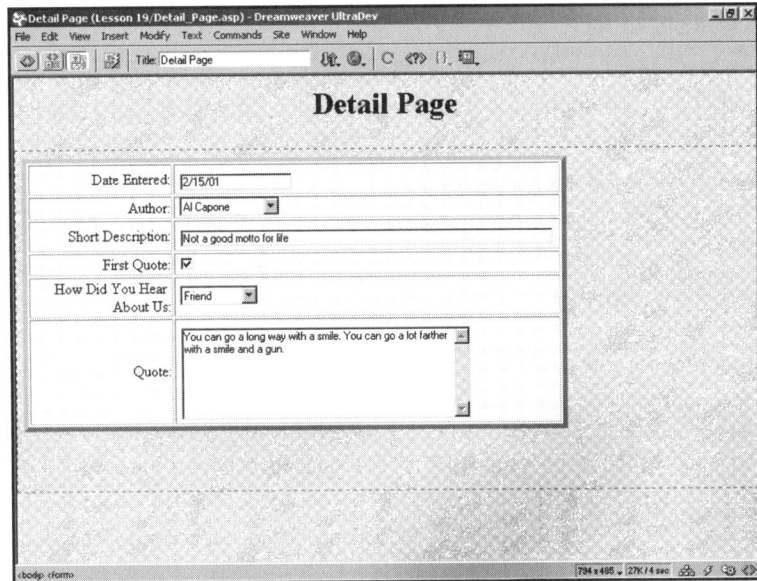

Figure 19.21

The detail page that you'll link to the page just created

There is nothing unique about this page that you have not already learned. What you will learn next is how to link the master page to the detail page.

You link a master page to a detail page by creating two Server Behaviors. One of these behaviors is on the master page and passes a parameter to the detail page so that the detail page can display with the correct record. The second of these behaviors is on the detail page, and its purpose is to accept the parameter received from the master page, locate the correct record in the recordset, and display that record.

Linking the Master Page to the Detail Page

The first step in the linking of a master page to a detail page is to create a Server Behavior on the master page that transfers an identifier (that uniquely identifies the record to display in the detail page) to the detail page.

In this lesson, the page named Results_List_Begin.asp is the master page, and a page named Detail_Page.asp is the detail page to which you will link.

To add a Server Behavior to the master page to pass a parameter to the detail page, perform these steps on the master page:

1. Click on the tag for the Short Description. This is directly under the column heading Short Description.

2. Click on the plus sign (+) icon to open the Server Behaviors menu list.

3. On the Server Behaviors menu list, select the Go To Detail Page option. UltraDev, in turn, will display the Go To Detail Page window with the name of the link that you are creating already inserted in the Link text box. Click on the Browse button next to the Detail Page text box. UltraDev will display the Select File window.

4. Within the Select File window, select the Detail_Page.asp page and click the OK button to return to the Go To Detail Page window.

<table>
<tr><td>

Figure 19.22

The Go To Detail Page window should look like this to properly create the link on the master page.

</td><td>

</td></tr>
</table>

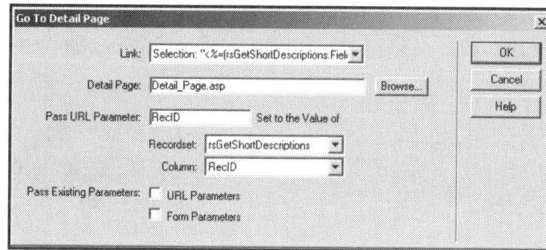

5. Within the Pass URL Parameter text box, supply a name for the tag that will be passed from one page to the next in the URL that contains the passed data. As you can see in Figure 19.22, I have chosen RecID.

6. Using the Recordset drop-down list, select the name of the recordset that contains the data element that you are passing. Because you usually will pass a data element that exists in the same recordset that was used to populate the master page, this is the name of the recordset you should specify in this control.

7. Within the Column drop-down list, specify the name of the column in the recordset that contains key data that uniquely identifies the record to load into the detail page. In the example

here, the column named RecID uniquely identifies each row of data in the recordset. This is the column name you should choose, too.

8. Click on the OK button to save the behavior. UltraDev will link the tag underneath the column heading Short Description.

Linking the Detail Page to the Master Page

Now that you have created the server behavior on the master page that sends a parameter on the URL to the detail page when a visitor clicks on the Short Description, you must create a server behavior on the detail page. The detail page will load the correct record into the page, based on the passed parameter.

To receive the passed parameter from the master page and load the correct record into the page, perform these steps:

1. Load the page Detail_Page.asp into the Document window.

2. Click your mouse anywhere in the editable portion of the page.

3. Click on the plus sign (+) icon to open the Server Behaviors list.

4. Within the Server Behaviors list, select the Move To option and choose Move To Specific Record. UltraDev, in turn, will display the Move To Specific Record window.

5. In the Move To Record In drop-down list, select the recordset named rsGetQuotes.

6. Within the Where Column drop-down list box, select the column named RecID.

Figure 19.23

The Move To Specific Record server behavior should be defined as you see here on the detail page.

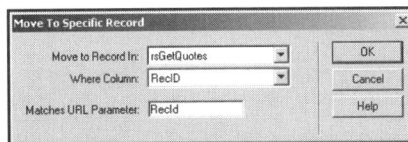

7. In the Matches URL Parameter text box, type the name of the passed parameter, which is RecID. After you are done, the Move To Specific Record window should look like Figure 19.23.

8. Click on the OK button.

That is it. Do not forget to save the pages you've been working on in the site. Test the quality of your work in a browser.

What You Must Know

In this lesson, you learned about some of the UltraDev's tools that allow dynamic access to data. In Lesson 20, "Extending Interactive Functions on Web Pages," you will learn how to add additional components on the Web page that extends the dynamic nature of the page.

Before you continue with Lesson 20, make sure you understand the following key concepts:

♦ Within UltraDev, you can easily define and use recordsets.

♦ Using a results list, you can display the results of a query on a Web page.

♦ By defining Server Behaviors, you make it easy for a visitor to navigate through a recordset.

♦ You use detail pages to view specific columns of a record in a recordset. Likewise, you use the master page to show the visitor the rows contained in the Recordset (Query).

♦ You can link a master page with a detail page to facilitate navigating through a recordset.

Lesson 20

Extending Interactive Functions on Web Pages

In Lesson 19, "Building Interactive Pages That Have Database Access," you learned how to pull data from live databases and use that data to build a highly interactive Web site. In this lesson, you will learn how to insert, update, and delete data to and from a database via a Web page. You will also learn how to build a Search function in your site. By the time you finish this lesson, you will understand the following key concepts:

◆ Within UltraDev, it is a very simple process to add an Update capability that lets you change database information via a Web page.

◆ UltraDev makes it easy for you to provide a Web page with the ability to add data to a database.

◆ When you add to a Web site a Delete function that removes data from a database, you need to provide ways to prevent users from maliciously destroying the information the database contains.

◆ Using UltraDev, you can quickly build Search functions into your Web site.

Updating a Database from a Web Page

In Lesson 19, you saw how to build a detail page that displays when a visitor clicks on a summary record displayed on a master page. Even though this is a valuable feature, frequently you want to perform certain maintenance functions on the detail record, such as these:

◆ **Update**. Modifies one or more columns of data, in one or more records.

◆ **Insert**. Places a new record into an existing database.

◆ **Delete**. Removes one or more records from an existing database.

In later sections in this lesson, you will learn how to add the Insert and Delete functions. To add an Update capability to a Web page, perform these steps:

1. Within the Detail_Page.asp page, click anywhere inside the form within which you want to place the Update button.

2. Using the Objects panel Forms panel, click on the Button icon to place a button on the form.

3. Double-click on the button just inserted. UltraDev, in turn, will display the Property Inspector.

4. Within the Property Inspector, enter the text values in the Button Name and Label fields, similar to those shown in Figure 20.1.

Figure 20.1

The Property Inspector window for the button that will trigger the Update Record server behavior.

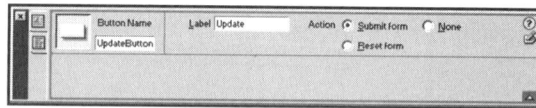

5. Click on the OK button to close the Property Inspector.

6. Click on the Update button to select it.

7. Within the Server Behaviors window, click on the plus (+) sign to add a new Server Behavior. UltraDev, in turn, will display the Server Behaviors window.

8. Within the Server Behavior window, click on the Update Record menu item. UltraDev will display the Update Record window.

9. Within the Update Record window Connection drop-down list, click on the connLesson item to select it.

10. Within the Table to Update drop-down list, click on the Quotes item to select this table as the table to update.

11. In the Select Record drop-down list box, click on the name of the recordset that contains the list of records to select from, which in this case is the rsGetQuotes recordset.

12. Within the Unique Key Column, click on the RecID column name to select it as the column that uniquely identifies each record.

13. Using the After Updating, Go To drop-down list, click on the name of the page to which the user will navigate after the database is updated. For this example, the page you select should be the page Results_List_Begin.asp.

14. Within the Get Values From drop-down list box, click on the form name form1 (this is the default name UltraDev assigns when you insert a form on a page).

15. Within the Form Elements list box, scroll through the list for the names of elements on the form that should be used to update a column in the database. When you click on an item in the Form Elements list, UltraDev will highlight the item, which lets you modify the item's values by clicking on the Column and Submit As drop-down list.

16. After you are done making these changes, the Update Record window should look similar to that shown in Figure 20.2.

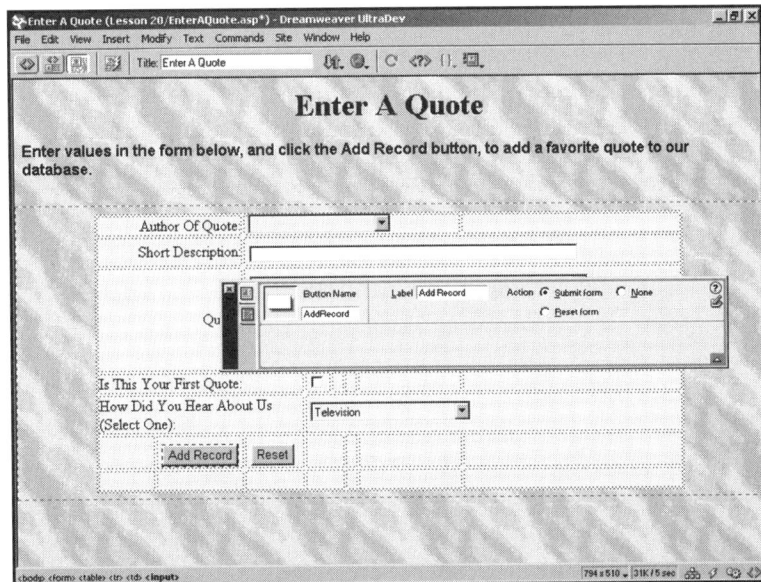

Figure 20.2

This is how the Update Record window should look after you have made the changes to define the Update Record server behavior.

17. Click on the OK button to save this server behavior and to return to the Document window.

Save the page and open the Results_List_Begin.asp page in your browser. After you click on Short Description for a quote, you will come to the detail page. Make a change on the detail page, and then click on the Update button. The site will take you back to the Results_List_Begin.asp page, where you can select another record to update by clicking on its Short Description.

Inserting a New Record in a Database

Updating a record to a database from a Web page is relatively easy to do in UltraDev. As you will see in this section, adding a record to a database from a Web page is just as easy (maybe easier).

Within the Lesson 20 folder on this book's companion disk, you will find a form named EnterAQuote.asp. Load that form into the Document window. To complete the processing necessary to insert a record into a database from this page, perform these steps:

1. Within each of two adjacent cells at the bottom of the table on the form, insert two form buttons, labeled **Add Record** and **Reset**.

2. Double-click on the Reset button. UltraDev, in turn, will display the Properties Inspector for this control.

3. Within the Properties Inspector for the Reset button, click on the Action radio button that reads Reset Form.

4. Double-click on the Add Record button to display the Properties Inspector for this control.

5. Within the Properties Inspector for the Add Record button, click on the Action radio button that reads Submit form to select it. Also, type a new Button Name of **AddRecord**. When done, your page should look similar to that shown in Figure 20.3.

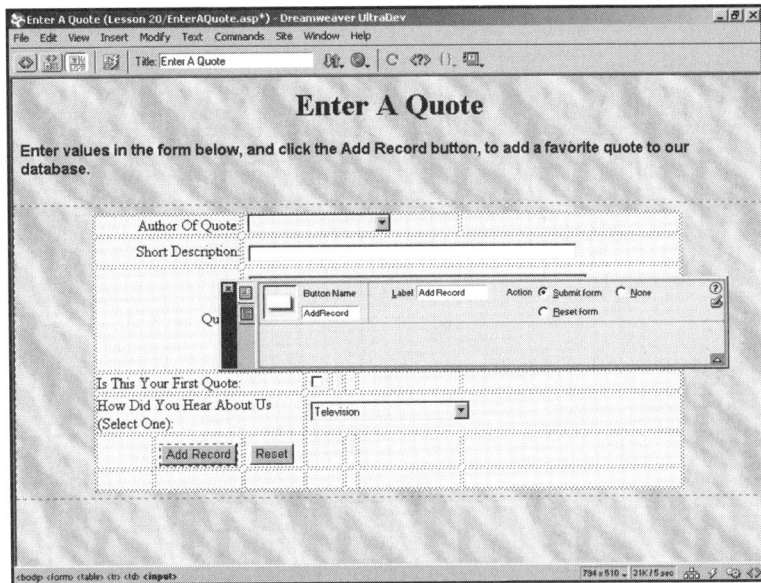

Figure 20.3

The Enter A Quote page with the Add Record and Reset buttons added.

The Reset button's behavior is controlled by the Action that you specified for it in Step 3. Next, you must create a server behavior for the Add Record button that inserts the record into the database and then displays the appropriate page to the visitor, by performing these steps:

1. Within the Enter A Quote Page, click on the Add Record button to select it.

2. Within the Server Behaviors window, click on the plus (+) icon to view the list of server behaviors you can create.

3. From within the list of behaviors, click on the Insert Record server behavior. UltraDev will display the Insert Record window, which is very similar to the Update Record window you saw in the last section.

4. Within the Connection drop-down list box, click on the connLesson item to select it.

5. Using the Insert Into Table drop-down list, click on the Quotes table name to select this as the table into which the page will insert data.

6. Within the After Inserting, Go To URL text box, enter the page name **index.html**.

7. Within the Get Values From drop-down list, click on the name of the form that contains the data that the page will insert into the database. This page only has one form, so click on the EnterQuote item.

8. Within the Form Elements list box, scroll through the list for the names of elements on the form that should be used to update the columns in the database. When you click on an item in the Form Elements list, UltraDev highlights the item, and you can modify values for that item by clicking on the Column and Submit As drop-down list boxes.

9. After you are done making these changes, the Insert Record window should look like Figure 20.4.

Figure 20.4

The Insert Record window after you have made the changes to define the Insert Record server behavior.

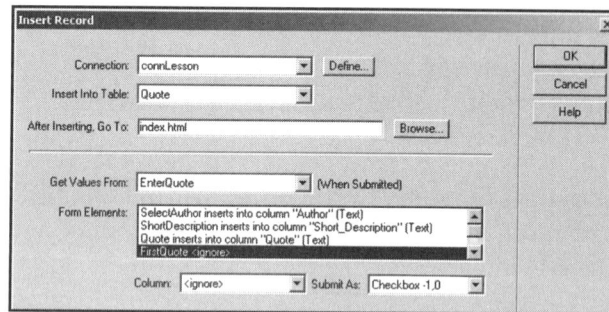

10. Within the Insert Record window, click on the OK button to save this server behavior and go back to the Document window.

Save the page and open the Results_List_Begin.asp page in your browser. After you click on the New Quote button at the top of the form, your browser should open the Enter A Quote page. Within that page, you should then be able to fill in the various controls on the page and then click on the Add Record button. After you click on the Add Record button, the page will add the record (whose values you supplied in the form) to the database, and your browser will display the Index.html page.

Deleting a Record from the Database

Within most applications, placing the Delete function on the detail page normally makes the most sense. Therefore, load that page into the Document window.

To delete a record from a database, you must trigger the Delete action using a form the user submits. The most common way to submit a form is to place a button on a form with the Submit form action.

NOTE: *You can only have one button on a form that has the Submit action. This is a UltraDev constraint. However, you can have reset buttons and buttons with the action "none" selected.*

To create the controls and behaviors to delete a record from the database, perform these steps:

1. Within the detail page, below the existing form, click your mouse to position the cursor.

2. Using the Objects Inspector Forms palette, click on the Form icon to place a Form object on the page at the current cursor location.

3. Again using the Forms palette, click on the Button icon to place a button inside the Form object just inserted.

4. Double-click on the button just inserted. UltraDev will display the Properties Inspector window for the button selected.

5. Within the Properties Inspector window, change the Label to **Delete**. Also, change the name of the button to **DeleteRecord**. After you are done, the page should look similar to that shown in Figure 20.5

6. Within the Property Inspector, click on the Delete button to select it.

7. Click on the plus (+) icon on the Server Behaviors Inspector. UltraDev, in turn, will display the various server behaviors you can select.

8. Within the Server Behaviors list, click on the Delete Record server behavior. UltraDev will display the Delete Record window.

9. Within the Connection drop-down list, click on the connLesson item to select it.

10. Within the Delete From Table drop-down list, click on the Quotes item to select this table as the table the Web page will update.

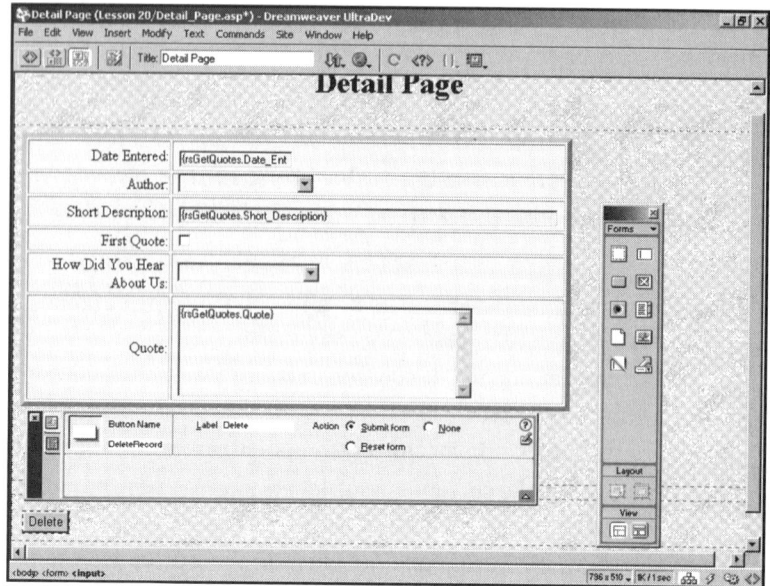

Figure 20.5

The Property Inspector with the values set for the Delete button.

11. Using the Select Record drop-down list, click on the name of the recordset that contains the list of records to select from, which in this case is the rsGetQuotes recordset.

12. Within the Unique Key Column, click on the RecID column name to select it as the column that uniquely identifies each record.

13. Using the After Deleting, Go To drop-down list, click on the name of the page to which the user will navigate after the Web site updates the database. For this example, the page you select should be Results_List_Begin.asp.

14. Within the Get Values From drop-down list, click on the form named form 1. (This is the default name UltraDev assigns when you insert a form on a page.)

15. Using the Delete By Submitting drop-down list, select the item form2, which is the form you just added that contains the Delete button.

16. After you are done making these changes, the Update Record window should look like Figure 20.6.

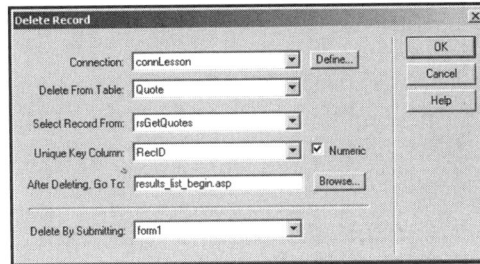

Figure 20.6

The Delete Record window after you have made the changes to define the Delete Record server behavior.

Save the page and open the Results_List_Begin.asp page in your browser. After you click on a Short Description for a quote, your Web site will display the detail page. After you click on the Delete button, the page will delete the record from the database, and your browser will display the Results_List_Begin.asp page, on which you can select another record to update or delete by clicking on its Short Description.

Adding a Search Component to Your Page

Building a Search capability on your site adds tremendous flexibility to it and makes finding information very easy for visitors. Using UltraDev, it is very easy to accomplish adding a Search page to the site. Now that you have added the Insert, Update, and Delete functions to the site, you can add a Search component.

Although you can search on any data element stored in your database, the three components you will search for within this application are the following:

◆ Date the quote was entered

◆ Words contained in the quote

◆ Author of the quote

NOTE: *The item(s) you search for does not need to display on the Results page. In this section, you will find that one of the components upon which you will search is contained within the quote—although you are not displaying the actual quote on the Results.asp page. The reason why you can do this is that the rsGetShortDescriptions recordset query retrieves the column named Quote from the database, although it's not actually displayed on the Results.asp page. Because the record is retrieved from the database, that gives you the ability to work with, and search on, the data contained in it.*

Building the Search Page

Within the Lesson 20 folder on this book's companion CD-ROM, you will find a page to get you started building the Search page, called Search.asp. Open that page in UltraDev. The page should look like the one shown in Figure 20.7.

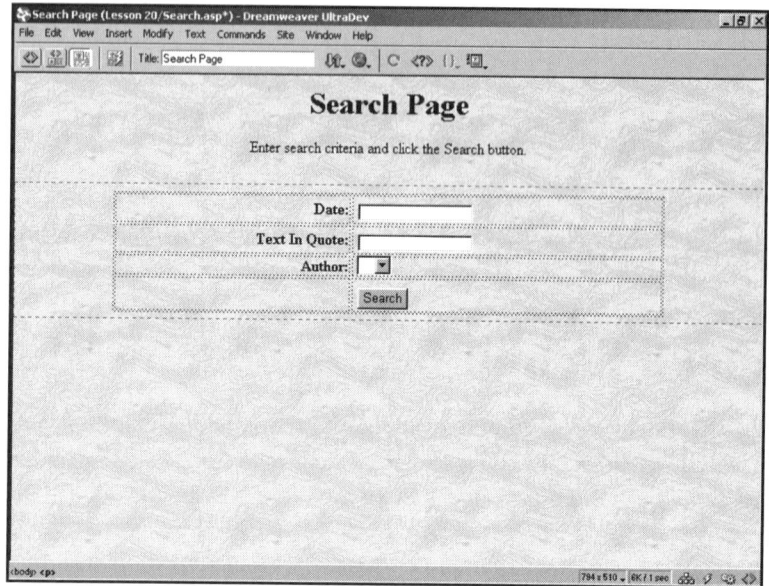

Figure 20.7

The Search page that you will build the functions on to initiate the search.

Within the page, the first thing you must do is to change the method the page uses to transfer data to and from other pages. As you recall, there are two standard methods: POST and GET.

Whereas the POST method is useful for transferring large amounts of data, the GET method is useful for transferring small amounts of data between pages. Because we'll be transferring only small amounts of data between the Search page and the Results page, the GET method is better for our purposes.

To modify the method the form uses to transfer data to other pages, perform these steps:

1. Within the Search page, click your mouse anywhere inside the form. UltraDev, in turn, will display the <form> tag within the status bar that appears at the bottom of the page, as shown in Figure 20.8.

Figure 20.8

The <form> tag within the status bar indicates the position in the Document window of the cursor.

`<body> <form> <table> <tr> <td>`

2. Within the status bar, click on the `<form>` tag. UltraDev, in turn, will display the Property Inspector for the form.

3. Within the Form Property Inspector, click on the Method drop-down list and select the GET method, as shown in Figure 20.9.

Figure 20.9

Use the GET method to transfer small amounts of data between Web pages.

Form Name
form1

Action

Method GET

Within the form, notice the drop-down list box named Author. When I created the form, I added a Recordset (Query) called rsAuthor for you. You will need to add a Dynamic Server behavior to the Author drop-down list box to attach the rsAuthor Recordset (Query) to it, by performing these steps:

1. Within the Document window, click on the Author drop-down list box to highlight it.

2. Within the Server Behaviors window, click on the plus (+) icon. UltraDev, in turn, will display a list of the various server behaviors you can select.

3. Within the Server Behaviors list, click on the Dynamic Elements Server Behavior, and then click on the Dynamic List/Menu server behavior. UltraDev will display the Dynamic List/Menu window.

4. Within the Dynamic List/Menu window, populate the controls so that they appear similar to those shown in Figure 20.10.

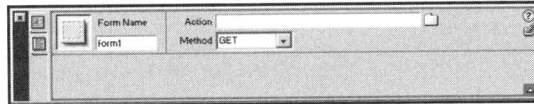

Figure 20.10

The Dynamic List/Menu associates the rsAuthor Recordset (Query) server behavior with the Author drop-down list box.

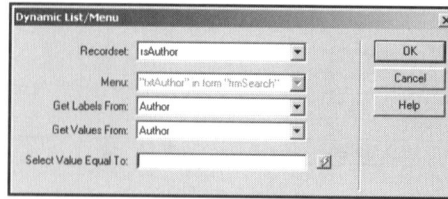

5. Click on the OK button to save the changes.

Because the GET method passes data from one page to the next by passing the name of the control creating the data element along with the actual data pulled from the control in the URL, you must change the names of the three controls on the form, by performing these steps:

1. Within the Document window, double-click on the Date text box. UltraDev, in turn, will display the Property Inspector for the text box.

2. Within the Property Inspector, change the name of the control to **txtDate**, as shown in Figure 20.11.

Figure 20.11

The txtDate text box control for the date

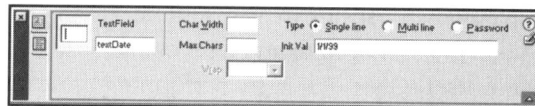

3. To make things easier for the site visitor, it is a good idea to place a value representing the earliest date possible in a control that is going to be used to search for a date in a database. Within the Init Val text box, type the value **1/1/99**.

4. Click on the OK button to close the Property Inspector and save the modifications.

5. Double-click on the Text In Quote text box. UltraDev will display the Property Inspector for the text box.

6. Within the Property Inspector, change the name of the control to **txtTextInQuote**.

7. Click on the OK button to close the Property Inspector and save your changes.

8. Double-click on the Author drop-down list box. UltraDev will display the Property Inspector for the drop-down list box.

9. Within the Property Inspector, change the name of the control to **txtAuthor**.

10. Click on the OK button to close the Property Inspector and save your changes.

Within the Author drop-down list box, the visitor will be able to select the name of an author from which to select a quote. In some cases, a visitor may not care about a specific author, but rather, may simply want to view the available quotes. For such cases, you must give the user the ability to select all the authors to search for a specific quote, by performing these steps:

1. Within the Document window, double-click on the Author drop-down list box. UltraDev will display the Property Inspector for the control, as shown in Figure 20.12.

Figure 20.12

The Property Inspector for the Author control, before adding the ALL List Value.

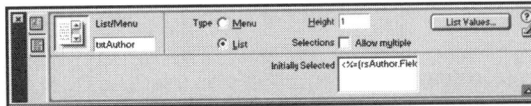

2. Within the List/Menu Property Inspector, click on the List Values button. UltraDev will display the List Values window, as shown in Figure 20.13.

Figure 20.13

The List Values window is where you will add an additional value to display in the list of available selections.

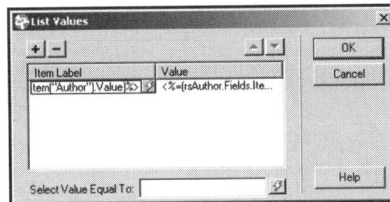

3. Within the List Values window, click on the plus (+) icon to add a new item to the list. UltraDev will open a cell below the Item Label column heading.

4. Within the cell, type the word **All** in the open cell, and press the Tab key. UltraDev will open a cell under the Value column heading.

5. Within the cell, type the percent sign, %, which is a wildcard character to an MS Access database that means the same as "Give me everything" or, in this case, "Use all the authors."

6. You still have a problem, though, in that the list item All is going to display at the bottom of the list of items in the Author drop-down list box. You can change the location that the word All displays in the list by clicking on the up arrow. After you do this, the List Values window should look like that shown in Figure 20.14.

Figure 20.14

The List Values window after you've inserted the word All to appear as the first item in the list.

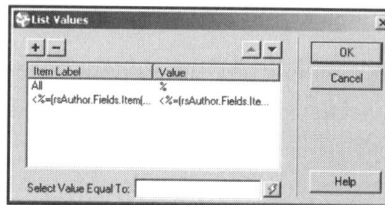

7. Click on the OK button to save your changes.

That is all the modifications that are necessary to the Search page to pass the necessary information to the Results page to do a search. Save your changes and open the Results_List_Begin.asp page in the Document window.

Modifying the Results Page

When you create pages to manage data that resides in a database, you must provide a page that the user can use to locate and update information.

Before you can do this, you need to make sure the form on the Results page uses the GET method. Using the process described previously for the modifications to the Search page, change the Method entry on the Results page to GET.

Next, you must modify the rsGetShortDescriptions Recordset (Query) to accept the passed URL parameters and to query the database applying the desired search criteria, by performing these steps:

1. Within the Server Behaviors window, double-click on the Recordset (rsGetShortDescriptions) behavior to open the Recordset window with the query displayed, as shown in Figure 20.15.

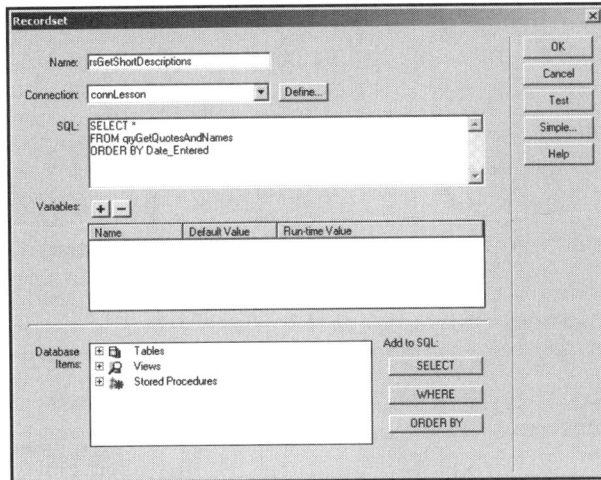

Figure 20.15

The rsGetShortDescriptions Recordset (Query) before any modifications are made.

2. Near the bottom of the Recordset window, within the Database Items tree display, click on the plus (+) sign that appears next to Views to expand the tree.

3. Within the expanded tree for the Views database item, click on the Date_Entered column, and then click on the WHERE button. The Recordset window should look similar to that shown in Figure 20.16.

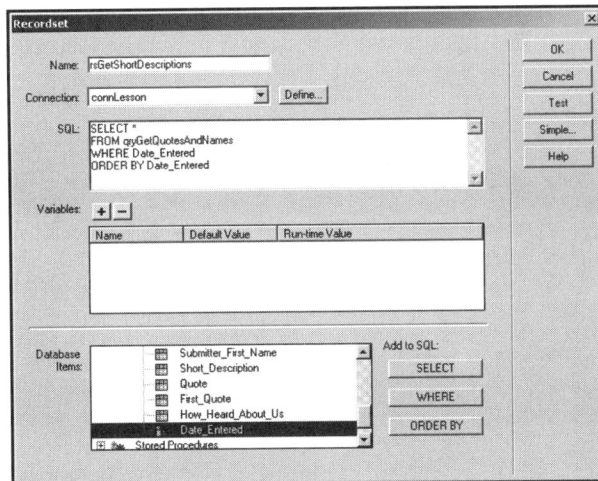

Figure 20.16

The Recordset window creating the first Where clause.

4. To identify the first variable passed to the Results page, which will then be the first selection criteria executed when the visitor queries the database, click on the plus (+) icon that appears next to the word Variables. Your cursor will move to an open cell underneath the Name column.

5. Within the cell, type the name **varDate**, which is the name of the Date control you specified on the Search page. Press the Tab key to move the cursor to the next column.

6. Within the Default Value cell, enter the characters: **1/1/99**. This is the value of the variable that will be placed in the SELECT statement. Press the Tab key to move the cursor to the next cell.

7. Within the Run-time Value cell, enter the text **Request("txtDate")**. This is the name of the Date control you specified on the Search page.

Next, you need to add this variable to the SQL statement by performing these steps:

1. Within the active Window, click immediately after the words WHERE Date_Entered to position the cursor there.

2. In this case, you will search for dates that are greater than or equal to (>=) the date passed in the URL parameters. Within the text box, type >= #**varDate**#. The pound sign in the variable name tells the MS Access database that the passed parameter is a date. You would not use this convention if you are not passing a date. The Recordset window should now look like Figure 20.17.

Next, you must add an additional selection item to the WHERE clause, which tells the query to search the actual quote, by performing these steps:

1. Within the active window, click on the Quote column that appears in the database tree at the bottom of the window. UltraDev, in turn, will highlight the column.

2. Click on the WHERE button. UltraDev will add the words AND Quote to the WHERE clause in the SQL window.

3. Because you want to search for quotes that contain the words the visitor enters within the Search window, you must add the reserved word **LIKE** in the SQL window, after the words

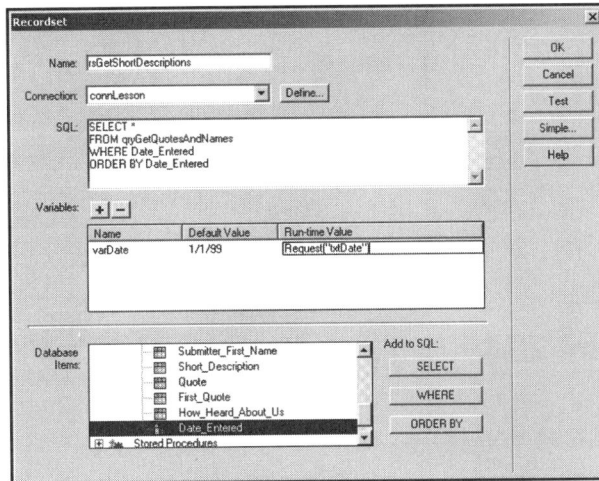

Figure 20.17

The Recordset window after the first selection criteria is added.

WHERE Date_Entered >= #varDate# AND Quote. The LIKE clause has special meaning to SQL: It allows you to query a database for values that are similar to the value entered.

4. You must identify the second variable that is transferred to the Results page that will be the second selection criteria when the page queries the database. You do this by clicking on the plus (+) icon next to the word Variables. Your cursor will move to an open cell in the next vacant row underneath the Name column.

5. Within the cell, type the name **varQuoteText**, which is the name of the control you specified on the Search page. Press the Tab key to move the cursor to the next column.

6. Within the Default Value cell, type % to extract *all* quotes if the visitor has not entered any text to search for in the control on the Search page.

7. Within the Run-time Value cell, enter the text **Request("txtTextInQuote")**, which is the name of the control you specified on the Search page.

Next, you must add this variable to the SQL statement:

1. Within the active window, click within the WHERE clause that immediately follows the words Quote LIKE.

2. Type the name of the variable for the quote text, enclosed in quotes and percent signs. The Recordset window should look similar to that shown in Figure 20.18.

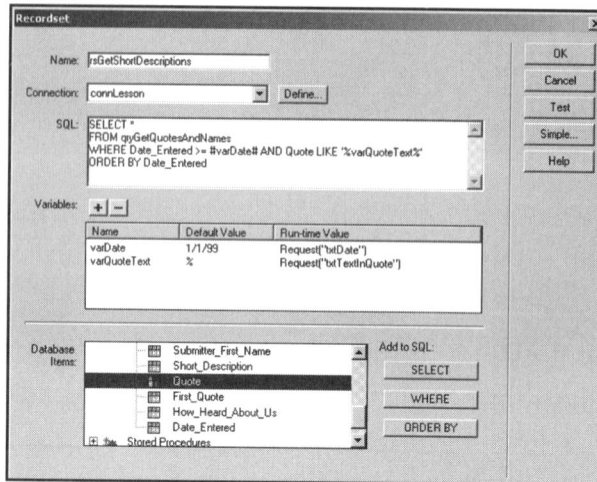

Figure 20.18

The Recordset window after you add the second selection criteria.

Next, you must add an additional selection item to the WHERE clause. The WHERE clause will allow you to retrieve the name of the quote that the site visitors select. You do this by performing these steps:

1. Within the database tree that appears at the bottom of the active window, click on the Author column. UltraDev, in turn, will highlight the column.

2. Click on the WHERE button, and UltraDev will add the words AND Author to the WHERE clause in the SQL window.

3. You must identify the third variable passed into the Results page that will be the third selection criteria when the page initiates a query to the database. You do this by clicking on the plus (+) icon that appears next to the word Variables. Your cursor will move to an open cell in the next vacant row underneath the Name column.

4. Within the cell, type the name **varAuthor**, which is the name of the control you specified on the Search page. Press the Tab key to move the cursor to the next column.

5. Within the Default Value cell, type % to extract all quotes if the visitor has not entered an author to search for in the control on the Search page.

6. Within the Run-time Value cell, enter the text **Request("txtAuthor")**, which is the name of the control you specified on the Search page.

Finally, you must add this variable to the SQL statement, by performing these steps:

1. Within the active window, click in the WHERE clause immediately after the words AND Author.

2. Type the word **LIKE**, followed by the name of the variable for the author, enclosed in quotes and percent (%) signs, as shown in Figure 20.19.

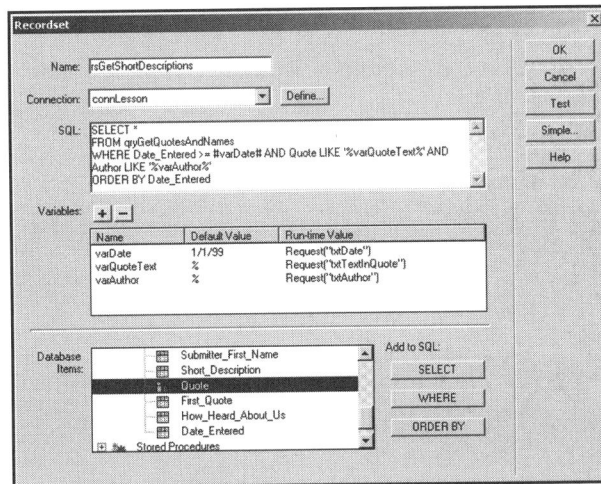

Figure 20.19

The Recordset window after the third selection criteria is added.

3. Click on the OK button to save the changes to the recordset.

Save and then open the Search page in a browser, enter search criteria, and view the filtered result set in the Results page.

NOTE: *Within the Lesson 20 directory of the CD-ROM accompanying this book, there are two pages that provide the completed Search and Results page for this site. You can use these as models if something does not work correctly on the modifications to the pages that you've made here. The Search page is named Search_Done.asp, and the Results page is named Results_List.asp.*

What You Must Know

In this lesson, you learned how to extend the capabilities on your site by adding Insert, Update, and Delete functions. In Lesson 21, "Using User Logins," you will learn how to incorporate site security using Login functionality into your site. Before you continue with Lesson 21, make sure you understand the following key concepts:

◆ Within UltraDev, it is easy to add a page to a Web site that inserts data into a database.

◆ Using server behaviors, you can implement Update and Delete functions on a Web page that let you modify or delete information a database contains.

◆ Search functions are easy to implement in UltraDev, and add great value to the visitor by giving them the ability to quickly locate information.

Lesson 21

Using User Logins

In Lesson 20, "Extending Interactive Functions on Web Pages," you learned how to extend capabilities via a Web page to insert, update, and delete information that resides in a database. You also learned how to build a Search function in your site. In this lesson, you will learn how to incorporate site security using Login functionality. By including security in your site, you can control which users can access what data. By the time you finish this lesson, you will understand the following key concepts:

◆ UltraDev version 4 has a number of very powerful features to control access to pages.

◆ Using a Login function, you can require that a user specify a username and password before he or she can access specific pages on your site.

◆ After a user logs in to your system, UltraDev tracks information about the user, which developers refer to as *session information*.

◆ UltraDev provides several built-in server behaviors you can use to implement and enforce site security.

◆ Within your site, you can use session information to prevent a user from navigating to certain pages unless they have successfully logged in.

Understanding User Authentication Server Behaviors

Beginning with version 4 of UltraDev, you have the ability to incorporate server sehaviors that greatly simplify the process of authenticating a user's access to your site, and controlling the access to certain pages after you have granted a user authorization. The server behaviors in Table 21.1 summarize each of these behaviors.

Table 21.1 Server behaviors that control access to your site and the pages on your site

Behavior Name	Description
Log In User	Verifies a username and password entered on a Web page against data stored in a database. If the username and password are verified, control passes to another page in the site. Otherwise, you can send the user to a different page.
Restrict Access To Page	Verifies that a user has the proper credentials to access a Web page before a browser displays the page contents.
Log Out User	Logs out the current user and terminates their session information. This is usually done as a preliminary step before another username is entered into the system by the same visitor. Often, this is done to control access to certain pages, depending on the username entered.
Check New Username	Enables the visitor to verify that a new username they would like to create currently does not exist in the authentication tables.

In the following sections, you will see how to create and use each of these server behaviors.

Using the Log In User Server Behavior

Within your site, you can use the Log In User server behavior to verify that the Login Name and Password a visitor enters reside within a user-access database table. After a user successfully logs in to your site (via the Log In User server behavior), UltraDev establishes for the user a session variable that remains active for as long as the user's browser is attached to your site. If the visitor leaves your site, or closes his or her browser, all session variables are lost, and the user will need to log in again should he or she return to your site.

To use the Login feature, you must first define a table in your database that contains valid Login Names and Passwords. As shown in Figure 21.1, I have created these columns in an MS Access table named Users.

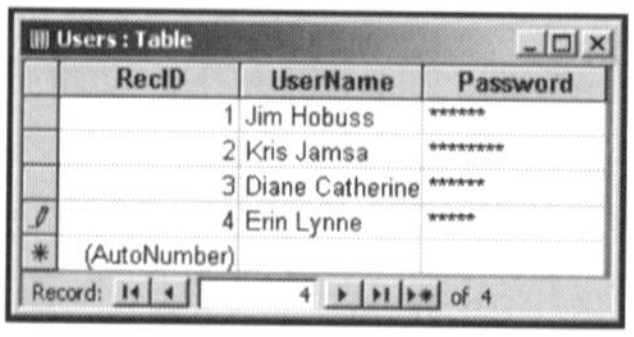
Users : Table

RecID	UserName	Password
1	Jim Hobuss	*******
2	Kris Jamsa	*********
3	Diane Catherine	*******
4	Erin Lynne	*****
(AutoNumber)		

Record: 4 of 4

Figure 21.1

The Users table contains a list of valid users to your site, with their passwords.

Your next step is to create a page that will hold the login controls and server behavior, which I have also done, as shown in Figure 21.2.

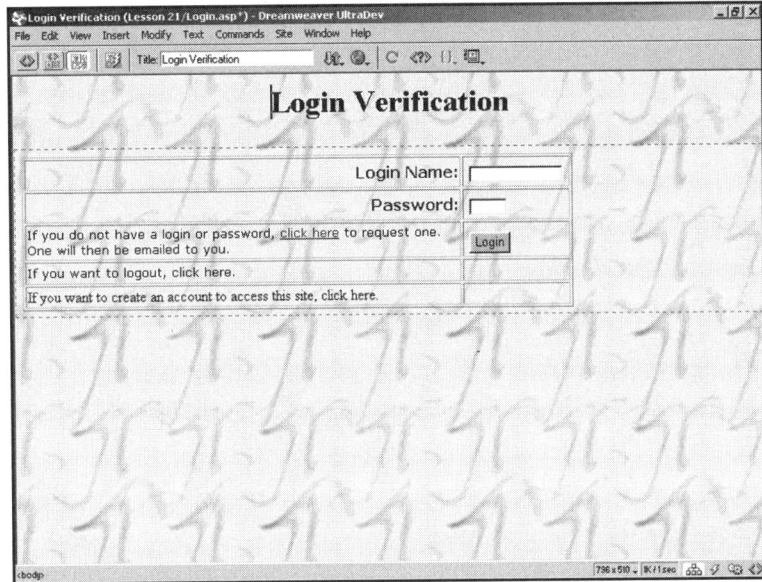

Figure 21.2

The Login Verification page gives visitors access to enter their Login Name and Passwords.

You can find the Login Verification page within the Lesson 21 directory on the CD-ROM that accompanies this book. The actual name for this page is Login.asp. It is a shell of a page, meaning there is really no functionality included on it. I created the page to save you the time of creating it for this lesson. You get the fun part, which is to add the behaviors and links to make the page's security function as it should.

To create a server behavior to verify the Login Name and Password a user enters, perform these steps:

1. Within the Login.asp page, click on the Login button to select it.

2. Access the Server Behaviors window by pressing Ctrl + F9. Within the Server Behaviors window, click on the plus (+) icon. UltraDev, in turn, will display a menu of the different server behaviors.

3. Within the menu, click on the User Authentication server behavior, and then click on the Log In User server behavior. UltraDev will display the Log In User window, as shown in Figure 21.3.

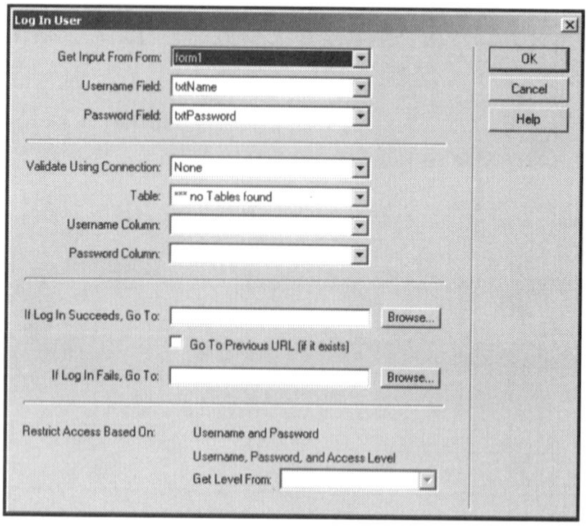

Figure 21.3

The Log In User window is where you describe how the site is to verify the Login Name and Password of someone visiting your site, and what the actions are if the authentication passes or fails.

4. Within the Get Input From Form drop-down list, click on the name of the form object that resides on the Web page that contains the Username and Password values you want to verify. In the example here, there is only one form on this page, form1.

5. Within the Username Field drop-down list, click on the name of the control on the form that contains the username text to validate, which in this case is the control txtName.

6. In the Password Field drop-down list, click on the name of the control on the form that contains the password text to validate. In this example, the control is txtPassword. I'll show you how to complete the remainder of the Login User window server behavior. Figure 21.4 shows you what the form should look like after you've completed the remaining steps.

7. Using the Validate Using Connection drop-down list, click on the name of the connection that contains access to the database table that the server behavior will check to validate the entered data. In this example, the connection is connLesson.

8. Within the Table drop-down list, click on the name of the database table the server behavior will check to validate the entered data. In the example here, the table is Users.

9. Using the Username Column drop-down list, click on the name of the column in the database table that contains the Username to validate against what was entered by the visitor. For this example, the field is UserName.

10. Within the Password Column drop-down list box, click on the name of the column in the database table that contains the Password to validate against what the user entered. In this example, the password field is Password.

11. In the If Log In Succeeds, Go To drop-down list, click on the Browse button. Then, click on the name of the page to which the visitor will navigate if the entered Login Name and Password are valid. In this example, the page is Search.asp.

12. Using the If Log In Fails, Go To drop-down list, click on the Browse button. Then, click on the name of the page to which the visitor will navigate if the Login Name and Password are not valid. In this example, the page is Index.html.

13. Within the Restrict Access Based On radio button group, click on the radio button that reads Username and Password. The radio button labeled Username, Password, and Access Level lets you further restrict access to pages based on a specified access level, as stored in a database.

14. The Log In User window should look similar to that shown in Figure 21.4. Click on the OK button to finish creating the server behavior.

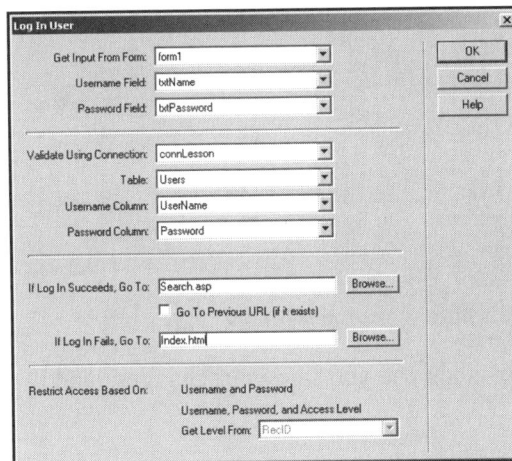

Figure 21.4

The Log In User window after all parameters are specified.

That is all there is to providing username and password protection to your site. Now, when the visitor accesses this page, they will have to enter a valid Username/Password combination to proceed forward through the site.

But, you are not quite done yet. You have to change the link on the Index.html page to go to the Login.asp page when the user clicks on the Find A Quote button, by performing these steps:

1. Within UltraDev, load the Index.html page into the Document window.

2. Double-click on the button at the bottom of the page that reads Find A Quote. UltraDev, in turn, will display the Insert Flash Button window.

3. Within the Insert Flash Button window, tab down to the Link control.

4. Click on the Browse button and then click on the Login.asp page as the name of the page to link to when a visitor clicks on the button. The Insert Flash Button window should look similar to that shown in Figure 21.5.

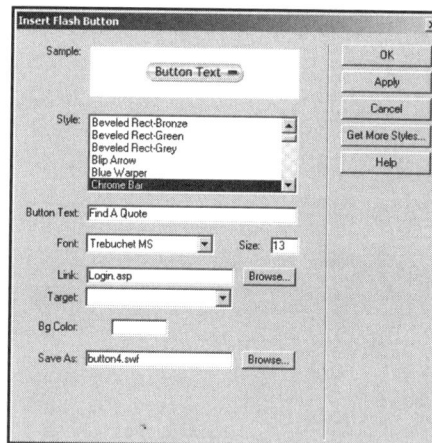

Figure 21.5

Change the page that is linked to when the visitor clicks on the button to force them to enter a Username and Password.

5. Click on the OK button to close the window.

After you have completed these steps and you save your changes, load the Index.html page into a browser and test the function added.

Restricting User Access to a Page

As you learned in the previous section, the Log In User server behavior verifies the Username and Password a user enters against data stored in a database table. In addition, this server behavior also establishes session variables when the visitor successfully enters a valid Username/Password combination.

When a visitor successfully logs in to your site, the session variable set by the server behavior has the major benefit of enabling you to check for and verify its existence before you grant access to pages on your site. The reason this is a major benefit may not be readily apparent, yet.

Do you know that potentially anybody can access any page on your site if they know the page name? They do not necessarily need to go through the scripted and linked process that you've built into your site to go from page to page. They merely enter the name of the page that they want access to in the URL address section of their browser and then press the Enter key.

What this means is that if you have a page on your site that is protected via the process described in the previous section, a visitor could potentially access that page merely by typing in the page name in their browser window.

You can stop this behavior, though, using a server behavior named Restrict Access To Page. This server behavior does not let anyone access the page it is associated with, unless the user has successfully logged in to your site and established the session variables.

In our quote site, the quote search page is named Search.asp. In the previous section, you placed a Login.asp page to display when a visitor clicks on the Find A Quote button on the Index.html page. But, at the present time, there is nothing stopping someone from accessing this page by typing the page name (preceded by the server name) in the URL address area of their browser. To place the Restrict Access To Page server behavior on the Search.asp page, perform these steps:

1. Within UltraDev, load the Search.asp page into the Document window.

2. Within the Document window, click anywhere in an editable portion of the page. Access the Server Behaviors window by pressing and holding the Ctrl key while pressing the F9 key. UltraDev will display the Server Behaviors window.

3. Within the Server Behaviors window, click on the plus (+) icon. UltraDev will display a menu of the different server behaviors.

4. Within the menu, click on the User Authentication server behavior, and then click on the Restrict Access To Page server behavior.

5. Click on the Username and Password radio button in the Restrict Based On radio group.

6. Within the If Access Denied, Go To text box, type the name of the page (**Index.html**) the browser will load if someone tries to access the page without having successfully logged in first. The Restrict Access To Page window should look similar to that shown in Figure 21.6.

Figure 21.6

The Restrict Access To Page window prevents someone from accessing the page it is associated with unless they have successfully logged in.

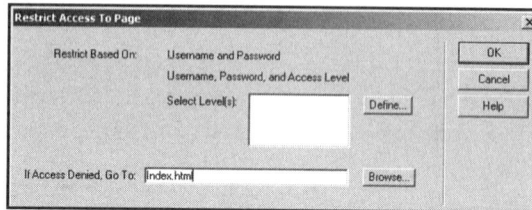

7. Click on the OK button to save this server behavior.

After you save your changes, test them out. The way to test this server behavior is to open a browser window and type the name **Search.asp**, after the server name, in the URL line. When you press the Enter key, you should go to the Index.html page, as described in Step 6 in the preceding list.

Using the Log Out User Server Behavior

The Log Out User server behavior has a very specific, albeit limited, function. It gives a visitor the ability to log out of the site under one username and log in under a different username, all in one session and without closing the browser. Here is why this function is sometimes valuable.

When a visitor logs in to the site using the Log In User server behavior, session variables are established for that Username/Password combination. These are in the form of session cookies that are set on their browser. The cookie lasts as long as the session, and the session can be terminated in one of two ways: the visitor closes their Internet Explorer or Netscape browser, or the Log Out User server behavior executes.

NOTE: *Most of the time, visitors to your site will never use a Logout capability if you make one available. I have visited many sites in the last four years, and the only site at which I use the Logout function is the site maintained by my bank. Certain functions I perform at this site require that I log in to gain access. Because of the sensitivity of the information, I always log out when I'm done on the site. I could effectively accomplish the same result by closing my browser, but I just feel safer logging out.*

To place the Log Out User server behavior on the Login.asp page, perform these steps:

1. Within UltraDev, load the Login.asp page in the Document window.

2. Within the page, highlight the words "click here" that appear in the sentence *If you want to logout, click here.* The page should look similar to that shown in Figure 21.7.

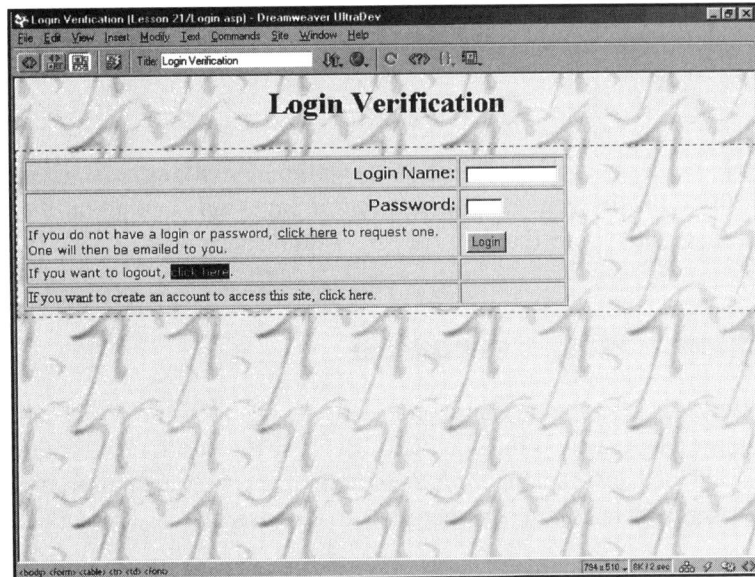

Figure 21.7

The words "click here" are highlighted and about to have a server behavior associated with them.

3. Within the Server Behaviors window, click on the plus (+) icon. UltraDev, in turn, will display a menu of the different behaviors.

4. Within the menu, click on the User Authentication server behavior, and then click on the Log Out User server behavior. UltraDev will display the Log Out User window.

5. Within the Log Out User window, the words "click here" are already specified in the Log Out When drop-down list, because you previously set up a link on "click here."

6. In the When Done, Go To text box, enter the page named Index.html. In this case, you want the visitor to go back to the Home page when they log out. The Log Out User window should look similar to that shown in Figure 21.8.

Figure 21.8

The Log Out User window after you have fully defined the server behavior for your site.

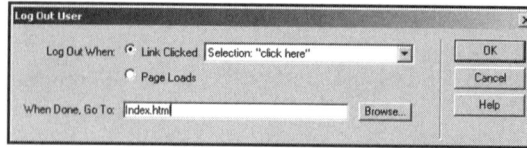

7. Click on the OK button to save your changes.

8. Finally, you must add a link to your Index.html page named Log Out, which you link to the Login.asp page.

When this is done, and you have saved the changes, test them. Especially test to make sure that when you click the hotlink that triggers the server behavior, you really kill the session variables that were set when you logged in. You can do this by going to the Index.html page and clicking on the Find A Quote button. If you see the Login.asp page, you know that you have not established a new session login yet.

Checking a New Username

Frequently, Web sites provide visitors the ability to create their own accounts. This is especially true on sites that do not charge a fee to access their contents. Because the Best Durn Random Quote Site On The Internet is a free site, it should include a capability for a visitor to create their own username. To do this, you use the Check New Username server behavior in conjunction with the Insert Record server behavior to perform the following tasks:

◆ Check the Username entered by a new visitor to make sure it is unique.

◆ If the Username entered by the visitor is unique, create an entry in the Users table.

NOTE: *UltraDev requires that you take a backward approach to defining the Check New Username server behavior. Before you actually create the Check New Username server behavior, you need to create the Insert Record server behavior. What UltraDev does, when a visitor clicks on the Create Login button in the page, is opposite of the order you create the behaviors. Ultra-Dev first executes the Check New Username server behavior. If the supplied Username is not currently in the Users table, then it executes the Insert Record server behavior.*

To provide your site with the ability to check new usernames, perform these steps:

1. Within the Login.asp page, you will see some text at the bottom of the table that reads *If you want to create an account to access this site, click here.* Using your mouse to highlight the words "click here."

2. Within the Property Inspector for this text string, type the linked page **Login_Create.asp** in the Link drop-down list box, as shown in Figure 21.9.

Figure 21.9

The first step in creating a Check New Username server behavior is to create a link to a page that will contain it.

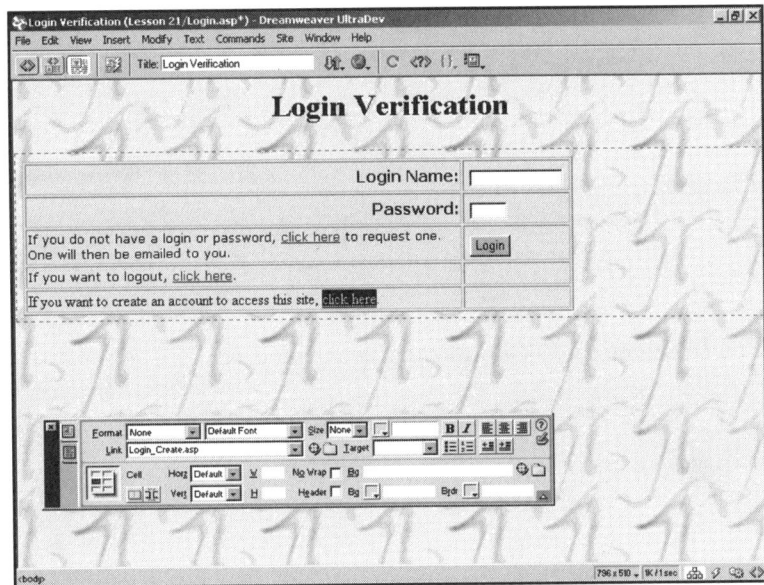

3. Save the modifications to the Login.asp page.

On book's companion CD-ROM, you will find the Login_Create.asp page. The page, however, does not have any server behaviors associated with it. To associate the behaviors with the page, perform these steps:

1. Within UltraDev, load the Login_Create.asp page into the Document window.

2. Click on the Create Login button. You will associate the Insert Record and User Authentication server behaviors to this control.

3. Within the Server Behaviors window, click on the plus (+) icon. UltraDev, in turn, will display a menu of the different behaviors.

4. Within the menu, click on the Insert Record server behavior. UltraDev will display the Insert Record window.

5. Within the Insert Record window, complete the fields as shown in Figure 21.10.

Figure 21.10

The Insert Record window defines the first step in the two-step process of using the Check New Username server behavior.

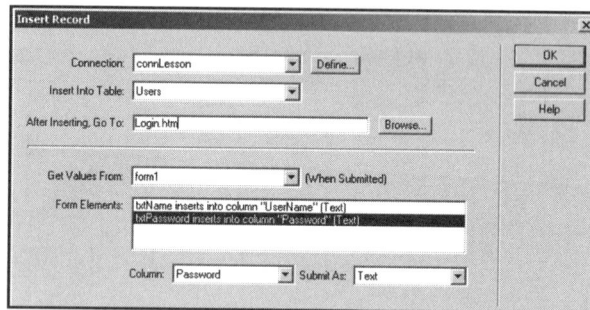

6. Click on the OK button to save the modifications to the Insert Record window.

7. Within the Server Behaviors window, click on the plus (+) icon. UltraDev, in turn, will display a menu of the different server behaviors.

8. Within the menu, select the User Authentication Server Behavior option and then choose Check New Username. UltraDev will display the Check New Username window.

9. Within the Check New Username window, the Username Field drop-down list should already have the name of the control on the form used to collect the visitor's suggestion for a new username. If this is not the case in your machine, type the name **txtName** within this control.

10. In the If Already Exists, Go To drop-down list, type the name of the current page, **Login_Create.asp**, because you want the visitor to be able to stay on the page to try to enter a new username. The Check New Username window should look similar to that shown in Figure 21.11.

Figure 21.11

The Check New Username window tells UltraDev what control on the page contains the visitor-supplied username, as well as what page to go to in the event the username selected already exists.

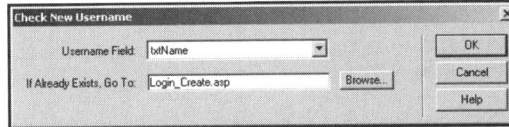

11. Click on the OK button to save your changes.

Save your changes and then test them out. You now have an entire user authentication and password verification system built into your site.

What You Must Know

In this lesson, you learned how to incorporate security and user login functions into your site. In Lesson 22, "Managing Your UltraDev Project," you will learn how to manage your UltraDev project by using several tools that improve your site organization and management

Before you continue to Lesson 22, make sure you understand the following key concepts:

◆ The current version of UltraDev includes certain server behaviors that maintain and manage user authentication.

◆ Using server behaviors, you can keep and pass session information from one page to the next.

◆ Within your site, you can use a Login function to require a user to specify a username and password before he or she can access specific pages on your site.

◆ After a user logs in to your system, UltraDev tracks session information, which your pages can use to restrict user access.

◆ You can use session information to prevent a user from navigating to certain pages unless they have successfully logged in.

Part IV

Extending Dreamweaver UltraDev

Lesson 22

Managing Your UltraDev Project

In Lesson 21, "Using User Logins," you learned how to incorporate site security by using Login functionality in your site. As your sites become larger and more complex, so too will your site management requirements. In this lesson, you will learn how to manage your UltraDev project. As you will learn, Ultra-Dev provides several tools you can use to improve your site organization and management. By the time you finish this lesson, you will understand the following key concepts:

◆ Within UltraDev, you can manage your project using the Site window.

◆ Synchronizing the site files on the local and remote sites is an important process to test your site, maintain security for archival purposes, and coordinate with others who are involved in the development process.

◆ Adding Design Notes to your site aids in the site's documentation, which makes your site easier for others to maintain and support.

Performing Site Management Within the Site Window

So far in this book, you have worked with many sites that this book provided to you on its companion CD-ROM. In this section, you will learn how to define a local site for a new project, and then how to manage that site.

Before you begin to define an UltraDev site, you should give some thought to the directory structure you want to create to hold all the site components. A fairly common hierarchical scheme is to make all the subdirectories of a site, containing various site components, subdirectories below the root folder. As shown in Figure 22.1, the directory structure for the lessons that accompany this book uses a similar structure.

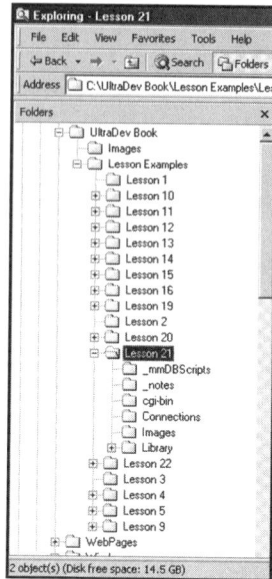

Figure 22.1

A common directory structure is to place all site components in their own directories under the root site directory.

NOTE: *If you establish a certain directory structure when you begin an UltraDev project, and then change your mind and move things around, UltraDev will update all the links in the various elements in your site, as long as you use the UltraDev interface to move things around. If you use Windows Explorer or some other such tool, then UltraDev has no way of knowing where things have moved.*

Creating a New Site in UltraDev

When you establish the directory structure for a new site, you can do that outside of UltraDev (using Windows Explorer, for example) or using the Site Definition window. Regardless of whether you create the directory structure inside or outside of UltraDev, you still use the Site Definition window in UltraDev to create the definitions for the site.

To create a new site in UltraDev, perform these steps:

1. With UltraDev, select the Site menu New Site option. UltraDev, in turn, will display the Site Definition window, as shown in Figure 22.2.

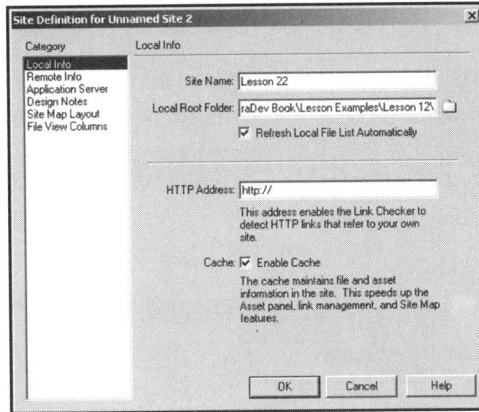

Figure 22.2

Use the Site Definition window to tell UltraDev all it needs to know to manage your local and remote sites.

2. Within the Site Definition window, you will complete the six categories listed in the Category pane, as described in the following sections.

Within the Category pane, you see six categories, described in Table 22.1. When you click on each category, UltraDev displays a different set of related controls.

Table 22.1   Each of the six categories and its purpose

Category Name	Description
Local Info	Sets up the site structure to contain the folders, assets, and other files for a particular site
Remote Info	Associates remote server information and Check In/Check Out preferences
Application Server	Organizes your site files to specify a server technology, an application server, and a URL prefix
Design Notes	Keeps track of extra file information associated with your documents, such as image source-file names and comments on file status, by using the Design Notes command
Site Map Layout	Customizes the appearance of your site map; you can specify the home page, the number of columns displayed, whether the icon labels display the file name or the page title, and whether to show hidden and dependent files
File View Columns	Customizes the columns displayed in the Site window's Local Folder and Remote Site lists. You can reorder columns, add new columns (for a maximum of 10 columns), delete columns, hide columns, associate Design Notes to column data, and designate columns to be shared with all users connected to a site

Local Info Category

Local Info is a term used in UltraDev that refers to the information residing on your computer which is specific to your site. Examples of Local Info are Web pages currently being created or modified.

Figure 22.3 illustrates a completed Site Definition window with the Local Info category selected. Table 22.2 describes each of the controls in this window.

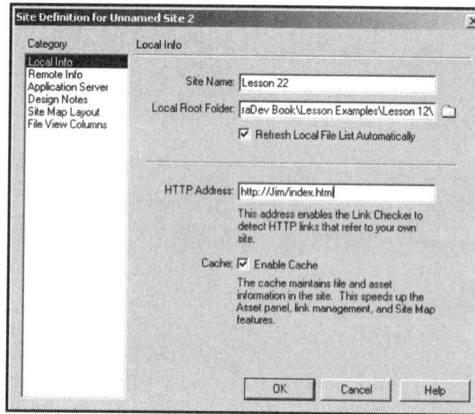

Figure 22.3

Use the Local Info category to set up the site structure that contains the folders, assets, and other files for a particular site.

Table 22.2 Controls in the Local Info category of the Site Definition window

Control Name	Description
Site Name	The name of the site that appears in the Site window. This name will *not* appear in a browser.
Local Root Folder	Specifies the name of the folder on a local (or network-attached) disk where site files, templates, and library items are stored.
Refresh Local File List Automatically	When checked, tells UltraDev to automatically refresh the local file list every time files are copied to the local site.
HTTP Address	Lists the URL that your completed Web site will use. This is used by UltraDev to verify links within the site that use absolute URLs.
Cache	When checked, tells UltraDev to create a local cache. A local cache improves the speed of link- and site-management tasks.

Remote Info Category

Remote Info is a term used in UltraDev that refers to the information specific to your site, which resides on a machine other than yours. An example of Remote Info is the database a site accesses, or perhaps the directory that contains the graphics used on the Web pages in your site.

Figure 22.4 is a completed Site Definition window with the Remote Info category selected. Table 22.3 describes each of the controls in this window.

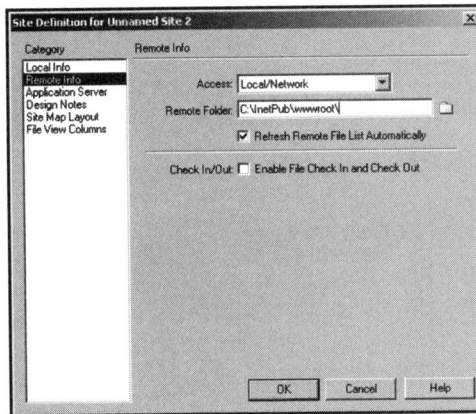

Figure 22.4

Use the Remote Info category to associate remote server information and Check In/Check Out preferences.

Table 22.3   Controls in the Remote Info category of the Site Definition window

Control Name	Description
Access	Specifies one of five different server access models: None, FTP, Local/Network, SourceSafe Database, or WebDAV. The controls that display on the page are based on which of these five models is selected.
Remote Folder	Specifies the name of a remote folder on a server that contains the completed site.
Refresh Remote File List Automatically	When checked, tells UltraDev to automatically refresh the remote file list every time files are copied to the local site.
Check In/Out	When checked, turns on UltraDev's source-level-tracking component to lock pages and site components from use by anyone other than the person checking out the component.

Application Server Category

The Application Server category is used to organize the files on your site and to identify the various technologies used to host the site.

Figure 22.5 is a completed Site Definition window with the Application Server category selected. Table 22.4 describes each of the controls in this window.

Figure 22.5

Use the Application Server category to organize your site files and specify a server technology, an application server, and a URL prefix.

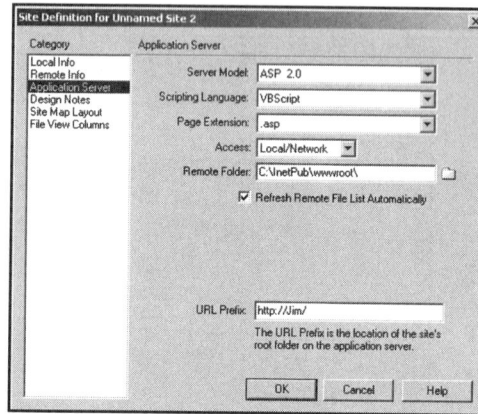

Table 22.4   Controls in the Application Server category of the Site Definition window

Control Name	Description
Server Model	Specifies one of four different server models: None, ASP 2.0, JSP 1.0, or ColdFusion 4.0. The controls that display on the page are based on which of these four models is selected.
Scripting Language	Specifies the scripting language UltraDev should use when creating scripts describing various behaviors.
Page Extension	Tells UltraDev what extension to use when creating pages containing code in the specified scripting language.
Access	Specifies the type of access used to move files between the local site folder and remote site folder.
Remote Folder	Specifies the name and location of the remote folder that contains the application-specific components.

(continued)

Table 22.4   *(continued)*

Control Name	Description
Refresh Remote File List Automatically	When checked, tells UltraDev to automatically refresh the remote file list every time application-server files are copied to the local site.
URL Prefix	Tells UltraDev what the URL prefix is for the remote application server.

Design Notes Category

The Design Notes category is used to house and maintain information specific to the pages on your site that helps to describe the pages on the site. These are free-form text in nature.

Figure 22.6 illustrates a completed Site Definition window with the Design Notes category selected. Table 22.5 describes each of the controls in this window.

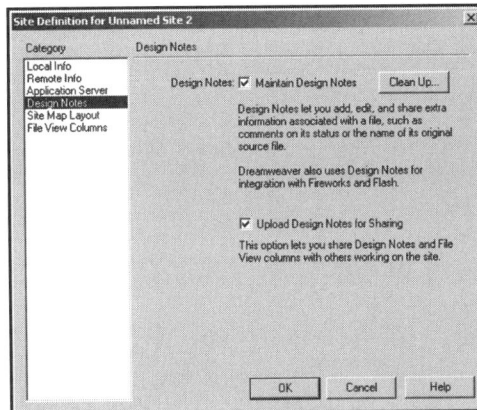

Figure 22.6

Use the Design Notes category to keep track of extra file information associated with your documents.

Table 22.5   Controls in the Design Notes category of the Site Definition window

Control Name	Description
Maintain Design Notes	When checked, tells UltraDev that you want to create, store, and review Design Notes specific to components on your site.
Clean Up	When clicked, causes UltraDev to remove Design Notes for pages that no longer exist.
Upload Design Notes for Sharing	When checked, tells UltraDev that Design Notes created on your local machine are to be uploaded to the remote server.

NOTE: *You can keep whatever type of information you want in Design Notes. For example, you can add a Design Note to a document that you copy from one site to the other, describing that it is indeed a copied document. You can also keep sensitive information in a Design Note for a page that you don't want to keep in the page itself, for security purposes.*

Site Map Layout Category

The Site Map Layout category is used to customize the appearance of the site map to suit personal preferences.

Figure 22.7 illustrates a completed Site Definition window with the site map layout category selected. Table 22.6 describes each of the controls in this window.

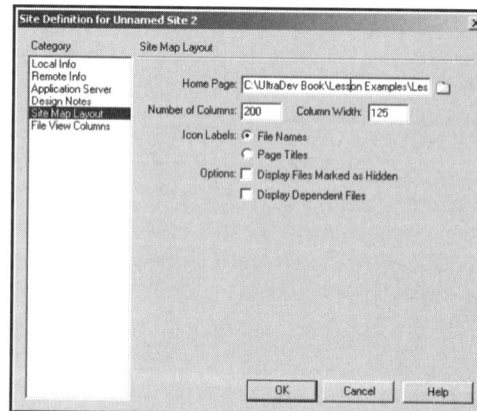

Figure 22.7

Use the site map layout category to customize the appearance of your site map.

Table 22.6   Controls in the Site Map Layout category of the Site Definition window

Control Name	Description
Home Page	Specifies the home page for the site.
Number of Columns	Specifies the number of pages to display per row in the site map window.
Column Width	Specifies the width, in pixels, of the site map columns.
Icon Labels	Specifies whether the names displayed with the document icons in the site map are represented as file names or as page titles.
Display Files Marked as Hidden	When checked, specifies that HTML files marked as hidden are to be displayed in the site map.
Display Dependent Files	When checked, specifies that all dependent files show in the site's hierarchy. A dependent file is an image or other non-HTML component that loads into a visitor's browser when the page is loaded.

File View Columns Category

The File View Columns category is used to individualize the display of columns in the Local Folder and Remote Site lists of the Site Definition window.

Figure 22.8 illustrates a completed Site Definition window with the File View Columns category selected. Table 22.7 describes each of the controls in this window.

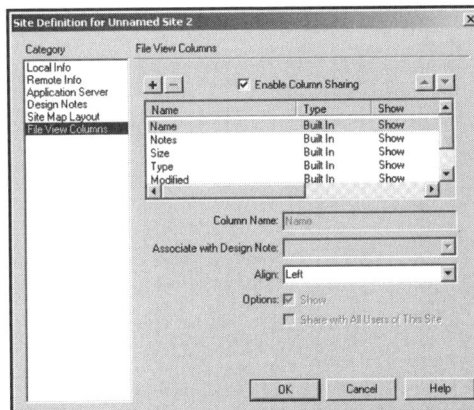

Figure 22.8

Use the File View Columns category to customize the columns displayed in the Site window's Local Folder and Remote Site lists.

Table 22.7   Controls in the File View Columns category of the Site Definition window

Control Name	Description
Enable Column Sharing	When checked, specifies that columns are to be shared in the site map.
Column Name	Specifies the name of the column to display in the site map.
Associate with Design Note	Specifies the name of the Design Note file to associate with the column selected.
Align	Specifies the alignment (Left, Center, or Right) of the Design Note relative to the column name in the site map.
Options	When checked, specifies whether to share design notes with all users of the site, and specifies whether to show Design Notes in the site maps of users.

Moving Your Site to a Remote Server

If you work in a corporate environment, the remote server is probably a computer that is attached to your network. If this is the case, then you access the remote site over a LAN. Otherwise, you are probably accessing your remote site over an FTP connection.

The Site Map window, shown in Figure 22.9, displays when you press Alt+F8.

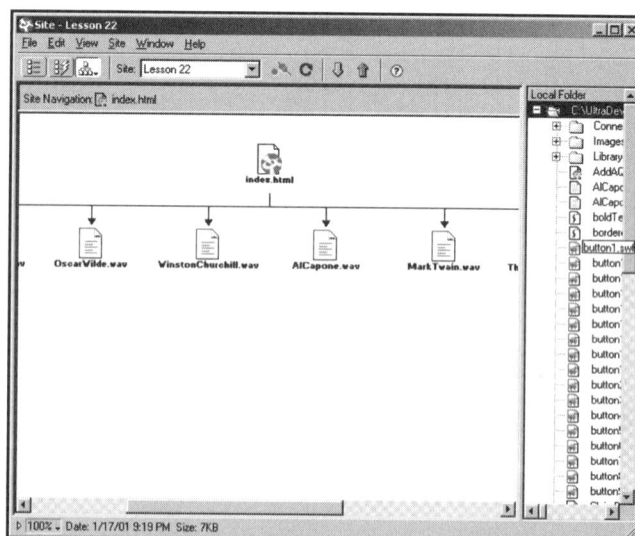

Figure 22.9

The site map provides access to many functions, including the ability to move ("Put") your site to a remote server.

The top-left portion of the site map has three icons, shown in Figure 22.10, that are significant to moving your site to the remote server, whether that be on a network-attached device or an FTP site.

Figure 22.10

These three icons determine the type of information displayed in the site map.

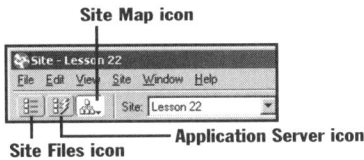

If you click on the Application Server icon, the site map will change its appearance and show you the files that are located in the directory identified as the root directory on the remote server, as well as the subdirectories, as shown in Figure 22.11.

Figure 22.11

The site map window showing the contents of the remote directory as well as the local directory

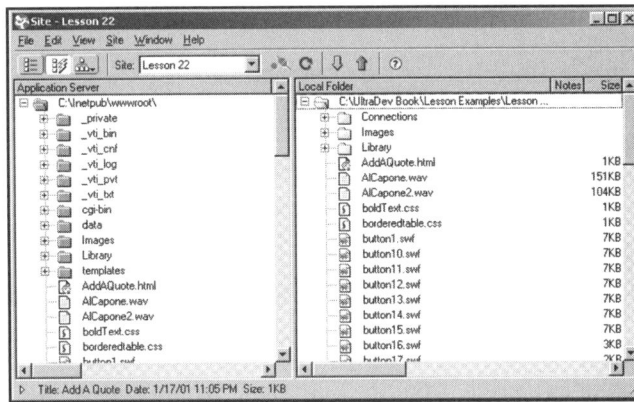

In UltraDev terminology, you "put" a site when you copy site files from a local folder to a remote folder.

To put your site, or files in your site, to a remote server, perform these steps:

1. Within UltraDev, open the Site window by pressing Alt+F8.

2. Within the Site window, click on the Application Server icon to display the contents of the root directory on the application server.

3. If you access the application server via an FTP connection, click on the Connect button. You will see messages flash on the status bar at the bottom of the window, indicating the status of the connection,.

4. Select the file(s) you want to transfer by clicking on it. To select the entire site, select the Edit menu Select All option.

5. Click on the Put icon (the arrow that is pointing up).

6. If you are putting an entire site, you may get a message similar to Figure 22.12. Click on the OK button to proceed if you want to Put the entire site; otherwise, click the Cancel button.

Figure 22.12

A warning message issued by UltraDev before an entire site is moved helps to prevent an unnecessarily long wait while an entire site is moved between machines.

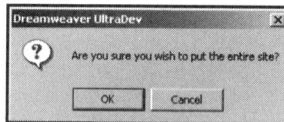

Moving the Current File to the Remote Server

UltraDev gives you the ability to put files to the remote server without having to go to the site map. You can access the put capabilities directly from the Document window.

You must be careful when moving a site, however, and remember that UltraDev transfers files from the local directory, not from the version you are working on in the document window. Therefore, always remember to save the current page before issuing a Put.

To initiate a Put of the page that is in the document window, perform these steps:

1. Save the file in the document window by selecting the File menu Save option.

2. Within the Save As window, click on the Site menu item and click Put.

That is it. You will find, as you get comfortable working with the UltraDev interface, that you will repeat these steps often and seamlessly.

Importing an Existing Site

As you manage sites, you will occasionally run into a situation where you have to do some maintenance to an existing site that you did not originally work on. In this case, you must import the site into UltraDev from the remote site.

Although the steps to import a site into UltraDev are straightforward and do not take too much time to initiate, the actual importing process may take some time, depending on the number and size of objects imported into UltraDev. As a rule of thumb, the larger the site, the longer it will take to transfer between the local machine and the remote server. To import an existing site into UltraDev, perform these steps:

1. Within UltraDev, select the Site menu Define Sites option. UltraDev will display the Define Sites window.

2. Within the Define Sites window, click on the New button. UltraDev will display the Site Definition window, as described in the beginning of this lesson.

3. Within the Site Definition window, complete the controls for the Local Info category, as described earlier in this lesson. Then, click your mouse on the Remote Server category.

4. Within the Remote Server category of the Site Definition window, click in the Access Method drop-down list and select the appropriate access method for your site.

5. Using the Remote Server drop down, select the location of the remote server that contains all the source components for the site that you are retrieving.

6. Complete the rest of the categories, as described previously in this lesson, and then click on the OK button. UltraDev, in turn, will display a site map for the newly defined site.

As you learned previously, the term *put* refers to the process of copying the site files from the local machine to the remote server. A complimentary process to this is the *get* process. This refers to the act of copying site files from the remote server to the local machine.

Now that you have defined the new site to UltraDev, you can get the files that are on the remote server into your local machine by performing these steps:

1. Within UltraDev, open the Site window by pressing Alt+F8.

2. Click on the Application Server icon. UltraDev will display the contents of the root directory on the application server.

3. If you access the application server via an FTP connection, and if you are no longer connected, click on the Connect button. You will see messages flash on the status bar at the bottom of the window, indicating the status of the connection.

4. In the Local Machine side of the window, select the file(s) you want to transfer by clicking on it. To select the entire site, select the Edit menu Select All item.

5. Click on the Get icon. This is the arrow that is pointing down.

6. You may get a warning message requesting you to verify that you in fact want to Get an entire site. Click on the OK button to proceed if you want to Get the entire site; otherwise, click the Cancel button.

Synchronizing the Local Site with the Remote Site

UltraDev includes a powerful component you can use to ensure that the files that exist on your remote and local sites are synchronized (in other words, to make sure the files on your local system are the same as those on your remote system, and vice versa). This component enables you to synchronize the remote site with the local site, or the local site with the remote site, thus giving you the ability to bring both sites up to the current level of synchronization concurrently.

To see which files are newer on the remote site, perform these steps:

1. Within the Site window, if you are using FTP, connect to the remote site by clicking on the Connect icon.

2. In the Remote Site pane in the Site window, click on the root folder to highlight the folder.

3. Within the Site window, select the Edit menu Select Newer Remote option. UltraDev will display the items on the selected remote site that are newer than the local site highlighted, or do not have counterparts on the local site, as shown in Figure 22.13.

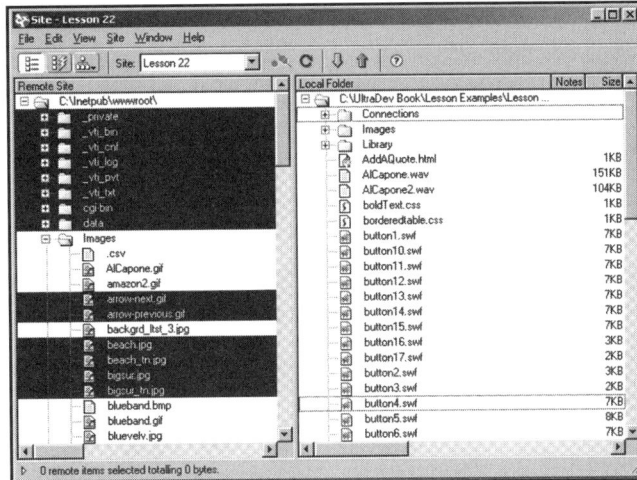

Figure 22.13

The highlighted items in the Remote Site pane are files that are newer or do not have counterparts on the local site.

To see which files are newer on the local site, perform these steps:

1. Within the Site window, if you are using FTP, connect to the remote site by clicking on the Connect icon.

2. In the Remote Site pane in the Site window, click on the root folder to highlight it.

3. Select the Edit menu Select Newer Local option. UltraDev, in turn, will display the items in the remote site that are newer than the local site highlighted, as shown in Figure 22.14.

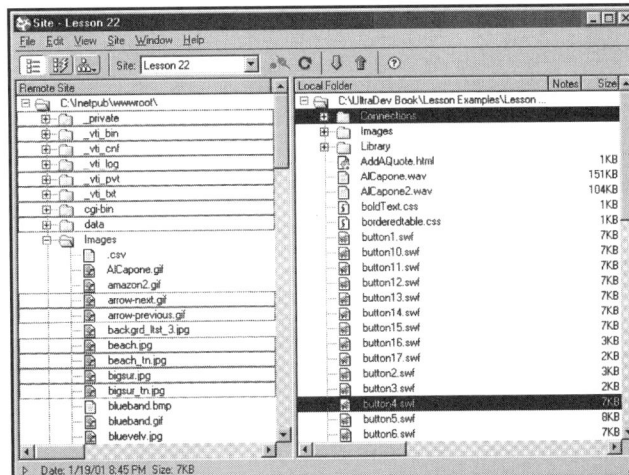

Figure 22.14

The highlighted items in the local site pane are files that are newer or don't have counterparts on the remote site.

Although you do not have to do either of the preceding two processes before you synchronize files, it is advisable to go through both of them to get an indication of the current level of synchronization between the remote and local sites. Then, to synchronize files between the remote and local sites, perform these steps:

1. Within the Site window, if you are using FTP, connect to the remote site by clicking on the Connect icon.

2. If you want to synchronize only certain files, you can select those files by holding down the Ctrl key while clicking on each file name. If you want to synchronize the entire site, you do not have to select any of the files.

3. Select the Site menu Synchronize option. UltraDev, in turn, will display the Synchronize Files window.

4. The Synchronize Files window has two drop-down list boxes. Synchronize lets you select whether to synchronize an entire site or only selected items. Direction lets you specify one of three options: Put newer files to remote, Get newer files from remote, or Get and Put newer files. Select the options in these two drop-down list boxes that are specific to your intent. An example of what this window will look like when an entire site is synchronized between a remote and local site is shown in Figure 22.15.

Figure 22.15

The settings chosen here will cause a synchronization to occur for an entire site between the remote and local site directories.

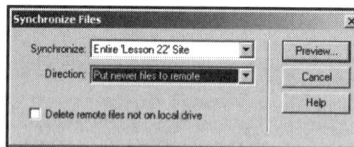

5. Click on the Preview button to begin the synchronization process. UltraDev, in turn, will begin a process that creates a Synchronization window containing the files that are subject to be moved, as shown in Figure 22.16.

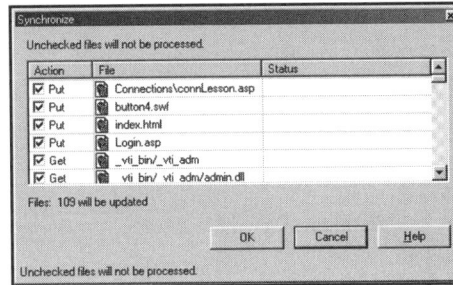

Figure 22.16

The Synchronization Verification window allows you to deselect any files before moving any files.

6. If you do *not* want a file to be moved that displays in the Synchronization Verification window, click in the check box directly to the left of the file name to deselect the file.

7. Click on the OK button to begin the synchronization.

Using Design Notes to Document Your Site

Design Notes is a great tool that is especially useful in site development projects where multiple people are working on the site concurrently. *Design Notes* are free-form text entries that provide the capability for one developer to pass communications about ideas or concerns specific to a page to other people that might be working on the same page. Design Notes are attached to each Web page, and, as you saw earlier in this lesson, that information can be transferred to the remote site and made available to other team members from there.

UltraDev keeps Design Notes in a subdirectory _notes, with a file extension of *.XML. If you look back to Figure 22.1, you will see this directory listed.

NOTE: *As you learned earlier in this lesson, you must first set up Design Notes for your site. You do this in the Design Notes category of the Define Site window.*

Adding a Design Note

After you have established the capability to store Design Notes in your site by using the Design Notes category of the Define Sites window, you can begin to add Design Notes to Web pages.

To add a Design Note to a Web page, perform these steps:

1. With the Web page active in the Document window, select the File menu Design Notes option. UltraDev, in turn, will display the Design Notes window, as shown in Figure 22.17.

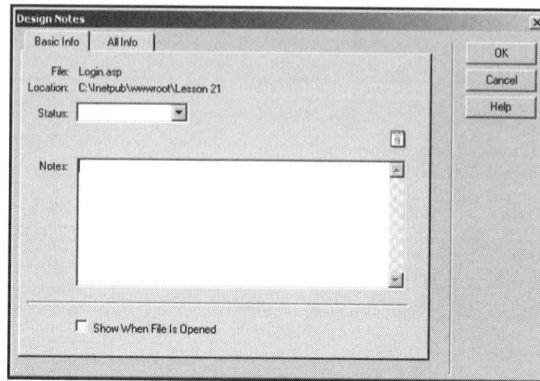

Figure 22.17

The Design Notes window is where you provide information that stays with the Web page for others to see and use.

2. Within the Status drop-down list, click on the status for the Web page for which you want to create the Design Note.

3. Click on the Calendar icon to insert a date stamp in the Notes text box. I strongly suggest you get into the habit of putting date stamps on your Design Notes, because they will remind you and others when and why you made a change.

4. Within the Notes text box, type any notes you desire.

5. If you want the Design Note file to appear every time the Web page is opened, click on the Show When File Is Opened check box to place a check mark in it.

6. In the All Info tab, you can add keys and values that are available to other people. For example, you could add a key of Requirements Version (in the Name field) and define a value of v1.5 (in the Value field). This is something you might do to tie certain features or Web pages to specific versions of Requirements Documents. Click on the plus (+) icon to add a new key/value pair, or you can click on a key/value pair to delete and then click on the minus (−) icon to delete it.

7. Click on the OK button to save the Design Note.

Figure 22.18 is an example of what a Design Notes window might look like after having information entered in it.

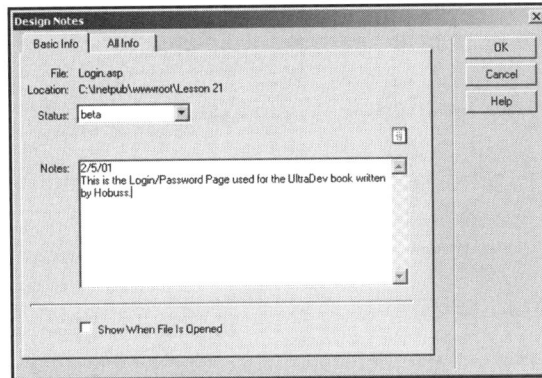

Figure 22.18

The Design Notes window with a Design Note visible

Viewing a Design Note

Viewing Design Notes is very easy. To view a Design Note for a page in the document window, select the File menu Design Notes option. UltraDev will display the Design Notes window. Figure 22.19 shows a Design Notes window with a note already entered.

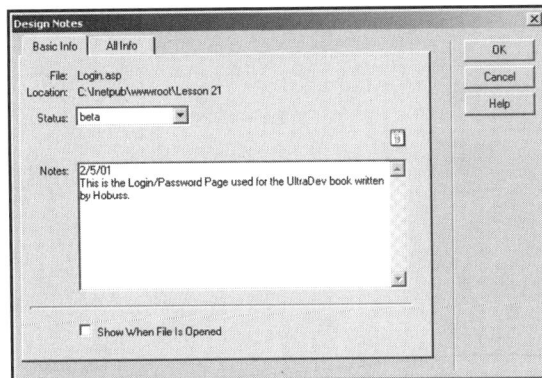

Figure 22.19

The Design Notes window with a Design Note displayed

What You Must Know

In this lesson, you learned how to manage your UltraDev project, including synchronizing a remote and local site. In Lesson 23, "Speeding Up Your Web Site Development by Reusing Elements," you will learn how to reuse items in your Web site and how to create and use a template.

Before you continue to Lesson 23, make sure you understand the following key concepts:

◆ Using the UltraDev Site window, you can manage certain functions for your site.

◆ Synchronizing the remote server with your local site is an important part of any site development project.

◆ Using Design Notes, you can document your site, which makes your site easier for you and others to maintain.

Lesson 23

Speeding Up Your Web Site Development by Reusing Elements

In Lesson 22, "Managing Your UltraDev Project," you learned how to use various features of the site map. Specifically, you learned how to create and manage a project in the Site window as well as how to use Design Notes to communicate with other developers who might be working on your site. In this lesson, you will learn how to reuse items in your Web site and how to create and use a template. By taking advantage of objects you created for other projects, you can quickly create new pages or even new sites. By the time you finish this lesson, you will understand the following key concepts:

◆ After you create an object for use by one Web site, you can store the object within a library, to simplify your use of the object later in a different site.

◆ A library is a collection of HTML snippets (pieces of code) or objects, such as graphics or Flash animations.

◆ The Library palette lets you add and modify components to your site, which facilitates consistency in how the site looks and performs.

◆ You can add items to the Library palette, as well as modify the attributes of existing items.

◆ Within UltraDev, templates let you build a base configuration for the sites you will create, which gives your sites consistent and controlled pages.

Understanding Libraries

A library is a collection of HTML snippets or page objects (such as Flash animations, graphics, and so on) that you use frequently on a Web site. Within UltraDev, you can create a library of such snippets and objects to make you more productive in creating the Web site, as well as to help you develop a consistent look and feel for your site.

A good example of an HTML snippet, which also includes graphics, is a navigation bar. A navigation bar is an element that appears on almost every Web page in a consistent location, and thus is a prime candidate you should consider as a library item.

Using a library item to define a navigation bar not only improves your productivity and provides a consistent look and feel to the site, but also assists you in making and maintaining the site. For example, if you define a navigation bar to be a library item, and then place that navigation bar on a number of pages, you can quickly and easily change its appearance on every page upon which you have placed it, simply by changing the bar's appearance in the Library palette.

When you place a library item in a document, UltraDev inserts a copy of the HTML source code for that item into the document and adds an HTML comment containing a reference to the original library item. The reference to the external library item makes it possible to update the content on an entire site all at once.

UltraDev stores library items in a Library folder within the local root folder for each site, as shown in Figure 23.1.

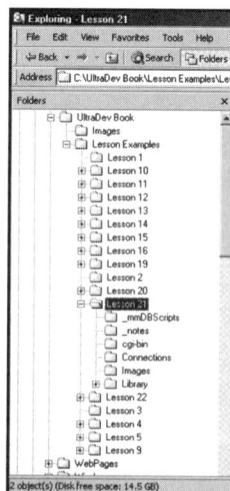

Figure 23.1

The Library folder contains the items defined on your site as being library items.

Each site has its own library, although UltraDev does give you the ability to copy a library from one site to the other.

Suppose, for example, you are building a large site for a company. The company has a slogan that it wants to appear on every page of the site, but the marketing department is still ironing out the details of just what the slogan should say. If you create a library item to contain the slogan and use that library item on every page, then when the marketing department provides the final slogan, you can change the library item and automatically update every page that uses it

Creating Library Items

You can create library items for any elements in the body of the Web page, including text, tables, forms, applets, navigation bars, and linked images. For linked images, the library stores a reference to the item, so that if the item changes location, you must update the link within the library.

To create a library item, perform these steps:

1. Within UltraDev, select the item, component, or portion of the Web page for which you want to create a library item.

2. Select the Window menu Library option. UltraDev, in turn, will display the Library palette.

3. Using your mouse, click and drag the selected item into the Library palette. You will then see something similar to Figure 23.2, in which I have placed a navigation bar into the Library palette.

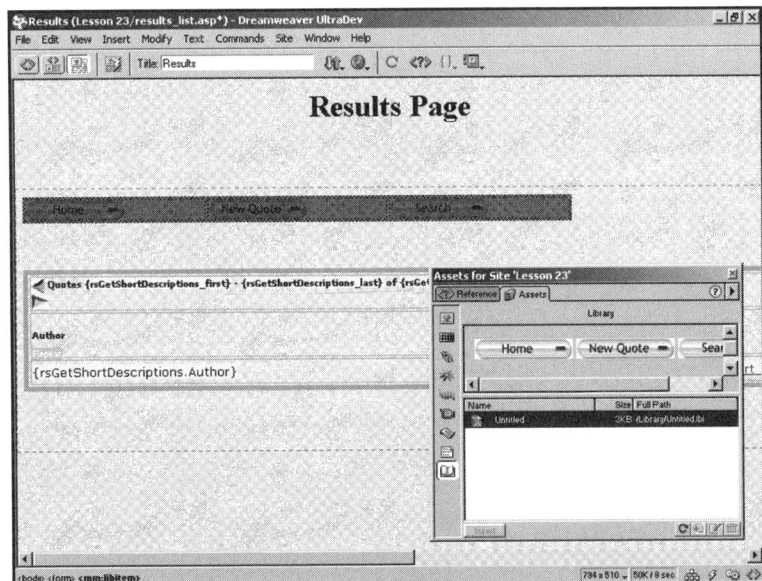

Figure 23.2

The Library palette is where UltraDev stores reusable library objects.

4. Within the Library palette, enter a name for the object.

NOTE: *When you create a library item, UltraDev saves the item in a file underneath the Library directory in a file with a name that corresponds to the object name you specify in Step 4 of the preceding list, with a file extension of .LBI.*

Highlighting Library Items

If you use libraries often, and incorporate many objects into the libraries, you may want to be able to identify which objects on a page are library objects. You can do this by setting a highlight color for library items in the Preferences window by performing these steps:

1. Within UltraDev, select the Edit menu Preferences option. UltraDev, in turn, will display the Preferences window.

2. Within the Preferences window, click on the Highlighting category. UltraDev will display the different Highlighting items.

3. As shown in Figure 23.3, one of the Highlighting items is Library Items. Click on the color box to change the color of library items placed on pages.

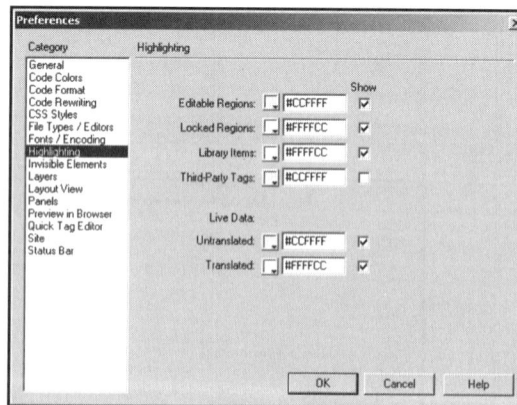

Figure 23.3

Change the color of library items appearing on a page in the Preferences window.

4. Click on the OK button to put your change into effect.

NOTE: *You can see the highlight colors only for library items placed on a page when you have Invisible Elements turned on. To turn on Invisible Elements, select the View menu Visual Aids option, and then click on Invisible Elements.*

Inserting Library Items in Web Pages

After you place an object in the Library palette, you can place that object on pages in your site. When you add a library item to a page, UltraDev inserts the actual content into the document along with a reference to the library item.

To insert a library item in a Web page, perform these steps:

1. Within the Document window, click at the location where you want to place the object.

2. Select the Window menu Library option. UltraDev will display the Library palette, with the Assets panel of the palette displayed.

3. Within the Assets panel, click on the library item you desire. UltraDev will highlight the item, as shown in Figure 23.4.

Figure 23.4

Clicking on the Insert button at the bottom of the Library palette will insert the selected object into the page in the Document window.

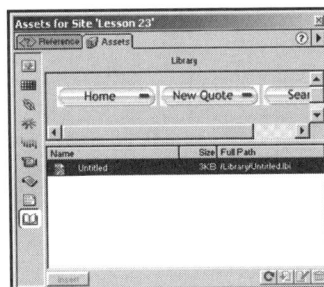

4 Within the Library palette, click on the Insert button. UltraDev will insert the selected object into the page.

Changing Library Items

After you create a library item, you may want to change something about the item. For example, assume you want to change a slogan that appears on every page of your site when the marketing department finalizes the slogan. When you make a change to the slogan in the library, you can subsequently apply those changes to either a page at a time or the entire site. To change a library item, perform these steps:

1. If the Library palette is not open, select the Window menu Library option.

2. Within the Library palette, click on the item you want to change. UltraDev, in turn, will highlight that item.

3. Within the Assets panel, click on the Edit button. UltraDev will open a new Document window with the selected item displayed, as shown in Figure 23.5.

NOTE: *You could optionally double-click on the item to edit in the Assets panel, which opens a new instance of the Document window with the selected item loaded.*

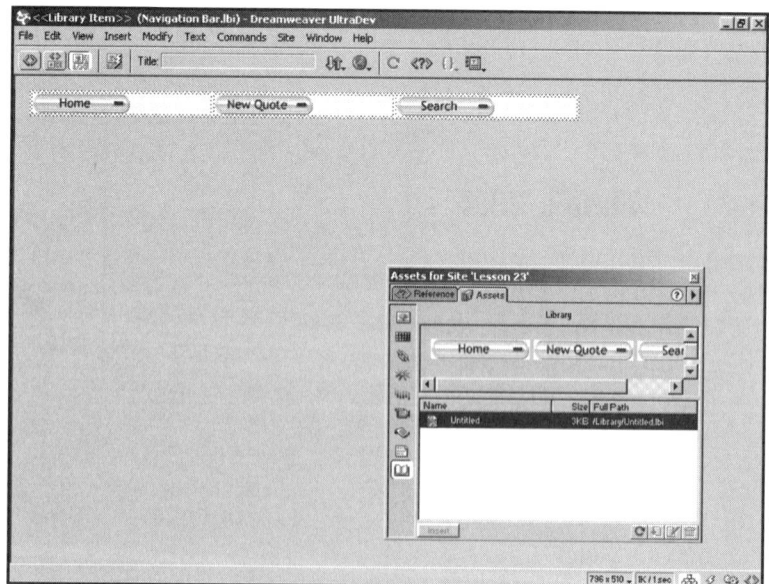

Figure 23.5

The Document window contains the library item that was selected to be edited.

4. Within the Document window, make the changes you desire to the item.

5. Select the File menu Save option. UltraDev will display a message box asking you to choose between updating or not updating the documents in the current site. If you choose to update the documents in the current site, all documents that include the edited library item will be updated. If you choose not to update the document, only the item in the Library will be updated.

Updating Your Site with the Changed Library Item

After you update a library item, you can populate your update throughout the entire site or to individual pages. To populate the changed library item throughout the site, perform these steps:

1. If the Library palette is not open, select the Window menu Library option.

2. Within the Library palette Assets panel, right-click on the item that you want to update across your site. UltraDev, in turn, will display an Item List of options that you can apply to that item.

3. Within the Item List, click on the Update Site option, and you will see the Update Pages window, as shown in Figure 23.6.

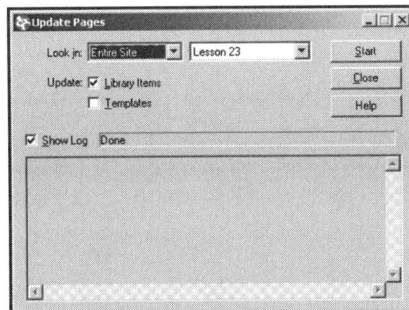

Figure 23.6

The Update Pages window allows you to specify that the entire site is to be updated with the selected library item.

4. Click on the Start button to update the site with the selected library item.

Updating a Single Page on Your Site with the Changed Library Item

You can also update a single page on your site with an updated library item by performing these steps:

1. Load the page you want to update into the Document window.

2. If the Library palette is not open, select the Window menu Library option.

3. Within the Library palette Assets panel, right-click on the item that you want to update. UltraDev, in turn, will display an Item List of options that you can apply to that item.

4. Within the Item List, click on the Update Current Page option. UltraDev will apply the updated library item to the current page.

Understanding Templates

Within UltraDev, a template is a document that designers use to create multiple pages that share the same layout. When you create a template, you can tell UltraDev which elements of a page should remain constant (noneditable, or locked) and which elements can be changed.

For example, if you are publishing a Web site that includes many pages that have the same style, a designer can create the layout of a master page and then save that layout as a template. The person putting together each page creates a new page based on the template, and replaces the placeholder text with the actual text of the new page.

You can modify a template even after you have created documents based on the template's contents. When you modify a template, the locked (noneditable) regions in documents that are based on the template are updated to match the changes to the template.

NOTE: *If you open a template file, you can edit everything in that file, whether it's marked as editable or locked. If you open a document that is based on a template file, you can edit only the regions that are marked as editable. So, the terms "editable" and "locked" refer to whether a region is editable in a document based on a template, not to whether the region is editable in the template file itself.*

An ideal situation in which to use templates is when you want a set of pages to have an identical layout; in other words, a situation in which you want to design the complete final layout for a set of pages first, and then add content later. If you simply want your pages to have the same headers and footers, with different layouts in between, use library items to store the headers and footers.

Templates are particularly useful in a collaborative environment in which a designer controls the page layouts, and other people add content to the pages but aren't allowed to change the layout.

NOTE: *Using a template may limit your later changes to design and layout. If you intend to make major layout changes to your pages later, you may want to use library items instead of templates.*

Creating Templates

There are two ways to create a template. The first is to create a template from an existing document and then modify it to suit your needs. The second is to create a template from scratch in a blank Document window.

NOTE: *UltraDev saves templates with a file extension of .DWT in a directory named Templates, which is directly below the site's root folder. You should neither move the templates in this directory nor put any nontemplate files in this directory. Also, you should not move the directory named Templates out of the local root directory. Doing this creates errors when you attempt to use the templates.*

You can use Design Notes with templates. Design Notes, discussed in Lesson 22, "Managing Your UltraDev Project," are a means to communicate information about a page object from one developer to others.

To save an existing document as a template, perform these steps:

1. With the Web page that you wish to have saved as a template visible in the Document window, select the File menu Save As Template option. UltraDev, in turn, will display the Save As Template window, as shown in Figure 23.7.

Figure 23.7

The Save As Template window lets you specify the site that the template is to be saved in.

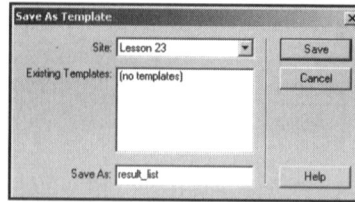

2. Within the Save As Template window Site drop-down list box, click on the name of the site to which you want to associate your template. You can select the current site, or you can select another site.

3. Within the Save As text box, you will see the file name that UltraDev has selected for the template. UltraDev uses a file extension of .DWT for templates, as shown in Figure 23.7. In this case, UltraDev will place a file named Results_List.dwt in a directory named Templates, under the root directory for the site named Lesson 23.

4. Click on the OK button to save the template.

To create a new template from scratch, perform these steps:

1. If the Templates palette is not open, select the Window menu Templates option.

2. Within the Templates window Assets panel, click on the New Template icon. UltraDev will display a new item added to the list of available templates, as shown in Figure 23.8.

Figure 23.8

After you add a new, blank template to the Templates palette, you can edit it.

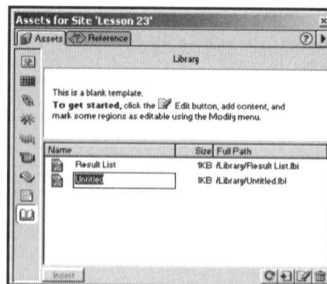

3. Within the Name column, notice that UltraDev highlights the name for the recently added blank template. Within this field, type a new, more descriptive name for the template and press Enter.

Editing an Existing Template

Occasionally, you will make changes to a Web page that is based on a template and decide that you also want to change the template. Other times, you will want to make changes to a template without working on a Web page that is based on the template. You can do both easily in UltraDev.

NOTE: *Remember that when you make changes to a template, even if you are making changes to a Web page based on a template by changing the template file itself, all the changes made will be reflected in pages across the site that use the template.*

To edit a template that a Web page is based on, perform these steps:

1. Open the Web page that contains the template to change within the Document window.

2. Within the Document window, select the Modify menu Templates option. UltraDev, in turn, will display a selection of actions you can perform on a template.

3. Within the list of actions, click on the Open Attached Template option. UltraDev, in turn, will open the template in a new Document window.

4. Within the Document window, make the changes you desire to the template and then select the File menu Save option.

To edit a template directly, perform these steps:

1. Select the Window menu Templates option. UltraDev will display the Templates palette.

2. Within the Templates palette Assets tab, click on the name of the template to edit.

3. Click on the Edit button at the bottom of the Assets panel. UltraDev will open a new Document window with the selected item displayed, as shown in Figure 23.9.

NOTE: *You could optionally double-click on the item to edit in the Assets panel, which will open a new instance of the Document window with the selected item loaded.*

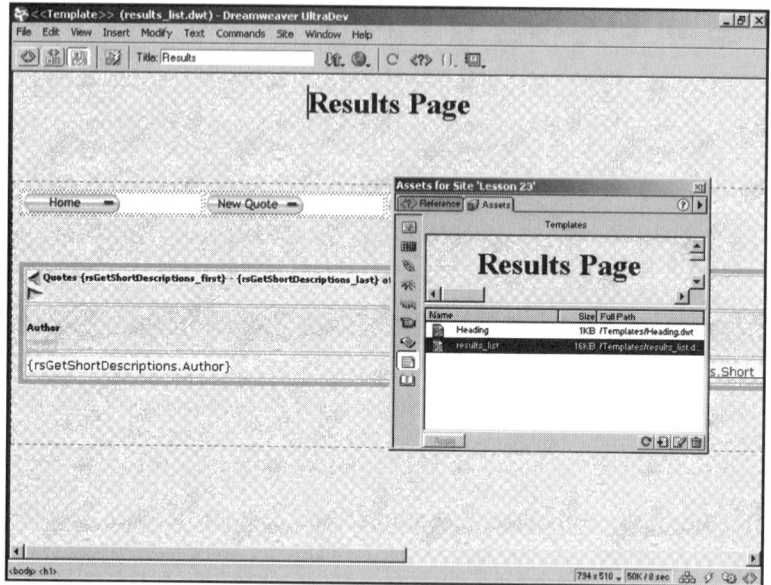

Figure 23.9

The Document window contains the template item to be edited.

4. Within the Document window, make the template changes you desire.

5. Select the File menu Save option to save your changes.

Applying a Template to a Web Page

Occasionally, you will have the need to apply a template to a Web page that is already under construction. For example, you might begin developing a site that you discover has a number of pages that contain the same heading elements. You don't have to go through the process of creating a template with the heading elements and then start over from scratch to create all the pages that use this template. Rather, you can create the template and then apply it to each page that it needs to appear on.

To apply a template to a Web page, perform these steps:

1. Load into a Document window the Web page to which you want to apply the template.

2. If the Templates palette is not open, select the Window menu Templates option.

3. Within the Templates palette, click on the template in the Assets pane that you want to apply to the Web page. UltraDev will highlight the template.

4. Click on the Apply button at the bottom of the Templates palette, and the selected template will be applied to the page.

What You Must Know

In this lesson, you learned how to reuse items in your Web site, as well as how to create and use templates. In Lesson 24, "Server-Side Includes and Add a Date," you will learn how to use server-side includes within your site to let the server easily update a site's contents each time a user requests a specific page.

Before you continue to Lesson 24, make sure you understand the following key concepts:

◆ A library is a collection of HTML entries and related Web objects.

◆ Within UltraDev, the Library palette maintains consistency in your Web site by letting you share design elements with other Web developers.

◆ Many different types of objects can be turned into library elements.

◆ Templates are a great way to build consistency and uniformity into your site, because making a change once to a template makes that change on every page that uses the template throughout the site.

Lesson 24

Server-Side Includes and Add a Date

In Lesson 23, "Speeding Up Your Web Site Development by Reusing Elements," you learned how to use libraries and templates to simplify your Web site development. Specifically, you learned how to use the Library and Templates palettes to add and modify components that facilitate a productive development effort and a consistent look and feel to your site. In this lesson, you will learn how to use server-side includes to save time and effort when developing a Web site. You will also learn how to add a "last modified" date to your site. By the time you finish this lesson, you will understand the following key concepts:

◆ Within a Web page, you should include comments that describe the processing your page performs. Using UltraDev, comments are easy to insert into Web pages.

◆ A server-side include is a set of instructions you insert into your Web page that directs the server to insert a specific file into the current page, before sending the page's contents to the user's browser. Within UltraDev, inserting a server-side include in a Web page is easy.

◆ Using a server-side include, you can insert files into Web pages immediately before the user views the page.

◆ Using a "last modified" date on Web pages lets everyone viewing the site easily see when the pages were last updated.

Understanding Server-Side Includes

Server-side includes (SSIs) are instructions you insert into your Web page that enable the Web server to place external data into your Web pages. The instructions direct the server to include a specified file in the current Web page before sending the page to the visitor who requested the page. The data that the server places in the page can be either a data string or the contents of a file.

When you open a Web page that contains a SSI on a server, the server processes the corresponding instructions and creates a new Web page in which the include instructions are replaced by the contents of the included file. The Web server then sends the new Web page to the visitor's browser.

Without using UltraDev, when a Web developer opens a local Web page in a browser, there is no server to process the instructions in the SSI embedded in the page, so the browser opens the Web page without processing the SSI instructions. Consequently, the file that is supposed to appear in the browser does not.

This situation is relieved with UltraDev. With UltraDev, you can preview the Web pages just as the pages will appear in a browser after the server has processed the instructions contained in the SSI. This is true when you view a page in the Document window as well as when you view it in a browser. To display the included file in the Document window, UltraDev uses a translator to mimic the way a server would process the SSI instructions.

There are five main events that can be done with an SSI, as Table 24.1 describes.

Table 24.1   The five main events you can do with server-side includes

Event	Description
Insert	Inserts another file directly into the Web page. UltraDev simulates the appearance of the Web page (appearing as it would after being processed on the Web server) so you do not have to check how the page will look by transferring it to the server and viewing it there.
Echo	Echos information back from the server to display information such as a date, a visitor's IP address, the URL of the previous Web page visited, or any other information that might exist on the server.
Configure	Includes information before another include to cause certain behaviors to apply. For example, you can control the appearance of a date by specifying that it display in a certain format.
Execute	Causes the Web server to execute a CGI script. For example, if you have an SSI that includes navigation buttons on a Web page, the SSI could call a CGI script that determines what the hyperlink is for the buttons.
Display	Displays the size of the current file or Web page using SSIs.

There are two types of SSIs: Virtual and File. The type of SSI you should use is dependent on the type of Web server you are using. If you are using an Apache Web Server, you should use the Virtual type of SSI. If you are using a Microsoft IIS Server, you should choose the File type of SSI. If you are not sure what type of Web server is being used on the machine that will function as the Web server, you should ask the system administrator to determine this for you.

NOTE: *The Virtual type of SSI only works with IIS in certain specific circumstances. For example, under most circumstances, it won't allow you to include a file that exists in a directory above the current directory in the directory hierarchy.*

To make SSIs work for you, you must know a little about the configuration of your Web server:

♦ The type of Web server you are using

♦ The name and location of the directory that is going to contain your Web pages

♦ The name and location of the subdirectories that will contain SSI include files

♦ The file extensions the Web server recognizes as potentially containing SSIs

Some servers are configured to examine all files to see if they contain SSIs. Other servers are configured to only examine files with a particular file extension, such as .SHTML, .HTML, or .INC. If an SSI is not working for you, ask your system administrator if you need to use special extensions in the name of the file that uses the SSI. (For example, if a Web page that contains an SSI is named AddAQuote.html and doesn't work as expected, you may have to rename it AddAQuote.shtml.)

The Web server on your site must know which files on your site to look through while it searches for SSIs. If your Web server is set up to look for SSIs in all file types, then this adds a lot of overhead to the site, because the Web server must search through every page to identify SSIs. Often, Web servers are configured to look for SSIs in files that have extensions of .SHTML, .SHTM, and .STM. The Web server that is set up to look in those files for SSIs will only parse files that have those file extensions while it looks for SSIs.

You should consider SSIs for use in many of the same situations in which you would consider using library items. You can update an included file and change every page in your site that references the included file. UltraDev inserts the contents of the library item into the Web page, but the contents of the file that is referenced in an SSI gets inserted when the visitor requests the Web page.

Inserting a Server-Side Include into Your Page

Viewing an SSI embedded in a Web page in the Document window is much like viewing an HTML comment. In fact, you insert an SSI in a Web page by first inserting a comment into the Web page. The information contained in the comment is what turns it from a comment into an SSI.

A comment in a Web page is usually text that explains or describes a snippet of code appearing on the page, or could even explain the Web page itself. As you create Web pages, you should make extensive use of comments to explain your processing. That way, if you (or another developer) must later change the page, you can read the comments to better understand the processing the page performs.

A comment, and an SSI, appears in a Web page as an invisible element, and you can view and edit the comment or SSI via the Property Inspector. To see how to insert an SSI, you will first learn how to insert a comment into a Web page.

To insert a comment into a Web page, perform these steps:

1. Within UltraDev, click at the location on the Web page where you want to insert the comment.

2. Select the Insert menu Invisible Tags option and choose Comment. UltraDev will display the Insert Comment window, as shown in Figure 24.1.

Figure 24.1

The Insert Comment window is where you enter text to describe something about the Web page, and where you enter the SSI text.

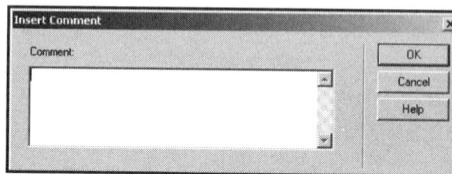

3. Within the Insert Comment window, enter descriptive text in the text box to meet whatever needs you have. As shown in Figure 24.2, I have inserted text as a comment that describes what the links that play audio files do when a visitor clicks on one of them.

Figure 24.2

Entering text in the text window to describe something about the Web page. In this case, I've described what occurs when a visitor clicks on one of the linked author names on the page.

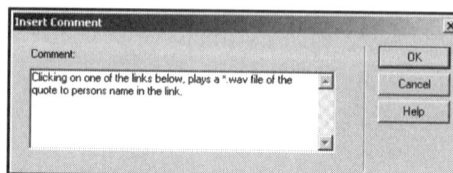

4. Click on the OK button to close the window and insert the comment into your Web page.

When you click on the OK button in the Insert Comment window, you insert the comment into the Web page. But, because UltraDev stores the comment as an invisible element, you cannot view the comment on the Web page. What does show for you is an invisible-comment icon in the Document window. If you do click (either a single or double click will work) on the invisible-comment icon, UltraDev will display the Comment Properties Inspector that contains the comment, as shown in Figure 24.3.

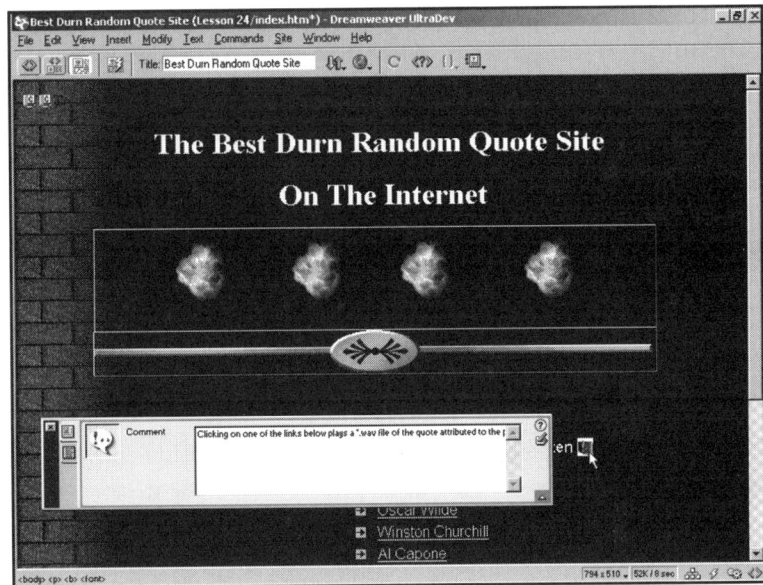

Figure 24.3

The cursor is pointing to the invisible-comment icon that, when you double-click on it, will pop up a Comment window.

Within the Comments Property Inspector that pops up, you will see an icon in the upper-right corner that looks like a pencil on a piece of paper. If you click on this icon, UltraDev will display the Quick Tag editor, which lets you view the HTML tag pair that contains the comment. In between the tag pair is the comment itself, as shown in Figure 24.4.

You will notice in the Quick Tag editor window the text that appears as follows:

```
<!—Clicking on one of the links below plays a *.wav file of the quote
attributed to the persons name in the link.>
```

The symbols < ! — tell the browser that what follows is a comment. The character —> ends the comment.

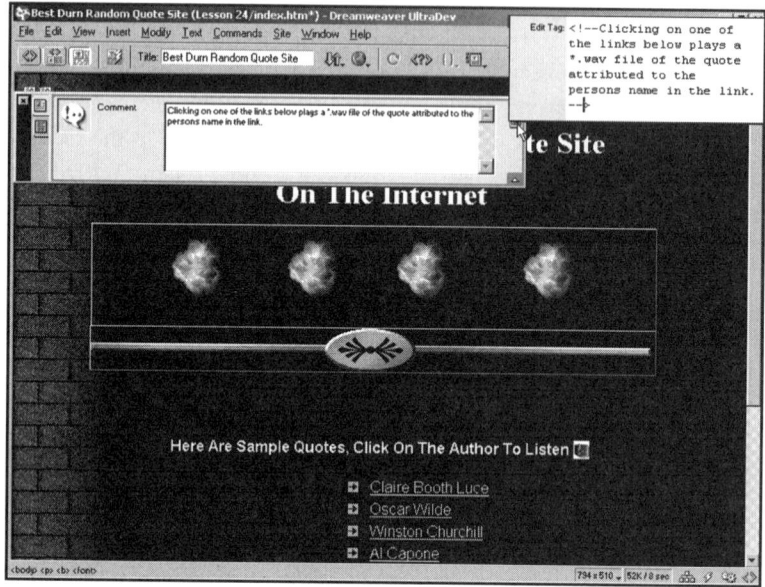

Figure 24.4

Clicking on the Quick Tag editor opens a window that shows the contents of the comment tag.

Creating a Server-Side Include from a Comment

After you have inserted a comment into the Web page, you can convert the comment into an SSI. Table 24.2 lists some of the SSI commands you can insert into your document.

Table 24.2 Some SSIs that you can include in your Web page as a comment

SSI Code	Description
#echo var="DATE_LOCAL"	Displays the current date and time
#echo var="DOCUMENT_NAME"	Displays the name of the Web page
#echo var="HTTP_REFERER"	Displays the URL of the Web page just visited
#echo var="HTTP_USER_AGENT"	Displays the visitor's browser name and version, and their operating system
#echo var="REMOTE_ADDR"	Displays the visitor's IP number

As the table describes, an SSI appears different from a comment insofar as the SSI begins with a pound (#) sign. The pound sign character instructs the Web server that what follows is an SSI that the server must process.

As you create your sites, you can enter one of the commands, or any of the other SSI commands, directly into the Comment window. Then, you will save the Web page to the local machine and to the remote location. Next, when you visit the Web site and the page executes, the server will process the SSI before the server sends the page to the visitor's browser. Figure 24.5 shows an SSI within the Comment window that will direct the server to display the date and time within the Web page.

Figure 24.5

The SSI to display the date and time is placed in the Comment window. Because of the pound (#) sign, the Web server will identify this as an SSI and process it accordingly.

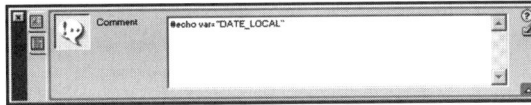

Creating a Server-Side Include of a File

As you just learned, within a Web page, you create an SSI by inserting a comment into the Web page. In addition to inserting individual commands into an SSI, you can also direct the SSI to include a file into the Web page. Including a file in a Web page gives you tremendous capability to dynamically change the information that appears on a Web page without having to change the Web page itself. Because you can change the contents of the file without changing the Web page itself, the next time a visitor accesses the page, they will retrieve the current contents of the included file.

To create an SSI that places an external file into a Web page, perform these steps:

1. Open a text editor (such as Windows Notepad) and enter some text. Next, save the file to the same directory on the server in which the Web page will reside. In the example in Figure 24.6, I have created the file LinkExplain.txt.

Figure 24.6

Create text to be included in the SSI in a text file using an external editor, such as Notepad.

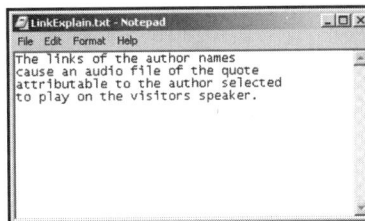

2. Within UltraDev, open the Web page that will contain the SSI.

3. Within the Document window, click at the location where you want to insert the SSI.

4. Select the Insert menu Server Side Include option. UltraDev, in turn, will display the Select File window.

5. Within the Select File window, locate and click on the name of the text file you created in Step 1. As shown in Figure 24.7, I have selected the file LinkExplain.txt.

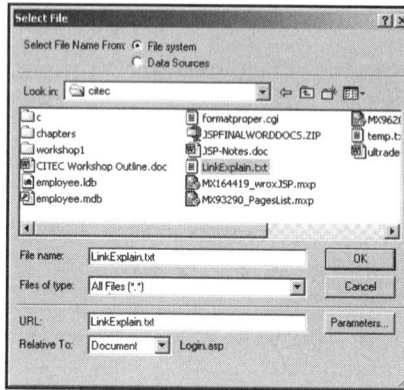

Figure 24.7

Select the name of the file containing the SSI text in the Select File window.

6. Click on the OK button.

7. The text within the LinkExplain.txt file will now appear within the Web page, as shown in Figure 24.8.

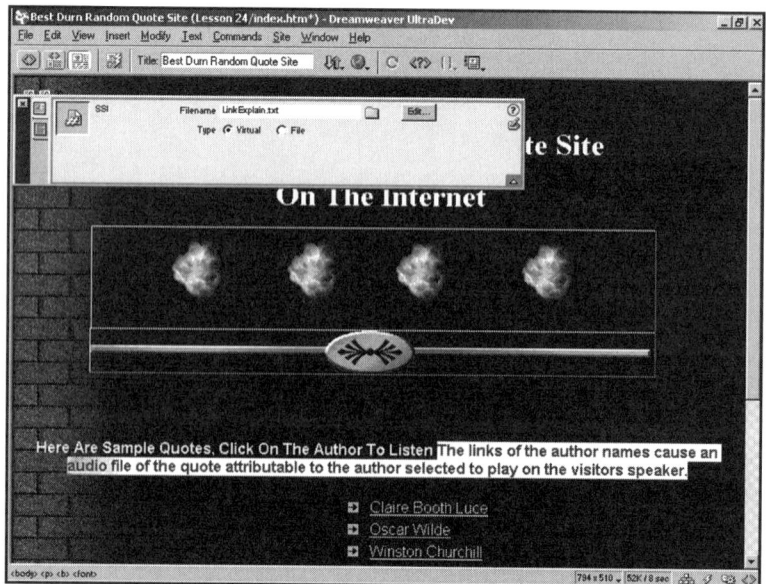

Figure 24.8

The Document window shows the SSI in the document.

Later, when a visitor accesses the page, he or she will see the contents of the included file, as shown in Figure 24.9.

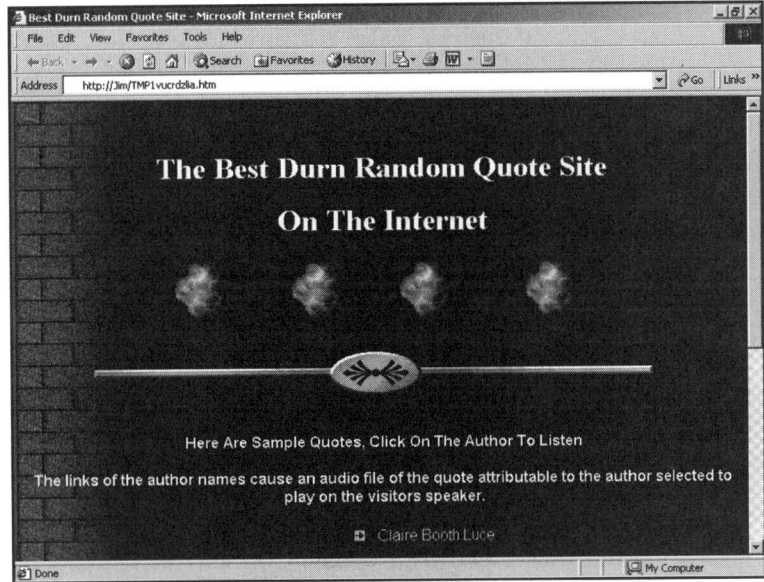

Figure 24.9

The included SSI file is displayed on the Web page.

Including a Last Modified Date on Your Site

On many sites, the developer of the site provides a "last modified" item on the site to let visitors know when the site was last updated. Personally, I do not like to see such a message appear on any site that is not frequently updated. The reason is that visitors to a site will return to that site and browse it only if the site offers something new to see. If they see a "last modified" date on the Web page they're viewing, and if that date is old (in their minds), then they probably will not look any further.

The problem of a visitor seeing an old "last modified" date and then deciding to look at other sites is exacerbated by the fact that some Web site developers put a "last modified" date on every page of the site. Wow! This is really asking for trouble, unless the developer is sure that each of the pages on the site is going to be updated frequently, thus keeping the "last modified" date updated.

Fortunately, UltraDev provides a really easy way to add a "last modified" date to a site that will set the date to the date that the Web page it appears on was last saved.

Add an UltraDev Date Object to a Page

To add an UltraDev Date object to a page, perform these steps:

1. Within UltraDev, open the page within which you want to place a Date object.

2. Within the page, click at the location where you want to place the Date object, as shown in Figure 24.10.

Figure 24.10

The UltraDev date object will appear at the cursor location.

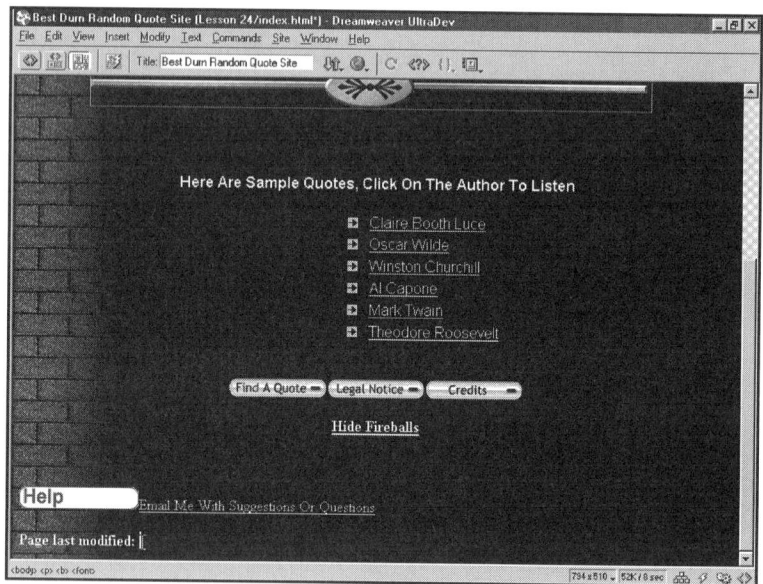

3. If the Objects palette is not visible, press the Ctrl+F2 keyboard combination. UltraDev will display the Objects palette.

4. Within the Objects palette, click on the Insert Date icon. UltraDev, in turn, will display the Insert Date window, as shown in Figure 24.11.

Figure 24.11

The Insert Date window lets you specify a format for the date that is inserted as an UltraDev object on the Web page.

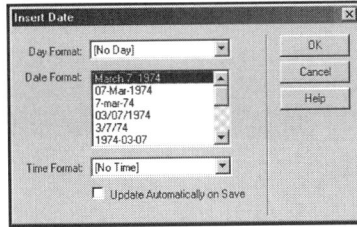

5. Within the Insert Date window, click on the date format that meets your needs and then click on the OK button to close the window and insert the object onto the Web page. UltraDev, in turn, will display the date inserted onto your Web page, as shown in Figure 24.12.

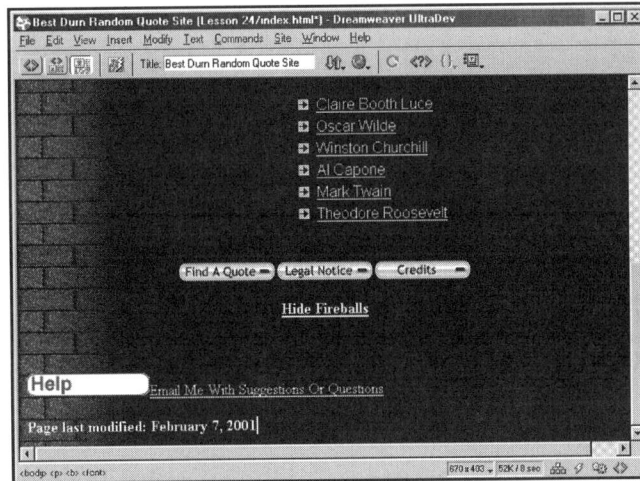

Figure 24.12

The Web page with the Date UltraDev object, as it appears in the Document window.

What You Must Know

In this lesson, you learned how to reuse items in your Web site, as well as how to use server-side includes and the "last modified" date Web page element. In Lesson 25, "Viewing and Modifying HTML," you will learn how to work with HTML on your Web pages.

◆ Before you continue to Lesson 25, make sure you understand the following key concepts: Within your Web pages, you should insert comments that describe the page's processing. Comments help you or another developer who must change the page to better understand the page's processing.

◆ A server-side include is a set of instructions you insert into a page that directs the server to perform specific processing before it downloads the page's contents to a visitor's browser.

◆ To create a server-side include using UltraDev, you first create a comment, and then, within the comment, you insert the corresponding instructions.

◆ You can insert files into a page using server-side includes to give your site the ability to show updated content without changing the actual page in UltraDev.

◆ Using an UltraDev Date object, you can easily provide a "last modified" date on a Web page.

Lesson 25

Viewing and Modifying HTML

In Lesson 24, "Server-Side Includes and Add a Date," you learned how to use server-side includes to direct the server to perform specific processing before it downloads a page to a visitor's browser. You also learned how to comment your Web pages to provide meaningful notes for yourself or another Web designer who must later modify the site.

Across the Web, all sites are built around HTML tags. When you create a site using UltraDev, you often do not have to worry about specific HTML entries. Instead, UltraDev handles the HTML for you, behind the scenes. As your sites become more complex, however, there will be times when you must edit one or more HTML entries to fine-tune your site's processing. In this lesson, you will learn how to work with HTML on your Web pages. By the time you finish this lesson, you will understand the following key concepts:

♦ Within UltraDev, you can view and edit HTML tags using the UltraDev Quick Tag Editor.

♦ The UltraDev Code Inspector displays the HTML source of a Web page.

♦ In addition to letting you view a site's HTML entries, UltraDev provides facilities you can use to customize the HTML preferences.

♦ If you are already familiar with a specific HTML editor, you can configure UltraDev to use it.

Viewing and Editing HTML Tags

HTML (*Hypertext Markup Language*) is the language that Web pages use to communicate their layout and composition to browsers. The language usually consists of paired tags, which are references that describe the content and layout of the information that resides between the two tag pairs. Although this book does not intend to teach you HTML, it does introduce you to the facilities in UltraDev that allow you to view and edit HTML.

HTML tags are contained in angled brackets (< and >) and surround objects on a Web page, such as text, images, and so on. Some tags, such as the <img> tag you use to insert images into a Web page, are single tags, meaning you only use one tag. Other tags, in contrast, require a starting and ending tag. You might, for example, use one tag to tell a browser when to start using a bold font and a second tag to tell the browser to turn off bolding. The beginning tag of a tag-paired set contains the tag name, such as `<form>`. The ending tag precedes the name with a forward slash, such as `</form>`. Tags also often contain attribute values that modify the way objects look on a page.

When you work on a Web page within the Document window, UltraDev inserts all the HTML code for you. With UltraDev's What You See Is What You Get (WYSIWYG) interface, you do not have to memorize the various HTML tag pairs. However, sometimes you will need to view the HTML code created by UltraDev, and other times you will need to edit the HTML code. The facility you use to view and edit HTML code in UltraDev is the Quick Tag Editor.

Accessing the Quick Tag Editor

UltraDev gives you two ways to access the Quick Tag Editor. The method you use is really up to individual preferences. To access the Quick Tag Editor from the Property Inspector, perform these steps:

1. Within UltraDev, click on the object in the Web page for which you want to view the HTML code.

2. If the Property Inspector is not active, press the Ctrl+F3 key combination.

3. Within the Property Inspector, click on the Quick Tag Editor icon, shown in Figure 25.1.

Figure 25.1

The Quick Tag Editor icon on the Property Inspector gives quick access to the Quick Tag Editor.

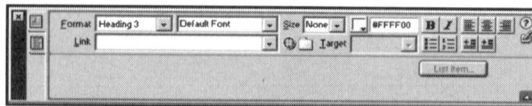

4. When you activate the Quick Tag Editor, UltraDev will display the Quick Tag Editor window, shown in Figure 25.2.

Figure 25.2

The Quick Tag Editor displays as a small pop-up window in the document window.

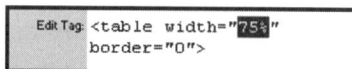

The other way to access the Quick Tag Editor is a preferred method if you do not have the Property Inspector visible in the document window. To access the Quick Tag Editor this way, perform these steps:

1. Within the Document window, right-click on any item on the Web page. UltraDev, in turn, will display a context pop-up menu for that object.

2. Within the menu, click on Edit Tag <a>. UltraDev, in turn, will display the Quick Tag Editor, previously shown in Figure 25.2.

Understanding Quick Tag Editor Modes

The three modes in which you can use the Quick Tag Editor are described in Table 25.1. The following sections describe each mode in detail.

Table 25.1   The three Quick Tag Editor modes

Mode Name	Description
Edit	Lets you edit the code in the HTML tag
Insert	Lets you insert code into the HTML tag
Wrap Tag	Lets you wrap another HTML tag around the selected tag

UltraDev gives you the ability to toggle through each of these modes while viewing the Quick Tag Editor. To toggle through these modes, press Ctrl+T.

Using Edit Mode Within the Quick Tag Editor

As you create Web pages, sometimes you may need to edit an HTML tag or the tag's contents. Using the Quick Tag Editor's Edit mode, you can edit not only the HTML tag, but also the contents within the HTML tag.

After you open the Quick Tag Editor for a section of the Web page within the document window, and have toggled to Edit mode, you make the changes directly in the Quick Tag Editor window, shown in Figure 25.3.

Many HTML tags let you specify attributes that control certain aspects of the HTML tag. For example, the <h1> tag specifies that the text that follows is to be formatted in the Heading 1 style. However, you can also specify alignment attributes with this tag. With this in mind, you can write an HTML tag that centers a line of text formatted in the Heading 1 style as: <h1 align="Center">.

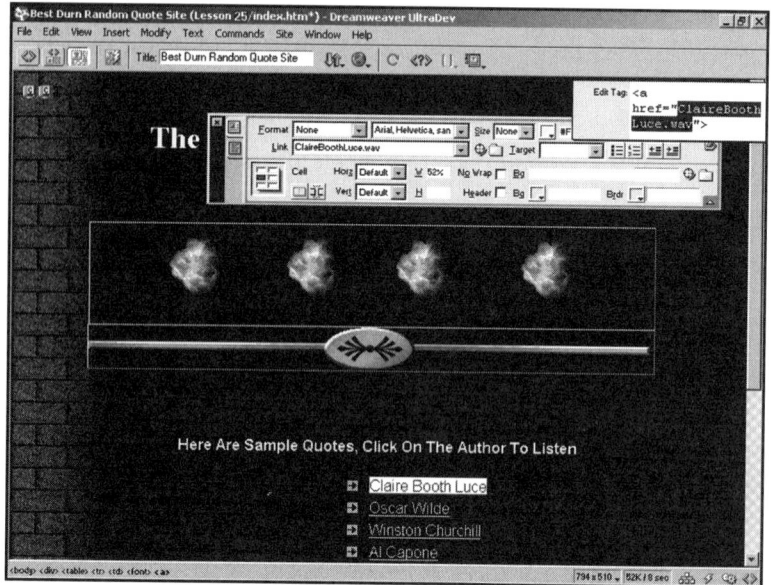

Figure 25.3

In Edit mode on the Quick Tag Editor, you can edit the HTML tag as well as the contents within the tag.

UltraDev gives you the ability to quickly add attributes to an HTML tag. To add attributes to a tag, perform these steps:

1. Within the Quick Tag Editor window, right-click at the end of the tag contents. UltraDev, in turn, will display a pop-up window of the various attributes that you can select for the HTML tag, as shown in Figure 25.4.

2. Within the attribute window, scroll down the list of attributes until you find the one you want. Next, click on the attribute. UltraDev will append the attribute you selected to the selected HTML tag in the Quick Tag Editor.

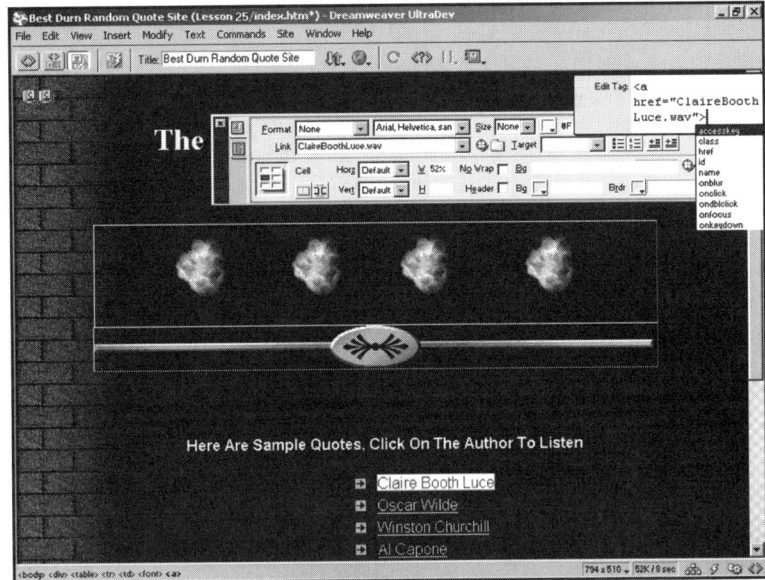

Figure 25.4

You can add attributes specific to the selected HTML tag from within the Quick Tag Editor.

Using Insert Mode Within the Quick Tag Editor

Within the Quick Tag Editor's Insert mode, you can insert HTML tag pairs directly into the Web page that resides in the document window. This is a very useful feature for those developers who are comfortable with HTML and want the control afforded by working directly with HTML in their Web pages.

After you open the Quick Tag Editor for a section of the Web page within the Document window, and have toggled to Insert mode, you can add the HTML tag pairs directly in the Quick Tag Editor window. To add an HTML tag pair to your page using the Quick Tag Editor, perform these steps:

1. Within the Quick Tag Editor window, right-click at the location in your Web page where you want to insert the HTML tag pair. UltraDev, in turn, will display a pop-up window of the various HTML tag pairs that you can insert, as shown in Figure 25.5.

2. Within the tag-pair pop-up window, scroll down the list of HTML tag pairs until you find the one you want. Click on the tag you desire. UltraDev, in turn, will place the tag or tag pair within the Quick Tag Editor.

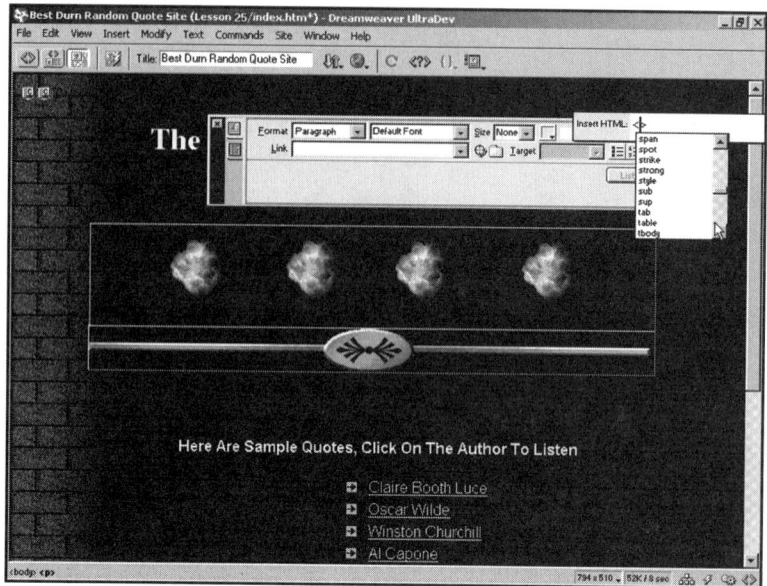

Figure 25.5

You can add specific HTML tag pairs from within the Quick Tag Editor.

Using Wrap Tag Mode Within the Quick Tag Editor

Within the Quick Tag Editor, Wrap Tag mode lets you wrap HTML tag pairs directly around the HTML tag selected and displayed in the Quick Tag Editor. You might, for example, wrap an HTML tag pair around an existing HTML tag pair when you want to make a link out of an item heading line. The ability to wrap tags in this way is another very useful feature for developers who are comfortable working with HTML.

After you open the Quick Tag Editor for a section of the Web page within the Document window, and have toggled to Wrap mode, you can add the HTML tag pairs directly to the page from within the Quick Tag editor window, by performing these steps:

1. Within the Quick Tag Editor window, right-click at the location in your Web page where you want to wrap the HTML tag pair. UltraDev will display a pop-up window of the various HTML tag pairs that you can add to the existing HTML tag pair, as shown in Figure 25.6.

2. Within the tag-pair list, click on the tag you desire. UltraDev, in turn, will display the HTML tag pair within the Quick Tag Editor, and the item will appear in the document window with the new HTML tag applied to it.

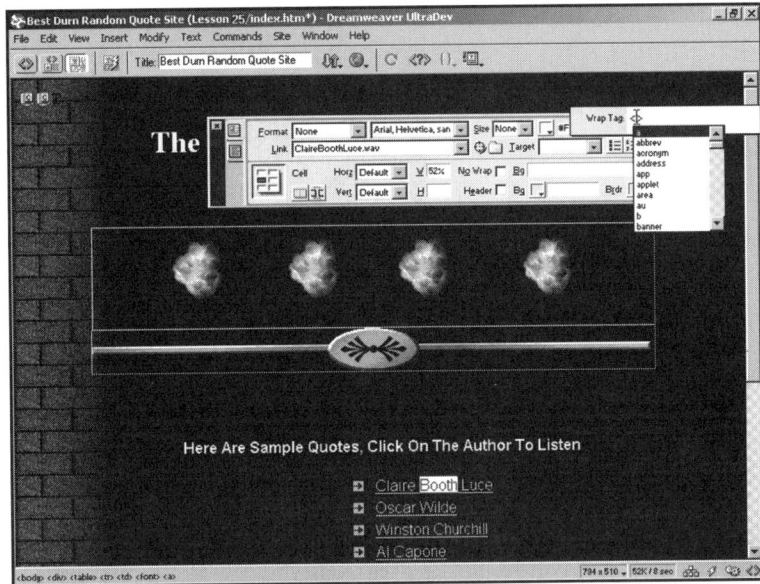

Figure 25.6

You can add specific HTML tag pairs to an existing HTML tag from within the Quick Tag Editor.

Using the Code Inspector

Within UltraDev, the Code Inspector displays the HTML source code for a Web page currently displayed in the document window. A developer can use the Code Inspector to quickly view the HTML code that surrounds a selected object. As the number of objects on a Web page increases, and as the HTML code to support those objects increases, the Code Inspector becomes even more valuable as a way to view and navigate through the HTML code.

Launching the Code Inspector is very easy. You simply press the F10 key from within the Document window. UltraDev, in turn, will display the document window with the cursor positioned at the HTML code that supports the object that resides where the cursor is located. For example, before I launched the Code Inspector, I positioned the cursor directly before the words "Page last modified" at the bottom of the Index.html page. As you can see in Figure 25.7, the cursor in the Code Inspector is positioned inside the tag pair, before the words "Page last modified."

NOTE: *You can change the text that displays on the page in the Code Inspector, but you cannot change any of the HTML tag pairs. To do that, you have to use the Quick Tag Editor.*

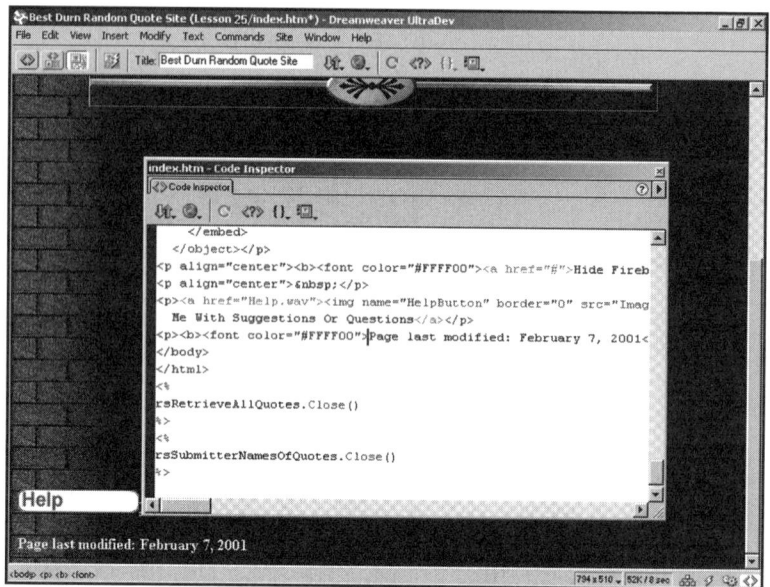

Figure 25.7

The Code Inspector is useful for viewing the HTML code that supports the objects on a Web page.

Setting HTML Preferences

UltraDev gives you a lot of freedom to change the appearance of HTML tags and code. You must be very careful when you change any of the preferences described in this section unless you are very sure of what you are doing. Setting an UltraDev HTML preference does give you the ability to customize how UltraDev works with HTML on your machine.

> **NOTE:** *The changes you make to the HTML preferences are applicable to your machine only. In other words, if you modify the HTML preferences and change the pages that appear on a site, another developer working on the site will not view the site using your preferences. Those are unique to your machine.*

Within UltraDev, there are three sets of HTML preferences that you can modify, as described in Table 25.2. The following sections describe each of these categories in detail as well as how to adjust the properties in each category.

Table 25.2   *The three HTML preferences categories*

Category	Description
Code Colors	Controls the background, text, tag, and reserved keyword colors of HTML in the Code Inspector
Code Format	Controls code formatting, such as indentation, line length, and the case of tag and attribute names
Code Rewriting	Controls what UltraDev does while opening HTML documents

Setting Code Color Preferences

Many developers like to use colors to represent various types of HTML tags. This is particularly true if you're looking at a page of HTML that is lengthy, or complex. Using Code Color Preferences, you can assign specific colors to certain HTML tags.

To set Code Colors preferences for HTML, perform these steps:

1. Within the Document window, select the Edit menu Preferences option. UltraDev, in turn, will display the Preferences window.

2. Within the Preferences window Category list, click on the Code Colors category. UltraDev will display the Code Colors Preferences window, as shown in Figure 25.8.

Figure 25.8

The Code Colors category of the Preferences window is where you control the background, text, tag, and reserved keyword colors of HTML in the Code Inspector.

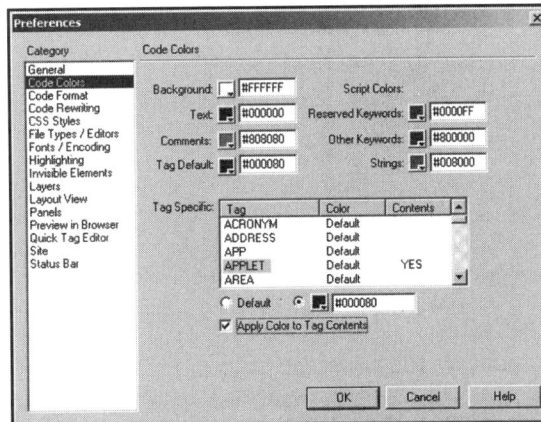

3. Within the Code Colors Preferences window, change colors for the settings you desire and then click on the OK button to save the preferences.

Table 25.3 lists the various controls on the Code Colors Preferences window and what they do.

Table 25.3   The Code Colors category controls of the Preferences window

Control Name	Description
Background	Specifies the background color of the Code Inspector window
Text	Specifies the color of the text that appears between HTML tag pairs
Comments	Specifies the color of the HTML comment tags (i.e., the < ! -- tags)
Tag Default	Specifies the color for all the tags except HTML comment tags
Reserved Keywords	Specifies the color for all reserved keywords
Other Keywords	Specifies the color for all keywords except reserved keywords
Strings	Specifies the color for all strings in your code
Tag Specific	Lets you specify a color for special tags that overrides the other color settings

Setting Code Format Preferences

Just as some developers prefer to use different colors to represent specific HTML tags, some people also prefer to view HTML code in set formats. By using Code Format Preferences, you can create a format to display HTML code.

To set Code Format preferences for HTML, perform these steps:

1. Within the Document window, select the Edit menu Preferences option. UltraDev will display the Preferences window.

2. Within the Preferences window Category list, click on the Code Format category. UltraDev, in turn, will display the Code Format Preferences window, as shown in Figure 25.9.

3. Within the Code Format Preferences window, change the formats you desire and then click on the OK button to save the preferences.

Table 25.4 lists the various controls on the Code Format Preferences window and what they do.

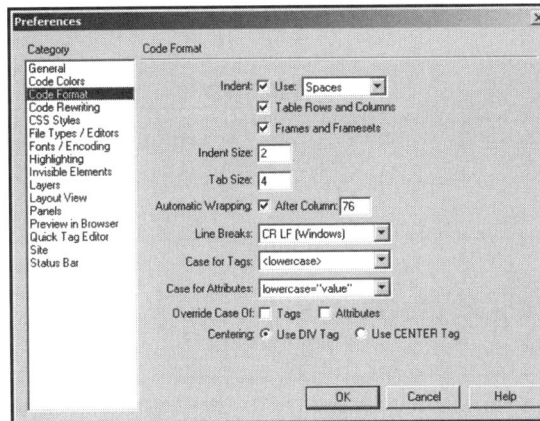

Figure 25.9

The Code Format category of the Preferences window is where you control code formatting, such as indentation, line length, and the case of tag and attribute names.

Table 25.4   The Code Format category controls of the Preferences window

Control Name	Description
Indents	Specifies whether to turn on indentation of all tags using the `<indent></indent>` HTML tag pair. With this option turned on, text that appears within the HTML `<indent></indent>` tag pair will indented when viewed in the editor.
Use	Specifies whether to indent using a space character or a tab.
Table Rows and Columns	Specifies whether to automatically indent the HTML tag pairs `<tr></tr>` and `<td></td>`,which makes tables easier to read in many situations.
Frames and Framesets	Specifies whether to automatically indent the HTML tag pairs `<frame></frame>`and `<frame></frameset>`,which makes tables easier to read in many situations.
Indent Size	Specifies the size of the indentations, if indentations are used. The number specified here relates to what is specified in the Use control.
Tab Size	Specifies the length of the tabs.
Automatic Wrapping	Specifies whether to add soft returns to a line of HTML code once that line reaches the specified column width.
Line Breaks	Specifies the type of remote server that hosts the remote site. The correct line break character specific to the remote server is important to ensure that HTML source code is viewed correctly.
Case for Tags and Case for Attributes	Let you control the capitalization of tag and attribute names, respectively.

(continued)

Table 25.4 (continued)

Control Name	Description
Override Case Of: Tags and Attributes	Lets you control whether to enforce specified case options at all times, including when an existing HTML document is opened.
Centering	Specifies whether elements should appear centered.

Setting Code Rewriting Preferences

Code Rewriting Preferences are set within UltraDev to allow you to keep a record and view the history of code modifications. This function works much the same as the Revisions feature in Microsoft Word.

To set Code Rewriting preferences for HTML, perform these steps:

1. Within the Document window, select the Edit menu Preferences option. UltraDev will display the Preferences window.

2. Within the Preferences window Category list, click on the Code Rewriting category. UltraDev, in turn, will display the Code Rewriting Preferences window, as shown in Figure 25.10.

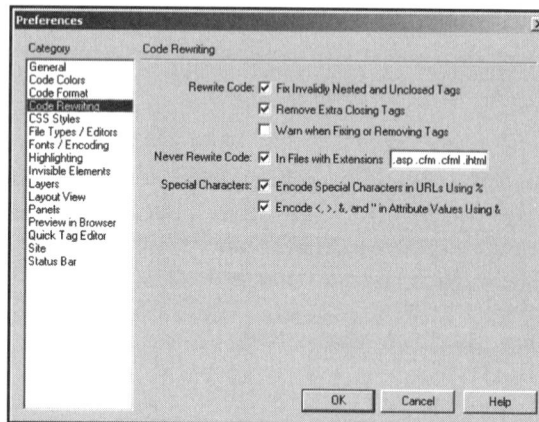

Figure 25.10

The Code Rewriting category of the Preferences window is where you control what UltraDev does while opening HTML documents.

3. Within the Code Rewriting Preferences window, change the preferences option as desired and then click on the OK button to save the preferences.

Table 25.5 lists the various controls on the Code Rewriting Preferences window and what they do.

Table 25.5   The Code Rewriting category controls of the Preferences window

Control Name	Description
Fix Invalidly Nested and Unclosed Tags	Instructs UltraDev to automatically fix overlapping tags. For example, if you have a set of HTML tag pairs appearing as `<b><I> This is bold, italicized text </b><I>`, UltraDev will re-write it as `<b><I> This is bold, italicized text </i><b>`.
Remove Extra Closing Tags	Instructs UltraDev to delete closing tags that have no opening tag.
Warn when Fixing or Removing Tags	Instructs UltraDev to display a warning message when either of the previous two options are turned on.
Never Rewrite HTML: In Files with Extensions	Instructs UltraDev to not rewrite HTML in files with the file name extensions specified in the text box.
Special Characters	These two options control whether UltraDev encodes certain characters in certain contexts.

Additional HTML Facilities

In addition to the facilities discussed so far in this lesson, UltraDev provides three additional components:

♦ The Clean Up HTML facility

♦ The Clean Up Word HTML facility

♦ The capability to launch an external HTML editor

The following sections describe each of these three facilities.

Using the Clean Up HTML Facility

Within UltraDev, you use the Clean Up HTML facility to remove empty HTML tags, combine nested `<font></font>` tag pairs, and otherwise improve messy or improperly formatted HTML. To clean up HTML using the Clean Up HTML facility in UltraDev, perform these steps:

1. Within the Document window, with a Web page loaded, select the Commands menu Clean Up HTML option. UltraDev, in turn, will launch the Clean Up HTML window, as shown in Figure 25.11.

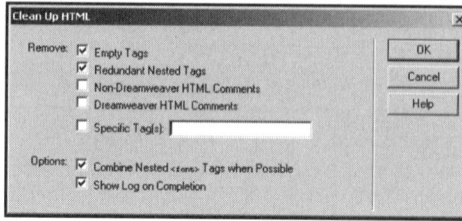

Figure 25.11

The Clean Up HTML window lets you specify what actions to perform when HTML is cleaned up.

2. Within the Clean Up HTML window, click your mouse on one of the desired cleanup options, as described in Table 25.6, and then click on the OK button to begin the cleanup process.

Table 25.6   The Clean Up HTML window options

Control Name	Description
Remove Empty Tags	Removes HTML tag pairs that have no code or text between them.
Remove Redundant Nested Tags	Removes HTML tag pairs that are redundant and superfluous.
Remove Non-Dreamweaver HTML Comments	Removes all comments that exist in the HTML code that were not inserted by Dreamweaver.
Remove Dreamweaver HTML Comments	Removes all comments that exist in the HTML code that were inserted by Dreamweaver.
Remove Specific Tag(s)	Removes the HTML tags that are specified in the adjacent text box.
Combine Nested <font> Tags when Possible	Instructs UltraDev to consolidate two or more `<font></font>` tag pairs when they control the same range of text.
Show Log on Completion	Displays a message box with details about the changes made after the OK button is clicked. If the changes are not acceptable, close the document window without saving the changes, which causes the window to revert to the previously saved version of the Web page.

Using the Clean Up Word HTML Facility

Microsoft Word has a component called Doc-to-HTML that allows you to create an HTML page from a Word document by clicking a couple of options from within Word. This capability was designed and developed to work closely with Microsoft's FrontPage Web development tool. Consequently, there are a number of HTML tags and tag pairs that get created when using Doc-to-HTML in Word that can be removed if the HTML page is imported into UltraDev.

You would use the Clean Up Word HTML facility in UltraDev to remove extraneous HTML code generated by Word. This facility is only useful if the page that is displayed in the document window was created or last saved using a version of Microsoft Word. The code that UltraDev cleans up is primarily code that is used by Microsoft Word to format and display documents in Word but that is not needed to display an HTML file.

To clean up HTML using the Clean Up Word HTML facility in UltraDev, perform these steps:

1. Within the document window, with a Web page loaded, select the Commands menu Clean Up Word HTML option. If UltraDev cannot identify whether the page loaded in the document window was created using Microsoft Word, you will see a warning message as shown in Figure 25.12.

Figure 25.12

If UltraDev cannot identify that Microsoft Word was used to create the Web page loaded in the document window, you will see this warning message.

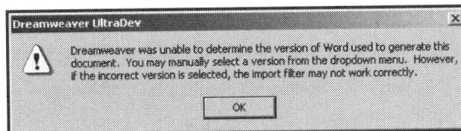

2. If you click on the OK button on the warning message, or if you do not see this message, UltraDev will launch the Clean Up Word HTML window, as shown in Figures 25.13. As seen in Figure 25.14, UltraDev presents you with a window that allows you to select which cleanup options you want to invoke.

Figure 25.13

The options on the Basic tab instruct UltraDev how to handle certain conditions that may occur in the HTML code existing on a Web page created using MS Word.

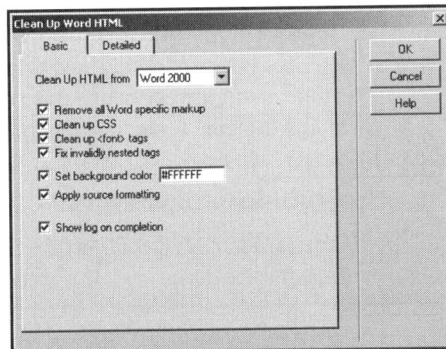

Figure 25.14

The options on the Detailed tab further instruct UltraDev how to handle certain conditions that may occur in the HTML code existing on a Web page created using MS Word.

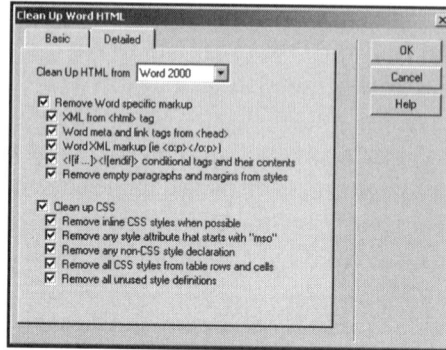

3. Within the Clean Up Word HTML window, as described in Table 25.7, click your mouse on the desired options to invoke to cleanup the HTML document, and then on the OK button to begin the cleanup process.

Table 25.7   The Clean Up Word HTML window options

Control Name	Description
Remove all Word specific markup	Instructs UltraDev to remove all MS Word–specific HTML markup.
Clean up CSS	Instructs UltraDev to remove all MS Word–specific CSS code, including inline CSS styles.
Clean up <font> tags	Instructs UltraDev to remove HTML font tags and convert the text to the default body text size of 2 HTML text.
Fix invalidly nested tags	Instructs UltraDev to remove the font markup tags inserted by MS Word that exist outside the paragraph and heading tags.
Set background color	Allows you to enter a background color that UltraDev uses in your document.
Apply source formatting	Applies the source code formatting options that are specified in the HTML Format Preferences window.
Show log on completion	Displays a message box with details about the changes made after the OK button is clicked. If the changes are not acceptable, close the document window without saving the changes, which causes the window to revert to the previously saved version of the Web page.
Remove Word specific markup	Instructs UltraDev to remove all HTML markup in the source Web page that is specific to MS Word.
Clean up <font> tags (Conversion drop-down list boxes)	Instructs UltraDev to convert the font size attributes to the ones selected in the drop-down list boxes.

Launching an External Editor

Given all the strengths of UltraDev as a Web site development tool, including those that make it a decent HTML editing tool, some people still prefer to use another HTML editor over the one provided in UltraDev. Fortunately, the developers at Macromedia have recognized this and have built the capability into UltraDev to let you define another HTML editor to use seamlessly with UltraDev. You do this by defining the editor to UltraDev in the Preferences panel.

After you define an external HTML editor and select the editor to edit the HTML from within the HTML Source Inspector, UltraDev launches the external editor defined, with the HTML pages already loaded.

To define an external editor to use with UltraDev, perform these steps:

1. Select the Edit menu Preferences option. UltraDev will display the Preferences window.

2. Within the Preferences window, click on File Types/Editors in the Category list. UltraDev will display the File Types/Editors Preferences window.

3. Within the File Types/Editors Preferences window, click on the Browse button to open the Select External Editor window.

4. Within the Select External Editor window, browse your machine's directories to select the name of the executable relating to the external editor you want to use.

5. After you locate the external editor you want to use in UltraDev, click the Open button to place the name of the external editor's executable in the File Types/Editors Preferences window. Your File Types/Editors Preferences window will look like Figure 25.15.

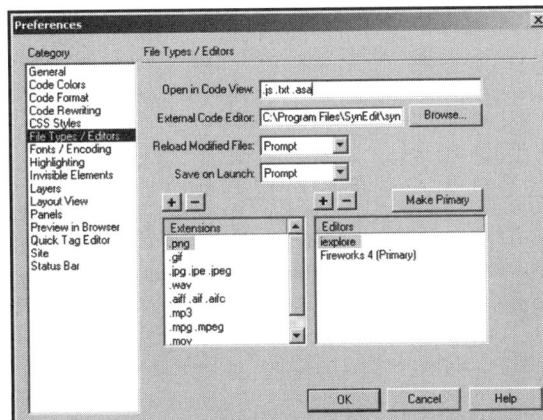

Figure 25.15

Select the name of the executable for your HTML editor and place it in the File Types/Editors Preferences window.

6. Click on the OK button to save the selection.

Defining the executable to execute when you want to launch an external editor for HTML is only half of the battle. You then need to open a Web page in the Document window and launch the external editor. To do that, perform these steps:

1. Open the Web page to edit within the Document window.

2. Press Ctrl+E. UltraDev, in turn, will launch the external editor and load the HTML for the current Web page into the editor.

What You Must Know

In this lesson, you learned how to work with HTML that exists in your Web pages. You also learned how to configure the look of the HTML in the HTML Source Inspector and how to configure an external HTML editor to work in conjunction with UltraDev. In Lesson 26, "Customizing Dreamweaver UltraDev," you will learn how to customize the UltraDev interface to better suit our needs.

Before you continue to Lesson 26, make sure you understand the following key concepts:

◆ You use the UltraDev Quick Tag Editor to view and edit HTML tags.

◆ The Code Inspector displays the HTML source code that defines a Web page.

◆ Using UltraDev preferences, you can configure the look of HTML code in the HTML Source Inspector.

◆ If you have a favorite HTML editor, you can easily configure UltraDev to use the editor.

Lesson 26

Customizing
Dreamweaver UltraDev

In Lesson 25, "Viewing and Modifying HTML," you learned how to work with HTML on your Web pages. Specifically, you learned how to view and edit HTML tags, how to use and customize the Code Inspector, and how to define and use an external HTML editor. In this lesson, you will learn how to customize the UltraDev interface to suit your needs. As you will learn, UltraDev lets you customize many of its components by modifying the Objects palette, the command menu, or one or more behaviors. By the time you finish this lesson, you will understand the following key concepts:

◆ Using the Objects palette, you can create custom objects within UltraDev. Such objects might be used to add objects on a page with unique behaviors.

◆ Within UltraDev, you can create new Menu commands that assist you in using the UltraDev interface in becoming more productive.

◆ A behavior is a customized entity that allows you to quickly place specific controls that predefined events that occur. Using UltraDev, you can easily edit behavior actions.

Modifying the Objects Palette

When shipped from Macromedia, Inc., the Objects palette of UltraDev contains seven panes:

◆ Characters

◆ Common

◆ Forms

◆ Frames

- ◆ Head

- ◆ Invisibles

- ◆ Live

- ◆ Special

The objects that are contained on each of these seven panes reside in subdirectories beneath the UltraDev directory on your hard drive, as shown in Figure 26.1.

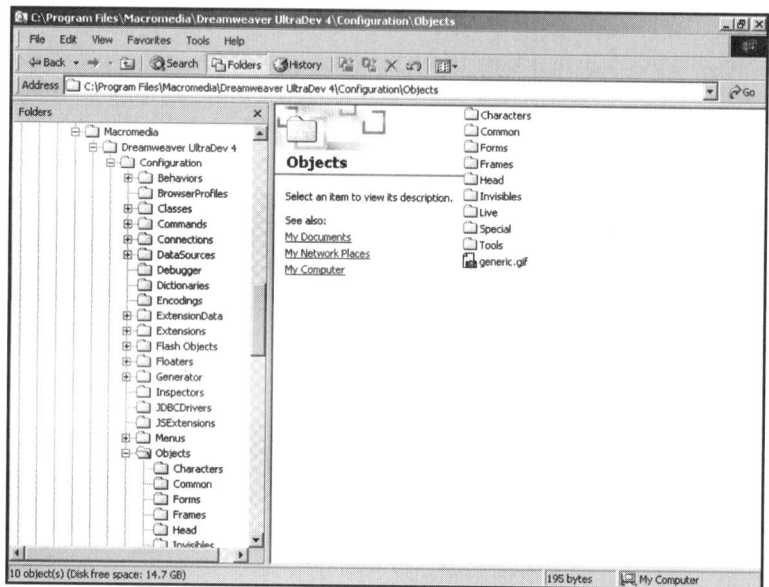

Figure 26.1

Each subdirectory beneath the Objects directory in the UltraDev directory contains the objects that appear in the panes on the Objects palette.

Given what you see in this figure, you could rightly conclude that UltraDev derives the panes that display in the Objects palette from the directories that exist below the Objects directory. You could also conclude that the contents of each of these subdirectories comprise the objects that appear on each of the panes in the Objects palette.

For example, if you open the Frames subdirectory, you will find the objects that appear in the Frames pane of the Objects palette. As shown in Figure 26.2, the Frames subdirectory contains eight pairs of files, each pair comprising a file with the extension .GIF and another with the extension .HTM.

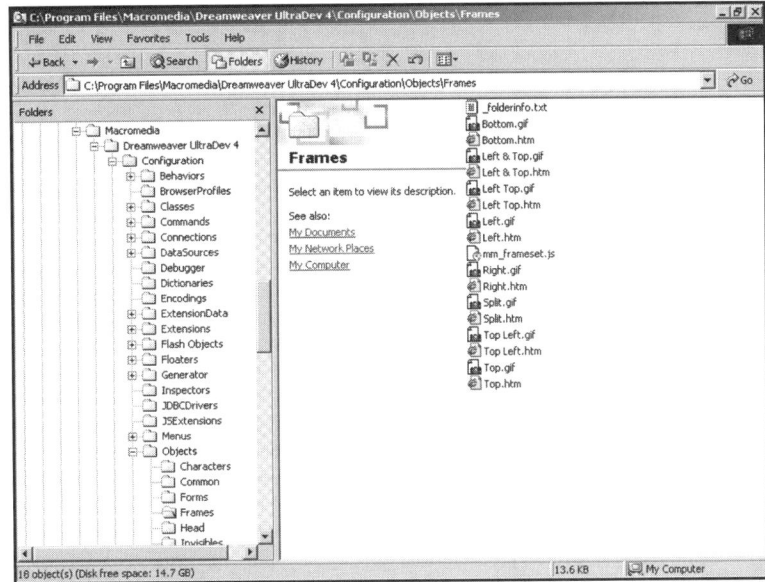

Figure 26.2

The paired files in the Frames subdirectory comprise the objects that appear on the Frames pane of the Objects palette.

The *.GIF portion of the pair of common files is the image that appears on the Frames pane of the Objects palette. The *.HTM portion of the pair of common files is the content that gets inserted into the Web page when the developer clicks on the objects icon in the Objects palette.

You will also notice a file in the Frames subdirectory with the file extension .JS. This is a JavaScript file, written by a developer, that contains code necessary to cause a certain behavior to execute when the developer clicks on the icon.

NOTE: *If you will be adding objects that you create to the Objects palette, and if these objects require a behavior that can only be accommodated with code (such as formatting a table in a certain fashion based on a parameter input by a developer), then you have to create this behavior in a JavaScript file, using JavaScript. Therefore, you need to be proficient with JavaScript to create certain custom objects.*

To modify the Objects palette, perform these steps:

1. Create a subdirectory underneath the Objects directory in the UltraDev folder on your hard drive. As shown in Figure 26.3, I've created a subdirectory named Personal. You can name your subdirectory whatever you like.

Figure 26.3

I've created a subdirectory named Personal that will contain the objects that will appear on the Personal pane of the Objects palette.

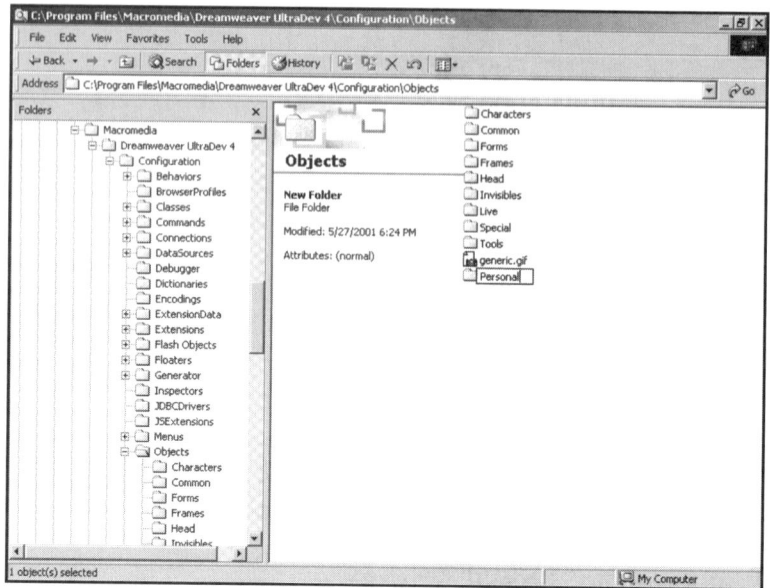

2. Within your newly created directory, place the graphics file (*.GIF), the content file (*.HTML), and a behavior file (*.JS), if one exists, that you want to appear in the new Objects palette pane. As you can see in Figure 26.4, I have placed four sets of files, which will represent four icons on the Personal pane of the Objects palette.

Figure 26.4

Place the graphics and content file, plus any applicable behavior files (.JS) in the new subdirectory. These will appear as icons on the new pane.*

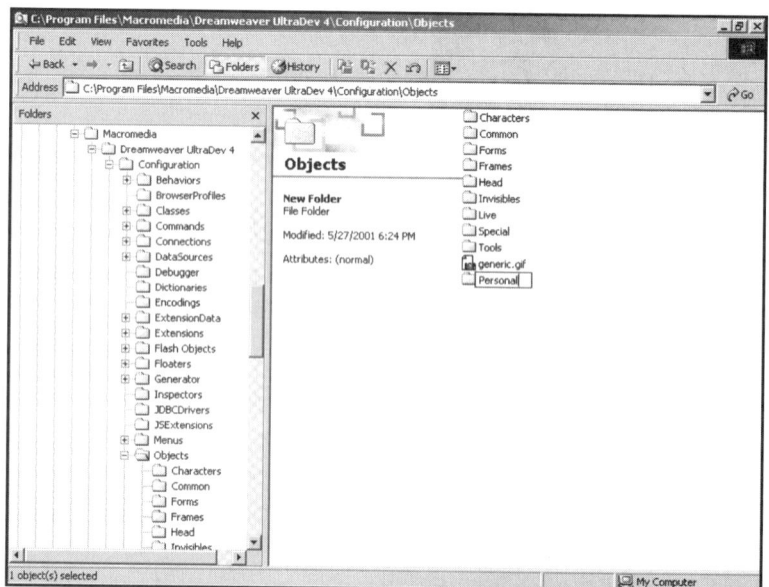

3. Within UltraDev, launch the Objects palette, if it is not already open, by pressing the Ctrl+F2 keyboard combination.

4. Within the Objects palette, position the mouse cursor within the name of the pane that shows immediately below the title bar. Then, press and hold down the Ctrl key and click your mouse button. UltraDev, in turn, will display the Objects palette pop-up, with an extra item added at the bottom of the list of panes, labeled Reload Extensions.

5. Click on Reload Extensions. UltraDev will take a few seconds to reformat the Objects palette for the new pane and information contained on the pane.

6. Click on the pane name drop-down list. You will now see the name of the new pane. If you click on the pane name, UltraDev will display the new pane with its objects listed. As you can see in Figure 26.5, a pane named Personal now is on my Objects palette, and this pane contains four icons, each representing a different object.

Figure 26.5

My Objects palette now has a pane named Personal, and this pane contains the four objects I placed in the Personal subdirectory to the Objects directory that is beneath the UltraDev directory.

Edit an Object on the Objects Palette

As you have learned, some of the objects on the Objects palette are supported by a JavaScript (.JS) file, whose execution causes a certain behavior to occur. Fortunately, JavaScript is a non-compiled language, so you can edit the JavaScript file of an existing behavior to modify the behavior of that object.

NOTE: *Exercise extreme caution when you make changes to JavaScript pro-grams. It is best to make a backup copy of the JavaScript code before you make any changes, to ensure that you can recover from a catastrophe if needed.*

You make the changes to an existing JavaScript file using whatever editor you prefer, and then save the changes using the same file name and in the same directory. As shown in Figure 26.6, I have made some changes to the Image.js file.

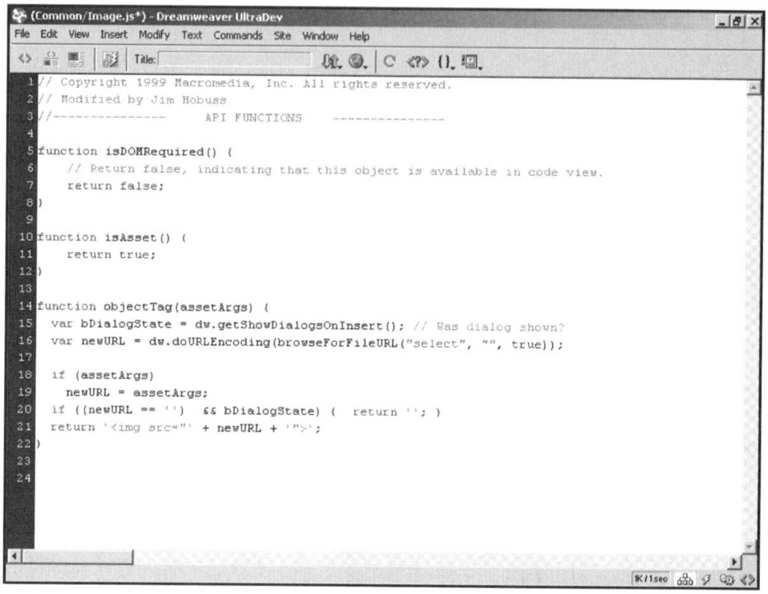

Figure 26.6

You can make changes to the JavaScript files associated with certain objects, but you must be careful and make a backup copy before you begin making any changes.

In addition to editing the JavaScript file that accompanies an object, you can also edit the HTM file associated with the object. You do this the same way you would edit any other Web page: open the HTM file in UltraDev, make the necessary changes, and then save the changes by overwriting the previous file. Figure 26.7 shows the Table.htm page, which is associated with the Table icon on the Common pane of the Objects palette, ready to receive updates.

As you can see in Figure 26.7, I have changed the default number of rows that appear in a table inserted into a Web page from 3 to 5.

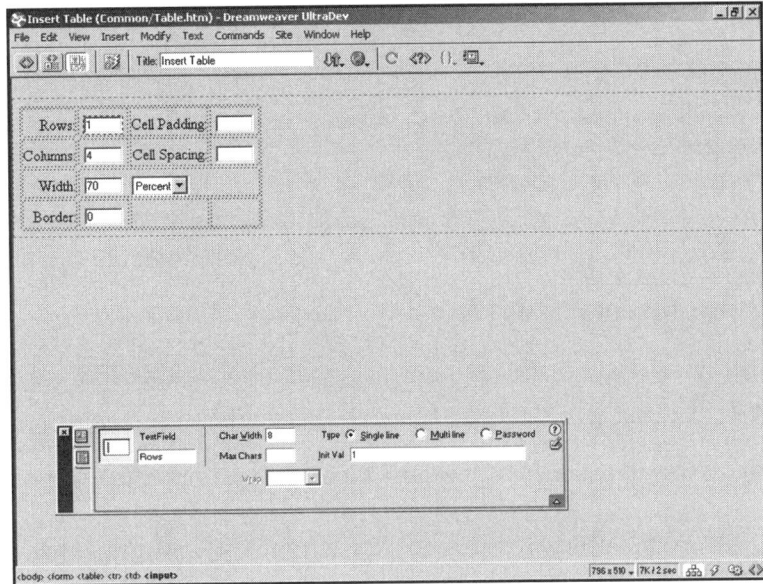

Figure 26.7

Make changes to the HTM file associated with an object in the same way you would make changes to any other Web page.

Creating a Menu Command

A menu command provides an option that, when a user invokes it, causes one or more steps to occur automatically. You can, for example, create a command that appears on a UltraDev menu that directs UltraDev to automatically perform the steps that correspond to an operation you perform on a regular basis.

Using UltraDev, you have the ability to create and execute a menu command. In fact, you have two ways to do this:

◆ Select a step, or series of steps, from the History palette and save it as a command.

◆ Record a step, or series of steps, as you perform it, and play it back later.

Understanding the History Palette

Within UltraDev, the History palette displays a list of all the steps performed on a Web page since it was created or opened in the Document window. The History palette does not show steps performed in other frames, Document windows, or the Site window. Using the History palette, you can undo one or more steps, or replay steps to create new commands and/or repetitive steps. To open the History palette, select the Window menu History option. An example of the History palette is shown in Figure 26.8.

Figure 26.8

The History palette displays all the steps performed on a Web page since it was created or opened in the Document window.

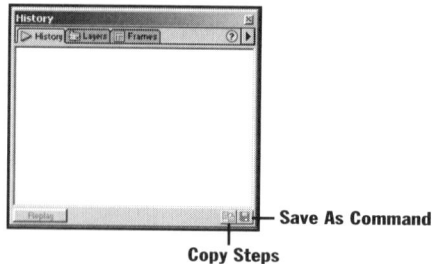

— Save As Command

Copy Steps

Using the History Palette

The History palette is a special component within the UltraDev interface that allows you to review and re-execute a command or function.

To undo the last edit step, using the History palette, perform these steps:

1. Within the Document window, select the Window menu History option to open the History palette.

2. Within the History palette slider bar, drag your mouse along the left side of the History palette. As you move the slider bar up one position, you will see the corresponding command or action disappear from the Document window.

NOTE: *You could also easily undo the previous operation by selecting the Edit menu Undo option.*

Using the History palette, you can easily undo a series of operations by using your mouse to drag the slider bar up as many steps as you want to undo. As you drag the slider bar, UltraDev removes the corresponding commands and actions.

Setting the Number of Steps the History Palette Retains

As with so many other components in UltraDev, you can customize the number of history items that UltraDev retains and displays in the History palette. By default, UltraDev retains the last 50 steps in the History palette. To modify the number of steps UltraDev retains and displays in the History palette, perform these steps:

1. Select the Edit menu Preferences option. UltraDev, in turn, will display the Preferences window.

2. Within the Preferences window, click on the General option in the Category list to see the options specific to the General category, as shown in Figure 26.9.

Figure 26.9

You can adjust the maximum number of history steps that display in the History palette in the General category of the Preferences window.

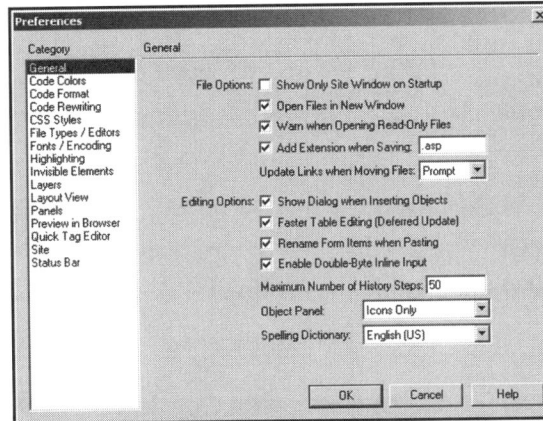

3. Within the General window, change the value in the Maximum Number of History Steps text box to the number of steps you want UltraDev to retain.

4. Click on the OK button to close the Preferences window.

Saving Steps Within the History Palette

When you save steps that appear on the History palette, UltraDev lets you name the saved steps and later re-execute the steps as a command that appears on the Command menu. To save a step or steps that appear in the History palette as a menu command, perform these steps:

1. If the History palette is not open, press Shift+F10.

2. Within the History palette, click on the step you want to save as a command. If there is more than one step, hold down the Ctrl key as you click on each step. As you select a step, Ultra-Dev will highlight the step within the palette.

3. Click on the Save As Command button that appears in the lower-right corner of the History palette. UltraDev will display the Save As Command window, shown in Figure 26.10.

Figure 26.10

The Save As Command window lets you save one or more steps that appear in the History palette as a command that is accessible as a menu item.

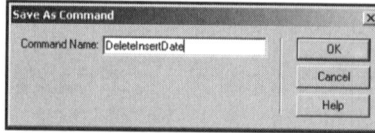

4. Within the Save As Command window, specify a meaningful name for the Command and then click on the OK button. UltraDev, in turn, will save your command to the Commands subdirectory that resides within the Configuration directory on your hard drive, as shown in Figure 26.11.

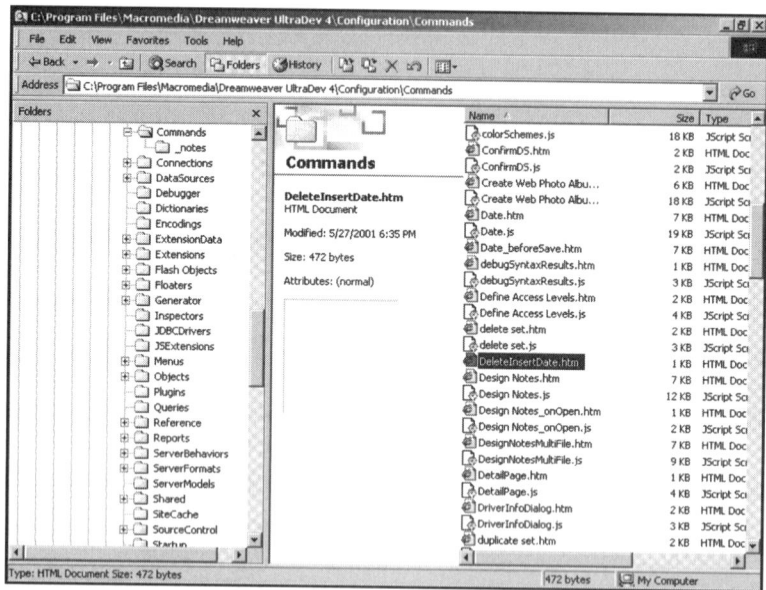

Figure 26.11

A command file that is saved is stored in the Commands subdirectory to the Configuration directory for the UltraDev directory on your hard drive.

Playing a Command Saved from the History Palette

After you create and save a command by selecting items from the History palette, the name of the command you provided in the Save As Command window will appear on the Commands menu.

For example, Figure 26.12 shows the command named DeleteInsertDate listed at the bottom of the Commands menu.

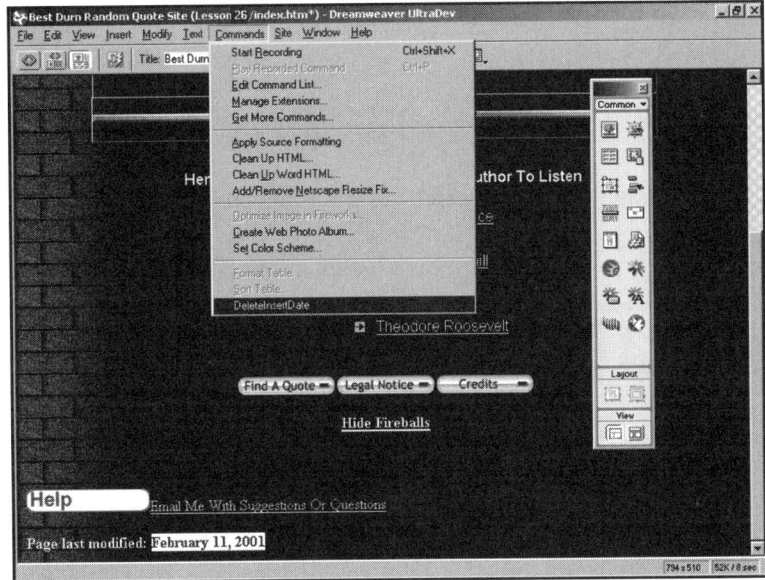

Figure 26.12

The DeleteInsertDate *command listed as an option on the Commands menu.*

To play a command previously saved in the History palette, simply select the Commands menu and choose the command you desire. UltraDev, in turn, will execute the steps that correspond to the command.

NOTE: *Because UltraDev stores saved commands in a subdirectory on your hard drive, saved commands are visible and usable on any page or site that you work on later. The only way to remove a saved command from the menu is to delete the corresponding files from the Commands directory on your hard drive.*

Recording a Command As You Work

In addition to saving a series of steps from the History palette as a command, you can also record a series of steps as you execute them, and save those as a command that you can later execute as a menu option. To record and save a series of steps as a command, perform these steps:

1. When you are ready to begin recording the steps, click on the object in the Web page for which you want to begin recording the steps. You will not be able to select that object after you begin recording.

2. Select the Commands menu Start Recording option. UltraDev will change the cursor to a small cassette icon.

3. Perform the steps you want to record as you would ordinarily perform them.

4. After you execute the steps you want to record, select the Commands menu Stop Recording option.

NOTE: *The steps you execute to record the command are listed on the History palette that you learned about in the previous section. Therefore, if you record and execute a series of steps and want to make those available in other UltraDev sessions, you can save the steps from the History palette with a command name, which will then show as an executable command on the Commands menu.*

Playing a Recorded Command

After you record a command, you can play that command on the current page, or on any page you open in UltraDev. To play a recorded command, perform these steps:

1. Within the Document window, click on the object upon which you want to perform the recorded command. UltraDev will display a border around the object.

2. Select the Commands menu and choose the option that corresponds to the command you desire.

Editing Behaviors

As you have learned, within UltraDev, objects have one or more behaviors that are triggered upon the activation of certain events (such as a mouse click, moving the mouse over a control, and so on).

The developers at Macromedia give you the ability to modify behaviors in a way very similar to the way you modify objects that appear on the Objects palette. As is the case when you modify the Objects palette, you must be very careful when you edit behaviors supplied in the base UltraDev product. You should always make a backup copy of the system directories before you begin to make any changes, in the event you need to recover the original settings.

UltraDev stores behaviors in the Actions subdirectory that resides beneath Configuration/Behaviors, as shown in Figure 26.13.

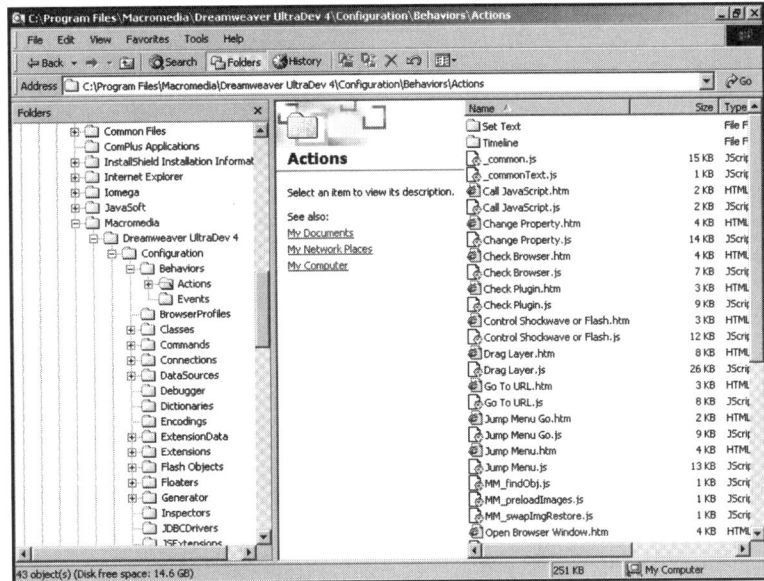

Figure 26.13

The Actions subdirectory contains the behaviors used by UltraDev.

Notice in Figure 26.13 that many of the behaviors have two related files. One file is an HTM file that contains the HTML code specific to the Web page, while the other is a JavaScript (JS) file that defines the behaviors specific to the page as written in JavaScript code. To edit a behavior, you may have to make changes to the JavaScript code as well as to the HTML statements.

To edit a behavior that does not require changes to the JavaScript code, perform these steps:

1. Open the HTML file that corresponds to the behavior you want to modify (*Behavior_name*.htm) within the Document window.

2. Make the modifications to the HTML that will accomplish the changes you desire. In Figure 26.14, for example, I have changed the text that appears on a message pop-up window from "Message" to "Message To Display."

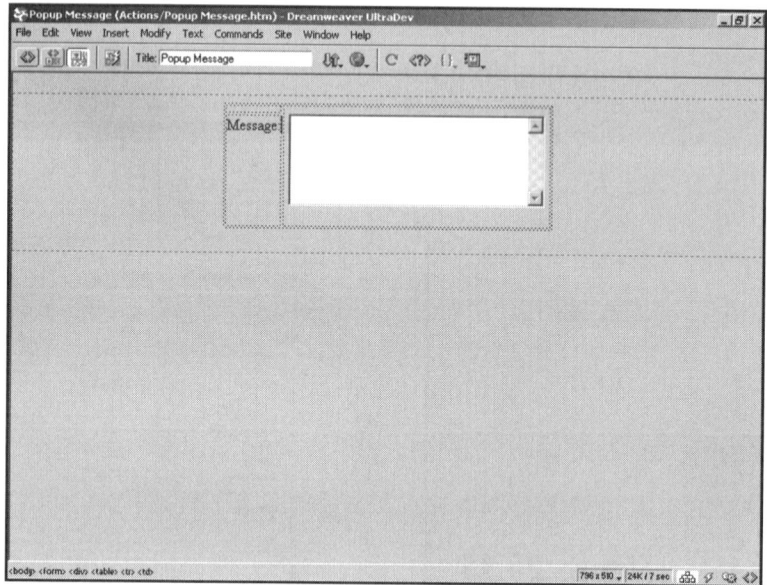

Figure 26.14

The HTML code associated with a behavior is edited in the Document window just as any other character.

3. Save your changes by selecting the File menu Save option.

The next time you use the behavior just modified, the modified JavaScript code will execute.

What You Must Know

In this lesson, you learned how to customize the UltraDev interface to suit the specific needs of the project you're working on, or to suit your individual preferences. Specifically, you learned how to modify the Objects palette, the Commands menu, and one or more object behaviors. In Lesson 27, "Accessing External Programs," you will learn how to use CGI-based applications to interact with the user, and how to place Java applets and ActiveX controls as well as JavaScript and VBScript statements into a Web page. Before you continue with Lesson 27, make sure you understand the following key concepts:

◆ The UltraDev Objects palette is not static. You can modify the Objects palette and create custom objects to be included in the Objects palette.

◆ Just as you can create custom objects for the Objects palette, you can also create custom menu commands.

◆ Behaviors are easy to create, modify, and delete in UltraDev.

Part V

Finatus

Accessing External Programs

In Lesson 26, "Customizing Dreamweaver UltraDev," you learned how to customize the UltraDev interface to better suit your needs. Specifically, you learned how to modify the Objects palette, create and execute menu commands, and edit behaviors. In this lesson, you will learn how to incorporate plug-ins, work with ActiveX components, add Java applets, and add JavaScript and VBScript to your Web pages. By the time you finish this lesson, you will understand the following key concepts:

♦ Using CGI-based programs, you can link your Web site to programs running on the Web or application server.

♦ A plug-in is an object that lets Web pages take advantage of third-party products. Within UltraDev, you can place plug-ins on a page by using the Objects palette.

♦ ActiveX components are program objects that you can place on a Web page to perform a specific task.

♦ Java applets are programs that a Web browser can execute to perform a specific task. Java applets are unique in that the same applet can run on a Windows-based system, a Mac, as well as a system running Linux.

♦ Within a Web page, you can use JavaScript and VBScript code to perform specific processing, such as responding to user keyboard and mouse operations.

Understanding CGI Programs

Within a Web page, Common Gateway Interface (CGI) programs accept data that a user enters (normally using fields that appear on a form) and then processes that information on the Web or application server. Additionally, CGI programs can format and write data back to the page that the visitor is viewing. In fact, it is common for a CGI program to include code that writes the HTML code around data that is then sent back to a visitor's browser. CGI programs can be written in almost any computer language, from COBOL to Perl. The following are some of the more common languages used to write CGI programs:

◆ Perl (Practical Extraction and Report Language)

◆ Visual Basic

◆ PL/SQL (Programming Language/Structured Query Language)

◆ TCL (Tool Command Language)

A Web or application server launches a CGI program when a visitor's Web page issues a POST or GET command that specifies the name of the CGI program in the URL it sends to the server. The Web server either redirects the request to launch the program to an application server for processing, or launches the CGI program directly. When the CGI program finishes executing, it usually sends a Web page back to the visitor's browser.

CGI programs usually are not written by the person developing the Web site, because the language used to write CGI programs is usually different than the language(s) used to develop Web sites. The developer is quite likely using HTML to create a site, whereas a programmer will use a language such as Perl to create the CGI program. However, some points of interaction must occur between the CGI developer and the Web site developer:

◆ The CGI developer must understand the purpose of the CGI program. He or she must also understand how the page will pass data to the CGI program in the form of variables that the CGI program uses to perform its processing.

◆ The Web developer must understand where the CGI program will be located in the architecture of the site. He or she must also understand the format of the data that the CGI program will pass back to the visitor's browser.

After these two communication components are done, and the CGI program and Web site pages accessing the CGI program are written, the Web developer must complete three items:

1. Place the CGI program in a directory accessible from the Web server. Frequently, these directories are named cgi-bin.

2. Set file permissions on the directory containing the CGI program based on the function of the programs in the directory.

3. Write the Web page in such a way as to call or reference the CGI program, and pass data to the program.

The system or network administrator in your company is the person who will establish the directory structure for your Web site, including the directory containing CGI programs. Also, the system or network administrator is the person who assigns the correct permissions. You should communicate the needs of your site to this person. As the developer of the site, you are the right person to create the Web page in a way that correctly calls the CGI program and passes data to it.

Sending Data to CGI Programs

There are two ways in which you, the Web developer, can request the execution of a Web page and pass parameters to it: the POST method and the GET method. The method you intend to use is specified when you create the form on the Web page that will collect the data. Examine Figure 27.1, which shows the Property Inspector for a form on the Login.asp page. Within the figure, you will see two areas of interest. First, the Action drop-down list box specifies the location and name of the CGI program to execute. In this case, the program location and name is www.bestquote.com/cgi-bin/login.pl. Second, the Method drop-down list box specifies the POST method for communication to the CGI program.

Figure 27.1

The Property Inspector is where you specify the method used to communicate to a CGI program, as well as the location of the CGI program.

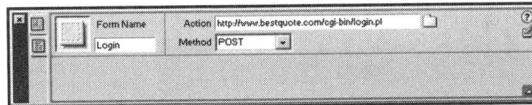

Using the POST method, the Web page appends the data it will send to the CGI program to the URL you specify in the Action drop-down list box. For example, assume you have two fields that the page will pass to the CGI program, which consist of a person's first and last name. To start, you must provide the two field names to the CGI developer, because the CGI developer must write code in the CGI program to extract the data from the URL it receives from the page.

In this case, assume you assign the name *first_name* to the First Name control and *last_name* to the Last Name control. In this scenario, and assuming the page passes the name James Smith to the CGI program, the entire URL will look like this:

```
www.bestquote.com/cgi-bin/login.pl?first_name=James+last_name=Smith
```

When the CGI program, Login.pl, executes, the program will interpret the command string first_name=James+last_name=Smith and Smithdetermine that the value for the variable *first_name* is James and the value for the variable *last_name* is Smith.

> **NOTE:** *The Web page sends a text string to the Web server when the visitor clicks on the Submit button on the form. The event that triggers the data being sent is the onClick event. You do not need to use the Submit form button, however, to cause this behavior to occur. Instead, you can use any graphics button, and write the necessary code to trigger the onClick event by using JavaScript.*

Passing Hidden Fields

When you work with CGI programs, sometimes you will want to pass information to the CGI program that does not appear on the form. For example, you might want to pass to the CGI program the name of the Web page the user visited immediately before he or she arrived on the page that contains the Submit button. As you learned in Lesson 24, "Server-Side Includes and Add a Date," you can perform this operation using a server-side include. In this case, you would use `#echo var="HTTP_REFERER"`.

Figure 27.2 shows that I have placed on the login page a Hidden Field, which the page passes as a single parameter to the CGI program using a variable named last_url. The value of this variable is contained in a server-side include with the format `#echo var="HTTP_REFERER"`.

Figure 27.2

You can use a Hidden Field, contained in the body of the form, to pass hidden information to the CGI program. In this case, the name of the last visited URL is being sent to the CGI program in a variable named `last_url`.

Understanding Plug-ins

Plug-ins are software objects that a browser can use to extend its own capabilities. First introduced by Netscape Communications for inclusion in its Netscape browser, and then incorporated by Microsoft in Internet Explorer, plug-ins have become very popular. In general, a plug-in is a small program that lets a visitor's browser work with different types of files, such as audio files, graphics files, Word documents, Adobe Acrobat files, and so on.

When you insert a plug-in into a Web page, you are not really inserting the actual small program. Rather, you insert the file that requires the small program to execute. For example, if you include an Adobe Acrobat file, in the format *.pdf, on a page in your Web site, the visitor to that page must have the Adobe Acrobat Reader software program installed on his or her machine before he or she can read the PDF file that exists on your Web page.

Because a plug-in requires a software program to work correctly (in the case of the PDF file, the browser must use the Adobe Acrobat Reader to view the contents of the PDF file), it is good practice to place a link on your page that your visitors can navigate to locate, download, and install the plug-in software.

Embedding a Plug-in-based Object on Your Page

There are two ways that you can embed a plug-in-based object on a Web page. The first is to put a link to the plug-in directly in an object (or text) that appears on the Web page. The other is to directly embed the plug-in object in your Web page. To embed a plug-in via a link, perform these steps:

1. Within the Document window, select the item (or text) to which you will link the plug-in.

2. Launch the Property Inspector by pressing the Ctrl+F3 keyboard combination. UltraDev, in turn, will launch the Property Inspector for the object (or text) you selected in Step 1.

3. Within the Property Inspector Link text box, enter the path to the embedded plug-in object. As shown in Figure 27.3, I have linked the text Click Here to the plug-in object Images/napsterop0212.pdf.

4. Save the page and transfer it to the Web server.

5. When you view the site within your browser and click on the link (and assuming the necessary plug-in is installed on your machine), you will see something very similar to Figure 27.4.

The other way you can place a plug-in-based object on your page is to embed the plug-in object. To do that, perform these steps:

1. Within the Document window, click at the location where you want to embed the plug-in.

2. Select the Insert menu Media option and choose Plugin. UltraDev, in turn, will display the Select File window, as shown in Figure 27.5.

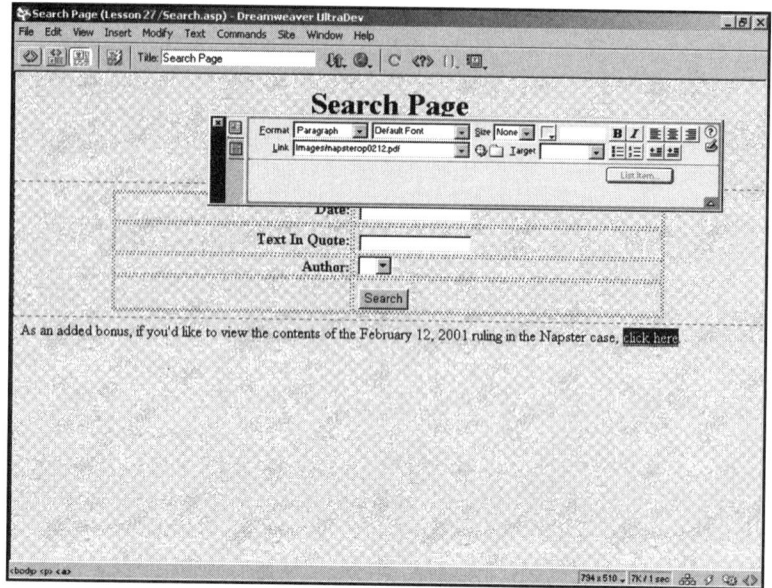

Figure 27.3

The file named napsterop0212.pdf requires a plug-in to view.

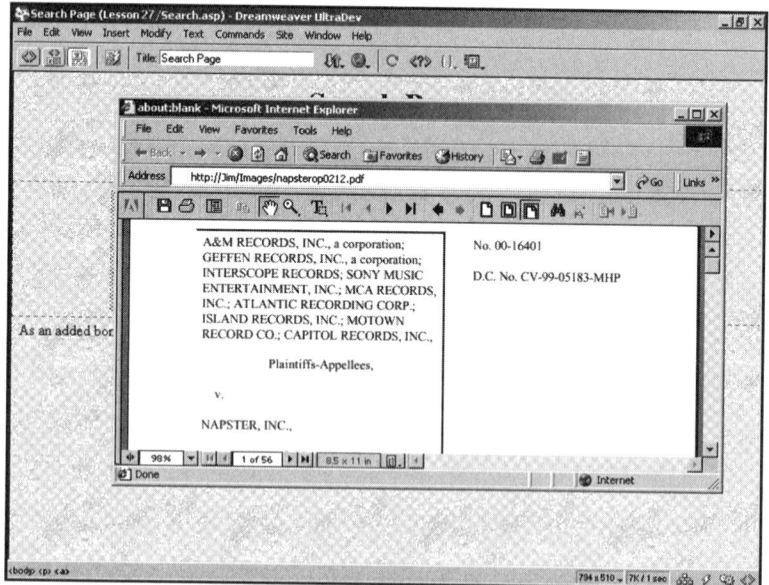

Figure 27.4

The Adobe Acrobat PDF file as viewed in the plug-in.

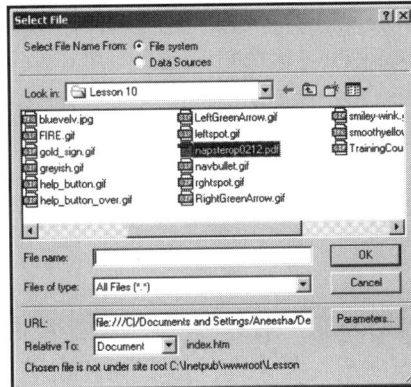

Figure 27.5

Select the file to load with the plug-in on the Web page.

3. Within the Select File window, click your mouse on the name of the file to load in the plug-in, and then click on the OK button. UltraDev will display the plug-in object, which looks like a jigsaw puzzle piece, on the Web page, as shown in Figure 27.6.

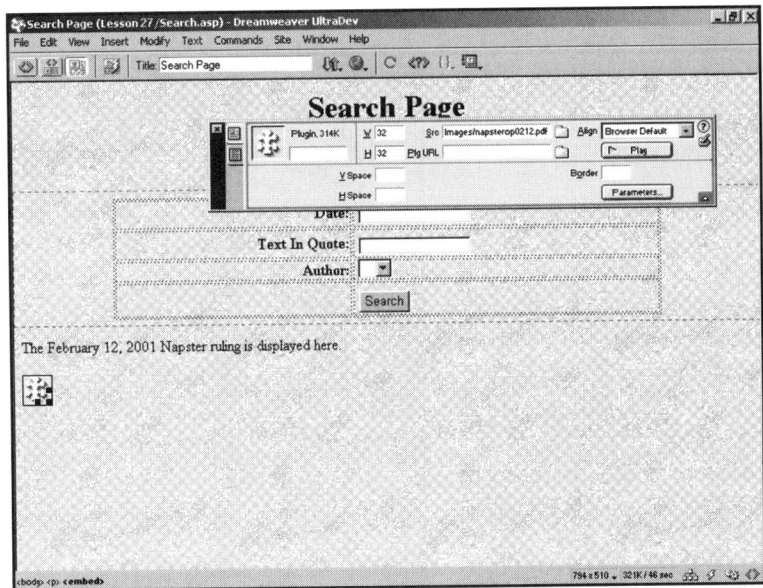

Figure 27.6

The plug-in object appears as a jigsaw puzzle piece on a Web page.

4. Within the Property Inspector for the plug-in object, you can adjust the size of the plug-in placeholder either by entering values in the W (width) and H (height) text boxes or by clicking on the object itself and sliding the resizing handle to the correct location on the page.

5. Using the Plg URL text box on the Property Inspector, specify the URL address to where the page will redirect visitors in the event the visitor does not have the correct plug-in to access the object.

6. You can change the alignment of the plug-in in relation to other objects on the page by clicking on the Align drop-down button and then choosing one of the options on the drop-down list that appears.

7. You can surround the entire plug-in with a border by specifying a value in the Border text box on the Property Inspector. The value you supply represents the thickness of the border in pixels.

As you can see in Figure 27.7, the plug-in object displays in the browser as if it were included on the Web page.

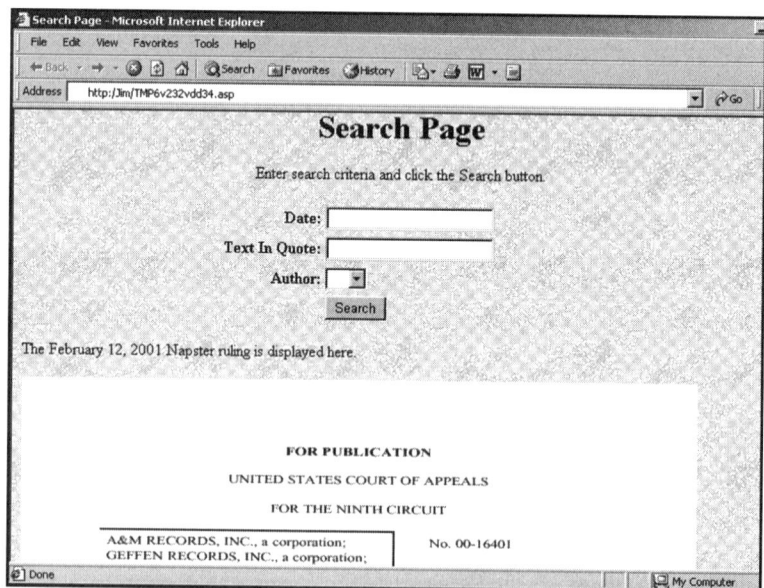

Figure 27.7

The plug-in object displays in the Web page as if it were a part of the page, assuming the correct plug-in is installed on the visitor's machine.

Using ActiveX Components

Soon after Netscape Communications developed its support for plug-ins in its browser, Microsoft developed its own flavor of support for external objects in browsers: ActiveX components. Although the two technologies are similar, and have similar value on a Web site, there are some significant differences between the two.

For example, ActiveX controls only work with Internet Explorer version 3.0 and beyond. However, a plug-in is available that lets Netscape browsers view and use ActiveX controls. ActiveX controls only work with browsers running on the Windows platform.

ActiveX controls are quite easy to place on a Web page, although not quite as easy as a plug-in-based object. One of the major differences is that each ActiveX control requires that you identify the control on the Web page by stating the component's Class ID. Each ActiveX control has a unique Class ID. A Web page accesses the ActiveX control by referencing the Class ID.

Additionally, ActiveX controls require a codebase that specifies a location on the Internet where a visitor can retrieve the ActiveX control (which the browser will automatically download and install). The primary difference between a plug-in-based object's *pluginspage* attribute and the ActiveX object's *codebase* parameter is that the ActiveX control can be transferred and installed without the visitor's browser having to close and restart. Another important distinction is that the ActiveX control is available for use for as long as the browser session is active. When the visitor closes their browser, the ActiveX control can be removed from their machine.

UltraDev provides a separate object for adding ActiveX controls and objects to a Web page. Additionally, it is easy to add complex Class ID codes by maintaining a user-definable list that is accessible from the ActiveX Property Inspector.

Adding an ActiveX Control to a Web Page

To insert an ActiveX control on a Web page, perform these steps:

1. Within the Document window, click at the location where you want to insert the ActiveX control.

2. Select the Insert menu Media option and choose ActiveX. UltraDev, in turn, will place an ActiveX icon on the page, and will display the ActiveX Property Inspector, as shown in Figure 27.8.

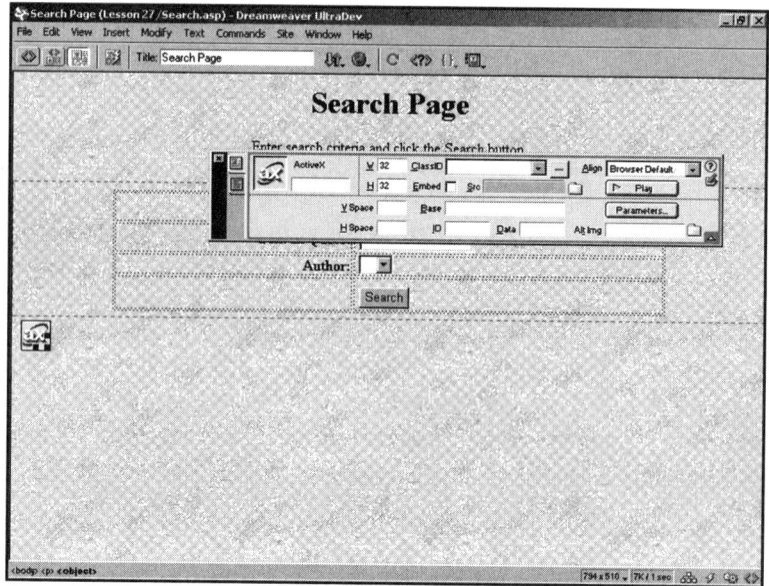

Figure 27.8

The ActiveX icon is visible on the page where the cursor used to be, along with a blank Property Inspector, which is where you specify attributes specific to the ActiveX control.

3. Within the Property Inspector ClassID text box, enter the object's Class ID (which the object's programmer can provide you, or the company that created the object will specify).

4. Within the W (width) and H (height) text boxes, specify the width and height for the control, as it should appear on the Web page when viewed in a browser.

5. Using the Base text box, enter the codebase URL from which the user can automatically download and install the object. This is *not* a required parameter, but it does make the page a lot more useable.

After you have specified the attributes to your liking, save the Web page and preview it in a browser. Make sure you use Internet Explorer, version 3.0 or above, to do this.

Table 27.1 provides some useful links to ActiveX sites you may find useful to expand your understanding and use of ActiveX objects on your Web site.

Table 27.1   ActiveX sites and useful links

Site URL	Description
www.asna.com/activeX_sites.asp	This site contains thousands of ActiveX components available from many reputable 3rd party providers.
www.shorrock.u-net.com/activex.html	The self-billed "unofficial" ActiveX authority on the Web.
www.cuinl.tripod.com/links-activex-1.htm	Many useful links to other sites and resources can be found here.
www.mvps.org/vbnet/links/activex/ax-abc.htm	This is a Visual Basic developers site specific to the usage of ActiveX objects.

Understanding Java Applets

Java is a platform-independent programming language that has become very popular across the Web. Java is platform-independent because the same Java program can run on a Windows-based system, a Mac, as well as a system running Linux. Programmers refer to Java programs as *applets*.

Developers can insert a Java applet into a Web page in much the same way as a plug-in-based object or an ActiveX component is inserted. As you place a Java applet on your page, it may have numerous configuration parameters that you can specify to elicit a certain behavior from the program.

Adding a Java Applet to a Web Page

To insert a Java applet on your page, perform these steps:

1. Within the Document window, click at the location where you want to place the Java applet.

2. Select the Insert menu Media option and choose Applet. UltraDev, in turn, will display the File Locate window.

3. Within the File Locate window, select the name of the Java class file (.CLASS) that contains the Java applet you want to insert. As shown in Figure 27.9, I have selected Upscroll.class.

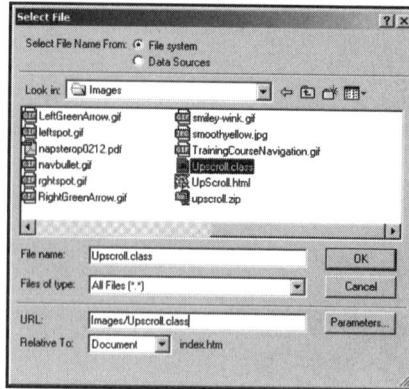

Figure 27.9

The Upscroll.class file is the Java class object that contains the applet I want to place on the page.

4. After you select the class that contains the Java applet, you will see the Java applet icon on the Web page, along with the Property Inspector open for the Java applet, as shown in Figure 27.10.

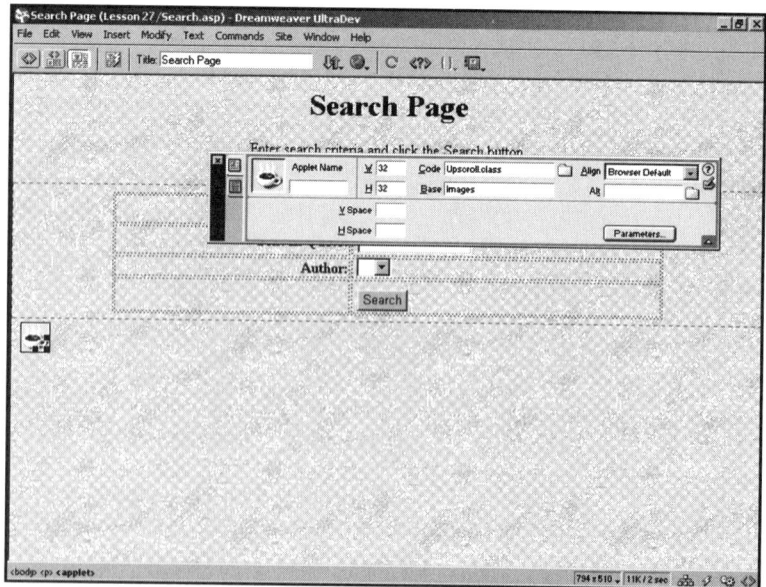

Figure 27.10

The Java applet icon is displayed on the page where I inserted the object, along with the Property Inspector.

5. Within the Property Inspector, specify a height (H) and width (W) for the applet object. You can also resize the Java applet object by clicking and dragging any of its sizing handles.

6. You can also specify parameters that are often required for an applet to work properly. To do this, click on the Property Inspector Parameters button. UltraDev, in turn, will launch the Parameters window, as shown in Figure 27.11.

Figure 27.11

The Parameters window allows you to specify parameters passed to the Java applet class.

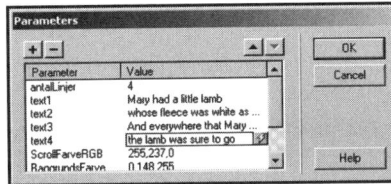

7. Within the Parameters window, specify the parameters and their values as necessary and then click on the OK button to add the Java applet to your Web page.

The Java applet in this example was written by Karsten Mandrup Nielsen, who is German. I found the applet on the Internet and, as is the nature of many of the Java applets written by others, it is available for distribution and use without charge. The purpose of the applet is to provide a scrolling marquee of text lines on a Web page. The following is an example of sample HTML code for this class:

```
<applet code="Upscroll.class" height="50" width="400">
<param name="antalLinjer" value="4"> <! Number of lines in the scroll>
<param name="text1" value="Java Boutique is your place for Java applets.">
<param name="text2" value="Try some of our tutorials">
<param name="text3" value="... and don't miss our servlets and applications">
<param name="text4" value="Remember to pass it along!"> <! texten.. you can
put in a blank: value=" ".. >
<param name="ScrollFarveRGB" value="255,237,0"> <!Color of scroll R G B >
<param name="BaggrundsFarveRGB" value="0,148,255"> <! Color of background
R G B >
<param name="farveSkift" value="0"> <! Colorchange - 0 = no, 1 = yes>
<param name="fontStorrelse" value="14"> <!Size of font>
</applet>
```

As you can see, the parameters are specified in German. Java applets that are available on the Web frequently require you to use parameter values in the language of the person who originally wrote the Java applet. In this case, Karsten did us a favor by supplying the English translation for each parameter. The point is that when you use a Java applet that requires parameters, you must define those parameters either by using HTML entries or within UltraDev.

Table 27.2 provides some useful links to Java sites you may find useful to expand your understanding and use of Java on your Web site.

Table 27.2   Useful Java sites you can explore to expand your knowledge of Java

Site URL	Description
www.freewarejava.com/javasites/index.shtml	A valuable site that contains many useful links to other sites, grouped by category.
www.jspinsider.com/links/javalinks.html	A site developed and sponsored by *JSP Insider* magazine that contains current information on the latest release of Java.
www.euroyellowpages.com/exhibitn/javasite.html	A site that contains many useful links to resources on the Web.

Understanding JavaScript and VBScript

When you create complex Web pages, the pages often will require specific processing. For example, you might want a page to perform a specific operation each time it loads or specific processing each time the user clicks on the page. In such cases, you can define the processing you want the page to perform by using the JavaScript or VBScript programming languages.

Although the names are very similar, the JavaScript language is nothing like Java. Its primary use is to add functionality on the client side of the browser (by placing statements within the Web page that the browser executes) for tasks such as verifying form data and adding interactivity to interface elements. VBScript, which is similar to JavaScript, expands a Web site's capabilities by providing access to many Windows-based programming features. A major difference between JavaScript and VBScript is that JavaScript can run on virtually any browser, whereas VBScript is targeted to systems using Internet Explorer running on Windows.

JavaScript and VBScript are both scripting languages, which programmers use to specify the processing that a Web page is to perform when specific actions occur. Normally, unless you are a programmer, you will have a programmer develop and insert the scripting code for you.

Inserting JavaScript or VBScript Code

Although you can create some nice Web sites without writing a line of JavaScript or VBScript code, you will find that expertise in one of these languages will be a requirement if you want to become a developer of large Web sites. After you have written JavaScript or VBScript code, you can add the code to your Web page by performing these steps:

1. Within the Document window, click at the location where you want to place the JavaScript or VBScript.

2. Select the Insert menu Invisible Tags option and choose Script. UltraDev, in turn, will display the Insert Script window, as shown in Figure 27.12.

Figure 27.12

The Insert Script window is where you can specify the JavaScript or VBScript code to insert at the cursor location. As you can see here, I'm inserting an alert box.

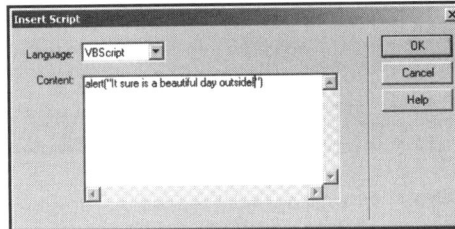

3. Within the Insert Script window, type the JavaScript or VBScript code you want the browser to execute. After you are done, click on the OK button. UltraDev, in turn, will display an icon on the Web page to mark the existence and location of the code.

To edit or modify the code, perform these steps:

1. Click on the Invisible Tag icon that corresponds to the JavaScript or VBScript code.

2. If the Property Inspector is not visible, launch it by pressing the Ctrl+F3 keyboard combination.

3. Within the Property Inspector, click on the Edit button. UltraDev will display the Script Properties window, as shown in Figure 27.13.

4. Within the Script Properties window, make whatever changes you require and then click on the OK button to close the window.

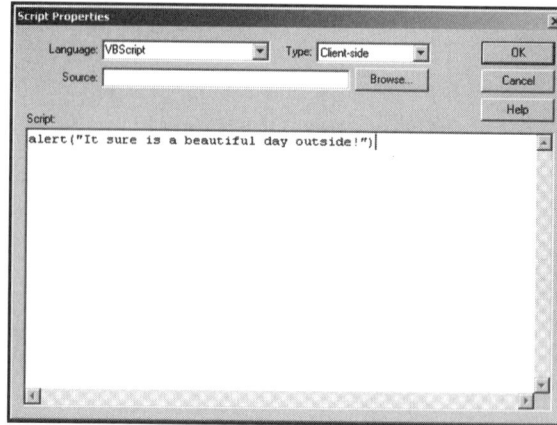

Figure 27.13

The Script Properties window is where you can edit the selected JavaScript or VBScript.

What You Must Know

In this lesson, you learned how to access and use external programs in the pages of your Web site. In Lesson 28, "Adding Multimedia to Your Site," you will learn how to place audio, video, and Flash-based animations on your Web pages. Before you continue with Lesson 28, make sure you understand the following key concepts:

◆ CGI-based programs link your Web pages to external programs that process user-entered data.

◆ Plug-ins are small software programs that extend a browser's functionality.

◆ ActiveX components are another object type that extends the capabilities and features of your site.

◆ Java applets are programs written to perform specific tasks. Using UltraDev, you can easily insert Java applets into a Web page.

◆ Using JavaScript and VBScript, you can place programming statements within a Web page that direct the page to perform specific processing.

Lesson 28

Adding Multimedia
to Your Site

In Lesson 27, "Accessing External Programs," you learned how to make your Web pages work with external programs. Specifically, you learned how to access CGI programs, incorporate plug-ins, work with ActiveX components, add Java applets, and work with JavaScript and VBScript. In this lesson, you will learn how to add multimedia components to your site. By the time you finish this lesson, you will understand the following key concepts:

◆ Fireworks is a Macromedia product that you can use to create Web graphics.

◆ Using UltraDev, incorporating Fireworks into your site is easy.

◆ On many sites across the Web, video is an important audio-visual element. Using UltraDev, you can easily integrate video into your pages.

◆ UltraDev also makes it easy for you to add audio clips to the Web pages that comprise your site.

Understanding Fireworks

Fireworks is a product developed and sold by Macromedia that you can use to create Web graphics. The graphics you create using Fireworks can be static images or animated GIF files. Because both Fireworks and UltraDev are sold and supported by Macromedia, Inc., a very tight degree of interaction exists between the two products.

Across the Web, developers are increasingly expanding their Fireworks skills, which rounds out their Web-development skill set. Many developers will find that having skills in Fireworks is more valuable than having skills in JavaScript or VBScript. This is not to say that skills in Fireworks will earn you as much income as skills in JavaScript or VBScript. For the most part, having skills in a programming language such as Java, JavaScript, or VBScript will earn you a higher income than having skills in a graphics program such as Fireworks. The reason that having skills in Fireworks is so valuable is that, as a Web developer, you will probably use your Fireworks skills more than your language skills. If this is not the case, it certainly is true that the output from a graphics program such as Fireworks is more visible, and consequently you will be more visible, than the output from a JavaScript or VBScript routine.

This book is not intended to teach you how to use the Fireworks program. Rather, this lesson will show you how to integrate the graphics created from Fireworks into your site, and how to integrate the Fireworks application itself into the UltraDev user interface.

Integrating Fireworks with UltraDev

Using the UltraDev Preferences window, you can establish many of the components that control your experience within UltraDev. One such component is the definition of a graphics program to use when you want to edit an image that appears on a Web page. To modify the Preferences window so that Fireworks is integrated with UltraDev, perform these steps:

1. Install Fireworks onto your system.

2. Within UltraDev, select the Edit menu Preferences option. UltraDev, in turn, will display the Preferences window.

3. Within the Preferences window, click on the Category named File Types/Editors. The Preferences window will appear as shown in Figure 28.1.

Figure 28.1

The File Types/Editors category of the Preferences window is where you instruct UltraDev to use Fireworks to edit graphics.

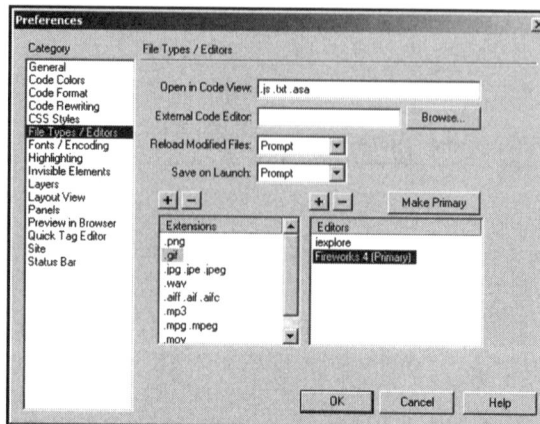

4. Within the Extensions window, click on a row that shows one or more of the file type extension(s) you will be using on your site.

5. Within the Editors window, click on the row named Fireworks to highlight it. Next, click on the Make Primary button.

6. Repeat Steps 3 and 4 for each graphics extension you will use Fireworks to edit.

7. Click on the OK button to save your settings.

Editing an Image in Fireworks

After you have Fireworks integrated into UltraDev, you can use Fireworks to edit graphics with just a few mouse clicks. To edit an image appearing on a Web page using Fireworks, perform these steps:

1. Within your Document window, right-click on the image you want to edit. UltraDev, in turn, will display a pop-up menu.

2. Within the Edit pop-up menu, select the Edit With Fireworks option. UltraDev will launch the Fireworks application with the selected image already loaded, as shown in Figure 28.2.

Figure 28.2

After the image is loaded into Fireworks, use that product to make whatever changes you desire, and then update the image and close Fireworks to go back into UltraDev.

3. Within Fireworks, make the changes you desire and then select the File menu Update option.

4. Close Fireworks to return to the UltraDev page you were viewing when you launched Fireworks.

5. Repeat Steps 1 through 4 until you have the image exactly the way you want it.

Optimizing an Image in Fireworks

Occasionally, you will use graphics on your Web sites that were created using tools other than Fireworks. Frequently, the optimization for those graphics will not be as good as it could be had you created the graphic using Fireworks, because Fireworks optimizes all the graphics it creates for viewing over the Web. In the process of this optimization, Fireworks creates an export file.

Using the Optimize Image in Fireworks option within UltraDev, you can modify either the source or exported file. In most situations, you will achieve better results from using the source file, especially when optimization includes rescaling or resampling.

To optimize an image for an UltraDev site using Fireworks, perform these steps:

1. Within the Document window, right-click on the image you want to optimize. UltraDev will display a border around the image and a pop-up menu.

2. Within the pop-up menu, select Optimize in Fireworks. UltraDev will display the Find Source window, as shown in Figure 28.3.

Figure 28.3

Select where Fireworks should locate the source file in the Find Source window.

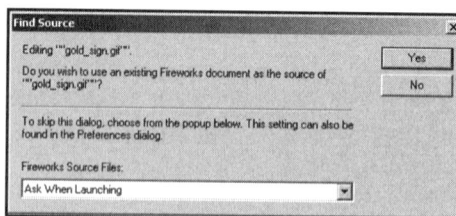

3. Within the Find Source window, click on the Yes button if you would prefer to use the PNG format for the source file, or click the No button if you would prefer to work with the exported file format. When you click the Yes or No button, UltraDev will display the Optimize Images window, with the selected image loaded, as shown in Figure 28.4.

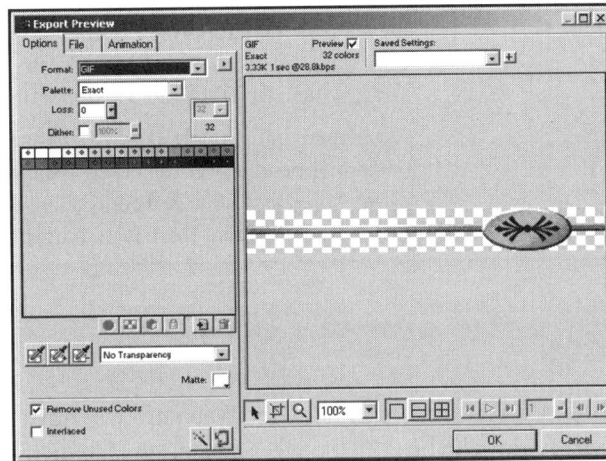

Figure 28.4

The Optimize Images window is where Fireworks optimizes the graphics used on your Web pages for viewing over the Web.

4. Within the Optimize Images window, make the changes you desire by using the Options, File, and Animation tabs. Then, click on the Update button to save your changes and close the window.

Integrating Video

Integration of video into a Web site is not too complex using UltraDev. It is almost as easy as integrating graphics. The issue with placing video into a Web site is not *how* to do it, but *whether* to do it, because video files tend to be quite large, and therefore take a lot of time to download to the visitor's browser, especially if they are accessing your site over a slow connection.

However, after you decide your need for including video on your site is great enough to ask your visitors to suffer the pains of waiting for the video to transfer from your server to their browsers, the next decision is which of the three major video formats to use. Table 28.1 briefly describes the three major video formats.

Table 28.1   The three major media types for video over the Web

Media Type	Description
RealMedia	Developed and supported by RealNetworks, this technology first appeared as RealAudio in 1995, and quickly evolved to support other media formats, such as video, Flash movies, and MP3.
QuickTime	Developed and supported by Apple, this technology is very popular on both the Macintosh and PC platforms. This media type now supports audio, video, MIDI music, Flash movies, and MP3 audio.
Windows Media	Developed and supported by Microsoft Corporation, this technology has one major benefit over the other two media types: the Windows media player ships as a standard component with every copy of Windows. The benefit to this is that there is no plug-in to download and install.

Linking to Video

Regardless of the media type you are using on your Web site, you have a couple of options when it comes to deciding how to include a video clip on a Web page. One option is to include the video clip as a linked item. The second option is to include the video as a plug-in or ActiveX object. To include the video clip as a linked item, perform these steps:

1. Within the Document window, click on the text or object to which you want link the video.

2. Press the Ctrl+F3 keyboard combination to launch the Property Inspector.

3. Within the Property Inspector Link text box, specify the name of the video file you want to launch. As shown in Figure 28.5, I have specified a file named Sample.mov.

Another way to include a video clip in your Web site is to include it as a plug-in or an ActiveX object. To include a video clip as a plug-in (or ActiveX object), perform these steps:

1. Within the Document window, click at the location on the page where you want to place the plug-in object.

2. Select the Insert menu Media item and choose Plugin. UltraDev, in turn, will display the Select File window.

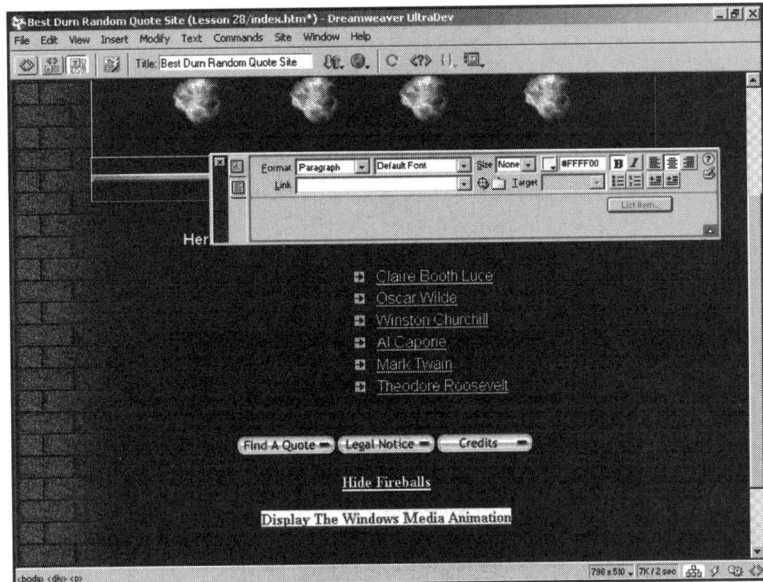

Figure 28.5

The Property Inspector is where you specify a video file to play when a visitor clicks their mouse on a linked text or image.

3. Within the Select File window, locate and select the video file to include on the Web page. Then, click on the OK button to close the Select File window. UltraDev, in turn, will display the plug-in object, which looks like a jigsaw puzzle piece, on the Web page, as shown in Figure 28.6.

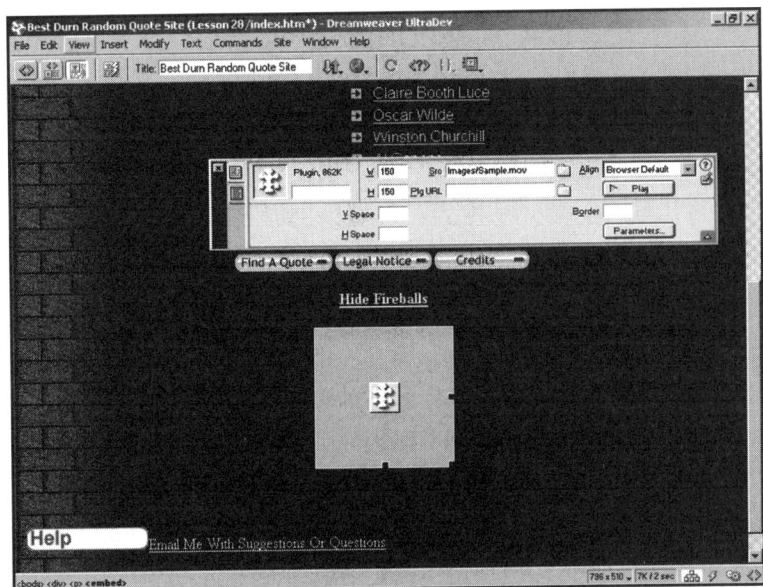

Figure 28.6

The plug-in object appears as a jigsaw puzzle piece on a Web page.

4. Within the Property Inspector for the plug-in object, you can adjust the size of the plug-in placeholder either by entering values in the W (width) and H (height) text boxes or by clicking on the object itself and sliding the resizing handle to the correct location on the page.

5. Within the Property Inspector window Plg URL text box, specify the URL address to where the browser will redirect visitors in the event they do not have the correct plug-in to access the plug-in.

6. You can change the alignment of the plug-in in relation to other objects on the page by clicking on the Align drop-down button and then choosing one of the options on the drop-down list that appears.

7. You can surround the entire plug-in with a border by specifying a value in the Border text box on the Property Inspector. The value you supply represents the thickness of the border in pixels.

Integrating Audio

Using the facilities in UltraDev, you can add audio (sound) files to your site in a way similar to how you add video. Although audio files can add pop to your site, be careful about using them if you are not sure whether your site visitors have a sound card and speakers.

You can add audio files to a number of different places. For example, you can add a sound file to play when any of the following occurs:

♦ A page first displays

♦ A visitor clicks on a control

♦ A certain visitor-triggered event occurs, such as entering an invalid amount in a text box

Linking to Audio Files

Assume, for example, you want to add a sound file that plays when a visitor clicks on a control on your site. In this case, you will link the sound file to specific text, by performing these steps:

1. Within the Document window, drag your mouse to highlight the text you want to serve as the link.

2. If you do not see the Property Inspector, press the Ctrl+F3 keyboard combination.

3. To link a sound file to play when a visitor clicks on the linked text, you are really creating a hyperlink for the text. Therefore, you must associate the sound file with the text as a link. Click on the icon of the folder next to the Link text box. UltraDev, in turn, will display the Select File window.

4. Within the Select File window, locate and select the file named Greeting.wav, as shown in Figure 28.7. Click on the OK button to close the window.

Figure 28.7

Select the name of the audio file to play when the link is clicked in the Select File window, and then click on the OK button.

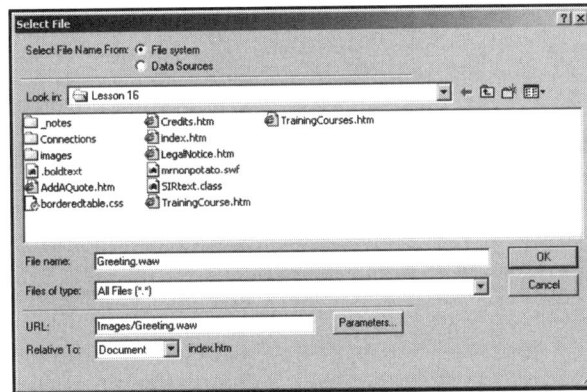

5. UltraDev will now list the Greeting.wav file within the Property Inspector's Link text box for the linked text, as shown in Figure 28.8.

That is it! You've just associated an audio file as a link that plays when a user clicks on the linked text item on a Web page.

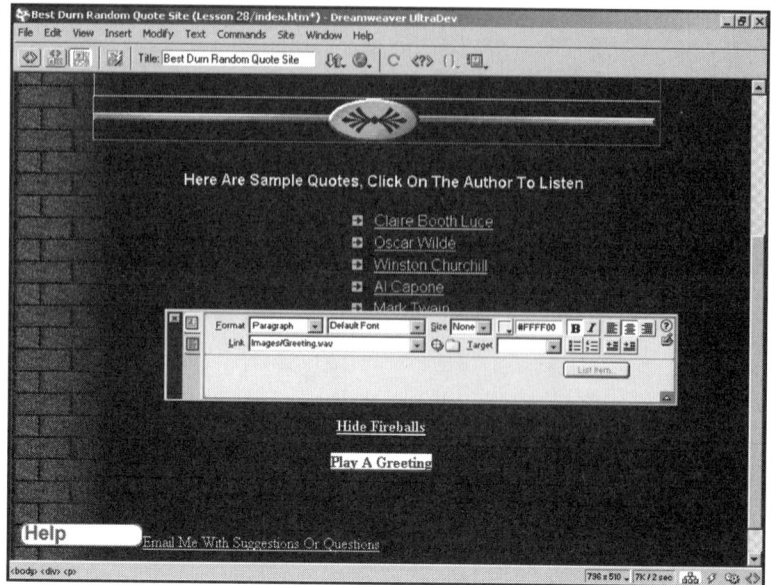

Figure 28.8

The Property Inspector after associating a sound file as a link with a graphic.

What You Must Know

In this lesson, you learned how to add multimedia components to your site. In Lesson 29, "Browser Targeting," you will learn how to customize your site so that it supports various browsers. Before you continue with Lesson 29, make sure you understand the following key concepts:

◆ Using Fireworks, you can create or edit graphics files.

◆ Fireworks files are simple to add and manipulate in UltraDev.

◆ Although video files can slow down the performance of pages they appear on, they are simple to add and use in UltraDev.

◆ Using UltraDev, you can easily add audio files to a Web site.

Lesson 29

Browser Targeting

In Lesson 28, "Adding Multimedia to Your Site," you learned how to add multimedia components to your site. Specifically, you learned how to integrate Fireworks into UltraDev and how to work with the three major formats of video. You also learned how to easily incorporate audio into your site. In this lesson, you'll learn how to use UltraDev to build a site suitable for specific browsers. By the time you finish this lesson, you will understand the following key concepts:

- ◆ Not all browsers are created equal. As you build a site, you need to take browser nuances into consideration.

- ◆ Using UltraDev, you can quickly convert a Web page you created for one browser into a page that a different browser supports.

- ◆ UltraDev provides several tools that facilitate browser checking.

- ◆ Using UltraDev, you can perform Web site testing for browser compatibility.

Understanding Page Conversion

As you create Web sites, there are a few features in UltraDev that you may find quite tempting to use and that offer valuable features to a Web site, but that will reek havoc to certain browser types. A couple of these features are layers and cascading style sheets. For years, Web developers have avoided using these components because some browsers, especially Netscape Navigator and Internet Explorer prior to version 4.0, could not handle them.

UltraDev includes a powerful component to convert a Web page with layers or cascading style sheets into a page that renders properly in browsers prior to version 4.0. Additionally, UltraDev has a component that converts nested tables into layers. Using this facility preserves the Web developer's desire to have absolute control over position and layout of page objects, while ensuring browser compatibility.

To state that UltraDev converts a Web page from one format to another is a misstatement. Rather, UltraDev creates a new page that is suitable for viewing in a different browser, thus preserving the attributes and characteristics of the original page. When a page conversion is done, the result is two pages: the original page, and the newly converted page that is suitable for viewing in a different browser.

Being able to convert a Web page from one browser-supported type to another is only half the battle. The other half of the battle is being able to determine which browser type and version a visitor is using, and redirecting the visitor to the correct page based on their browser type and version. In a later section of this lesson, I'll show you how you can use a feature in UltraDev to determine the browser type of the visitor before the first page is shown to them, and redirect them to the appropriate pages based on their browser type.

Conversion Considerations

Page conversion is a great feature, but there are some important considerations, briefly described in Table 29.1, that you must plan and provide for in the source Web pages that you convert.

Table 29.1   Considerations when converting source Web pages to a different browser type or version

Consideration	Description
Content must be in layers	Browser types prior to version 4.0 use tables to position page elements. The UltraDev conversion utility requires all page content to be in layers in the source Web page so that tables, and nested tables, can be constructed to maintain positioning.
Layers can't overlap	UltraDev does not know how to resolve overlapping layers when it constructs the tables that define the layout of the converted page. Consequently, the conversion utility issues a warning message when overlapping layers are encountered.
Layers can't be nested	Because the nested layer's position is determined by the position on a Web page of the other layer, the conversion utility does not know where to position the nested layer when it is converted to a table. Consequently, nested layers are not accepted.
`<ilayer>` tag can't be used	One of the attributes displayed in the Property Inspector when you place a layer on a page is how you want that layer positioned. One of the options you can choose to determine the placement is to use the `<ilayer>` tag. Because this tag relies on relative positioning, it cannot be converted. A Web page that has a layer that relies on this tag will not be accepted in the conversion.

Converting Pages to 3.0 Compatibility

After you make sure the Web page to convert is compliant with the considerations in Table 29.1, converting the pages is a relatively straightforward process. To convert a Web page to a 3.0-compatible version, perform these steps:

1. Within UltraDev, open the Web page you want to convert within the Document window.

2. Select the File menu Convert option and choose the 3.0 Browser Compatible option. Ultra Dev, in turn, will display the Convert to 3.0 Browser Compatible window, as shown in Figure 29.1.

Figure 29.1

The Convert to 3.0 Browser Compatible window is where you convert a Web page into a formatted Web page viewable by version 3.0 browsers.

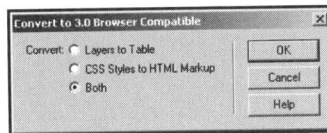

3. Within the Convert to 3.0 Browser Compatible window, click on the layers to Table radio button, if you are only converting layers to tables. Or, click on the CSS Styles to HTML Markup radio button if you are only converting cascading style sheets to HTML markup. Or, click on the Both radio button if you are converting layers to tables and cascading style sheets to HTML markup.

4. Click on the OK button to begin the conversion process.

If there are no problems with the conversion, UltraDev creates the converted page and places it in a new Document window. You can then save the converted page using a different file name from the source Web page. If there are problems with the conversion, UltraDev will notify you of the problem in a dialog box.

NOTE: *You must perform this conversion procedure each time you change the original Web page in order to update the 3.0-compatible file. For this reason, it's best to perform this procedure only after you are completely satisfied with your original Web page.*

Converting Tables to Layers

Web developers used to create sites by using tables extensively to control the positioning of objects on a page. Although positioning of an object on a Web page using tables can never equal the control you have by positioning the same object using layers, the capability of browsers to support layers is much more recent than their capability to support tables.

Additionally, some tools used to create complex Web graphics still produce those graphics in tables, not in layers. For example, I recently worked on a Web development project where the creation of a page title and navigation bar elements was contracted out to a graphic arts company. They did an excellent job in creating a beautiful title and navigation bar. They used Adobe Photoshop to create the graphics, and exported the graphics in a table format. Consequently, when we imported those graphics into the Web page, our Web page consisted of 14 different tables, with up to three layers of nested tables. This was a nightmare to maintain, especially when we wanted to make some minor changes to the graphics.

Fortunately, UltraDev has a nice conversion utility for converting tables to layers. After a Web page that contains a large number of tables is converted to a Web page using layers, it is much easier to maintain.

To convert a Web page using tables into one using layers, perform these steps:

1. Open the Web page you want to convert within the Document window.

2. Select the Modify menu Layout Mode option and choose Convert Tables to Layers. UltraDev, in turn, will display the Convert Tables to Layers window, as shown in Figure 29.2.

Figure 29.2

The Convert Tables to Layers window is used to remove the tables that appear on a Web page and replace them with layers.

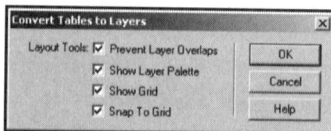

3. Within the Convert Tables to Layers window, click on the Show Grid and Snap To Grid check boxes if you want to use a grid to control the positioning of the layers on the page. Or, click on the Prevent Layer Overlaps check box to constrain the position of layers when they are created, moved, and resized so that they don't overlap.

4. Click on the Show Layer Palette check box to show the Layers palette during the conversion to establish attributes for the layers that are converted.

5. Click on the OK button to begin the conversion process. When done, the converted page will display in the Document window.

> **NOTE:** *Unlike the process whereby you can convert a Web page to a 3.0-compatible version that opens the converted page in a new Document window, the Convert Tables to Layers process does the conversion on the source page and does not open a new Document window. If you want to maintain the source page for some reason, you should save the converted page with a new name.*

Ensuring Browser Compatibility

As mentioned earlier in this lesson, UltraDev provides a convenient facility to ensure that visitors to your site have a compatible browser. Using this facility, you can test the compatibility of the visitor's browser before they see the first page, and direct them to an alternate page if their browser is not current enough to view the site. For example, you could have your visitors go to one page if they have Navigator 4.0 or later, go to another page if they have Internet Explorer 4.0 or later, and stay on the current page if they have some other browser.

This feature is attached to an object on a page using a Behavior. It is best to attach this behavior to the `<body>` tag because even if the visitor coming to your site has JavaScript support turned off, they will see something. To use the feature that checks for browser compatibility, perform these steps:

1. Open a Web page within the Document window.

2. Within the Document window, click on an object on the Web page to which you will attach a behavior. UltraDev will display a border around the object.

3. Open the Behavior Inspector by pressing Shift+F3. UltraDev will display the Behaviors window, as shown in Figure 29.3.

Figure 29.3

The Behavior Inspector is where you add the browser-compatibility check.

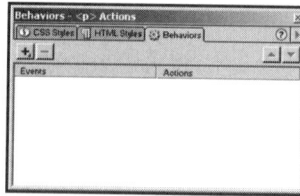

4. Within the Behavior Inspector, click on the plus (+) icon to open the Behavior menu list.

5. Within the Behavior menu list, click on the Check Browser item. UltraDev, in turn, will open the Check Browser window, as shown in Figure 29.4.

Figure 29.4

The Check Browser window is where you control what page the visitor goes to based on their browser type and version.

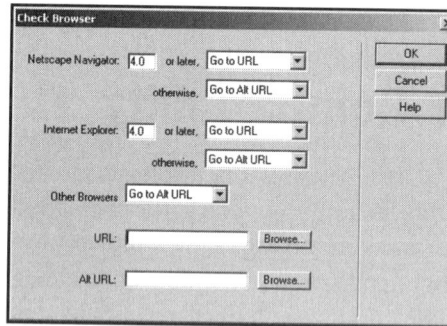

6. Determine how you want to separate your visitors. The choices are by browser brand, browser version, or both.

7. Within the Check Browser window, specify a version of Netscape Navigator and where the visitor should go if they are accessing your site using a version equal to or later than the version specified. Then, specify where a visitor should go if they are using a version of Netscape Navigator that is earlier than the version specified.

8. Specify a version of Internet Explorer and where the visitor should go if they are accessing your site using a version equal to or later than the version specified. Then, specify where a visitor should go if they are using a version of Internet Explorer that is earlier than the version specified.

9. Within the Other Browsers drop-down list box, choose an option to direct the visitor to in the event that they are accessing your site using a browser other than the version of Netscape Navigator and Internet Explorer specified.

10. In the URL text box, specify the name of the page that visitors are to be directed to when you have selected the Go To URL option in the drop-down list boxes on the Check Browser window.

11. In the Alt URL text box, specify the name of the page that visitors are to be directed to when you have selected the Go To Alt URL option in the drop-down list boxes on the Check Browser window.

12. Click on the OK button to save the behavior and apply it to the selected object.

Testing Pages with Targeted Browsers

I started my career by building computer systems that ran on IBM mainframe computers. I then began building computer systems that ran on PCs in a client/server architecture in the early 1990s. When Web technology became popular, I transferred my skill set to develop Web sites. In the years that I have been building computer systems, I have never witnessed less time and attention spent to testing than in the business of building Web sites. Unfortunately, because of global reach and inconsistent browsers, testing should be even more of a significant event in the construction of a Web site than it is in building other types of computer systems.

One of the easiest and most fundamental tests you can perform on a Web site you are constructing is to test the pages of the site with targeted browsers. UltraDev provides a nice interface that you can use to test a page, or pages, in a site with various browsers. Currently, UltraDev supports testing your site pages against the following browsers:

◆ Microsoft Internet Explorer versions 2.0 through 5.0

◆ Netscape Navigator versions 2.0 through 5.0

Using the UltraDev browser-checking facility, you can check a page against one or more of the preceding browser types. You can also check the entire site against one or more of the preceding browser types in one operation.

To check a single page against one or more browser types, perform these steps:

1. Open the page in the Document window.

2. Select the File menu Check Target Browsers option. UltraDev, in turn, will display the Check Target Browsers window, as shown in Figure 29.5.

Figure 29.5

The Check Target Browsers window is where you specify the target browsers against which to check the current page.

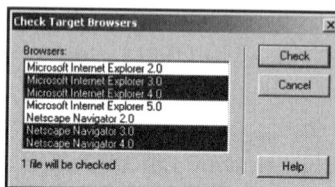

3. Within the Browsers list box of the Check Target Browsers window, click on the name of the target browser to check the current page against. If there is more than one target browser for which you want to check the compatibility, hold down the Ctrl key while clicking on each browser name.

4. Click on the Check button to begin the browser check.

5. When the browser checking is done, UltraDev will launch a browser window and display a report of its results, as shown in Figure 29.6, which you can then print.

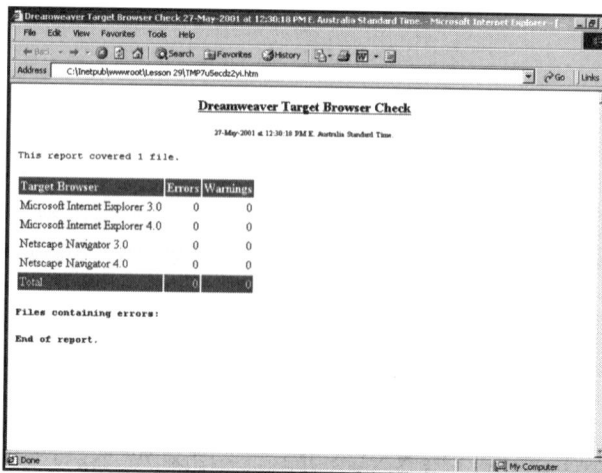

Figure 29.6

The Dreamweaver Target Browser Check report displays the results of the target browser-check process.

In addition to checking the browser compatibility for a page, you can also test the compatibility of your entire site against one or more browser types, by performing these steps:

1. Select the Window menu Site Files option. UltraDev, in turn, will display the Site window, as shown in Figure 29.7.

Figure 29.7

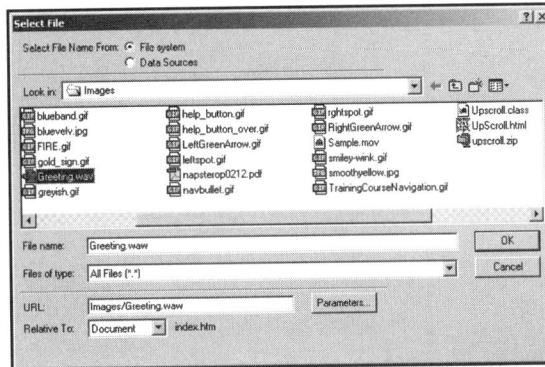

The Site window is where you select the local or remote location to perform a browser check on.

2. Within the Site window, if you want to check all the pages on the site that exists on the remote server, click on the name of the folder on the remote server that contains the site. If you want to check all the pages for the site on your local hard drive, click on the name of the folder on the local hard drive that contains the site. You will see the selected folder highlighted.

3. Select the File menu Check Target Browsers option. UltraDev will display the Check Target Browsers window.

4. Within the Browsers list box, click on the name of the target browser to check the current page against. If there is more than one target browser for which you want to check the compatibility, hold down the Ctrl key while clicking on each browser name.

5. Click on the Check button to begin the browser check.

6. When the browser checking is done, UltraDev will launch a browser window and display a report of its results, as shown in Figure 29.8. As you can see in this figure, multiple errors were discovered. If you scroll down the page displayed in the browser, you will see a description of each error, as shown in Figure 29.9.

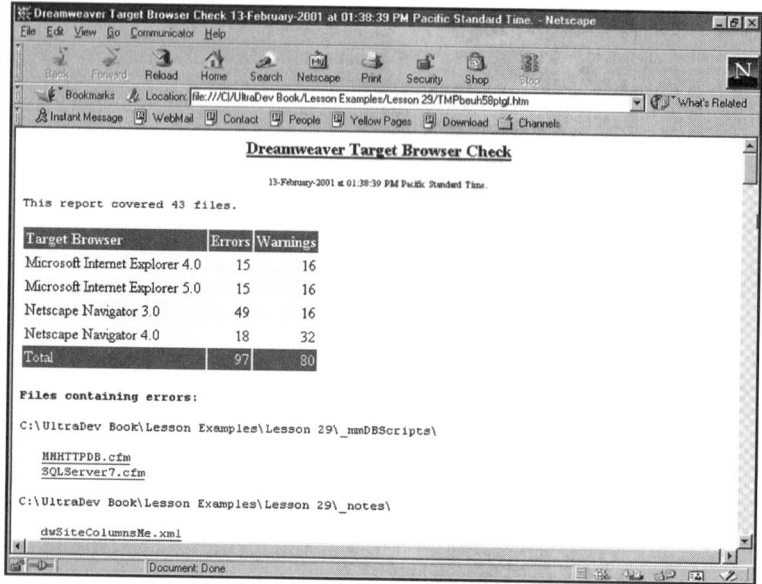

Figure 29.8

The results of the entire site browser check reveal a number of errors.

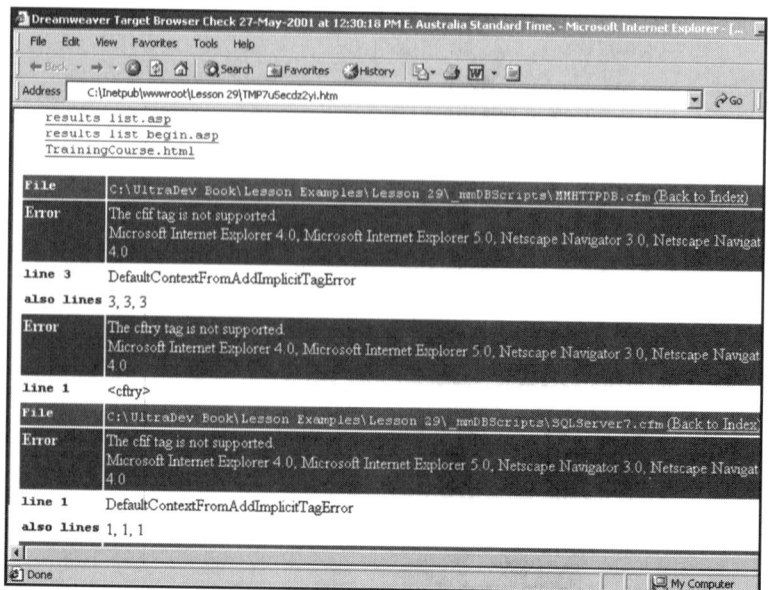

Figure 29.9

The report that is shown following the browser check also describes each of the errors.

Using the Browser Check Results

All the errors encountered by UltraDev during the browser check will display in the Browser Check report. However, not all the errors that display in this report are errors that need to be resolved.

For example, you may have a design specification that calls for the base-level browser support for the site you develop to be version 3.0 of Netscape Navigator and Internet Explorer. When you do the browser check, you could specify the check process to include version 2.0 browsers, just to see how compatible the site will be for this version of browser. Because your target browser version is 3.0, you may be able to ignore all the errors that are attributable to version 2.0 browsers.

What You Must Know

In this lesson, you learned how to create Web sites suitable and viewable for different browsers, as well as how to test the site, and pages in the site, against different browser types and versions. Before you continue with this book's appendixes, make sure you understand the following key concepts:

◆ By using UltraDev you can quickly convert a Web page you created for one browser into a page a different browser supports.

◆ By using UltraDev you can establish parameters that make page conversion from one browser to the other simple.

◆ UltraDev provides several tools to help you check your site for browser compatibility.

Appendix A

Understanding XML

XML, the Extensible Markup Language, is a markup language for Web pages containing structured information. Such structured information contains both content (words, pictures, and so on) and some indication of what role that content plays (for example, content in a section heading has a different meaning than content in a footnote, which means something different than content in a figure caption or content in a database table, and so on). Almost all Web pages have some structure.

A markup language is a mechanism to identify structures in a Web page. The XML specification defines a standard way to add markup to Web pages.

The number of Web sites currently being developed that are based on, or make use of, XML is truly amazing (particularly when you consider that XML is barely three years old).

XML is not like HTML. In HTML, both the tag semantics and the tag set are fixed. An <h1> tag is always a first-level heading, and the tag <ati.product.code> is meaningless. The World Wide Web Consortium (W3C), which is the governing body over the Web, in conjunction with browser vendors and the Web community, is constantly working to extend the definition of HTML to allow new tags to keep pace with changing technology and to bring variations in presentation to the Web. However, these changes are always rigidly confined by what the browser vendors have implemented and by the fact that backward compatibility is paramount. And for people who want to disseminate information widely, features supported by only the latest releases of Netscape Navigator and Internet Explorer are not useful.

XML specifies neither semantics nor a tag set. In fact, XML is really a *metalanguage* for describing markup languages. In other words, XML provides a facility to define tags and the structural relationships between them. Since there is no predefined tag set, there cannot be any preconceived semantics. All of the semantics of an XML Web page will be defined either by the applications that process them or by style sheets.

To appreciate XML, it is important to understand why it was created. XML was created so that richly structured pages could be used over the Web. HTML is not a viable alternative for this purpose.

HTML, as you have already read, comes bound with a set of semantics and does not provide arbitrary structure. This is not to say that XML can be expected to completely replace HTML.

Whereas HTML has a rigid set of tags that control the way content appears on a Web page, XML has a very flexible tag structure that controls the content that moves between a Web page and a data store.

For example, consider the following HTML code that formats a name and address:

```
<h2 align="left"><bold>Name and Address</bold></h2>

<p align="left">Name:</p>

<p>Jim Hobuss</p>

<p align="left">City, State:</p>

<p>Portland, Oregon</p>
```

Notice all the tags that control the display and placement of the data. Now consider the following XML:

```
<contentType>Name And Address</contentType>

<name>Jim Hobuss</name>

<cityState>Portland, Oregon</cityState>
```

Like HTML, you will notice that XML uses the tag-pair concept. That is, each beginning tag is closed with an ending tag. Where XML is different from HTML is that each beginning tag in XML *must* have an ending tag. Failure to follow this will generate an error.

Another important distinction you will notice in XML is that the names of the tag pairs are completely arbitrary, whereas the names of the tag pairs for HTML are quite rigid. When you place a value inside a tag pair in XML, you can reuse that value on the Web page merely by referencing the tag pair.

Table A.1 describes the six different kinds of markup that XML recognizes.

Table A.1   The types of markups recognized by XML

Markup Type	Description
Elements	More commonly referred to as tag pairs, elements are delimited by a set of angle brackets (< >).
Entity references	Certain characters in XML are reserved to preserve the integrity of the language. Angle brackets are examples of these. For example, the XML code to represent the HTML code `<body>` is `&lt;body&gt;`.
Comments	HTML comments and XML comments are identical. They begin with the `<!–` characters and end with the `–>` characters.
Processing instructions	Server-side includes (SSIs) are a facility incorporated in UltraDev and represented in HTML. Processing Instructions is an XML facility similar to SSIs.
Markup sections	Using XML, you can pass blocks of code or other data without parsing the markup and content. These blocks of code and data are identified by the characters `<![CDATA[` at the beginning of the block, and the characters `]]>` at the end.
Document type	Document Type declarations are used to define and describe elements, attributes, character entities, and notations in Web pages.

Many of the features in UltraDev are built and supported using XML. For example, Menus and Commands are built using XML. Figure A.1 shows the content of the Menus.xml file, which is used to display the menu options.

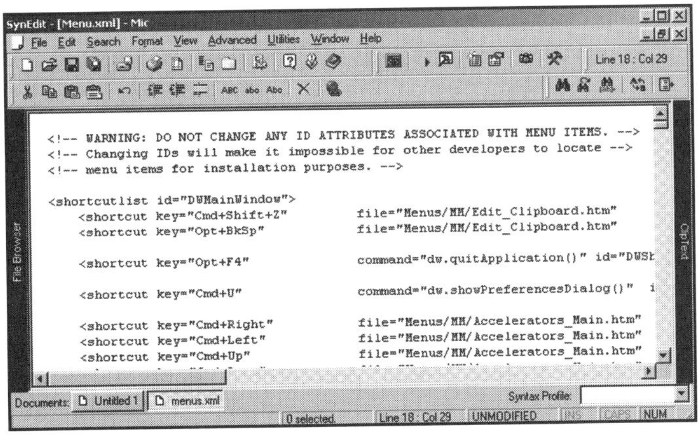

Figure A.1

UltraDev uses XML in the way it manages and displays menus in the UltraDev interface.

Appendix B

E-Commerce and UltraDev

When companies first started putting up Web sites, their motivation was to provide customers with information about the company. Frequently, these sites consisted of marketing information, contact information, and maybe a brochure of the company's products. The early Web sites did not include the capability for a customer to order products from that company.

The second generation of Web sites included features and capabilities allowing companies to sell their products to customers over the Web. When a customer, or company, orders products over the Web, this is customarily described as an *e-commerce transaction*. E-commerce transactions on Web sites are the payday that companies are searching for in trying to understand how to make the Web a profitable environment in which to do business.

NOTE: *We're not done in the evolution of how companies use the Web to conduct business. I think the next big evolutionary step of companies using the Web is when two or more companies get together and develop a customized Web site where these companies, and only the companies that are part of this consortium, can do business. For example, a supplier of bumpers to General Motors, as well as General Motors, would benefit significantly if that supplier could look into the inventory levels of bumpers at GM plants via a Web interface and automatically replenish the factories with bumpers. Although we see that companies are beginning to use the Web in this way, I believe this will become quite common in the next few years.*

E-commerce sites are definitely on the rise. More and more companies are using them as a portal in which to conduct business. Forrester Research estimates that consumers purchased 46 percent more goods over the Internet for Christmas 2000 than they did for Christmas 1999. With the proliferation of e-commerce sites, and the probability of continued movement in this direction, it is wise to develop an understanding of e-commerce.

Understanding e-Commerce

There is about as many ways that e-commerce sites function as there are e-commerce sites. Each Web site that includes an e-commerce capability follows a very similar path, though. The following describes a typical e-commerce transaction:

1. A site visitor enters the e-commerce pages. Typically, this starts with an online store where the goods for sale by the company are displayed, along with a description and price. When the visitor sees something they want to purchase, they click on a Buy button. When the user clicks on the Buy button, a cookie that contains the item number is written in the cookie file on their machine.

2. After clicking on the Buy button, the visitor is redirected back to the catalog pages to do more shopping. They repeat Steps 1 and 2 until they are done shopping, and then click on a button that says Proceed to Checkout.

3. When the visitor clicks on the Proceed to Checkout button, they are redirected to a page or pages secured using Secure Sockets Layer (SSL) technology. SSL technology controls the information passed between a Web page and a server by encrypting and decrypting all information transferred.

4. The visitor is given an opportunity to confirm the current order. They can change the quantity of any of the items selected, or they can remove any of the items selected. The visitor then confirms their order, which prompts the Web site to search for payment information for the visitor.

5. The Web site searches for payment information specific to the visitor. If payment information records are not located, the visitor is asked to supply credit card information, which is then verified through one of a number of online credit card verification services. This information is then saved in a database for the visitor. If payment information is located, the visitor is asked to confirm the information stored, and is given an opportunity to change the credit card used for the purchase of the goods.

6. The credit card information is sent to a credit card clearinghouse service, where the purchase amount is verified against the credit limit of the card. This is done via secure phone lines and encrypted transactions. At the same time this occurs, the visitor is sent an automatically generated e-mail thanking them for their order.

7. If the credit card purchase is validated and approved by the credit card clearinghouse, the order is placed into a database of orders. This order database is then referenced and used as part of the company's normal order-fulfillment processing. Usually, this entails one or more client/server applications that use the information in the database.

8. The information received by the credit card clearinghouse is sent to the visitor's bank for processing. The bank accepts the charge and sends a record of this back to the credit card clearinghouse.

9. The credit card clearinghouse receives the acceptance from the bank.

10. When the goods purchased by the visitor are shipped, an e-mail message is automatically generated to the visitor, telling them of the shipment and supplying them with a tracking number in the event the shipment is lost.

Assuming the visitor receives the goods, this ends the transaction (with the exception of the visitor seeing the item[s]) show up on their next credit card statement).

Authentication

The Web is a dangerous place to do business, and it is an even more dangerous place for people to shop. There are people who enjoy breaking into sites, stealing secure information (such as credit card information, social security numbers, and so forth), and creating havoc for the businesses they hack into as well as the customers whose private information they steal.

Authentication allows a higher level of security on Web sites, especially when used in conjunction with SSL. The most prevalent form of authentication involves using digital certificates. A digital certificate is purchased from a company and is automatically transferred to a Web browser once a visitor is authorized to access the site. When a company or individual applies for a digital certificate, they must prove their identity to the company issuing the certificate. Once a digital certificate is issued to a company or an individual, that company or individual can use that certificate on their Web site and transfer that certificate to a visitor's browser. When the certificate comes back to the server from a different page, the Web site can interpret the certificate and verify its authenticity. If the certificate is not authenticated, or if it is not present at all, the site restricts access to that page that requires authentication.

Encryption

Encryption is another method used to provide security for e-commerce transactions conducted on the Web. Encryption is what the SSL technology described earlier in this appendix performs.

Hackers have tools that allow them to read transactions and data strings passed over the Internet. They use this capability to search for useful information, such as social security numbers, credit card numbers, telephone number, and so forth. Once they have this information, they can use it in a number of ways, all of which are illegal and potentially very damaging to you and your credit.

Encryption foils hackers. It does this by changing the value of characters that are sent from a visitor's browser, before they are sent. Then, should a hacker intercept the string of data traveling over the Internet, they can't do anything with it because they don't know how to decrypt it. Current encryption technology makes it virtually impossible for a hacker to decipher an encryption algorithm. When the Web server receives the character stream, it is decrypted according to a logarithm stored in the decryption software used by the company. Transactions sent from the company to the visitor's Web browser are likewise encrypted and decrypted. The software used by the company to perform this encryption and decryption is termed Secure Sockets Layer.

Shopping Carts

The shopping cart function is a critical element of any e-commerce site. This function is the one that keeps track of the items a visitor has selected to purchase, and also allows the visitor to alter the quantity of an item or delete an item from their shopping cart prior to checkout.

The way in which most shopping carts work is to store a small cookie on the visitor's machine that contains the item number and purchase quantity for the current shopping session. The information in a cookie is then passed to the Web server in the form of a set of parameters on the URL. If the site uses encryption, then the information contained in the cookie is encrypted before it leaves the visitor's browser. The Web server receives this information, decrypts it if it needs to be, and then parses the passed parameters to perform whatever action needs to be performed based on the items and quantity of items ordered. Most e-commerce sites include a function to delete the cookie containing this information from the visitor's machine when the visitor receives and views the Order Confirmation window.

Appendix C

Internet Resources

The Web is a wonderful resource of information. Just about every bit of knowledge ever written, and most forward-thinking thought, is available on a site attached to the Web. The difficulty a person has in using this vast amount of information is first finding it.

I have compiled the following list of resources as a way to help you get started finding useful information. If you can't find what you're looking for in one of the links here, then follow the links to related sites, provided on most of the sites listed. One of the things I've found to be almost universally true about the people who host these "information" type sites is that they include links to related sites.

The links to the Web sites are categorized and placed in Tables C.1 through C.9 according to the type of information you'll find on them.

Table C.1 *Active Server Pages Web sites*

Site URL	Site Description
www.4guysfromrolla.com/	Frequently updated, with access to many FAQs and Internet resources.
www.activeserverpages.com/activeserverpages/	Hosted by Charles Carroll, with a few useful links.
www.aspfaq.com/faq/faq.asp	Includes links to various FAQ pages on other ASP sites.
www.asptoday.com/	A wonderful site that is well designed for quick access to a lot of useful information.
www.serverobjects.com/	Hosted by ServerObjects, a company with products to sell. Some useful information is available on the site, but you have to search for it.
www.15seconds.com/	Another frequently updated site. The Webmaster promotes the site as giving you the tools necessary to keep up with the latest in the world of Microsoft Internet technology.

(continued)

Table C.1 (continued)

Site URL	Site Description
www.asp-zone.com/default1.asp?Area=ASP	The layout of the home page on this site is very busy. Take note: Do not design home pages on your site to be as busy as this site's home page. However, there is a lot of valuable information. The site includes an "Ask Question" component, where someone will answer any ASP-related question that you e-mail to them.
www4.tcp-ip.com/	A great site that is frequently updated with content. Check out the search engine to find an ASP to host your Web site!

Table C.2   Browser Web sites

Site URL	Site Description
browserwatch.internet.com/	Useful and current information on different browser technologies, created and supported by Brian Proffitt.
browsers.evolt.org/	Information on what I believe to be every browser available. Although the information is sparse for some of the browser types, this site is a great place to start searching for information on obscure browser types.

Table C.3   CGI script Web sites

Site URL	Site Description
www.itm.com/cgicollection/	A great site at which to begin your search for CGI scripts. The navigation is easy, and useful information is readily accessible.
www.cgi-resources.com/Programs_and_Scripts/	Lists the CGI scripts available by programming language.
www.worldwidemart.com/scripts/	Matt's Script Archie Site, which is probably the most frequently visited CGI site on the Web. You'll find lots of free and nearly free scripts here segmented into functional categories.

Table C.4   ColdFusion Web sites

Site URL	Site Description
www.allaire.com/products/coldfusion/	A set of pages hosted by Allaire that gives useful information on the ColdFusion product.
www.allaire.com/Support/KnowledgeBase/SearchForm.cfm	Another set of pages on the Allaire site that gives you access to the Knowledge Base of technical notes kept by Allaire.
www.allaire.com/Documents/cf4docs.cfm	Includes a search page that will give you access to product and technical documentation on ColdFusion.

Table C.5   Database and SQL fundamentals Web sites

Site URL	Site Description
www.builder.com/Programming/SQL/ ?tag=st.bl.3880cd3.promo3.bl	Hosted by CNET.com, this site gives 12 tips for using SQL with ASP pages, as well as useful links to other sites.
www.sqlcourse.com/	Supplies a free training course on SQL, and provides links to many other SQL-specific Web resources.
www.citilink.com/%7Ejgarrick/vbasic/ database/fundamentals.html	Privately supported site that contains some useful information on RDBMS technology and using the Microsoft Jet database engine.
clubs.yahoo.com/clubs/structuredquerylanguage	A Yahoo! club whose purpose is to provide technical support, assistance, and information specific to SQL. It is wholly supported by individual contributors.
willcam.com/sql/default.htm	Includes a free course to teach you the fundamentals of SQL. For additional information and links, visit **willcam.com/sql/**.

Table C.6   HTML and cascading style sheet Web sites

Site URL	Site Description
www.blooberry.com/indexdot/html/index.html	A great site with an awesome user interface. It's worth checking out if for no other reason than to see what the designers have done with the user interface design.
www.htmlcompendium.org/Menu/0framefn.htm	The user interface on this site is not nearly as inviting as the blooberry.com site, but it offers a lot of valuable information, including a substantial amount of information on cascading style sheets (CSS).
www.webreview.com/style/	An informative site with sample style guides you can use to design the user interface.
builder.cnet.com/webbuilding/0-7258.htm	Everything you wanted to know about CSS is here.

Table C.7   JavaScript Web sites

Site URL	Site Description
www.web-hosting.com/javalinks.html	Links, links, and more links to resources on the Web that the author feels is important to JavaScript developers.
www.geocities.com/SiliconValley/Park/2554/index.html	Appropriately billed as a beginner's introduction to JavaScript. There aren't a lot of links on this site that are valuable, but this is a great place to start if you're just beginning to learn about JavaScript.
www.serve.com/hotsyte/	Promotes JavaScript knowledge through the open exchange of ideas, research, scripts, and links.
developer.netscape.com/docs/manuals/communicator/jsguide4/index.htm	An e-book that is the definitive guide to JavaScript.
developer.netscape.com/docs/manuals/jsframe.html	Offers lots of links to resources on the Web that support an understanding of and development in the JavaScript language.

Table C.8   *JavaServer Pages Web sites*

Site URL	Site Description
java.sun.com/products/jsp/download.html	This set of pages is boring reading to many, but it contains the specifications for the JSP environment.
java.sun.com/products/servlet/index.html	These pages are related to the previous set, and include the specifications for the Java Servlet environment.
developer.netscape.com/viewsource/ kuslich_jsp/kuslich_jsp.html	These pages are an introduction to JSP, as espoused by Netscape Communications.
www.webtechniques.com/archives/1999/11/note/	Contains many useful resources and links to JSP technologies.

Table C.9   *UltraDev Web sites and extensions*

Site URL	Site Description
ultradevfaq.com/	Developed and maintained by Nic Skitt. It includes useful information, but you have to spend some time looking for it. A nice Search capability has just been added that not only makes it easier to find information on the site, but demonstrates how a Search function ought to look on a site.
www.dreamweaverfever.com/default.asp	In the words of the site's developer, it was developed both to make his extensions for Dreamweaver available for download, and to provide some useful and interesting reading about Dreamweaver and Dreamweaver UltraDev topics.
www.powerclimb.com/	Sells and supports a shopping cart function to use if you build an e-commerce site. There's not a lot of information on this site of value if you're not looking for a shopping cart head start.
www.magicbeat.com/mb/	A pretty good site if you're looking for UltraDev extensions. In fact, Macromedia named the developers of this site the nominee as the Best Extension Developer.

(continued)

Table C.9 *(continued)*

Site URL	Site Description
www.ultradevextensions.com/xcdirectory/XcDirectory.asp	Provides a lot of information about UltraDev extensions, grouped by category. The site also boosts a nice selection of links to other sites of interest.
home.att.net/~JCB.BEI/Dreamweaver/	You have to check out this site if for no other reason than to see how a very nicely done Flash animation can be very engaging.
ultradevguru.com/	Site of Bill Kennelley, an UltraDev developer extraordinaire. This site offers a nice selection of behaviors and links.

Index

License Agreement/Notice of Limited Warranty

By opening the sealed disk container in this book, you agree to the following terms and conditions. If upon reading the following license agreement and notice of limited warranty, you cannot agree to the terms and conditions set forth, return the unused book with unopened disk to the place where you purchased it for a refund.

License:

The enclosed software is copyrighted by the copyright holder(s) indicated on the software disk. You are licensed to copy the software onto a single computer for use by a single concurrent user and to a backup disk. You may not reproduce, make copies, or distribute copies or rent or lease the software in whole or in part, except with written permission of the copyright holder(s). You may transfer the enclosed disk only together with this license and only if you destroy all other copies of the software and the transferee agrees to the terms of the license. You may not decompile, reverse assemble, or reverse engineer the software.

Notice of Limited Warranty:

The enclosed disk is warranted by Prima Publishing to be free of physical defects in materials and workmanship for a period of sixty (60) days from end user's purchase of the book/disk combination. During the sixty-day term of the limited warranty, Prima will provide a replacement disk upon the return of a defective disk.

Limited Liability:

THE SOLE REMEDY FOR BREACH OF THIS LIMITED WARRANTY SHALL CONSIST ENTIRELY OF REPLACEMENT OF THE DEFECTIVE DISK. IN NO EVENT SHALL PRIMA OR THE AUTHORS BE LIABLE FOR ANY OTHER DAMAGES, INCLUDING LOSS OR CORRUPTION OF DATA, CHANGES IN THE FUNCTIONAL CHARACTERISTICS OF THE HARDWARE OR OPERATING SYSTEM, DELETERIOUS INTERACTION WITH OTHER SOFTWARE, OR ANY OTHER SPECIAL, INCIDENTAL, OR CONSEQUENTIAL DAMAGES THAT MAY ARISE, EVEN IF PRIMA AND/OR THE AUTHOR HAVE PREVIOUSLY BEEN NOTIFIED THAT THE POSSIBILITY OF SUCH DAMAGES EXISTS.

Disclaimer of Warranties:

PRIMA AND THE AUTHORS SPECIFICALLY DISCLAIM ANY AND ALL OTHER WARRANTIES, EITHER EXPRESS OR IMPLIED, INCLUDING WARRANTIES OF MERCHANTABILITY, SUITABILITY TO A PARTICULAR TASK OR PURPOSE, OR FREEDOM FROM ERRORS. SOME STATES DO NOT ALLOW FOR EXCLUSION OF IMPLIED WARRANTIES OR LIMITATION OF INCIDENTAL OR CONSEQUENTIAL DAMAGES, SO THESE LIMITATIONS MAY NOT APPLY TO YOU.

Other:

This Agreement is governed by the laws of the State of California without regard to choice of law principles. The United Convention of Contracts for the International Sale of Goods is specifically disclaimed. This Agreement constitutes the entire agreement between you and Prima Publishing regarding use of the software.